Comment on *The Life and Times of Grigorii Rasputin:*

"Alex de Jonge—an Oxford professor of Russian ancestry—takes Grigorii Efimovich Rasputin's rise to power to be one of history's tragic jokes. The Tsarina thought Rasputin a saint because he could apparently heal her son; and because he was a saint, he must be heeded in all matters. The Tsar did not lag far behind in credulity. Little is known about Rasputin's early life. . . . Yet this drunken lecher with insolent ambitions had the power to make troubled people feel better—to lighten souls, as De Jonge puts it. . . . In his own way he wanted to be what the Tsar and Tsarina believed him to be: the savior of Holy Russia . . ."—*Time*

THE LIFE AND TIMES OF GRIGORII RASPUTIN

ALEX DE JONGE

Carroll & Graf Publishers, Inc.
New York

First Carroll & Graf edition 1989
Published by arrangement with The Putnam Berkley Publishing Group

Carroll & Graf Publishers, Inc.
260 Fifth Avenue
New York, N.Y. 10001

ISBN: 0-88184-484-5

Manufactured in the United States of America

To my wife

Regarding our earthly life as a transition I would observe that this transition is especially difficult in Russia.

NIKOLAI LESKOV

Our land is broad and fruitful but we have no order here.

THE CHRONICLE OF NESTOR,
EARLY TWELFTH CENTURY

When will there at last be order, which in every sense our poor country needs, and which is not in the Slave (sic) nature!

ALEXANDRA TO NICHOLAS, MAY 29, 1916.

PREFACE

A GREAT MANY PEOPLE *have helped me with this book. I have sometimes learnt more from a brief conversation than from hundreds of pages of reading. In particular I should like to thank Sophie Lund, her mother and late grandmother, variously, for their recollections and their help. I owe a special debt to Kyril Fitzlyon, who went to such trouble to vet my manuscript, and who made so many helpful suggestions and corrections. I am deeply appreciative of the trouble he took, although of course I remain entirely responsible for any mistakes the book may still contain. I should also like to thank George Katkov for talking to me, and for the insights and information he was kind enough to provide. I owe a very special debt to Richard Tempest and his parents, for all the help and hospitality they gave me. If this book has worked at all it is in great measure thanks to them, and the doors they opened for me. I should also like to thank those scholars and writers I met in the Soviet Union for their enthusiastic help and hospitality, particularly the generous host and collector who was ready to give me items of his collection be-*

cause "I needed them more than he did." I am very grateful to Kathleen and Russell Sharp for their hospitality when I was working on the first draft. I owe a second very special debt to the late Michael Astor. Not only did he give me a place to live in the country when I started work on the project, he also persuaded me to join the London Library. Finally I should like to thank my wife for laboriously picking her way through my manuscript, pointing out errors and offering helpful and vociferous criticism.

A. DE J.

INTRODUCTION

RASPUTIN WAS BORN in the early 1860s, which makes him about ten years older than Churchill, some fourteen years older than Lenin, and nearly twenty years older than Stalin. He was born in the reign of the Tsar-Emperor Alexander the Second, absolute ruler over an empire occupying a sixth of the world's land mass, its inhabitants numbering some hundred million, consisting of over fifty different nationalities and speaking nearly two hundred different languages or dialects. The empire stretched from the Prussian border to beyond the Pacific Ocean–Russia sold Alaska to the U.S.A. in 1867. The tsar's wish was absolute; he was the Autocrat, who ruled by his will alone, free to appoint and dismiss ministers as he wished. It was Tsar Alexander himself who, in the early 1860s, initiated the most radical set of reforms that the Russian people had ever known. By far and away the most important of these was the emancipation of the serfs in 1861, which conferred personal freedom upon the thirty-seven percent of the population that had hitherto been state or private property. Emancipation was accompanied by grants of land made collectively to individual peasant communities, to be redeemed by payments extending over half a century. Other reforms included the creation of an independent judiciary, trial by jury, elements of local government in both town and country, and the liberalisation of the universities.

Although the emancipation may have anticipated the abolition of slavery in the U.S.A. by a few years, the reforms came too late and granted too little to satisfy the radicals. The 1860s saw the rise of a revolutionary intelligentsia, fierce, uncompromising and with a stern belief in science, socialism, materialism and the emancipation of women; a generation whose sincere enthusiasms were not always matched by the intellectual sophistication required to understand the German and French philosophers they read so avidly. Impatient with reforms and the liberals who wished to bring change about gradually, they clamoured for immediate results, and believed that, in order to secure them, all means were justified. Their objective was the destruction of the existing system of government in its entirety, their chief weapon was assassination, their ultimate target was the tsar.

Alexander II survived a first attempt in April 1866, when a young student named Karakozov shot at him and missed from close range. One of the more bizarre consequences of his action was an attempt by the reactionaries to check the spread of higher education by making university entrance depend upon a knowledge of Latin and Greek. Seven years later, virtually to the day, in April 1873, Alexander survived a second attack, by A. K. Solovyev, who also shot and missed, and was subsequently hanged.

Alexander was preparing a second round of reforms, which would include elected elements in the process of government, another major step forward. He had indeed just signed the substantive proposals when, on March 13, 1881, the "Tsar-Liberator," as he was known, was blown up by a terrorist bomb, which destroyed his legs, tore open his stomach and disfigured him. "Home to the palace, to die there" were his last words, and all hope of further reform went with him.

He was succeeded by his son, Alexander III, a man of huge physical strength (he liked bending and straightening horseshoes) and reactionary temperament. His faith in the crack of firm government was encouraged by his old tutor, Konstantin Pobedonostsev, now over-procurator, or minister for religion. Alexander's abhorrence for reform was based upon his lack of faith in human nature and the possibilities of human intellect. This made him opposed to liberalisation of any kind, as he believed that any change was probably for the worse. During his reign the tightest hold was kept upon public opinion, the press and the universities.

However, in other important respects Russia was stirring. She was rapidly becoming an important industrial country. Vast deposits of iron and coal had been discovered in southwest Russia, in the Donets basin, and iron production grew at tremendous speed. The textile industry had also developed rapidly after the American Civil War had checked the import of cotton. Industry developed faster still in the nineties, thanks largely to the work of one of the great ministers of the age. Sergei Witte had begun life as a railway clerk in Tiflis, and worked his way up to become head of the South Western Railways. He was subsequently appointed minister of communications and did much to develop the imperial railway system, helping to initiate the Trans-Siberian Railway in the early 1890s. In 1892 he was appointed minister of finance, in which post he helped to create the vast influx of foreign capital which funded Russia's industrial expansion, giving her the highest industrial growth rate in Europe from 1890 to 1914. Major European and American companies began to invest generously in Russia. On St. Petersburg's Nevsky Prospekt, the smartest street in the empire, one could see advertisements for Singer sewing machines and International Harvester. Some years later the consortium of Shibayev, Nobel, and Rothschild were the principal exploiters of the Baku oilfields, where oil could be seen seeping out of the ground in puddles. Rothschild also owned all the petrol stations between Moscow, Kiev and Warsaw.

Alexander III, who was married to Princess Marie, daughter of the king of Denmark, had a temperament to match his physique. He was a man of great determination, a hard-working ruler who always knew his own mind. Although narrow in outlook and determined to fight the revolutionaries who had murdered his father, rather than isolate them by judicious reforms, absolute power suited him. He had the strength of character and determination needed to make it work.

Unhappily for the Romanov dynasty, these were not characteristics which he succeeded in passing on to his eldest son. Alexander died unexpectedly in his Crimean residence in the autumn of 1894, a death which left the twenty-six-year-old tsarevich Nicholas Alexandrovich singularly ill-equipped to succeed to the throne as ruler of all the Russias and master of the Russian land. The last of the Romanovs would rule for just twenty-three years before dying, with his wife and five children, at the hands of a Bolshevik firing squad.

✧ ✧ ✧

Russian peasants used to have a revealing saying: "God is on high and the tsar a long way off." It implies that while they look to God and the tsar for protection, they recognise that neither protector is readily available. Yet although the saying is a warning not to expect help from anyone, it also reminds us that the great mass of the population of old Russia felt that their lives were, at least in theory, regulated by the two great powers of the autocracy and the church.

The Eastern, or Orthodox, church differs in many ways from Western counterparts as we know them today. The Eastern church, which came to be centered in Constantinople, grew steadily away from Rome between the sixth and eleventh centuries, a final break coming in 1054. Unlike the Catholic church, which places itself under the supreme authority of the pope, the Eastern church consists of a series of more or less autonomous bodies, or patriarchates, of which there were originally four–Constantinople, Alexandria, Antioch, and Jerusalem–to which have since been added those of Cyprus, Russia, Roumania, Yugoslavia, Greece, Bulgaria, Poland, Georgia, Albania and Sinai. There also have grown up a series of other independent, or autocephalous, churches–Finland, Estonia, Latvia, Czechoslovakia. When the Russian grand dukes of Kiev assumed the Christian faith in 989, the patriarch of Constantinople was considered the senior or ecumenical patriarch.

Unlike the Western churches, which would undergo continuing theological development from the beginnings, through the Middle Ages, Reformation, and Counter-Reformation to the present day, the Eastern church had resolved all its major theological issues by the time of the Kievan conversion. Strict adherence to traditional patterns is one of its most important characteristics, and is even reflected in the name; Orthodoxy, in Russian *Pravoslavie,* meaning "correct worship." Central to the faith is the liturgy, or mass, and by participating in its correct forms of worship the Orthodox Christian joins in a communal ritual that unites him with all other Orthodox throughout the world and throughout time, reaching back to the earliest days of Christianity.

Where the Roman Catholic mass was until recently said in Latin, the Orthodox liturgy has tended to be performed in the vernacular. Today it may be heard in Old Church Slavonic, Greek, Georgian, Arabic, Roumanian, Estonian, Lettish, various Finnish and Tartar dialects, Japanese, Chinese and English. There are flourishing Orthodox communities both in the United Kingdom and the United States, and these are by no means limited to persons of Greek or Russian antecedents. Yet despite its obvious claims to universality as a faith, the history of the Orthodox church is closely associated with nationalism. Situated on Christendom's eastern frontier, and frequently under attack from non-Christians, it has often happened that keeping the faith and remaining true to one's country have become bound up with one another. This is very much the case in Russia. For more than two hundred years, from 1237 to 1448, while first Italy and then northern Europe were experiencing the intellectual and scientific renewals of the Renaissance, Russia was occupied by a foreign and heathen power, an occupation which ensured that Russia would remain cut off from the crucial developments of European civilization and go a very different way. To give one example, Moscow's first printing press was established a century after the invention of printing in the West.

Throughout the period of the Tartar occupation the church had provided an important rallying point for both Christian and patriotic values, although it must be said that it frequently cooperated with its Tartar overlords, rather as it does with the regime of today, although the Tartars were more tolerant of Christianity than the Communist party. After the Turks captured Constantinople in 1453, Russia, which had just rid itself of the last vestiges of Tartar rule, assumed leadership of the Eastern church. Although Russia was autocephalous even then, it was governed not by a patriarch, but by a metropolitan or senior bishop. It was at this time that there emerged the heady doctrine of "Moscow the Third Rome." Two Romes (i.e., Rome and Constantinople) had fallen to barbarians; Moscow was the third and last citadel of Orthodoxy. "Two Romes have fallen, and a fourth there will not be," wrote a monk, Philotheus of Pskov, in 1510. Henceforward Russia would consider herself the champion of Orthodoxy, defender of the faith. Religion and nationalism became bound up with one another for rulers and ruled alike. It was this that gave the Russians their unshakeable belief in their own superiority over all other races, a superiority that would always be with them, whatever their superficial shortcomings and failures, and which would ensure that one day Russia would save the world.

Moscow's identity as the Third Rome was confirmed in 1589, when, with the approval of the patriarch of Constantinople, the Russian church was granted a patriarch of its own. However, the office only existed, in the first instance, for a little more than a century. When the post fell vacant in 1700, during the reign of Peter the Great, the tsar did not make a new appointment. Instead, in 1721, he established a governing body that would endure up to the revolution, when once more it was replaced by a patriarch. Peter's Holy Synod was a collective governing body, consisting of three bishops and nine monks or members of the married clergy. It was supervised by a government official, the over-procurator, who was in effect minister for religion. The result of Peter's reform was to turn the church into a branch of the state, and destroy its independence. Indeed, by the early nineteenth century, during the reign of Nicholas I, the "gendarme of Europe," the political role of the church was fully recognised. Nicholas advanced the doctrine of "Official Christianity," which stated that the basis of Russia's greatness lay in acceptance of an ideology founded on the "joint spirit of Orthodoxy, Autocracy and Nationality."

It is from the belief in the moral and political rightness of Orthodoxy and Nationality, i.e., Russianness, that tsarist anti-Semitism was derived. This was religious, as opposed to racial by nature. Practising Jews were denied a whole range of rights. The vast majority of the Empire's Jewish population were required to reside within the so-called Pale of Settlement in southwest Russia, and had to live in cities and towns, being forbidden to farm. There were further restrictions; admission to institutes of secondary and higher education was on a quota system: five percent for high schools and three for universities in the capital, ten percent for schools and five for universities in the rest of Russia, except for the Pale, which admitted fifteen percent to its high schools, ten percent to the universities. Jews were not allowed to become civil servants, and although subject to conscription in the army they could not become officers. No Christian could enter a legal marital bond with a person of the Jewish faith. However, these restrictions only applied to practising Jews; conversion to Orthodoxy sufficed to entitle the convert to all the freedoms enjoyed by those born Christians. Yet the convert had to pay a terrible price. Every Jew was brought up to believe that by betraying the faith of his fathers he would bring disgrace to his family and community. A father who refused to sever all links with a daughter converted to Christianity would be driven from his community. In such circumstances conversion was understandably rare. In the early twentieth century fifty percent of the world's Jewish population lived within the boundaries of the Russian Empire.

The Orthodox clergy are divided into two groups, the "white" or married clergy, which provides the church's parish priests, and the "black" or monastic clergy. Those intending to marry must do so before ordination; others become monks. In prerevolutionary Russia the white parochial clergy formed an independent class, or rather estate, with priests' sons habitually marrying priests' daughters. They were usually persons of relatively limited education, who frequently lived a life that differed little enough from that of their peasant parishioners, supporting themselves in part at least by cultivating the plot of land allotted them. Scope for advancement was limited to one rung of the ladder, from priest to archpriest, unless the priest were to be widowed, and become a monk.

Monasticism has always had a vital part to play in Orthodoxy. Eastern monasticism is essentially contemplative and inward looking, whether the monks lived alone, as hermits, or in loosely knit communities. It does not have the emphasis on active works that is found in many Western orders. Above all the Eastern monk seeks, through prayer and contemplation, for knowledge of God. For over a thousand years the heart of Eastern monasticism has been Athos, a rocky peninsula in northern Greece that ends in a six-thousand-foot mountain known as the Holy Mountain. The whole peninsula consists entirely of monasteries, and in its heyday it contained over forty thousand monks, although by 1930 there were scarcely more than a tenth of that number. Early in this century Russian monks were very much in the majority, although this is no longer the case. The entire population of the Holy Mountain is male, no females of any kind, including animals, being allowed upon it, although in latter years a relaxation has been made in the case of hens.

Monks and holy men have always been prominent in Russian Orthodoxy. In 1914 the empire contained no fewer than 1,025 monasteries, although the number is sadly reduced today; one of the very few still functioning is the famous Trinity St. Sergius monastery at Zagorsk, just outside Moscow, a massive establishment and fortified place that has been a bastion of faith, and sometimes of resistance to foreign powers too, for some four centuries. Before the revolution itinerant monks and ordinary pilgrims from every walk of life, literally in the thousands, could be seen wandering across the face of Russia, going from one holy place to the next, worshipping at the shrines of saints, or visiting a particularly holy icon, in fulfillment of a vow or in search of salvation. For the great majority of the population, religion was still a vital driving force that brought people of every level together as they observed the patterns of ritual and of worship, the Lenten fast that culminates in the Easter celebrations, the supreme moment of the Orthodox year, with the joyous announcement that "Christ is risen, He is truly risen." Orthodoxy was then, as it has remained for many within and outside Russia, a truly active faith, one which does not seek to maintain contact with the faithful by "keeping abreast of the times" and pandering to modes and fashions. It offers a community of faith and worship that embraces its faithful, providing them, by its magnificent rituals, with a glorious mediation between man and God.

THE LIFE AND TIMES OF GRIGORII RASPUTIN

CHAPTER 1

My country, O my country
Distant Siberia
You are rich in forests,
Your animals are countless.
Your people, O my country,
Come from all over Russia,
From the Don and from the Volga,
Came people bold in spirit,
Came people rich in courage.

SIBERIAN FOLK SONG

IT IS SAID that if you stand on top of a certain hill more or less in the middle of England and look east, the next piece of high ground you see will be the Urals, the mountain range that marks the eastern boundary of Europe. Anyone travelling in that direction might suppose, after passing through Germany, Poland and European Russia, that he knew all there was to know about monotony; the monotony of unrelieved flatness, unrelieved, unaltering vistas that stretched endlessly away from the carriage window, expanses of flat, grey, thinly wooded countryside, crossed now and again by a muddy road. Yet however oppressive and overpowering European Russia might appear to a visitor, once across the Urals and into Siberia even European Russians were overpowered and oppressed by the sheer scale, uniformity and sense of unchecked expanse that they encountered in the land that lay before them, reaching four thousand miles to the Pacific Ocean, its total area exceeding that of the United States of America combined with Europe, less European Russia and Poland. The Western Siberian province of Tobolsk alone, only one among nine, was larger than France, Germany, and Great Britain put together.

In the early twentieth century it took about three and a half days to travel from St. Petersburg to the Urals, a distance of some fifteen hundred miles. The journey was not without charm, as the train moved sedately along the line. One reason the train moved so slowly, averaging about eighteen miles an hour, was the primitive signalling system that stretched from St. Petersburg to the Pacific. Every *verst* (.66 of a mile) there was a yellow-painted log cabin, with a signaller and his family. They would display a green flag by day to show the line was clear, a green lamp by night. The train actually moved at rather more than eighteen miles an hour between stops, but these could be protracted, thanks to the excellent refreshment rooms to be found at each station. As an English traveller of the time wrote:

> If ever the Muscovite thanks the Great White Czar for anything he should thank him for the food on the railways. Foreigners grumble about the slowness of the Russian trains. They are not particularly slow, the time is spent at the railway station while the passengers eat.[1]

As you entered Siberia by train the first, indeed the only thing to be seen was forest, the *taiga,* three million square miles of boggy woodland; Siberian poplars, spruces, Scotch pines, alder and birch trees, growing close together and reaching out in all directions as far as the eye could see. In Western Siberia, and close to the railway line, there were occasional villages and signs of agriculture; forest would be interrupted by the odd ploughed field, usually with a tree or two left standing in it. Even to Russian eyes man's impact upon the environment appeared unimpressive. Even to Russian eyes it all appeared hopeless and run down, particularly since the cultivation of a particular patch of land was usually a short-term affair. A field of black earth would be cleared of forest, farmed intensively for five or six years, and then left to lie fallow for another decade. Animal husbandry was also conducted on a fairly haphazard basis, the cattle being allowed to fend for themselves without additional feed, which made them poor in quality, ill-favoured and bad milk producers.

The climate was no help. From May to September the boggy *taiga,* with its swamps and its mosquitoes, produced bad water and all manner of fever and disease. Although the first signs of winter came with the nightly hoar frosts of late August, heavy autumn rains made the roads impassable until the snows came in October, shortly to be accompanied by frosts of up to −50° Fahrenheit, which would remain for the next six months before melting to render travel impossible again until the end of April. The Siberians are proud of their cold but dry winter. "One of our winters is worth nine summers," they boast.

Russia first began to settle the huge eastern territory in the sixteenth century, when a cossack adventurer, Ermak, in dangerously bad standing with Ivan the Terrible, led a series of expeditions into Western Siberia, allegedly regaining the tsarist favour by presenting him with new-won territories, as an Elizabethan pirate might present new conquests to his queen. From then on there was a steady drift to the east of adventurers, soldiers, trappers, traders, runaway serfs and anyone anxious to escape the heavy hand of the central government, for reasons of politics, or as we shall see, more often and more significantly, religion. It would long be possible for whole communities to up and migrate east to settle deep in the *taiga,* without the authorities even knowing that they were there. In many respects Siberia was to European Russia what the West was to Eastern seaboard America, creating its own version of the frontier mentality–but with important differences in treatment of the native population, for example. Thus, although by 1900 more than eighty-five percent of the population of Western Siberia was European, Europeans and the indigenous population had lived together in harmony for centuries, without the need for reservations. Yet there were "reservations" of a different kind. While the tsarist government's penal settlements may never have matched the scale of the USSR's gulag archipelago, which includes several areas the size of France devoted exclusively to camps, there can be no doubt that the steady stream of convicts that had been trudging east without interruption for nearly four centuries, to the tune, by 1885, of nearly twelve thousand a year, had left its mark upon the land. Moreover, to prove that in Russia some things do not change, descriptions of prison conditions on *étape,* that is, on the road to Siberia, could well have been written by Solzhenitsyn. George Kennan, a Western Union man turned journalist from Ohio, describes conditions in a Siberian forwarding prison in 1887:

> "You see how it is," said the warden, addressing me. "This cell contains more than four times the number of prisoners it was intended to hold, and the same condition of things exists throughout the prison." I looked around the cell. There was practically no ventilation whatever, and the air was so poisoned and foul that I could scarcely bring myself to breathe it. We visited successively in the yard six cells essentially like the first, and found in every one of them three or four times the number of prisoners for which it was intended . . . In most cells there was not room enough on the sleeping platforms for all of the convicts, and scores of men slept every night on the foul, muddy floors, under the *nary* (plank beds), and in the gangways between them and the walls.[2]

Siberia, then, was at one time a refuge and a place of penal servitude and exile. The land was settled by pioneers, fugitives and ex-convicts, and it evolved a peasant culture and cast of mind that differed markedly from its Russian counterpart, and for good reason. Throughout Russia the entire peasant population had known increasingly severe degrees of servitude from the beginnings until 1861. Some serfs were private property, to be bought, sold, flogged within an inch of their lives, if not further, by their owners. Others belonged to the state, working on state farms or in state factories. Centuries of servitude had left their mark, in the shape of a passive acceptance of authority, however cruel or unjust, since authority could no more be avoided than a force of nature, and justice was a long way off. This fatalistic acceptance of cruelty and misrule was accompanied by a capacity to endure conditions of physical hardship that any other European would have found intolerable. The attitude was assisted by the Orthodox religion, which encourages the faithful to "accept suffering" as a God-sent burden. The preposterous capacity for submission and endurance found in the people has helped to shape an important characteristic of Russian public life—a feature found in tsarist times, and still found today—namely a disregard for the interests, well-being or indeed life of one's fellow men, together with a resigned tolerance of administrative incompetence at every level; attitudes shared by governors and governed alike.

The Siberian peasant was different. He lacked the *pokornost'*—meek submission—that marked his Great Russian counterpart, and this because although there had been factory serfs aplenty in Siberia, agricultural serfdom, and more especially serf-owning landowners, or *pomeshchik,* were unknown. The Siberian peasant had always owned his own land and was immensely proud of the fact: "Siberia never knew the *pomeshchik,* here all is from God and for the people,"[3] as one peasant saying went. To Great Russians, Siberians appeared dour, uncommunicative, awkward and highly insular, displaying little interest in anything taking place west of the Urals. They were conscious of being a people apart, and would describe crossing the Urals as "going to Russia." The peasants were stubborn and independent-minded, they never fawned before authority and "addressed highly placed officials as equals, not superiors."[4]

As one might expect from a huge decentralised agricultural society, Siberia abounded in different dialects, varying in accent and in idiom, although to Great Russian ears there is a certain manner of speech that sounds specifically Siberian; low in pitch, soft, with dark booming vowel sounds, very different from the singsong Moscow accent that is the standard spoken Russian of today.

Siberian peasants were generally more prosperous than their Russian counterparts. Like them they lived in village communities, and it was the community as a whole that controlled the allocation of land to individual farmers. Each village would be surrounded by several hundred acres of communal grazing. Rather than fence off individual fields, the Siberians preferred to leave them unfenced, simply enclosing the common pasture. Thus each village was ringed with a fence, and at the point at which it crossed the road on each side of the village there would be a gate and gatekeeper's hut. All farm buildings were contained within the villages, so that it was possible to drive for hours through cultivated land without seeing a single building of any kind.

The villages themselves were of miserable appearance. They consisted of two long rows of houses built of undressed and unpainted logs, caulked with moss. They would have elaborately carved window frames, however, and the shutters would often be brightly coloured. When there was not enough glass to fill the frames, the deficiency would be made up with birch bark. Cottages would be separated from one another by yards, containing sheds and stabling, and the houses were said to smell "like all the cats in the province."[5] Anyone getting his first glimpse of a Siberian village street would be entitled to think that it was a depressing, run-down affair:

> The wide street has no sidewalks; it is sometimes a sea of liquid mud from the walls of the houses on one side, to the walls of the houses on the other; and there is not a tree, nor a bush, nor a square yard of grass in the settlement. Bristly, slab-sided, razor-backed pigs lie here and there in the mud, and wander up and down the street in search of food, and the whole village makes an impression of shiftlessness, poverty and squalor.[6]

In a sense the impression was erroneous. The inhabitants might well be quite prosperous, but on the whole Siberian villagers saw little point in exerting themselves to improve the quality of public village life, as long as they found that life tolerable. Yet this is not to say that they led a cheerless existence, or one that lacked colour. On the contrary, not only did they like to fill their houses with flowers, they liked to dress as brightly as they could:

> Some of the peasant women had a strength of mind sufficient to carry a green bodice over a purple skirt, while red and pink, or heliotropes and browns of every shade, were largely fancied. Their dress is very uniform. Outside of all is an ordinary apron; below that a print skirt, often held up by two bands of the same material passing over the loose bodice, one over each shoulder. The men are content with a brightly coloured shirt, velveteen or cloth trousers, jack-boots and peak-cap, and a short pea-jacket in the cool evenings.[7]

Village life had its own steady agricultural rhythms; spring and summer in the fields, with harvest coming quite late in the year, and then the long winter months, when there was nothing to do but look after the animals. Some of the menfolk would go to work in the nearest towns as artisans or labourers. Others would have their cottage industry, wood carving mostly, or hunt and trap. Others still, like Rasputin's father, drove a horse and sleigh for the state.

The rhythms of the peasant year were not just seasonal, they were also set by saints' days and religious festivals, which were often accompanied by customs that were manifestly pagan in origin. On New Year's Eve unmarried girls would go to listen at the closed door of a neighbour's house; those who heard a man's name would be married by the end of the year. Midsummer's Day was an unashamedly pagan festival. Bonfires were lit, as they used to be all over Northern Europe, along river-banks wherever possible. Young girls would weave wreaths, which they donned before jumping over the fires and into the river, letting the wreaths float down the stream. The next morning they would go in search of them, hoping to tell from their position and condition whether or not they would get married that year.

For all the charm of such practices, they were really incidental to village life proper. In European Russia this centred around the inn, but since inns were less frequent in Siberia, entertainment usually began in private houses. However, as in the rest of Russia, the chief source of entertainment came in bottles. Drunkenness existed upon the scale of the land itself; long winters together with a staple of grain spirit saw to that. To get the feeling of a Siberian holiday one needs to imagine the sound of a wheezing accordion, sometimes drowned by loud voices shouting and cursing, accompanied by the hot reek of vodka, salt fish and raw onions, as the village drunks, in need of a little fresh air, tumble out of the house and move onto the streets:

> I saw a whole crowd of women singing and dancing, some of them had red ribbons pinned to their headscarves, some wore their sheep-skin coats inside out, others wore comic headgear and hats: they carried sticks and wreaths of flowers, one of them had a bale of straw. As they came to side streets they would set a handful of straw alight, jump over it, stamp out the fire and go on their way. They threw snow at any man they en-

> countered and tried to knock him to the ground; they were all perfectly drunk, stumbling into one another, falling over, four or five at a time, slipping over together shrieking on the ice, throwing up their legs and revealing the most remarkable sights. Their songs made use of words that are not to be found in any dictionary . . . The following day, and a terrible snowstorm notwithstanding, crowds of drunken and frenzied women were still staggering about the village.[8]

The Siberian judicial code laid down that the penalty for assaulting the humblest civil servant could be as harsh as two years hard labour–unless it could be established that the culprit was drunk. The worst a drunken aggressor could expect for, say, doing physical violence to a judge was three days in the local prison.[9]

Yet it should never be forgotten that this disregard for life's finer things went along with other qualities no more familiar in the West: that capacity for emotional warmth, tenderness, and spiritual cosiness which made Siberians describe convicts as "the unfortunates." This benevolence was reflected more tangibly in the dish of food and bowl of milk which most peasants would leave outside their well-bolted doors each night for vagrants and men on the run; the fact that they would not dare admit them into their homes did not mean that they were willing to let them go hungry.[10]

There was also to be found considerable practical intelligence or peasant cunning, which was restricted in its scope by the almost total lack of formal education, and the limitations of a society that had remained virtually unaffected by the culture of the West. The Siberian peasant of the early twentieth century was narrow-minded, conservative, with a deep and often less than Orthodox religious faith, and was frequently profoundly superstitious. He might have been born into this age, but at least until 1914 he was not a part of it. Siberia was altogether removed in time from the Europe of the twentieth century. The first motor car to be seen in Siberia, the property of a Danish agriculturalist, was also the cause of Siberia's first traffic accident–when an old woman who saw it took it for the chariot of Antichrist and died of a heart attack. When Siberian units first went into action in East Prussia in 1914 they panicked at the sight of enemy aircraft, taking them as the sure and certain sign that God was fighting for the other side.[11]

It is appropriate that the most famous and powerful Siberian of modern history, Grigorii Efimovich Rasputin, should have been a peasant, who, along with his own remarkable qualities and powers, preserved a peasant's intuitive cunning and narrowness, a peasant's love of drink, dance, and unbridled celebration, a peasant's capacity for warmth and for superstition, and above all, perhaps, the Siberian peasant's readiness to address his superiors as equals—a readiness Rasputin took to unheard-of lengths, when, wearing his peasant boots and embroidered blouses, he addressed the tsar and tsarina as "Papa" and "Mama." Rasputin died as he was born, a peasant of Western Siberia, only the second of his class to get close to the Russian throne. The first man to do so, Patriarch Nikon in the seventeenth century, can be said with some justification to have destroyed the unity of the Orthodox church forever.[12] The second, Rasputin, may be said with more justification still to have destroyed the dynasty. In neither case was the destruction intentional.

The village of Pokrovskoe, Rasputin's birthplace, is in Western Siberia, not far beyond the Ural Mountains, and some sixteen hundred miles from St. Petersburg. The village lies on a river, the Toura, which forms part of the Ob basin, a network of navigable rivers that played an important part in the Western Siberian communications system. Especially in spring and autumn, when the roads were impassable, axle-deep in mud, the wide, fast-flowing rivers of Siberia, which had the draft to accommodate steamers of considerable size, offered the only means of long-distance travel in the area. Since the Trans-Siberian Railway passed well to the south, a traveller from the capital wishing to journey to Pokrovskoe would take a train which would bring him in three-and-a-half days to the end of the line, the Siberian town of Tyumen. Before the laying of the Trans-Siberian Railway all exiles from northern and central Russia travelling east to Siberia used to pass through Tyumen, and Baedeker's guide for 1914 estimates that in the sixty years preceding the opening of the railway an astonishing total of 908,266 persons had passed that way.

How the traveller would continue his journey depended on the season. If it was winter, and the rivers were frozen, he would have the misfortune to go by road, along the so-called Trakt No. 4. It was a miserable journey and all images of sleighs gliding smoothly over a carpet of snow, sleigh bells jingling and cheerful driver calling to his galloping horses, should be put aside. The *trakt* was in constant use by convoys of heavy transports, and the journey was slow and anything but smooth:

> Bump jolt, bump, jolt, over huge frozen lumps of snow, and into holes, and up and down those dreadful waves and furrows made by the traffic. Your head seems to belong to every part of the sledge! It is first bumped at the top; then the conveyance gives a lurch, and you get an unexpected knock against the side . . . Bright memories of asphalt and the omnibus spring up to diversify your thoughts. Little gleams of light which you pass on your way seem to come from tiny hut windows in the forest.
>
> "Driver, can't we stop a minute at one of those huts, where the lights are?"
>
> "Lights! They're wolves."[13]

The river journey was easier:

> The S.S. *Irkutsk* plied its way between Tyumen and Tobolsk. In the first class there were Russian officials and officers on their way to take up positions in the far North, Siberian merchants dealing in dairy produce, fish and skins, and by no means least important, furs, squirrel, fox, sable, etc. In the steerage, there was a motley collection of peasants, soldiers and workers, and, among them a group of extremely distinguished-looking young Russians who were students of both sexes, on their way to serve terms of penal servitude in the far North, for political offences . . . For hours the ship passed enormous pine forests on the port side and an endless wilderness of wild steppe on the starboard, with cultivation only at rare intervals.[14]

Anyone wishing to reach Tobolsk, the capital of Western Siberia, would travel 257 *versts* along the *trakt,* or 403½ by river. It was by the latter route that the imperial family went on their last journey east in 1917, before retracing their steps west as far as Ekaterinburg, some two hundred miles west of Tyumen, where they met a Bolshevik firing squad. One hundred and five miles to the east of Tyumen, just before the Toura River joins the river Tobol, it makes a wide curve to the south. The northern bank rises steeply at that point, and, as the boat moves slowly round the bend, there is plenty of time to observe the village of Pokrovskoe standing above the river. Pokrovskoe was a village of considerable size. It was a river stop, between the villages of Monastyrskaya and Podbulyga, and also a staging post or station upon the *trakt,* between the stations of Yuzhekovskaya and Sazonovskaya. A contemporary travel guide to Western Siberia describes it as a village, *selo,* as opposed to a hamlet, *derevnya,* and one can gain a sense of its relative importance from the fact that of the seventy-five stops along the river between Tyumen and Tobolsk, only eight are accorded *selo* status.[15] As the steamer moved slowly round the Pokrovskoe bend, the imperial family made the most of this splendid opportunity to inspect the birthplace of their murdered friend, healer, and councillor as they took their last journey back along the river, thereby fulfilling a prophecy of Rasputin's. In 1916 he had announced to an astonished lady-in-waiting that the imperial family would see his village before they died.[16]

Pokrovskoe consisted of several streets of spacious wooden houses of one or sometimes two stories, with ornately carved and painted beams and window frames. The village was dominated by a large white church with a gilded dome. All the streets met at the church, which was set on a slight prominence, and was easily seen from the river. In most respects it was an ordinary village, more prosperous perhaps and more lively than most since it was on both the road and the river. It was also distinguished by another feature that has survived to this day; Pokrovskoe is part of an area known as *Zatatarskoe Boloto,* "The marsh beyond the Tartars," which was, and remains, well known for its wealth of legend and enduring superstition. Today, as an ex-resident told the author, the spot is famous for a particular kind of hunter, known as a *khvostitel'* or "tailer"; they are said to be able to transport themselves to different parts of the forest by teleportation, unpowered flight, although their name suggests that in earlier times they probably relied on broomsticks.

The village, as one would expect from the name of the region, is surrounded by marshland, with thick growths of black, dank conifers on slightly higher ground, the trees growing at all angles, and the space between them littered with fallen branches and tops broken off by lightning.

A description of the village published in a Petrograd newspaper in 1915, part of an attack upon Rasputin, describes Pokrovskoe as a poor village, a wretched boggy place, remote and wild, inhabited by dour Siberian "*zhigany,*" or rogues, a race capable of anything.[17] Nevertheless there is nothing to suggest that Pokrovskoe's record of drunkenness, violence and horse stealing was worse than that of any other Siberian village. Siberia was, after all, Russia's Wild West.

✧ ✧ ✧

We do not know when Rasputin was born, for peasant culture keeps no records, and it must be admitted that we know next to nothing about the first forty years of his life, because he lived in a world beyond the reach of the written word. There are a few landmarks, one piece of official testimony, and apart from that virtually nothing but hearsay evidence from various prejudiced sources, such as a daughter and a number of old men trying to reach forty years back in time. Yet however unsatisfactory this might appear at first glance, there is a strange propriety about this lack of hard factual framework. The part Rasputin played in Russian history has little to do with facts; it derives from the tangled mass of hearsay and innuendo in which he was wrapped. It was not so much what Rasputin did but what he was rumoured to do that mattered. In this respect he was, literally, a legend in his own time. The legend was known to the whole of Russia, the man to very few. Even the manner of his death was legendary, nor do the legends end with his death.

In many respects the life of Rasputin resembles the life of a saint, in the sense that hagiography is a stylized form of narrative that only touches on those aspects of the saint's life that pertain to saintliness: anything else is irrelevant. The man is hidden by his legend. It is out of this accumulation of legend and rumour, none of which can be believed without question, although none can be altogether discounted, that we must watch the real, the historical Rasputin gradually emerge.

CHAPTER 2

Ra Ra Raspoutine
Lover of the Russian Queen.
POP SONG 1979

IF BY LEGEND one means the smothering of hard fact by fantasy, the projection of what people want to believe upon a core of truth, then the legend of "the mad monk" (he was neither a monk nor mad), "lover of the Russian queen" (he was not her lover and the lady in question was an empress), is already contained in the very name of "Russia's greatest love machine." To Russian ears "Rasputin" has an uncannily appropriate ring, tailor-made for the sexually hyperactive peasant who brought down the dynasty. In "Rasputin" he will immediately hear *"rasputstvo,"* or debauch, sexual licence. The association sounds too good to be true, and strictly speaking it is incorrect. There are two other words close to "Rasputin," each of which, however, also has a certain relevance: *rasputitsa,* a word used to describe the state of roads in spring and autumn, when they were and often still are rendered impassable by mud and melting snow, and also *rasput'e,* which describes a fork in the road. It is from the latter word that "Rasputin" is probably derived, and the name is a common one in Western Siberia, presumably describing the inhabitants of villages located at such spots. Thus, today there is a Soviet Rasputin, an author who is a well-known member of the so-called "village prose" school. Yet inevitably it is the name's sexual connotations that are the most striking, and this was the case even in Grigorii Efimovich's lifetime; for in 1907 he made a valiant but unsuccessful attempt to modify his name to Rasputin-Novykh, Rasputin-Newman. (*Novykh* is a plural form of the adjective *noviy,* or new.)

We know little about Rasputin's family background. The most detailed account of his father, Efimii or Evimii Andreevich, suggests that he came to Siberia from Saratov, where he had had trouble with the law. A carter working for the state, he had passed out dead drunk by his horse on the way back from a fair, only to find when he came to that the horse had been stolen. As the animal was state property he was imprisoned for a year and subsequently moved east to Pokrovskoe. The author of this account gives a convincing description of how he established himself there, stopped drinking, won the respect of his neighbours, and began to prosper. However, after the death of his wife and two of his children, he took to drink again and his affairs went into a decline. He took to thieving and was frequently beaten senseless by his fellow peasants in retribution. This altogether plausible story loses some of its credibility when we go on to learn that one day he was beaten so badly that his young son was obliged to take him to hospital in Tyumen, where he died, leaving the future mad monk an orphan in the late nineteenth century. Rasputin's father actually lived well on into the next century, dying less than a year before his son. Besides, Rasputin himself liked to claim that he came from old Siberian stock: "There were Rasputins living in Pokrovskoe before Ermak conquered Siberia for Ivan the Terrible," he used to boast.

All versions agree that Evimii was indeed a carter, driving a sleigh in winter, a *telega* or springless cart in summer along the east-west highway, Trakt No. 4. He was employed by the state once more, driving between the post stations set some sixteen miles to the east and west of Pokrovskoe. His official status was betokened by a badge tied to his left arm bearing the imperial eagle, and a round metal plate with the same device attached to his cap. By all accounts he was fairly prosperous, but not rich. Together with his driving he farmed on a modest scale. As was the local custom, he took care of the grain crop, leaving his wife, Anna Egorovna, to do the rest of the household and agricultural work. The family house was large, with a gently sloping roof and double wooden walls, but it was not the house of a wealthy peasant, having only one story. Made of thick dressed logs it had a hall and two rooms, the *izba* and the *gornitsa,* the former containing the stove, which reached to the ceiling except for an area on which one could stretch out. Close to the stove and just under the roof was a platform that served as the family sleeping area. The room was lined with wooden benches, and the left-hand corner, looking from the door, the so-called "red" or beautiful corner, had an icon hanging there. This was the room in which the family lived, slept and ate. The smaller *gornitsa* was for guests. It held a bed and a much smaller stove. Beside the house was an enclosed yard with stabling for two horses, a bathhouse and a small cellar.[1]

We do not know the exact date of Rasputin's birth. One fairly reliable source suggests 1864 or 1865,[2] another claims that it was 1863.[3] Rasputin himself said that he was aged twenty-eight in 1892, so that it would appear that he was born after 1862 and before 1865.

The little we know about his childhood has more than a slight ring of legend to it. It seems that his mother died when he was quite young, though we cannot say when. The biographer who killed his father off gives him an elder sister, Maria, who was an epileptic and who died young. While walking beside the river Toura she had a fit, fell in and drowned. This version of the legend may well be a convenient way of slipping epilepsy into Rasputin's family background. However, nothing in his own life suggests that he was epileptic, and had there been the slightest suggestion that he was, one may be certain that his detractors would have made the most of it. The only plausible element in the story is the name Maria. That was the name of Rasputin's own daughter, whom he could have named after a dead sister, just as he named a son, Dmitri, after his brother, who certainly did exist, and who really came to grief in the Toura.

Dmitri was two years older than Grigorii. All we know about him is that he died young. It would seem that the two brothers were playing by the river when he fell in. Grigorii allegedly jumped to his rescue, and they were both fished out by a passing peasant. Grigorii was none the worse for his immersion, but Dmitri caught pneumonia and died soon after. This much is a matter of well-attested fact, but hereafter legend, or something closely akin to it, takes over. Grigorii was deeply affected by his brother's death. He was about eleven years old at the time, and it was now that he first began to reveal his powers of second sight.

The delicate question of Rasputin's "powers" has to be faced. Powers there certainly were, although they were less extensive than has usually been supposed. Matters are complicated by the fact that it is hard to keep an open mind when dealing with paranormal phenomena. Those who want them to exist clutch at anything that supports their belief, while those who take the opposing view are consistently dismissive. As we shall see, two kinds of "extrasensory" power have been attributed to Rasputin: healing and precognition. Since it is important that the reader know where his author stands on such issues, suffice it to say that I believe that both faith healing and precognition are possible, in the sense that I do not reject evidence of their existence *a priori,* as being against nature. But in the case of Rasputin I have been careful throughout, in so far as is possible, to separate fact from hearsay, and to allow the facts to speak for themselves. There are, as we shall see, well-attested instances of "miraculous" healing, and some instances of something close to prophecy, but the account we have of Rasputin's childhood clairvoyance is not among them. Whether he was indeed clairvoyant as a child we cannot say, but what is certain is that the account of these powers has a ring of hagiography about it, and must be treated with the utmost caution.

The story of Rasputin the clairvoyant child comes from his daughter Maria, who has written three books about her father. The first two are on the whole sober if obviously sympathetic accounts, while the third and most recent is more sensational in tone and content, and differs in some of its detail from the earlier works. We cannot verify her description of her father's childhood and youth: she is the sole source and there is no possibility of cross-checking. This is particularly the case in her description of Rasputin's childhood powers.

It would seem that after the death of his brother the boy became strangely withdrawn. He spent a great deal of time with the animals in his father's yard, and established an uncanny degree of rapport with them. He was especially good with the horses. Throughout his life Rasputin had the power to calm troubled minds with a few soothing words and gestures, displaying the kind of gentle authority that wins the trust of a nervous animal even more readily than that of humans. Anyone who could calm the hysterical ladies of St. Petersburg as easily as Rasputin would have had little trouble with the most highly strung thoroughbred filly, let alone the stocky Siberian ponies in his father's yard. However, according to his daughter, who sounds as if she is relaying a family tradition, it was not just a question of the eleven-year-old Rasputin having a strange hold over animals. She says that he also possessed second sight. When something about the house was missing Rasputin would regularly be able to see where it had got to and recover it. He was also able to apply these powers to people. According to his daughter, he said of his childhood: "I used to play with the children of Pokrovskoe and quarrelled with them, but I never dared to steal the smallest thing. I used to believe that everybody would at once see that I had stolen something, since I, myself, was aware of it as soon as one of my comrades had stolen. Even when he had stolen in a distant place and hidden the object I would always see that object behind him."[4]

He claimed that at the time he attached no importance to his gift, assuming that everybody could do as much. As we shall see, he soon came to realise that this was not the case, and that it was quite possible to take other people's property and get away with it, provided that one was not caught in the act.

The most famous instance of his childhood power concerns a theft. In the course of an evening gathering in the Rasputin house a villager announced that someone had stolen his horse. The young Rasputin was lying on the stove with a fever. He interrupted the discussion and pointed to one of the most prosperous peasants in the village, quietly observing that he was the culprit. Such an implausible charge was indignantly dismissed. However, later that night some of the villagers followed the accused to his home and saw him lead the horse in question out of his yard. They promptly fell on him and administered the standard Siberian justice for horse thieves, beating him as close as they could get to death. There is no way in which the story can be verified, but it has become an integral part of the Rasputin legend—the first time the great man revealed his powers.

It must be said that in later life Rasputin did not often reveal specifically clairvoyant powers. He tended to have more generalised intuitions, and in that sense the episode does not accord with what we know of him. In years to come he did not go in for the recovery of lost property, and there is no doubt that had he possessed that talent in any degree, both he and his admirers would have made much of it, although it may be argued that this was a faculty he possessed as a child, which waned as he grew older. There is, however, one feature of the story that does ring true: throughout his life Rasputin would possess an uncanny ability to read character and make instant assessments of the strengths and weaknesses of a personality; to smell out guilt. He was by no means infallible, or he could never have accepted an invitation to the Yusupov palace late on the night of December 16, 1916, yet his remarkable rise from a small Siberian village to closest proximity to the throne was largely founded on his capacity for instant and accurate reading of others.

The picture Maria Rasputin paints for us of an introverted boy with strange psychic powers does not accord well with other accounts of his youth and adolescence—which is perfectly understandable, since Maria was very much the loyal daughter. In 1917 the Provisional Government set up the so-called Muravyev Commission to look into the abuses of the last years of the imperial regime. The poet Alexander Blok acted as its secretary. The commission interviewed a great many figures prominent in tsarist politics, and other less distinguished persons. The six volumes of its findings, and certain supplementary sections published later, provide an extraordinary picture of the age.

In the course of its work the commission interviewed a handful of Rasputin's village contemporaries, who recalled what they could of his childhood, looking back over a span of some forty years. The picture they paint is of a turbulent, dirty and sexually precocious boy, unruly, disagreeable, and widely known as *soplyak,* or "snot-nose." As adolescence came on, Rasputin grew wilder still, began to drink and tumble girls, and fast acquired the reputation of a drunk and a lecher. Although it may be a case of peasants telling their superiors what they might want to hear about the "evil genius," the stories ring true. Rasputin possessed to a high degree the Russian capacity for wild indulgence of appetite, which transcends mere coarseness by the exuberant quality of its excess. It comes as no surprise to find him pushing his celebrations beyond the norms of acceptable peasant behaviour from an early age. His contemporaries remember that already at the age of fifteen he was a drinker of vodka.

Where Western culture distinguishes between drinkers and non-drinkers, peasant Russia distinguishes between vodka drinkers and the rest. "My man never touches vodka" was the peasant woman's proudest boast. Whereas wine or beer usually made for an acceptable degree of intoxication, vodka provided its consumer with the quickest possible path to oblivion. The point of the stuff was to get falling-down drunk as quickly as possible. Throughout imperial Russia the state had a monopoly upon the sale of vodka, which played a vital part in balancing the annual budget. It was sold at state liquor shops, and its consumption, just off the premises, was something of a ritual:

> A crowd of drunken carters and barefoot vagrants were opening their various sized bottles. This is how it was done: first of all the wax had to be scraped off the top by means of a tin grater driven into a tree trunk in a spot where the drunks would not spoil the town's flora. The bearded carters with transparent blue eyes and red noses, in oilskin or cardboard hats with side buckles, and blue cloaks down to their ankles, together with barefoot tramps, literally bare footed, or occasionally wearing some kind of incredible bast shoes tied to their feet with strings, in denim trousers and torn shirts, through the holes of which one could see their naked bodies . . . crowded round the grater and scraped the wax off till the grater seemed to be covered in blood. Then, after a skillful knock on the bottom of the noggin with the palm of their hands had shot out the cork, they threw their heads back and poured the pure liquid, which had a sweet,

> slightly narcotic smell . . . straight down their thin throats. When satisfied they wiped their hairy mouths on their sleeves and bit into appetising, yellow-green salted cucumbers, from which brine and the colourless seeds sprouted profusely.[5]

Drinking vodka encourages ruthless pursuit of a "high," and shortly after this is attained the vodka drinker is frequently known to fall over. In Rasputin's case it had other no less unfortunate consequences, for it would seem that he took to thieving in order to satisfy his thirst. E. I. Kartashev, a neighbour some fourteen years his senior, remembers for the commission:

> I caught Grigorii stealing pieces of my fence. He broke them up and put the sticks on his cart and was about to tie them up and take them away when I caught him and ordered him to come to the village elder with the stolen property. When he refused, and in order to get away tried to hit me with his axe, I gave him such a blow with my pitchfork that the blood poured from his nose and mouth and he fell to the ground unconscious. At first I thought I'd killed him, but when he began to move I brought him round and took him to the elder. He didn't want to go but I hit him a few more times in the face, and then he went of his own accord. Shortly after the theft of the fencing I had a pair of horses stolen out of the meadow. I'd had my eye on them on the night of the theft and noticed that Rasputin had been nearby with his friends Konstantin and Trofim, but had paid no attention until I discovered the loss of the horses some hours later. I immediately went back to see if Rasputin was at home. He was back by morning but his friends were nowhere to be found.[6]

Kartashev describes the young Rasputin as guileful, insolent, but possessed of a wild excess-seeking and expansive temperament—all words which in Russian have a ring of grudging admiration to them, since Russians consider moderation and caution to signify a meanness of the spirit. It is with a blend of reproof and covert admiration that Kartashev portrays him staggering drunkenly about, harnessing his horses and going for wild whooping drives through the village, or using the foulest language and fighting with friends and family alike. Frequently he would come to drunken blows with his father, and continued to do so for the next thirty years, conducting himself like a peasant version of Dmitri Karamazov. His neighbours held him in fairly low regard. They considered him a fool and suspected him of being a *varnak* or horse thief, a crime Siberian peasants took very seriously. As an adolescent Rasputin was already sexually active. He would always be attractive to women, projecting an immediate and unspoken authority over members of the opposite sex, making them feel that compliance to his demands was a pleasure in itself. However, on the whole he dissociated sex from feeling. Making love for him was part of the quest for totality of experience through excess, like drink or the gypsy music which he grew to love in later years. Yet although his physical relations with women were almost invariably transitory and purely carnal, they seem to have left remarkably little bitterness in their wake. He had the rare capacity to love and leave women without making them feel rejected. It is true that in later years we shall find women complaining, in a state of bemused retrospective shock, that he had taken advantage of them, but his women never seem to have felt scorned. It says much for his natural authority that he could make his lovers feel that to sleep with him once or twice was enough in itself. He had the gift of making women happy when he was with them, and the still greater gift of soothing away complaints when he moved on.

We know of only one serious emotional attachment in Rasputin's life. At the age of nineteen he met Praskovia Dubrovina, a slightly older girl from a neighbouring village, strikingly good-looking, with the unusual combination of fair hair and dark eyes. She also had remarkable strength of character, resisting all Rasputin's attempts to seduce her, and obliging him to court her assiduously for over six months before she would agree to marry him. The marriage took place in 1883 or 1884. They made a handsome couple. The young Rasputin was very good-looking. A young man of a little over medium height, he held himself very straight, and there was great strength in his broad shoulders. He was beardless in those days, with an open, somewhat weatherbeaten face without a hint of weakness. Everything about him radiated health and physical force, down to his massive calloused hands.

In its way the marriage was a great success. Praskovia was a practical-minded woman, and Rasputin remained attached to her, in his fashion, for the remainder of his life. She kept the household going during his frequent absences, and remained calmly tolerant of his sexual excesses. "Grigorii has enough to go round for everybody," she was known to observe in later years. In due course she gave birth to three children, Dmitri in 1897, Maria in 1898, and Varvara in 1900.

Marriage did not make Rasputin settle down. He had married Praskovia because he desired her, not because he felt that it was time to mend his ways. According to his neighbour Kartashev he grew wilder still and stepped up his drinking appreciably. In fact it would seem that it was as a married man that he was knocked senseless for stealing fenceposts. The villagers' view of him as a fool and a wastrel was no different from Rasputin's own; looking back on his youth he once observed: "I was a drunkard and smoked tobacco, but then I repented and just look what I made of myself."[7]

There can be no doubt that at some time in early manhood Rasputin underwent a genuine spiritual transformation. Now transformations and turning points are the very stuff of hagiography; whether it be Saul's encounter on the road to Damascus, or St. Julian the Hospitaller's killing of his parents, lives of saints regularly feature critical events that turn hitherto ordinary mortals onto the path to sainthood. However, no attempt to de-mythify the man, to separate him from his legend, can escape the fact that something very similar seems to have happened to Rasputin.

> The Russian is never settled; he is so frequently stung with the mania for travelling that it seems to be the call of the blood. He will sometimes rise up suddenly, start off as if in response to a mystic impulse, and wander for days or months or years. The lower orders are oftener possessed by this overmastering passion than their superiors. They are constantly changing their places of abode . . . Thousands of them flit from Western Russia to Eastern Siberia, others pilgrimage to Jerusalem and back again to their respective hamlets, then after an interval they trudge off to Kiev, afterwards to Svyatye Gory, next to the

> northern shrines, and so on, they keep roving until they lie down and die.
>
> Sectarians scour the countryside in every direction preaching, teaching, proselytising. One sect has a rigid rule forbidding its members to tarry longer than three days in one place . . . A well-to-do Russian whose sons were grown up would often distribute his property among his children, take a wallet and a staff, and spend the remainder of his days pilgrimaging from shrine to shrine.[8]

A regular stream of pilgrims or *stranniki* (wanderers) passed through Pokrovskoe along the *trakt:* some travelling east to visit the Abalatsky monastery near Tobolsk, where there was a famous icon of the Virgin, others going some 260 miles northwest to Verkhoturye, one of the most famous monasteries in Russia, which held the relics of St. Simeon the Just. In the previous century it had been immensely wealthy, with an income of over one hundred thousand roubles a year, but in recent years it had declined. However, it was still well-known for its extraordinarily restful atmosphere, quiet, clean and set in a beautiful wood of pine trees and magnificent cedars.[9] Wandering pilgrims were an essential feature of Russian life; they could be seen on any major road, with a bag on their shoulders and a staff in their hands, going from one holy place to another, in expiation of a crime, to render thanks to God, to fulfill a vow, or just to save their souls. As late as 1914 Russia was still predominantly a country of illiterate peasants who lived in a way that in some respects appears closer to the Middle Ages than the twentieth century.

Pilgrims were accorded hospitality as a matter of course, and many of them stayed in the Rasputin household, paying their way by telling stories of their wandering. On the whole these people were sincere and devout, but there were always a fair number of rogues and opportunistic vagabonds who preferred life on the road to a settled existence, and who could expect a crust of bread and a dry place to sleep in the next village.

Legend would have it that as a boy Rasputin was stirred by the pilgrims' accounts of holy places, and it was their tales that developed his religious sense at an early age. His daughter claims that he went to the monastery of Verkhoturye at the age of fifteen, and paid regular return visits over the ensuing years. This is perfectly possible, if only out of curiosity and an urge to wander that would grow stronger and stronger as the years went by. That he should have been womanising and drinking vodka at the age of fifteen was not in itself proof that the young Rasputin lacked a spiritual sense. For someone of Rasputin's temperament riotous living was perfectly compatible with aspiration towards spiritual excellence. Yet whether or not he made such pilgrimages they did not constitute any kind of turning point, encourage him to mend his ways and cease to be a drunkard and smoker of tobacco. The turning point came later.

It came as a direct consequence of the encounter with his neighbour Kartashev, whose horses he and his friends Konstantin and Trofim had stolen. The affair blew up into a major scandal and there was talk in the village of sending the three lads away to eastern Siberia. In the event only Trofim and Konstantin had to go; Rasputin escaped. However, matters did not rest there. He was summoned to appear in court on charges of stealing wood and possible complicity in horse stealing. The case went onto the record, although it was never heard, for Rasputin felt that the moment had come to spend a little time away from Pokrovskoe. He went to the monastery of Verkhoturye for three months, and on his return he was unrecognisable. No longer the wild young man of the village, he had abandoned tobacco forever, and would not touch vodka again for many years. His manner too had changed, so much so that Kartashev concluded that his beating had affected his brain, which may indeed have been the case. He no longer spoke normally, but held forth in sudden nervous bursts, as he discoursed on spiritual topics in garbled, jerky and frequently incomprehensible phrases. He never looked his interlocutor in the eye, kept turning away and leapt nervously from topic to topic.[10] An eyewitness recalls that he conversed not in sentences but in disjointed, syntactically incomplete fragments,[11] and as he talked he twisted his fingers nervously through his sparse beard and kept casting glances at his listeners,[12] all characteristics he would retain for the rest of his life.

Friends who saw him on his return found him mentally disturbed, in a state of high nervous stress. Another neighbour, named V. K. Podshivalov, met him on the homeward journey:

> Some time after Rasputin went to Verkhoturye my mother and I went to Tyumen, and we met Rasputin on his way home. To me he seemed not in his right mind. He was walking home bare-headed, his hair had grown long, and as he went he kept singing some sort of song and waving his arms about.[13]

When he got home he made a similar impression on others: another villager, V. K. Raspopov, recalls seeing him in church. He too felt that the young man was disturbed, singing in a "wild voice" and staring around with an unsettling expression.[14] Not only did he give up drink and tobacco, he also became a vegetarian, and never again would he touch meat, although in later years he would happily eat fish. He also became a recluse, and whereas before he had been totally illiterate, he now proved able to read fairly easily and even to write a little, although he would never learn to spell and his handwriting was no more than an illiterate and barely legible scrawl. He also attempted to study Old Church Slavonic, the Southern Slav language of the Orthodox liturgy, although there is no evidence that he ever got far with it. His personality was altered in other respects; no longer consistently wild and lecherous, he seems to have taken a manic turn, with rapidly alternating moods of nervous exaltation and deep depression, as if he were permanently under some kind of stress while experiencing the urgent need to come to terms with himself.

Rasputin had clearly experienced some kind of conversion during his three months' stay in the monastery. Whether this was the culmination of earlier surges towards the Good we cannot say. Moreover, the conversion seems to have caused considerable emotional disturbance, setting the erstwhile sinner, who had retained his powerful appetites, very much at odds with himself, and inaugurating a struggle between spirit and flesh which would continue for the rest of his life; a struggle in which the flesh would frequently but by no means invariably triumph.

Verkhoturye was not renowned for its relics alone. It had other distinguishing features, one of which was the number of hermits who lived in tiny wooden huts in the forests surrounding the monastery. We have a glimpse of the kind of life such persons continued to live right up to the revolution:

> The hermit lived in the heart of the forest and his hermitage might easily be taken for a poultry farm. He was surrounded by fowls of all descriptions. Perhaps he considered fowls akin to holiness; he gave quantities of eggs to the monastery, but we supped frugally off cold water and black bread. The hermit had no use for beds so we slept miserably on the hard unyielding floor of dried mud, and I must confess that I was very glad when we returned to Verkhoturye where we were able to sleep and bathe in comfort.[15]

It was such a man who gave Rasputin his sense of spiritual vocation, while also teaching him an important lesson in self-discipline, the nature and exercise of authority. The hermit was named Makarii, and he was what is known in the Orthodox church as a *starets,* or elder. Readers familiar with *The Brothers Karamazov* will recall Dostoevsky's description of the *starets* Zosima, a character based upon Dostoevsky's own experience. The *starets* is a monk, who functions as an unofficial spiritual guide, outside the monastic hierarchy. He tends to live on the outskirts of the community. He is especially graced by God, having the power to see into the hearts of men and explain their secret selves to them. Sometimes he is credited with extraordinary powers, notably precognition. Essentially he gives men the additional strength of self-knowledge to assist them in their struggle for spiritual improvement. The *starets* has disciples, as Zosima had Alyesha Karamazov, and the authority he exercises over them is total. He absorbs their will into his own, commanding abdication of the self; the aim being to attain eventual liberation through obedience. He could be a person of the humblest origins, or, like Zosima, an ex-officer who had changed his ways. Acting as an individual, and impelled by the grace of God, he assumes responsibility for his disciples' quest for perfection. He possesses an extraordinary power to bring comfort and lift burdens from those coming to him heavily laden, and to remit sins. He is a healer of the spirit. Makarii was a *starets* of very considerable repute, who in earlier years had travelled extensively over Russia, and had even been received by the tsar and tsarina at Tsarskoe Selo. It is just possible that it was Makarii who sowed in Rasputin the first seed of his future ambition, or at the very least gave him an inkling of just how high a peasant man of God might aspire.

There can be no question of Rasputin's actually becoming Makarii's disciple. Three months would never have sufficed for that. However, he would say in later years that it was Makarii who gave him his sense of vocation and who brought about his transformation. More important still, perhaps, was his experience of the nature of spiritual authority and the manner in which it was exerted. His daughter suggests that it was to his experience of *starchestvo* that he:

> owed his gradual acquisition of that authority which many people completely failed to understand, that strange force of will, and that almost magnetic glance to which all who knew him well have subsequently testified.[16]

It is important to realise that Rasputin did not undergo any long period of spiritual training. Mystics, holy men, gurus, indeed certain kinds of creative artist, devote years to the disciplined development of their gifts; a sense of the spiritual alone is not enough. The power requires training and guidance to be brought to the peak of its fulfillment. Rasputin had little guidance. He was always to remain something of a snapper-up of holy trifles—a line or two of the Scriptures here, a flash of wisdom there, developing a ragbag of garbled pieces of theology and doctrine. Essentially he was a self-educated peasant possessed of a confused jumble of facts and occasional insights. Mental discipline would never be his strong suit, any more than he would prove capable of sustaining a coherent framework of ideas. His talent lay elsewhere, in surges of intuition and healing power, and above all in his capacity to bring comfort and reassurance to others.

CHAPTER 3

I have never met anyone who understood Russians.
GRAND DUKE ALEXANDER MIKHAILOVICH

ALTHOUGH THE TRADITION of *starchestvo* was not universally approved of by the Orthodox church it was in no sense considered heretical. It fell within the bounds of official Christianity. Nevertheless official religion was not the only or even the strongest spiritual force in the Russia of Rasputin's time, and Verkhoturye itself was a centre for a religious movement of a very different kind, so different that it has been suggested that it was not Christian at all, but pagan. Russia's unofficial Christianity had his origins in the seventeenth century, when Patriarch Nikon destroyed the unity of the Orthodox church forever through the imposition of certain reforms, creating a division of faith and allegiance from which it has never recovered.

Nikon sought to revise ecclesiastical ritual and the Old Church Slavonic liturgy, which was full of inaccurate renderings from the original Greek. To many devout Russians this seemed nothing less than sacrilege. As obstinate fundamentalists, they believed in the supremacy of the letter of the law over its spirit. Nonetheless the reforms were accepted by the state, thereby creating a schism or *raskol* in the church, which endures to the present day. Thousands of Christians stayed with the old ways; rather than accept seemingly trivial adjustments, such as making the sign of the cross with three as opposed to two fingers, or an alteration in the spelling of "Jesus," schismatics ran away, fleeing to the lower Volga or the wilds of Siberia, underwent martyrdom, or burnt themselves alive, literally in the thousands–twenty thousand within the first five years.

The Old Believers were schismatics, not heretics. They refused to accept the official church with its reforms and stuck to the old ways with obstinate devotion. Although the schism was not based on class divisions initially, in latter years the Old Belief came to be associated with the arch-conservative merchant class, especially in Moscow, and with communities that had fled to the Siberian forests to escape authority. It is vital to the understanding of their mentality to appreciate that they believed that with the reforms, first of Nikon, later of Peter the Great, the reign of Antichrist had arrived, and that any deviation from their rigid observance of the old ways would imperil their immortal souls; a belief held so profoundly that martyrdom or self-immolation was deemed preferable to any form of compromise.

The conflict between the Old Belief and Orthodoxy was very much alive at the beginning of this century.

> In the early years of the last tsar's reign they were treated with a harshness that smacks of the persecutions of a bygone age. These pillars of conservatism and religious faith, fervent supporters of so much that the old regime stood for, were treated like public enemies and given a harder time than many a future Bolshevik.
>
> An Old Believers' monastery was seized by an Orthodox archimandrite [abbot] who, at the head of fifty cossacks, drove out the monks and took possession of their dwelling. One of their bishops . . . was thrown into prison . . . The Orthodox archimandrite dug up the tombs of two Old Believers held to be saints . . . and breaking their coffins he saturated the boards with petroleum and then burned the remains of the Holy Men to ashes. . . .
>
> Bishop Methodius, one of the pillars of the Old Believers

. . . administered the sacraments to a man who, born in the State Church, had joined the community of Old Believers . . . Methodius was denounced, arrested, tried, found guilty and condemned to banishment in Siberia. And the sentence was carried out with needless brutality. With irons on his feet, penned up together with murderers and other criminals of the worst type, he was sent by *étape* from prison to prison to the government of Yakutsk. [He was then sent on to a still further place of exile.] The aged bishop—he was 78 years old—was set astride a horse, tied down to the animal, and told he must ride thus to his new place of exile about 700 miles distant. "This sentence is death by torture," said Methodius' flock. And they were not mistaken. The old man gave up the ghost on the road [1898] but when, where and how he died and was buried has never been made known.[1]

It was not until 1905 that the Old Believers were accorded legal freedom of worship, and long after that they were ostracised by the official church and subject to much illegal official harassment. Often living in almost complete isolation, they were closer in spirit to the unchanging world of a Tibetan monastery than to modern Europe, as can be seen from the following account of a provincial governor's visit to an isolated Old Believers' community in 1912:

After a pleasant journey along a forest road the police chief and I came to the monastery. We were greeted from afar by the sound of bells. The abbot met me and took me to the church, which was old, of crude design, made of wood and undistinguished. Bishop Militii met us at the steps, dressed in his vestments, together with a double file of monks in cowls and habits decorated with representations of the instruments of Christ's torture and the face of Adam. They were all hundred year old *startsy,* with long white beards, heavy brows over faded eyes, looking like figures from Byzantine icons, having long observed vows of silence and the strictest asceticism. As I approached they fell to their knees and bowed down to the ground before me.

I must confess that the spectacle which was simply steeped in tradition sent a shiver down my spine.[2]

The Old Believers were devout Christians who adhered punctiliously to their rituals, and who lived by a rigid discipline even though they stood outside the official church. However, the consequences of the schism went far beyond the Old Belief. Just as a language requires the support of strong centralised authority to maintain its purity of form, so that it disperses into a multitude of widely differing dialects once that authority begins to lose its hold–as with the history of Latin after the decline of Rome, for example–so it is with religious faiths. The Orthodox church lost much of its authority as a religious power with carefully maintained doctrines and rituals, as peasants in the hundreds of thousands moved away from central Russia rather than accept the new teaching. Some remained with the Old Belief, others started to found increasingly eccentric faiths of their own, constituting the so-called peasant "sects," an infinitely varied series of faiths, one splintering off from another in continuous variation without any "high cultural" guidance from central ecclesiastical authority–in a manner that recalls the development of popular sects in rural America. It was this native peasant sectarianism that shaped the attitudes and the subsequent teachings of Rasputin.

Sectarianism was a specifically peasant form of that search for God, the quest for righteousness, salvation, and justice that so often dominates the Russian consciousness; Gogol, Tolstoy, Dostoevsky, Solzhenitsyn being some of the more obvious examples that spring to mind. It was specifically a popular phenomenon, as one of its historians writes:

> In our history sectarianism was the only occasion on which the Russian people, not as individuals, but in the mass, without leadership or encouragement from the governing powers or the educated made its own contribution to ideas and values.[8]

It was a brand of spirituality which owed as little to high cultural tradition as folklore does to literature, and this accounts both for its intensity and its eccentricity.

About the intensity of these heterodox beliefs there can be no doubt. There are innumerable examples of fervour combined with obstinacy and superstition that make it clear that peasant culture in the last years of the old regime was as far removed from us in its psychological climate as any dark age. It was in a milieu in which events such as the following were possible that Rasputin spent his formative years.

A sectarian peasant named Kovalev had news of an impending state census. He at once assumed that this heralded the advent of Antichrist, who was anxious to have a list of the names of all the damned. Feeling there was little time to lose he dug graves for himself and his family. He buried the latter alive, mother, wife and young children, and as the earth fell on them they uttered prayers for the dead. The idea caught on in Kovalev's village and he had to bury some twenty more persons before he was able to commit suicide himself. In the same year, and for similar reasons, a community of sixty sectarians deemed it necessary to die. The men first killed their wives and children, and were then decapitated by their leader, who afterward cut his own throat. The year was 1897.[4]

Another late nineteenth-century sectarian, Nikitin, a peasant from Vladimir, burnt his house and two children after cutting their throats in an overzealous emulation of Abraham sacrificing Isaac. As he was killing them, his wife and their mother talked to them, carefully explaining his motives. He was sent to Siberia, where he was found some time later on Good Friday, wearing a crown of thorns and hanging from a cross of his own construction. He had contrived to nail his feet to it with his right hand, holding on with his left—which he subsequently drove against the point of a nail he had hammered through the back of the crosspiece. He lacked the strength to do as much for his right. He announced that he had wished to sacrifice himself for the sins of the world.[5]

Russian sectarianism embraces a wide range of practices and beliefs. In a novel tracing the sectarian movement in Siberia Andrei Cherkasov describes the fortunes of a group of dissidents from the lower Volga who flee to Siberia as a sectarian unit, or "fortress" (*krepost'*), and who gradually undergo a process of fragmentation after the death of their leader, breaking up into a series of fortresses adhering to differing faiths (*tolki*) that come close to paganism. Thus the *dyrniki* (literally, holers) worship the sky through a hole in the roof, another faith worships a particular tree, another the river, but whatever the *tolk,* they all displayed an obstinate attachment to their particular faith. This kind of belief persisted at least up to 1917; radical in its rejection of official religion, and highly unstable in the sense that at any moment fission or secession to a new form of worship could be expected.

It is for that reason that one cannot be specific about sectarian doctrine and practice; the sects were heterodox by definition. There are common features, however, above all hatred of the official church, which persecuted them even more savagely than it did the Old Belief. One even finds cases of mass antisectarian trials being conducted as late as the summer of 1915 when, after three retrials, forty-eight men and women were found guilty of belonging to a sect and were sentenced to eight months' imprisonment in a military fortress.[6] In the eyes of the Orthodox church sectarianism was part of the primitive side of the peasant soul, with powerful and not always unfounded connotations of heresy, paganism, and savage, not to say licentious, practices. Sectarianism was viewed as part of the Russian heart of darkness, the spiritual version of a terrible secret vice.

In some respects the picture was distorted. Many of the sects, Baptists, Stundists, Dukhobors, Molokane (milk drinkers), were much closer to Germanic nonconformists than to any heart of darkness. They could only be considered dangerous in a land of official Christianity, which considered dissent of any kind dangerous in itself. But a much more powerful case can be made against the particular range of underground sects that shaped the attitudes of Rasputin, the so-called *khlysty,* or as they preferred to be known, the *Bozhie lyudi,* or people of God.

Khlyst means "whip" in Russian and it is usually assumed that the *khlysty* were so called because of the role of flagellation in their rituals. However, it is more likely that the word is a distorted form of *khristy,* or Christs, particularly since the notion of a succession of Christs is central to the doctrine, the role of flagellation incidental.

The *khlysty* were not simply schismatics; at best they might be considered heretics, but it is possible to argue that they were not Christians at all, despite the ardour of their faith and their determination to search for perfection of the spirit. As far as we can tell, the sect dates from the early seventeenth century, and was allegedly founded by a certain Danila Philippov, a peasant from Kostroma and an army deserter. One of the sect's sacred texts describes him as follows:

> Once he climbed to the top of a mountain, and there, surrounded by angels, archangels, seraphim and other celestial beings the Lord Sabaoth himself came down to him. The heavenly beings rose up again and the Lord Sabaoth remained on earth incarnate in Danila Philippov.[7]

Philippov became the "living God" and his followers were God's people. He issued twelve commandments, proclaiming himself God and requiring that he be worshipped. He forbade the use of alcohol and bad language, prohibited theft, and also marriage or even attendance at weddings and christenings. The final commandment was to "believe in the Divine Spirit."

The sect caught on and some years later Philippov was joined by a "Christ," Ivan Suslov, to whom he transmitted his divine nature. Suslov in turn was joined by twelve apostles and a "Mother of God." Together they preached the *khlyst* doctrine, which maintained that all other forms of worship were without value. It was only through intense and fervent prayer according to their teaching that the Holy Spirit, the divine essence, would enter into one. Christianity was rejected; Jesus was dismissed as an "Old Christ," held in much lower esteem than more recent incarnations. The cult went to great lengths in pursuit of spiritual purity, but others went further still, witness a breakaway group, the *skoptsy,* or castrates. They believed that the original apostles were castrates who had undergone what they called baptism by fire, as opposed to John's baptism by water, and mutilated themselves accordingly. The first stage of mutilation, or "first stage of purity" or "little seal," as it was termed, consisted of the removal of the testicles and scrotum with a razor or knife; sometimes a red-hot instrument was used to cauterise the wound. The operation was sometimes succeeded by the "second degree of purity" or "great seal," which consisted in the removal of the penis. Under judicial interrogation many castrates described the process; the operation was usually performed when they were rendered unconscious by drink.

Some, however, maintained that they were castrated forcibly; arms and legs being tied down to rings so that they formed a cross. Not all sects considered actual castration essential; they admitted so-called spiritual castrates as well as actual ones. The *khlysty* tended to look down on the castrates, taking the view that castration made chastity too easy.[8]

The *skoptsy* founded their faith on the conviction that there was no indivisible barrier between the human and the divine, so that man could literally become The Lord Incarnate.[9] Through renunciation and mortification of the flesh, the burial of appetite, a secret resurrection could be achieved, man reborn as God,[10] or at the very least as a "secretly resurrected prophet." Such a man will have experienced complete annihilation of the will, its place being taken by the will of God. From that moment on it is the living God who speaks through him, so that he can do no wrong.

Despite, or perhaps because of the obsession with abstinence, sexuality plays an intermittent and peculiar role in the doctrine of the cult, notably with respect to the resurrected prophet or living God. Since he can do no wrong, his behaviour, however seemingly extreme or immoral, is venerated because he is "beyond sin" and cannot be judged by mortal man. He is omnipotent, and for him nothing is impossible. He can work miracles and foretell the future. He attracts disciples not by words alone but by a secret power. He can override all traditions and prohibitions, and his followers will accept his instructions without hesitating. Thus one resurrected prophet, a certain Radeev, maintained more than thirty lovers whom he ordered to obey him since such was the will of God. Chastity, he observed, in anticipation of Rasputin, was the sin of pride. His devotees were convinced of his innocence: "With him there can be no temptation for others since he gave himself unto this sin not of his own will but by the very will of the Holy Spirit."[11]

The Orthodox church persecuted the cult, but with varying degrees of success. Thus Tsar Aleksey Mikhailovich (father of Peter the Great) arrested Suslov, tortured and crucified him on the Kremlin wall. He was then put in a coffin by the place of execution on Red Square. However, the legend has it that Suslov rose from the dead and started to preach again. Once more he was tortured, flayed alive and crucified. His followers wrapped him in a shroud, which promptly turned into a new skin. He rose yet again and renewed his preaching until, in 1718 at the age of one hundred, he ascended to heaven.[12] Suslov was succeeded by another Christ, and so the tradition continued. In the course of the next 150 years the cult flourished and gained adherents among the merchant classes. Even some members of the aristocracy were drawn to its heterodox spirituality. Thus in 1800 there were castrate sects in both capitals among merchants, noblemen, the army and the civil service. Some years later the *Napoleonovtsy* believed that Christ had returned yet again, in the improbable form of Napoleon.[13] Other sectarians believed that Napoleon was none other than Antichrist, and the illegitimate son of Catherine the Great, who had sent him to be educated in France. They believed that he did not die upon St. Helena (the notion that great rulers live on in some mysterious way is a feature of Russian peasant superstition). Instead he had gone into hiding in Turkey, and on the Day of Judgment would return, and become a castrate.

Khlyst practices are based upon oscillation between self-denial and ecstasy; the one acting as catalyst to the other. Thus carnal relations are forbidden between husband and wife, but as we shall see, are encouraged in other circumstances. The sectarians group themselves in cells or "arks," each of which has its leader, the pilot or Christ, a Mother of God, angels, apostles, prophets, and prophetesses who come together with the simple brethren to guide them through rituals of ecstatic worship that are the essence of the faith. They would usually congregate in secret cellars especially dug to accommodate their practices, wearing special wide-sleeved white tunics with coloured girdles. Some would form circles and slowly begin to gyrate and dance, singing special songs and always moving from right to left, while the rest of the congregation sat round watching, slapping their knees in time to the music. The movements would continue, forming complex ritual patterns and building up excitement. The object was to attain the state of *radenie* or frenzy, which plunged you into a religous ecstasy as the Holy Spirit entered you. Sometimes in the course of the dance the worshippers would strike each other across the shoulders with cloths. They would turn faster and faster, becoming soaked in perspiration. As one sectarian put it: "The songs, the heat, the smell in which you bathe make you feel quite drunk, your face burns with a fever and you feel the fire in your heart."[14]

Finally everyone present joined in the dance with "convulsive movements crying 'Oh the Spirit, Oh the Spirit' until the whole ark was overcome with confusion and ecstatic joy."[15] Ecstasy was accompanied by prophecy and speaking in strange tongues, as in the following *radenie,* which took place in early twentieth-century Siberia:

> As they turned they behaved strangely and outrageously, some shook, bent over, fell down like lunatics, other stamped their feet, squatted down and danced, or cried out wildly and spoke in unknown tongues believing that the Holy Spirit had come upon them.[16]

Some claimed to talk "Indian" or "The language of Jerusalem," though it must be said that the examples of such speech provided by the eyewitness in question have a strong pseudo-Germanic ring to their gibberish:

> *Rente rente funtritut*
> *Nodir lisentrant entrofint.*[17]

It was at this point in the proceedings that abstinence could give way to its opposite with the so-called "communal sin," when fervour would turn into an indiscriminate sexual orgy among the celebrants. The practice was also known as "the love of Christ." However, it was by no means a regular feature of sectarian worship, occurring in some arks some of the time. Apparently its function was twofold: to engender children during the ritual, and also, a notion dear to Rasputin and the basis of his sexual casuistry, "to use sin to drive out sin." The sectarians believed that it was only through having sins to expiate that true salvation could be attained, so sin was necessarily the first step towards salvation.[18] Sin played a particularly important part in the doctrine of an extreme *khlyst* sect, the New Israel, which flourished right up to 1915 when its leader, Aleksey Shchetinin, an acquaintance of Rasputin, was arrested and deported. He preached that man is immersed in a sea of sin, but must not drown there; sin is the great equaliser. The more a man sinned the more he suffered and the greater were his chances of salvation.[19]

So far the *khlysty* do not seem so very different from such American pentecostal sects as the Snake Handlers or the Holy Rollers, rural forms of ecstatic worship which have evolved independently of ecclesiastical high culture. Yet for the Orthodox the sects had sinister connotations, "nameless practices" being attributed to them. Andrey Bely's novel *The Silver Dove,* set in early twentieth-century rural Russia, features a demonic "pilot" who uses his "Mother of God" to beguile a young member of the intelligentsia, captivating him with her dark sensuality to ensure that, when the time is ripe, the young man first impregnates her and then is sacrificed in ritual murder. It is a superb and prophetic novel which projects the most powerful "sense of an ending." It portrays life in cool country houses going on as it always had; gracious and venerable ladies being waited upon by loyal retainers oblivious of a new generation of aggressive, restless, half-aware peasants who had somehow discovered that only the old and the ignorant were content with their lot, that a time would soon come when they would have all the land they wanted, and even grow smart enough to be a match for any city dweller. In the meantime the old ladies would have done well to lend an ear to the songs the young men of the village sang to their accordions, songs of freedom, violence, and the red cockerel of arson. In so far as the book is a study of the fatal nature of contact between the peasantry and the intelligentsia, which portrays sectarianism as a revolutionary and destructive force, describing fervour and ecstasy mischannelled as an integral part of peasant rebellion, it is a strange anticipation of Rasputin and the role he would play in Russian history. As Bely wrote later:

> I sensed the spirit of Rasputin before Rasputin appeared on the scene. I fantasized him in the spirit of my pilot. He is Rasputin's village past.[20]

It has been alleged that the sects practised the ritual mutilation and circumcision of young adolescent girls. While the victim held on to an icon one of her breasts and the clitoris would be cut off, divided up and eaten. Alternatively a girl would be worshipped as a Mother of God and impregnated. Her left breast would be removed after *radenie* and eaten communally. If she were to give birth to a daughter it would be brought up as her successor, if a son he would be called a Little Christ, and on the sixth day after his birth his heart would be pierced with a spear and his blood drunk. His body was then reduced to a powder and used in the bread baked for communion.[21] In justice it must be said that these practices are described by only one source, and even this concedes that they had probably died out by the late nineteenth century. However, for our purposes the truth of the matter is less important than the fact that many educated Russians at the turn of the century believed the sects to be capable of such actions. This helps us to understand the sinister associations with which they were invested. The authority of rumour and extravagant allegation in late tsarist Russia was boundless. A striking example was the *cause célèbre* of a young Jew named Beylis, the unfortunate main protagonist in one of imperial Russia's numerous Dreyfus cases. He came within a hair's-breadth of being convicted of the totally imaginary ritual murder of a Christian baby, shortly before the First World War. When he heard that Beylis had been found not guilty, the tsar, whom some have accused of anti-Semitism, observed that although the murder undoubtedly took place, he was glad that Beylis was not convicted, since he was innocent. The case was the inspiration of Bernard Malamud's novel *The Fixer*.

Rumour apart, the hysterical atmosphere of the sects was responsible for unusual experiences, notably among the *khlyst* pilgrims who wandered from village to village, practising spiritual abstinence or giving themselves over to divinely directed promiscuity. Some of them travelled with "spiritual wives" who might share their beds without having intercourse, giving both partners a chance to prove their spiritual mettle. A case history published in 1912 gives an indication of the strange blend of delusion, exaltation, and the quest for truth which informed that world.

A male pilgrim met a woman, Pelageya, on his wanderings. She had a vision that informed her she was to meet three men carrying books who would be "higher than all other men." She had spent two years visiting holy places in search of them. The male pilgrim was also travelling as a result of a vision; it had promised him that if he went to a certain place angels would carry him from there into the wilderness. All he needed was the company of a "Blessed Mother" who would be the catalyst of his transportation. The couple eventually abandoned their separate quests and returned to the man's village, where they started a prayer circle. Their house was soon the source of strange portents witnessed by many, for example a pillar of fire reaching to the sky and surrounded by swallows. This, it emerged, was the devil tricking them into believing in their own sanctity. They were both accompanied by an invisible angel who told them one another's thoughts, as well as the thoughts of those present at their gatherings. They acquired a great reputation for holy wisdom, and encouraged others to emulate them, to leave their spouses and take spiritual partners.

Spirituality turned to sensuality when another prophetess, named Anastasia, urged the man to sleep with Pelageya after a prayer meeting, "when upon me descended in the form of a cloud a kind of vapour which smelt very sweet, and I felt delight course through my body convincing me that this could be no sin." From then on the meetings ended in orgies "without anyone noticing anything criminal about it. If sinners might comfort themselves with the pleasures of the flesh surely we the just and the righteous are the more to be forgiven for doing what we do out of necessity."

The man's legal wife begged him to return to her. This irritated him and he prayed for her death, whereupon an angel appeared to him saying that she would die in twelve days and her soul would be lost because of her disobedience. He began to pray for her soul and a second angel appeared, telling him that his prayer was answered, giving him three crowns, one for himself, one for Pelageya, the third for his wife, who would stand on his left hand in the Kingdom of Heaven. When he told her as much she began to cry. Shortly afterward she found her husband making love to Pelageya, fell over in the snow and went into a six-hour trance. On coming to she told of a vision she had had; devils were trying to keep her from her husband, the sky was on fire and he was barefoot, surrounded by devils, foaming at the mouth. Whenever he kissed one of his disciples the foam stuck to her lips and she was held to him as by an invisible force. The vision appears to have convinced the husband that he had been deceived by devilry, and he was persuaded to return to the Orthodox fold.[22]

Another convert, an ex-*khlyst starets* of great authority, made the following confession:

> For 17 years I preached the so called spiritual life, in actuality a life of secret vice which profited me greatly. Even now I have more than 300 followers. The devil came to me in the form of an angel each day, bringing a dozen books of a peculiar kind which he called gospels, which he had brought from heaven and which he read to me. They expounded on various devilish matters. When a novice would come to me hearing about my supposed saintliness and second sight devils revealed to me all his sins and thoughts. All I needed was to look him steadily in the eye for me to see, as in a mirror, all his sins and wrong-doings, which the devils made known to me at once. Consequently everyone had great faith in me, believing me to be a veritable saint and prophet. They all brought me presents and I profited greatly from my skills.[23]

As Rasputin comes into clearer focus in latter years it will be seen how deeply he was marked by various aspects of sectarian practice. He used their casuistry to persuade his female disciples to sleep with him, asserting that he wished to share their beds to test their capacity to resist temptation. Alternatively he would tell them that it was no sin to have sex with him since he was above sin, or that sin was the first stage on the path to repentance. He himself ranged from sincere belief to something approaching charlatanry, or at the very least an abuse of his spiritual authority in the interests of physical appetite.

Rasputin was drawn toward the sectarians for a number of reasons. As a popular faith it employed language and rituals that were readily acceptable to the peasant religious imagination, much more so than the rituals of the Orthodox church, which were executed in a foreign tongue; Old Church Slavonic is closer to Bulgarian than to Russian. The ritual search for ecstasy through *radenie* and the dance appealed to Rasputin; in later years he would end drinking bouts by dancing till he dropped, preferably to the accompaniment of gypsy guitars, violins, and rhythmic clapping. *Radenie* struck the deepest chords in his being. Sectarian attitudes answered another of his fundamental needs. It will be recalled that on his return from Verkhoturye Rasputin was a changed man. Yet he would never prove capable of sustained asceticism; however much he might crave perfection, and it was a craving that wavered considerably over the years, he would never succeed in transcending the world of appetite. Now the *khlystovshchina,* with its strange combination of abstinence and licence, its emphasis on spiritual purity combined with orgiastic coupling, the quest for salvation through sin itself, was perfectly suited to Rasputin's paradoxical blend of God and appetite, enabling him to strike a balance between the spirit and the flesh.

It would be a mistake not to take his God-seeking seriously, to dismiss him as a simple opportunist who exploited his talents to make a career for himself. True, he was as much an ambitious opportunist as any courtier, and peasant though he was, he was one of the most successful courtiers in history. But he was also, above all in his early adult years, a seeker after truth and holiness, who spent many hours at a time absorbed in his devotions; both then and in later years he was known to pray for hours at night, or could be found in an isolated part of a neighbouring wood absorbed in meditation.[24] But, Rasputin's powerful sexual appetites were not conducive to a quest for salvation conducted within the framework of Orthodoxy. Moreover, there was yet another reason why he could never have become a monk: Rasputin was incapable of accepting discipline. Throughout his life he arranged to go his own way, and it was inconceivable that he could live by a monastic rule. His "broad Russian nature," as Russian cliché would have it, needed more room to breathe than could ever be found within the walls of any institution. As an observer, drawing on recollections and police records, put it:

> From his early years Rasputin fully understood that he was a man with pathologically corrupt tendencies. He was quite aware that he would not last long in the narrow world of monastic life, which is why he chose to follow a course that suited him better —passing into the world of pseudo-Saints, pilgrims, Fools in

Christ which he had known from early childhood. Entering that world as a young man, Rasputin, ignoring the mockery and condemnation of his fellow villagers, who referred to him as "Grisha the prophet," became a clear and definite representative of the type, in true peasant style, being both coarse and eloquent, hypocritical, fanatical and holy, a sinner and an ascetic, a womaniser who put on an act for every minute of the day, arousing curiosity, wielding great influence and enjoying a knowledge of his fellow men that was tantamount to clairvoyance.[25]

CHAPTER 4

THE "NEW" Rasputin returned from the monastery and settled back into village life. However, according at least to official hagiography, in the form of one of his daughter's memoirs, the village could not hold him for long. One day when working in the fields he appears to have had a vision: the Virgin appeared to him, bathed in glory, walking just above the ground, and remained long enough to give him her blessing before disappearing. She appeared in unfamiliar form, and it was not until some years later that Rasputin recognised its basis in one of Orthodox Russia's holiest icons, the Black Virgin of Kazan. It is presumably her dark colouring that he recognised, since the icon portrays Our Lady with an infant Jesus, only her face being visible, the outline of the body being traced on the rich settings of the icon case. The icon was deemed to have extraordinary virtue; each summer it would go the rounds of village after village in procession. Inhabitants would go out to meet it, accompanying it to their church and even into private houses.[1] In 1904 the icon was desecrated by an escaped convict. It was torn from its setting, which was stolen, and the icon itself disappeared. It was seriously believed by many devout persons that Russia's subsequent misfortunes—defeat at the hands of the Japanese and the revolution of 1905—were direct consequences of this act of sacrilege. Some years later the convict's accomplice tried to talk his way out of gaol by persuading a gullible bishop that the icon lay hidden in an Old Believers' monastery deep in the woods of Siberia. However, it was suspected that the icon in question might be a fake, and his offer was not taken up—for the remarkable reason that should it be accepted as authentic when in fact a fake it would compound the nation's misfortunes. It would be a disaster if an unworthy object were mistaken for the genuine article, and venerated accordingly.[2]

However, the story does not end there. In the early 1950s there were persistent rumours that the icon was still intact, and was in private hands, in England. The icon in question was eventually tracked down and inspected by experts, who after subjecting it to every conceivable test and measurement concluded that it was indeed Our Lady of Kazan. In an attempt to discover how it came to be where it was a trail was followed that led back to a Polish Jew in West Germany. When asked how he came to have possession of one of the holiest objects of Russian Orthodoxy he showed the investigator the door with considerable vehemence, and the trail ended there. The icon is now in the United States of America.

Together with a friend, Dmitri Pecherkin, Rasputin returned to the monastery to ask the *starets* Makarii what the vision meant. Makarii seems to have told Rasputin that he should go on a pilgrimage to the Orthodox monasteries of Mount Athos.

Did Rasputin really have a vision? All we can say for sure is that he always maintained that he did. His daughter told one of his early biographers, General Spiridovich, one-time chief of the tsar's personal security service, about the experience in some detail. However, the general had his doubts—for the extraordinary reason that there was no place near Pokrovskoe where the Virgin was known to make regular appearances to peasants.[3] On the other hand we have seen from other accounts of sectarian religious experience that belief in supernatural portents was widespread. We can be sure of one thing; if Rasputin did have such an intense visionary experience it was a unique event in his life. Although he would have his moments of clairvoyance, nothing of this kind would ever happen to him again. If he had such a vision during his first enthusiastic practice of ascetic self-denial, as his daughter suggests, it is perfectly possible that he ascribed the lack of any repetition to the inability to master his own sensuality, making him experience his alternating bouts of indulgence and depressed remorse all the more acutely. A less charitable view of the experience would suggest that it was no more than a pretext to escape the drudgery of peasant labour and the banalities of married life; a splendid way to convince his wife that he was obliged to leave her and his young family to become a pilgrim.

It was in 1893, at the age of twenty-eight, that Rasputin set off on his wanderings. We are given a glimpse of the kind of figure he would have cut by another peasant, a genius who rose as high as Rasputin—and lived longer to tell the tale. As a performing artist he had a feel for Russian temperament, history, and mood that has never been equalled. One evening after a day's fishing as a young man, the future singer Feodor Chaliapin stayed in a miller's hut, where he saw:

> a figure stretched out in the corner wearing a threadbare grey garment and gaping felt boots . . . a beggar's pouch covered his face, a stout staff protruded from under his arm, and, in the midst of it all, he was sound asleep. At last it began to grow light. As soon as the night faded, the grey figure with the worn felt shoes began to stir unceasingly and stretched itself to the accompaniment of grunts; presently the visitor sat up, yawned, crossed himself, got to his feet and made for the door . . . [He washed himself] pouring water on his hands . . . soaked his beard, rubbed it and dried it . . . Next he took his staff, crossed himself again, bowed in three directions and departed. . . .
>
> The man was a pilgrim, a *strannik*. From time immemorial such wanderers have existed in Russia, nomads, homeless and hearthless, possessing no earthly ties, following no trade, driven onward by some nameless thought. Leading the life of gypsies, and yet not of the gypsy class, they roamed over the vast territories of Russia, from village to village, from country to country. They were to be seen going from one tavern to another,

dragging themselves to the fairs, entering a hostel for a brief moment. They rested and slept when and where they chose. Nobody knew the meaning of their pilgrimages. I am convinced that had any of them been asked whither he was going, and why, not one could have answered. Not one of them would have known. Not one of them had ever considered the reason of his wanderings.

All these pilgrims appeared to be in search of something. Their minds seemed to be filled with a confused idea of an unknown country where life would be kinder and more just. Perhaps they were escaping from something. Perhaps they were escaping from nothing more tangible than "*toska,*" that nostalgia that only Russians experience, utterly indescribable, utterly incomprehensible, and often without motive.[4]

Accompanied by Dmitri Pecherkin, Rasputin wandered on to Mount Athos–which was a disappointment. He was shocked to discover that the monks indulged in homosexual practices–it would appear that he came across someone enjoying a young novice in the woods. Shortly afterward he departed from the Holy Mountain in disgust, leaving behind an undeterred Pecherkin, who entered a monastery and remained there till his dying day. Rasputin henceforward invariably referred to Mount Athos as a hotbed of unnatural vice.

For the next three years Rasputin fades again from recorded history. Subsequently he claimed that he travelled on to Jerusalem—which is doubtful, since notes he made on a future visit to the Holy Places do not suggest that he had been there before. It is more likely that he simply travelled the length and breadth of Russia, living the pilgrim life, talking to others like himself, monks, priests, heretics, and sectarians, developing his knowledge of the Scriptures and his capacity for theological discourse and debate. In short, they were years of wandering and learning, in the course of which he turned from a simple God-seeking peasant with healthy appetites into a person who projected great spiritual authority and who appeared, to many eyes, to be a *starets* in his own right.

The mature Rasputin was a man of medium height, bony, tense, with a thin face, which was pale and yellowish, and a straggling, slightly curly beard. He could make a most powerful impression upon his listeners, staring at them with bright steady eyes that seemed to read their very souls. Everybody who described him in later years agrees that it was the eyes that made the greatest impression, and it was claimed by some that he was able to make his pupils expand and contract at will. The voice was strange too. He talked in a thick, almost incomprehensible Siberian accent, but without the booming sonority that its rounded vowel sounds usually impart to it. His conversation was desperately hard to follow, for he often spoke in riddles, accompanied by strings of spiritual adages and half-remembered passages from the Scriptures. As he talked and stared at his listeners, his face would frequently cloud over with an air of mistrust, a combination of hesitancy and arrogance: was he making a fool of himself or was it perhaps that his listener was unworthy of him?

He continued to struggle with his sensuality in encounters with peasant women, and female pilgrims too. He had already developed that extraordinary sexual dominance which was one of his most remarkable characteristics, effortlessly taking over a woman's will and persuading her that she would find salvation in her submission to his authority. Submission did not necessarily imply intercourse, however; Rasputin was equally prone to the testing of his self-control, and that of others. He liked to sleep with one or more naked women and struggle to overcome his and their desires—a struggle in which he was intermittently successful. He never, incidentally, seems to have admitted that a night spent "overcoming the demon of desire," as he put it, could produce a degree of sexual excitement exceeding that achieved when the demon of desire was actually triumphant.

Some years later Rasputin spoke about his wandering years to a priest, Iliodor. Initially a fervent admirer, Iliodor rapidly turned against Rasputin to the point of first attacking him publicly, then arranging an assassination attempt that nearly succeeded, and which, Rasputin claimed, was responsible for Russia's entry into the Great War, and hence for the revolution. Iliodor maintains that he based his account on some notes Rasputin dictated in 1907, *The Life of an Experienced Pilgrim;* although we have no way of checking the claim, the tone of the passage resembles that of Rasputin's only published work, with its half-educated echoings of the language of piety:

Up to the age of 28 I lived what people call a worldly life. I loved the world and everything in it, and I sought my consolations in worldly things. I drove, I fished, I ploughed, and my life was fairly easy for a peasant . . . In my heart I always cherished a hope of finding the road to salvation. I became a pilgrim and in my pilgrimages I often had to bear all kinds of calamity and misfortune. There were attempts to kill me but the Lord watched over me. More than once I was attacked by wolves but they did not harm me.

It is sweet to write about this now but I had to live through it all. I used to walk 40 or 50 *versts* a day, heeding neither storm, wind nor rain. Often I had to go hungry. More than once I wandered from Tobolsk without changing my underclothing for half a year and without touching my flesh with my hands. This I did for the sake of experience and trial. Often I walked for three days at a stretch eating very little. On hot days I imposed a fast on myself, drunk no *kvas,* and worked with the labourers, at intervals running into the bushes to pray. I liked to walk along the river banks, finding consolation in nature and thinking of the Saviour who also liked to walk near streams. Nature is a teacher of wisdom just as every tree teaches of spring.

I found comfort greater than all other comforts in daily readings from the Gospel, though I did more thinking than reading. Then for three years I wore shackles, but the evil one disturbed me, saying, "You are exalted, you have no peers." The shackles did me no good, but when I discovered the chains of love I loved everyone. . . .[5]

This account of his wanderings is not to be taken at face value: it is Rasputin who is writing hagiography here. It seems unlikely that he wore penitential chains for a span of three whole years, for example. Yet the overall picture of wandering, asceticism, prayer, and contact with nature rings true enough, even though the picture it presents is a partial one, omitting any reference to sectarian practices, or to the testing of his self-control by passing the night with unclothed pilgrims of the opposite sex.

Rasputin returned from his first bout of travelling three years later, in 1896. He gave eminently sensible reasons for his return; the pilgrim way was too easy, it failed to concentrate the spirit, and in the long run, made for an essentially aimless mode of existence that exposed one to the temptations of sectarian heresy:

> It is good to wander, but not for many years. I visited many a pilgrim's hostel, and I met pilgrims who had wandered not only for many years, but for a lifetime, and it happened that the enemy had sown his heresies among the poor souls, the chief among these being philosophising. They had become so lax and negligent that I found only one in a hundred following in the footsteps of Christ Himself. We wanderers fall an easy prey to the enemy. Lassitude breeds evil. That is why one should not wander for too long at a stretch, unless one has fortitude and power of will and is deaf and even a little dumb.[6]

Rasputin suggests that pilgrims are overexposed to the combined dangers of heresy and idleness—whether this was a piece of specious apologetic defending himself against charges of sectarianism we cannot say, but whatever his reasons he clearly decided that a life of perpetual pilgrimage was not for him. Early in 1896 he returned to Pokrovskoe. The family tradition, as related by his daughter, has it that he arrived unannounced and disguised as a pedlar, a Siberian Ulysses surprising his wife Praskovia, who duly failed to recognise the travel-stained, weather-beaten figure who stood smiling quietly before her.

Although he may have come home Rasputin did not settle back to the peasant life. He was deeply marked by his experiences, not to mention his release from manual labour, and had no intention of returning to work in the fields—an activity which any Russian peasant was all too happy to define as "woman's work" if he could, and spend summer lying on the hay piled up in the barn, winter on the stove. For all his seeking after truth and bouts of asceticism Rasputin would always remain reluctant to earn his bread by the sweat of his brow.

It was not physical laziness alone that kept him from the fields. He had a powerful if personal and unfocussed sense of vocation too; the need to save his own soul and to guide others towards their own salvation. We now see the beginning of a new phase in his development, as the pilgrim turns teacher while remaining the embodiment of a certain well-known type of peasant mentality:

> Religious, restless, anguished, seeking the path to salvation, often yielding to temptation but never discouraged by his moments of weakness.[7]

For all his moments of failure and anguish Rasputin was possessed from the outset of a remarkable capacity to impress his authority as spiritual guide and mentor, now in the first instance, upon his fellow villagers. He was and would remain a man of the people. He had forged his beliefs, his cast of thought, his manner of speaking and preaching in pilgrim circles that lay far beyond the reach of authority and the jargon of official Christianity. He expressed himself in a way that was immediately sympathetic to the peasant mind, and would subsequently impress others of infinitely higher rank precisely because his mode of expression had all the naive directness, the freedom from claptrap, which had made generations of educated Russians, who ought to have known better, believe that true wisdom, goodness, spirituality were to be found in the bosom of the great, good, and simple Russian people. This preposterous belief in the virtues of a peasant class who in 1905, 1917, and the Civil War proved themselves capable of extreme callousness and animal violence, was, if not engendered, then widely disseminated by Leo Tolstoy, who, in the courts of history, has a certain amount to answer for.

From now on Rasputin gave himself over entirely to preaching and to his personal quest. Soon after his return, acting, in his own words, in imitation of Christ, who had been born not in a palace but a manger, "I dug a cellar in the stables and went to pray there . . . Whenever I was free during the day I would return there, and I found that my thoughts did not scatter in that narrow place."[8] Although there was nothing intrinsically "wrong" with digging underground chambers, it will be recalled that this was a sectarian practice, and so bore distinct connotations of heresy. Rasputin turned his chamber into a tiny chapel, hung with icons that had lights burning before them. "Only there did it feel good to pray," his daughter once observed in late years.[9]

The Rasputin *izba* now became a kind of meeting house, where the *starets* held forth, telling stories of his travels, discoursing on the proper path to salvation, and exchanging interpretations of the Holy Scriptures with passing pilgrims. He was an eloquent, convincing speaker who already had a large number of disciples, the majority of whom were women. Although Rasputin would have his share of male followers, and gained his entry into the highest circles by his ability to impress some of the most distinguished churchmen in the land, he never inspired in men that uncritical devotion and obedience that he proved able to secure from women. His closest followers were always members of the opposite sex, while he made no close men friends. Talk of sexual magnetism rings with precisely the kind of sensationalism that has so often clouded earlier accounts of Rasputin, making him the "mad monk," an inexact cliché that conceals a subtler and more interesting personality. Yet it is perfectly clear that he presented himself, exercised his authority as a spiritual leader, in a way that impressed women more than men, inspiring a submissive trust that had a sexual base.

Rasputin's growing reputation as a guide and comforter did not go unnoticed, or unenvied, by ecclesiastical authority, in the shape of Father Peter, the village priest. He considered Rasputin a challenge to his own position, while the underground chamber and the following of spiritual "sisters" whose relationship to their leader was rumoured to be anything but spiritual sufficed to make the priest suspect that his rival could be the pilot of a sectarian ark–and in imperial Russia that was a serious offence. Accordingly Father Peter wrote to his biship in Tobolsk, accusing Rasputin of sectarian practices. His letter resulted in a combined operation by church and state in the shape of a police raid on Rasputin's cellar accompanied by an ecclesiastic who interrogated him on the articles of his faith.

The police were presumably looking for traces of *khlyst* rituals, white garments or coloured girdles; it is hard to say what else the raid might have yielded unless they seriously expected to interrupt Rasputin and his adepts in full *radenie*. In the event they found nothing but a small chamber decorated with icons and containing a few sacks of flour. The interrogator drew a blank too. He had a long conversation with Rasputin, who made a profound impression upon him as an Orthodox holy man of great piety. Father Peter's charges were dismissed as ridiculous, and Rasputin's reputation as a *starets* increased.

The priest had bitten off a great deal more than he could chew. It might have been possible to get the better of Rasputin but there is no record of anyone actually doing so. Where courtiers, ministers and princes of the church were all to fail, a village priest stood no chance. There is no reason to assume that he denounced Rasputin out of unfounded malice. Although it is unlikely that Rasputin was a full practising *khlyst,* since he could never exist happily within the framework of any system, he drew liberally upon practices, arguments and attitudes that derived from the sects. However, Rasputin was a highly intelligent man, with a strong sense of self-preservation and the ability to protect his flanks. He would never flaunt his sectarian leanings and was always capable of convincing churchmen and other investigators of his unswerving Orthodoxy in matters of religion. Even then in Pokrovskoe, to be seriously suspected, let alone convicted, of being a sectarian would have destroyed him, and he was more than a match for any local church investigator when it came to defending his own position.

Over the next few years Rasputin spent a lot of time in Pokrovskoe, steadily acquiring the reputation of a Siberian holy man. People began to travel long distances to talk with him, consult him, and seek comfort from him, bringing him presents of food or money in return. The *starets* did not disappoint his visitors. Although, in later years especially, he would abuse his authority in the interests of sexual gratification–which could give rise to complaint–no one ever complained that he was a quack or a charlatan; no one to whom he offered spiritual comfort has ever described himself as disappointed by him, and one may be sure that his enemies would have made much of any such instance. Unless from the outset one accepts that Rasputin really did possess genuine spiritual authority, the story of his astonishing rise will remain incomprehensible. The greatest of all his strengths, one which never left him and which was the real reason for the tsarina's dependence upon him, was his ability to calm people in distress, or, as Russian has it, "to lighten their souls." As a later female admirer, Mounya Golovina, put it: "Does one not feel at peace with Grigorii Efimovich, so that one forgets all the world's misery? He has the gift of bringing calm and serenity to the soul."[10]

However, Rasputin was not just an unorthodox holy man who gave spiritual comfort punctuated by occasional lapses into sensuality. He was also at this time, more than ever before or after, a family man, and it is as such that he first comes into clear focus, through his daughter's recollection of her own early years:

> My father would often take us on his knees, my brother Mitya, my sister Varvara and myself. He would tell us wonderful stories with the tenderness he always showed and that absent look in which seemed to be mirrored the countries he had visited and the strange adventures he had met with on the road . . . At other times he would speak of the deep silence of the Siberian forest and the wild beauty of the steppes. But he could also laugh with his children. I know well what good games of ball Varya and I had with him in the court or in front of the house, the rides we had in the *telega,* with father driving himself or teaching Dmitri the proper way to hold the reins. In October it was he who used to take us to the village fête where girls in embroidered dresses and bodices with coloured scarves used to dance to the accordion.[11]

Family man though he had now become, Rasputin did not abandon the wandering life. Every spring he would set off as soon as the roads were passable, travelling to monasteries and holy places all over Russia, coming back to Pokrovskoe in late summer–after harvest. He was profoundly attached to his village and would remain so. When he became an intimate of the imperial family, the highest courtier in the land, he would still leave the capital to spend spring and autumn at home. But even now at the turn of the century Pokrovskoe had grown too small to hold him.

✧ ✧ ✧

Rasputin took his first step into history proper in 1902, on his way back from a pilgrimage to the monasteries and shrines of Kiev, among the holiest places of Russia, when he spent some time in the city of Kazan. Situated on, or rather close to, the Volga, it had been the capital of the Tartar kingdom until Ivan the Terrible sacked it in 1552. It was a colourful city, and a flourishing river port, and it was from the river that Rasputin would have caught his first glimpse of it, as did the American telegraphist George Kennan:

> Presuming that we had arrived at Kazan, I went on deck. The sun was about an hour high and the river lay like a quivering mass of liquid silver between our steamer and the smooth, vividly green slopes of the high western bank. On the eastern side, and close at hand, was a line of the black hulls with yellow roofs and deck-houses that serve as landing stages, and beyond them and just above the high water mark on the barren sandy shore was a row of heterogeneous wooden shops and lodging-houses, which, but for a lavish display of colour in walls and roofs, would have suggested a street of a mining settlement in Idaho or Montana. . . .
>
> The builders of the shops, hotels and rooms for travellers along the river bank resolved to make it at least dazzling and attractive in colour . . . I noted a chocolate-brown house with yellow window shutters and a green roof; a lavender house with a shining tin roof; a crimson house with an emerald roof; a sky-blue house with a red roof; an orange house with an olive green and chocolate brown roof, and finally a most extraordinary building which displayed the whole chromatic scale within the compass of three stories and an attic . . .

Looking towards the river Kennan could observe great caravans of black barges passing down, towed by a single tug, and then:

> a little Russian hamlet of ready-made houses, with elaborately carved gables, standing on an enormous timber raft 100 feet in width by 500 in length, and intended for sale in the treeless region along the lower Volga. The bareheaded, red shirted, and blue gowned population of this floating settlement were gathered around a blazing camp-fire near one end of the raft, drinking tea.[12]

The actual city of Kazan was less exciting to look at. By Rasputin's time it bore virtually no architectural trace of its Asiatic past, although as a British traveller put it, "the number and brightness of the Greek churches helps to relieve the general air of modern and commonplace regularity."[13] Theologically and academically speaking, however, it was the most important city of Eastern Russia. It contained one of the empire's four theological academies, the others being in Kiev, Moscow, and St. Petersburg, an important university and an observatory. Besides its reputation for Orthodox theology, the city also had a high concentration of Old Believers, many of whom had settled in towns of the lower Volga centuries before. It also had a large Tartar population and was an important centre for Islamic studies. Despite its monotonous architecture the city was extraordinarily lively and colourful:

> All around us we could see characteristic oriental costumes: Tartars in overcoats of cloth of gold or silver with blue or yellow jackets; Chinamen in the wide, coloured pantaloons of their country, and wearing curious caps and shoes . . . Every type of Russian was also represented. There were faces and costumes from every district . . . Chinese, Bokharese, negroes, rubbed shoulders with Russian merchants, peasants, gentlemen.[14]

Rasputin already had a considerable word-of-mouth reputation as a peasant holy man, and this was enough to give him an entrée into church circles. The Orthodox church places great emphasis upon saints, holy men, miracle workers, and the growing sense that political and ideological developments of the nineteenth and early twentieth centuries had created something of a crisis of faith—the essential theme of the novels of Dostoevsky, for example—made churchmen anxious to discover new saints, new holy men, new workers of miracles, seeing in their existence the living proof that the faith was as strong as ever and things were as they had always been. This meant that many of its members were open-minded to the point of gullibility about those who came to them with a reputation for holiness.

In Kazan Rasputin made the accquaintance of at least three distinguished churchmen. The first was a teacher at the academy, a Jewish convert named Father Michael. A short, thin man, bald, with a thick black beard, he had a highly excitable temperament and was easily given to strange enthusiasms, while reputed to be very intelligent and a scholar of distinction. Some years later he abandoned the official church to join the Old Belief. He became a bishop and was known for his fulminations against the established church. Rasputin also made the acquaintance of a popular preacher, Chrisanthos, who rapidly became a great admirer. Rasputin for him was the embodiment of simple faith, a true Holy Man of the people.

Finally Rasputin met a much more important personage, none other than the bishop of Kazan, Bishop Andrey, who had in secular life been a Prince Ukhtinsky. Thus he had suddenly begun to move in the highest ecclesiastical circles of the city, which says much for the impression he was able to make. However, Bishop Andrey did not stay impressed for long. A more sophisticated judge of character than Michael or Chrisanthos, within a year he had begun to voice the gravest doubts about Rasputin's holiness. The doubts were inspired by another new step Rasputin took in Kazan; his ecclesiastical acquaintance had brought him to the notice of Kazan society, introducing him to several of the city's leading families. It was a crucial moment in Rasputin's life, the moment when he ceased to be just another peasant holy man, who had the ear of a handful of not altogether Orthodox churchmen, to be taken up by polite society, polite feminine society to be precise. He started social life as he would end it, in an aura of fervent adoration, coloured by more than a tinge of scandal.

In many ways this was the greatest step that Rasputin ever took. Hitherto he had been a religious vagabond, wandering from one holy place to another, sleeping in ecclesiastical hostels if he was lucky, sometimes sharing a foul-smelling peasant's hut, sometimes sleeping under the open sky. On his travels he might have seen trains, and perhaps even the occasional motor car bowling down dusty summer roads, but he had lived in the timeless, slowly moving world of peasant culture. Now, thanks to his ecclesiastical friends, he moved into a different world. For the first time he entered European houses, saw carpets, gas, electric light, telephones even. For the first time he found himself sitting in upholstered chairs. He saw people drink tea without sucking it through a piece of sugar they held in their mouths, nor did they pour it into their saucers to cool it. Yet great though the shift from the peasant world to civilisation might have been, Rasputin took it in his stride. As he sat, with his dirty boots, his threadbare overcoat with its bulging pockets, and his straggling beard, in drawing rooms hung with chintz and muslin, at tea tables covered with embroidered cloths, absentmindedly twisting his fingers through his napkin, he did not allow his surroundings to over-awe him, and took the veneration accorded him by his tea-gowned hostesses as no more than his due. He remained as ready to hold forth on spiritual matters or talk of his wanderings as he was in any peasant *izba.* In Kazan he revealed for the first time one of his most striking qualities, one that would take him to the heights of imperial Russian society, namely a complete indifference to the quality of his surroundings, and to the rank of his hosts, whether they were the wives of academics and government officials that made up what passed for high society in Kazan, or the "Master of the Russian land" himself, with his wife and children, an empress, four grand duchesses, and the heir to the throne.

That he should have come to the notice of society was not all that surprising. Kazan was a provincial town, with a provincial town's eagerness for new faces. Besides, there as elsewhere, many religiously minded households had their particular visiting priests and holy men of the people. Religion, more than any other force in imperial Russia, regularly bridged the gap between social classes. However, from the very start, Rasputin was something much more than a curiosity, a hanger-on at rich women's tables. Rapidly he built up a circle of disciples in polite society, who regarded him as a man of God and a *starets.*

They were quite wrong to do so. Although he possessed great insight, together with the talent to ease souls and remove the burden of guilt, Rasputin could never properly be termed a *starets.* His admirers' use of the word was a testimony to their ignorance and their enthusiasm. He could more properly be considered a so-called "Man of God":

> Along with the . . . official *starets* who obeys the monastic rule, there is in Russia yet another religious type unknown in Europe, the so-called Man of God . . . unlike the *startsy* they seldom remain in monasteries, travelling from place to place, preaching

> the will of God and calling on people to repent. You find "Men of God" outside holy orders but like the *startsy* they lead a rigidly ascetic life, and enjoy a comparable moral authority.[15]

Clearly Rasputin was no *starets;* he could not possibly be. To be a proper *starets* he would have to have been a monk, and Rasputin was married. However, there can be no doubt that he already wielded great authority over his would-be disciples, and it was this that earned him his unmerited title. An account of him in Kazan describes the impression he made there:

> He had an original approach, his language was simple, short sentences with lots of images. He had expressive eyes that seemed to see straight through you . . . and the *starets* seemed to exercise a certain hypnotic hold over those who came near him.[16]

But for all his authority Rasputin was no ascetic. He assisted women to struggle against the flesh in strange ways reminiscent of sectarian practices, and it was such assistance that sowed the seeds of doubt in the mind of Bishop Andrey. An eminent citizen of Kazan has left the following account of his behaviour:

> I do not know of any instances of a lady actually giving herself to him or joining him in orgies, but I do know of a most respectable lady, a wife and mother, who, though greatly surprised, yielded to Rasputin's request that he share a bed with her. It is true that they were not alone and that matters went no further, but the fact remains that share his bed she did.[17]

It appears that in many houses Rasputin was permitted to kiss young girls or women, or share their beds, in order to assist them in their struggle against sin. We get a glimpse of the kind of argument he used to persuade them from the testimony of Mme. E. A. Kazakova, who saw him in Pokrovskoe in the autumn of that year on his return from Kazan. It appeared that Rasputin warned village girls of the dangers of being seduced by pilgrims who would then forbid them to talk of their experience. In order to protect them from such temptation Rasputin would kiss and kiss them "until they should grow disgusted with kissing."[18] When Mme. Kazakova took him to task for his behaviour he replied that the girls had no cause to be ashamed, and went on to observe that, when repentant women confessed their sins to him, he took the whole burden of their guilt upon himself. Then in order to test the fullness of their repentance he would invite them to take baths with him and wash him.

Rasputin always loved the bathhouse, which plays such an important part in Russian life in villages and towns alike. In later years in the capital he would visit the bathhouse several times a week, sometimes in the company of prostitutes, sometimes simply to sober up. A simple peasant bathhouse consisted of a steaming room and a washing room with plenty of hot and cold water. Rasputin would go to the washing room first, and invite his companion to wash and scrub him, making use of a bast swab. He would perhaps invite her to see for herself that he was "beyond sin" by inviting her to wash his private parts, while he kept his self-control. They would then move on to the steam room, which would hold a stove and some red-hot stones over which they would pour buckets of water. The room had tiers of shelves around it, and Rasputin and his companion or companions would retire there to lie and steam themselves for hours. Later they would go back to the washing room, where once more they would give the *starets* a good soaping, and round the proceedings off by thrashing him gently with a leafy bunch of newly plucked birch twigs.[19]

When Rasputin kissed and fondled his disciples, in or out of the bathhouse, he claimed to be tempering them against passion. Mme. Kazakova revealed that he had already managed to entice a good number of well-to-do lady followers to Pokrovskoe. They took him to be a person of great sanctity, who also, it would seem, needed looking after. They combed his hair and beard, and were even known to trim his fingernails and toenails, devoutly preserving the parings. He would often put his arms around their waists, fondling and embracing them openly, observing that there was no harm in his actions, since they were all as sisters to him. The expression sister, or spiritual sister, again smacks of the sects.[20]

These then are our first glimpses of the mature Rasputin, the reputed *starets* or man of God, with his arms round the waists of adoring ladies who venerate his nail clippings and submit to unusual forms of trial by sexual ordeal. The picture tests belief but it has been repeated so often in various forms, described by so many different sources, that it must be accepted, and if possible explained. Rasputin's behaviour is comprehensible enough; it is his success that calls for comment. Rasputin was a highly sexed and fearless peasant, who retained his peasant abruptness and directness of approach: the man who would address tsar and tsarina in the intimate second person singular would never alter his manners to suit the company he kept. It was precisely those direct peasant qualities that helped to account for his appeal to women. He appeared to many a simple, unaffected man of the people, while others were drawn to him for reasons that recall that mysterious but indubitable attraction that certain types—jockeys, boxers, professional huntsmen—have been known to hold for ladies very much their social superiors. But of course there was more to it. Rasputin radiated an authority that both attracted and repelled. We can get an idea of the impression he made by seeing him, at a somewhat later date, through the eyes of Lili Dehn, an imperial lady-in-waiting. She went to him for advice—should she go abroad with her husband or stay at home with a convalescent son?

> I waited for some time alone in a little study until a man came in so noiselessly that I was almost unaware of his presence. It was Rasputin! Our eyes met and I was instantly struck by his uncanny appearance. At first he appeared to be a typical peasant from the frozen North, but his eyes held mine, those shining steel-like eyes which seemed to read one's inmost thoughts. His face was pale and thin, his hair long, and his beard a light chestnut. Rasputin was not tall but he gave the impression of being so; he was dressed as a Russian peasant and wore the high boots, loose shirt, and long, black coat of the moujik. He came forward and took my hand.
>
> "Ah . . . I see thou art worried . . . Well nothing in life is worth worrying over—everything passes—you understand—that's the best outlook."
>
> He became serious.

> "It is necessary to have Faith. God alone is thy help. Thou art torn between thy husband and thy child. Which of them is weaker? Thou thinkest thy child is the more helpless. This is not so. A child can do nothing in his weakness—a man can do much . . ."
>
> . . . the impression which Rasputin had produced on me was so vivid. I was at once attracted, repelled, disquieted and reassured; nevertheless his eyes were productive of a feeling of terror and repugnance. . . .[21]

He could undoubtedly exert great sexual authority—even though he might make a woman feel like a rabbit staring into the eyes of a stoat. He was also a remarkable lover. In later years his assassin Felix Yusupov once told Duff Cooper that as a lover Rasputin was exceptional in his ability to withhold orgasm for a very long time, and that moreover he had a large wart strategically situated on his penis, which vastly enhanced its capacity to stimulate. Persons who knew Yusupov well have dismissed this observation with a smile as "just the sort of preposterous thing Felix would say." Besides, the wart may not have been a permanent feature: venereal warts tend to come and go. However, one woman who submitted to Rasputin, allegedly in order to gain his protection for her husband, later confessed that the first time he made love to her her orgasm was so violent that she fainted. Subsequent encounters gave her "a marvellous, delicious" sensation the like of which she had never experienced before or, sadly, since. One only needed, she observed, to have been possessed by Rasputin once to belong to him body and soul.[22] Her reaction provides the key to his magnetism. A lover of such power does not need actually to possess a woman in order to convey to her a sense of his authority. His own knowledge of his ability is sufficient in itself for him to radiate an overpowering and easily sensed sexual confidence.

However, it takes more than magnetic personality, or even a wart, to account for Rasputin's hold over countless reputable women who did *not* become his lovers. It was not their sexuality as such that he appealed to, but an appetite of a very different kind.

The pilgrims who spent years on the road in search of salvation were by no means alone in their quest. This was born of a craving that has remained to this day an integral part of the Russian character–take the case of a distinguished if eccentric Marxist philosopher I recently encountered in Moscow who, aged fifty, observed that the time had come to abandon philosophy and, in his words, "set about saving his soul." The search for God has long played a vital part in Russian intellectual life. This was particularly the case in the early twentieth century, which saw a marked religious revival. Earlier decades had seen a fashion for ruthless materialistic radicalism and austere feminism, but by the 1900s the fashionable conscience of the age was more concerned with the life of the spirit. Yet it was a peculiar kind of concern. The age was suffused with something close to the sense of an ending: a sense which developed dramatically in the first fifteen years of the century. There was a widespread feeling that old, stable values, particularly the values of official Christianity, were played out. Sergei Witte feared that a decline in religion might herald revolution:

> In my opinion, the greatest danger confronting Russia is the degeneration of the official Orthodox church and the extinction of the living religious spirit of the people . . . No state can exist without higher spiritual ideals. These ideals can only sway the masses if they are simple, lofty and accessible to everyone, in a word if they bear the imprint of the Divine . . . Without religion the masses turn into herds of beasts, but beasts of a particularly evil type, for these beasts possess a greater intelligence than animals. Our church has unfortunately long since become a dead, bureaucratic institution; our priests serve not the high God, but earthly Gods; Orthodoxy has become Orthodox paganism.[23]

The poet Alexander Blok, who was remarkably sensitive to the climate of change, and could smell revolution on the wind, felt that official Christianity was finished, that, in his words, "The gypsy caravan was moving on." It was a restless time, when people looked for unorthodox solutions to their spiritual problems and worshipped strange gods. Many turned to theosophy, occultism, later anthroposophy, which grew increasingly fashionable; others, in avant-garde artistic circles, made half-hearted attempts to worship the ancient Slavic deities—Stravinsky's *Rite of Spring* (1913) is one of the trend's more successful manifestations. There was also a growing interest in heterodox Christianity, in wandering holy men and in the sects which began to find adherents among the lower and even the upper classes of the capital. One of the most intelligent observers of the contemporary scene, S. R. Mintslov, a civil servant and a writer of talent, was appalled by the veneration accorded certain popular churchmen, persons of physical coarseness and religious eccentricity. He considered their rise a symptom of decadence, a manifestation of spiritual sickness and the craving for strong sensation. Thus in 1903 he writes of a St. Petersburg priest, one Malinin, who commanded a huge following at St. Isaac's Cathedral. He was a coarse monster of a man, with a stentorian voice—and a great female following. Mintslov considered his success a sign that he was living in an age, in his words, of "female psychopaths."[24]

To understand Rasputin's success, to appreciate that his disciples sincerely believed that when he kissed and fondled them he was purging them of sin, that his kisses "were different from those of other men," he must be conceived of in the context of this unbalanced spiritual craving and sensation-seeking. His lady followers were guilty of silliness and gullibility rather than hypocrisy. They believed in Rasputin's holiness, evidence notwithstanding, because they wanted to believe in a holy man, and because of his authority. He was able to convince them all too easily that by obeying him they were advancing the course of their salvation in an unorthodox but by no means unhappy marriage of spirit and flesh.

CHAPTER 5

No mistake could have been made as to the ultimate nationality of the city that ordered its champagne by the magnum, never by the quart.

GRAND DUKE ALEXANDER OF RUSSIA

ST. PETERSBURG, PETROGRAD, LENINGRAD, whatever names the shifts of history may give it, remains one of the great cities of Europe. It has authority, scale, and above all a sense of identity, which it impresses upon its citizens and visitors alike, making them feel that they are in a very particular place which cannot be mistaken for any other. All accounts of the capital whether by distinguished novelists such as Pushkin, Gogol, Dostoevsky, or by less eminent observers, stress the city's special quality, its uniqueness. Thus Meriel Buchanan, the daughter of the last British ambassador to the court of the tsar, noticed first of all a combination of monotony and colour:

> A grey city St. Petersburg seemed that day. The wide streets covered with dirty half-melted snow, the houses huddled together as if trying to seek refuge in each other's company, crowded trams with shrill insistent bells, people hurrying along, so muffled in heavy coats that it was impossible to see their

faces. Then, as we drew nearer the better quarters of town, the streets grew more spacious, a little colour stole in amidst the surrounding greyness, a church with blue domes painted with golden stars, a huge red palace, carriages and coachmen with bright velvet caps, policemen in long black fur trimmed overcoats, a big yellow building with a pale green roof, a golden spire that shone against the sky, a huge bridge spanning an immensely broad river.[1]

A novelist, Hugh Walpole, fleshes this first impression out with a more detailed panorama of prewar St. Petersburg:

I was conscious of the town itself, in every one of its amazingly varied manifestations. I saw it all laid out as though I were at a great height above it–the fashionable streets, the Nevsky and the Morskaya, with carriages and motor cars and trams, the kiosks and the bazaars, the women with baskets of apples, the boys with the newspapers . . . the shops in the Morskaya with the coloured stones in the window, the oculist and the pastry cooks and the hairdressers and the large "English Shop" at the corner of the Nevsky . . . And I saw the Nevsky, that straight and proud rolling street filled with every kind of vehicle, and black masses of people, rolling like thick clouds up and down, here and there, the hum of their talk rising like mist from the snow. And there was the Kazan cathedral, haughty and proud, and . . . the bridges and the palaces and the square before the Alexander Theatre . . . I watched the Nevsky and saw how it slipped into the Neva with the Square on one side of it, and St. Isaac's on the other, and the great station on the far end of it, and about these two lines, the Neva and the Nevsky, the whole town sprawled and crept, ebbed and flowed. Away from the splendour it stretched, dirty and decrepit and unattended, here piles of evil flats, there old wooden buildings with cobbled courts, and the canals twisting and creeping up and down and through it all. It was all bathed, as I looked down upon it, in coloured mist. The air was purple and gold and light blue fading into the snow and ice and transforming it. Everywhere there were masts of ships and the smell of the sea and rough deserted places, and shadows moved behind the shadows, and yet more shadows behind *them,* so that it was all uncertain and unstable and only the river knew what it was all about.[2]

The Neva and the Nevsky set the feel of the city, a feel of great breadth; both the river and the street seem quite disproportionately wide. The feeling is increased by the flatness of the land on which the city is built, so flat that one feels dominated by an overpowering sky, which dwarfs the city for all its imposing palaces and government buildings. More than most, the city is at the mercy of its climate, which contrives to be unpleasant for some eleven months of the year —take the following entries from a 1903 diary which give glimpses of autumn, winter and finally summer.

> 4 ix 03.
> Petersburg is having peculiar sunsets, as if the whole horizon were bathed in fire, the sun sets purple and appears to flood the sky with smoke. Although the street lamps are lit the sky keeps on smouldering with a fiery tinge till late evening.[3]

By December the light was long gone:

> 9 xii 03.
> Not a sign of a sleigh yet [i.e., no snow]. Amazingly dark mornings, you get your first glimpse of dawn around half past eight; lamps lit everywhere. The air is thick not with darkness but with something heavy and brownish like peat smoke. They turn out the street lamps at a quarter past nine.[4]

Summer seems worse:

> 14 vii 04.
> Life is hard in Petersburg in the summer, in the heat of the day, and worse in the still summer evenings. The place is airless; out of doors there is a kind of blue grey pall of unhealthy vapours and even the smartest streets have begun to smell of rotting sewage.[5]

One of the first features to catch a visitor's eye in summer was the proliferation of notices and public warnings in bold red lettering telling citizens not to drink the water for fear of cholera, which regularly used to reach the level of an epidemic. Papers such as the *Petersburg Gazette* would solemnly exhort their readers to stick to beer–for safety's sake. Many of the inhabitants of the capital had never tasted fresh water, suggests one observer, since all drinking water was automatically boiled. During the cholera season free boiled water was to be had from huge containers that were wheeled from street to street. However, it must be said that many of the capital's humbler citizens treated such bids for health and hygiene with sublime disregard. It was quite usual to see "dirty workmen slaking their thirst with water dipped out in their greasy caps from the foulest canals of the city, while cautionary notices were staring them full in the face only a few yards off."[6] The workmen and working-class crowds of St. Petersburg in the early twentieth century would seem quite familiar to anyone who knows the Moscow or Leningrad of today. He would find the same blend of jostling, pushing, and squeezing, accompanied by hair-raising bad language from both sexes, and indignant squeals of protest from elderly women who suspect that they might not be getting their way. Then as now there was widespread drunkenness. On public holidays the city took on a colouring all its own, with drunks pouring down its main streets, while the air itself appeared to reek of vodka and bad language.[7] Although it was not a working-class city–indeed as late as 1910 ten percent of factory workers went home for harvest–the kind of Russian liable to end his celebrations by falling flat on his face in the street rather than being taken home in a cab was more in evidence in the centre of the town than he might be in other capitals. This is because the poorer classes were evenly distributed over the city. Rather than concentrate in slum areas on the outskirts, they tended to live in the attics or basements of houses which they shared with the more well-to-do.

Yet there was more to the capital than drunken workmen. It was distinguished from other Russian cities by its cosmopolitan quality. This was reflected in many ways–in its merchants, for example. The merchants of Moscow were conservatives of the old school, Russian to the core for all their fabulous wealth–it used to be said that their warehouses held enough furs to lay a path from Moscow to Paris. The merchants of St. Petersburg were different. English and German families had lived there for generations, and had their own independent communities. The city's smart set was equally cosmopolitan. Everybody had foreign governesses, and in the early twentieth century England was all the rage, English having replaced French as the fashionable language. However, members of society were usually at home in both languages, switching from English to French to Russian quite unconsciously. *"On govoril one sans-atout"*–he bid one no-trump–being the kind of trilingual phrase one could expect to hear at the bridge table. Anglomania had made Drew's English Shop the most popular store in the city. Its stock included Pears soap and football jerseys in the colours of Oxford and Cambridge colleges. The English habit came from the court, where everything English was in special favour. The aristocracy even used to get their suits made in London, but when it came to washing, France was still held to have the edge. It was the smart thing to have one's laundry done in Paris.

Although such gestures might suggest that the Russian aristocracy had a certain talent for conspicuous consumption, this does not mean that as a caste it possessed fabulous wealth. In fact even the tsar himself had to take care if he was to balance his domestic budget. There were, of course, great fortunes, among the grand dukes and a tiny handful of other families, such as the Yusupovs, but they were few in number, and would scarcely stand comparison with those of some of the leading English families of the age. Nevertheless the social life of the capital was brilliant enough. The St. Petersburg season opened on the morning of New Year's Day, when the emperor and empress made a ceremonial appearance in the Winter Palace. It ended on the Sunday before Lent. During this time hostesses vied with one another to give the most memorable ball of the season. There were highly formal *bals blancs* for unmarried debutantes and rather more relaxed *bals roses* for young married couples. The dancing season would culminate in a grand masked ball given by Countess Kleinmichel.

Yet private entertainments of this kind were eclipsed by the magnificent court balls, held in the enormous, and, it was generally agreed, forbidding Winter Palace. The most important of them was the ball that opened the season. There was a fixed guest list, which included the diplomatic corps, members of the first four of the fourteen classes into which all Russian government servants, civil and military, were divided, senior guards officers, and junior guards officers known to be good dancers. The ball began early, carriages arriving at appointed entrances to the palace at 8:30:

> January. Intense cold. The whole of the three vast blocks of the Winter Palace inundated with light. Braziers burning around the immense Alexander column, a granite monolith with an archangel on top of it. Carriages arriving in an unbroken line. Open sledges bringing those officers who did not fear the cold; the horses' harness covered with blue netting to prevent accumulations of snow from being blown into the passengers' faces.
>
> Motor-cars were regarded then as a capricious and undependable toy . . .
>
> The guests went up the grand staircases of white marble, on the soft and velvety carpets; white and scarlet uniforms; spread-eagle helmets in gold and silver; countless epaulettes . . . white dolmans bordered with precious beaver fur; finally the Court uniforms, heavy with gold embroidery and completed by short breeches and white silk stockings.[8]

Uniforms dominated at the balls, as they did at the opera and the ballet, occasions from which uniforms were quite indissociable. The author remembers many years ago taking an old Russian lady to the ballet at Covent Garden. The last time she had been to it was to see Kseshinskaya dance in Petrograd, just before the revolution. As we walked into the opera house she exclaimed, in a blend of shock and bitter undisguised disappointment: "But where are the uniforms?"

Whatever they may have looked like, the uniforms were a misery to their wearers, notably to the young officers on duty in the palace. They wore a full-dress uniform that consisted of a regulation jacket, a kind of extra waistcoat—for the Horse Guards, for example, this was scarlet with metallic eagles on the front and the back—and, worst of all, elk-skin breeches:

> It was essential that the breeches should have not the slightest crease. To attain this result they were damped, smeared with soap, and put on—after taking off the pants (ie drawers) if I

may venture to say so. The operation called for the services of a couple of vigorous soldiers.[9]

The ladies wore court dresses, cut very low, with bare shoulders and a long train. On the left of their bodice they would wear, according to rank, the imperial monogramme, if they were maids of honour, or even the imperial portrait, which was only granted to ladies of the greatest merit. The head of Nicholas's Court Chancellery, A. A. Mossolov, evokes a *grande dame* at the ball:

> She was already in her forties, but still slim, and her spangled dress displayed her figure wonderfully. Her light, almost chestnut hair was decorated with a diadem set with two rows of diamonds. A *ferronière* with a single diamond of two square centimetres crossed her forehead. A diamond necklace, the neck of her dress bordered with diamonds, with a flower at the back entirely of diamonds, set flat; two diamond chains leading, like enormous threads of fire, first to the front of the bodice, and then to the buckle at the waist.[10]

The tsar and tsarina would circulate freely through the crowds, and when supper was served they did not have their own table, but moved from one table to the next, at each one places being kept in reserve for them, while their itinerary, and just whom they would honour by joining, were of course all carefully determined in advance. Court balls, as may be imagined, were occasions that were taken very seriously indeed by the guests, and when, in later years, the tsarina insisted that the number of balls be drastically curtailed, since they put an intolerable strain upon her, shy and awkward as she was, it made her increasingly unpopular, and not just among the court nobility, but also among their juniors, the newly promoted civil servants who were only just eligible for an invitation, and who set that much more store by the whole occasion.

Besides balls and dances there were other social occasions which brought society into contact with the imperial family, notably the charity bazaars that were held during and after the Japanese war. They would be organised by leading figures such as the Grand Duchess Marie, who held hers annually in the Assemblée de la Noblesse, and at which the empress herself had a stall. St. Petersburg also had to offer the usual entertainments of a capital city. These were golden years for the opera and the ballet, which performed every Sunday night, while Saturdays were reserved for visits to the French Theatre. There was horse racing all the year round at the hippodrome, while an important centre for male social life was the Yacht Club, on Bolshaya Morskaya St., where it owned a smallish single-story building. The club was exclusive. Male members of the imperial family were elected automatically, other members were put up. It was a great thing for an up-and-coming guards officer to get in, and new members tended to make themselves conspicuous, looking proudly out over the busy street through the club's ample windows. It was a place where many useful contacts were made, and many rumours had their origins there, especially during the First World War.

As well as being a vital centre for trade, and the focus of social life, St. Petersburg was also the administrative capital of the empire, and hence the home of civil servants galore, and of still more uniforms, civil and military. Everyone in state service wore a uniform, and this included even students, their full dress consisting of a dark green tunic with gold buttons and a dark blue collar. Swords were plentiful too. One of the sounds to be heard on any smart street was the ring and rattle of sabres trailing and travelling along the pavement in the wake of cavalry officers temporarily on foot, for the capital was also a military city, and an imperial one, much given to parades:

> April 28. Just after eleven. I saw a splendid sight. Starting from the palace, along the embankment to the Summer Garden there were rows of Horse Guards; the bands were playing God Save the Tsar and the tsar rode along in a dark uniform with a blue sash beside the Empress's carriage; behind came the various uniforms of the aides-de-camp and generals. The regiments . . . began to cheer, but very much by numbers, giving one very little sense of enthusiasm. Of course no one was allowed near the embankment, on foot or otherwise, and the imperial procession went slowly by the ranks of soldiers moving down an apparently deserted street.[11]

Imperial protocol and security on such occasions was strict, since the danger of assassination was ever-present and the tsar the prime target. To those of us who believe terrorism to be a recent phenomenon it comes almost as a comfort to realise that, in the latter days of imperial Russia, countless government officials fell to the assassins' bombs and bullets. These included three ministers of the interior, D. S. Sipyagin, 1902, V. K. Plehve, 1904, and in 1911 Peter Stolypin —who had already survived a bomb attack on his house five years before. Another distinguished victim of terrorism was the governor-general of Moscow, Grand Duke Sergei, who was blown up by a revolutionary named Kalyaev in February 1905. Despite a visit from the grand duke's wife and the tsar's sister-in-law in prison, Kalyaev refused to express regret for his actions and went unrepentant to the scaffold.

Between 1905 and 1909 the total number of victims of terrorist attacks numbered 5,913, of which 2,691 were killed. Over the same period 4,630 terrorists were sentenced to death, 2,390 executed.

Tight though security was, it had its lapses, such as the occasion when the tsar came under the fire of his own guns. Each year, on the Feast of the Epiphany, the sixth of January, the tsar and the metropolitan of St. Petersburg would ceremoniously bless the waters of the Neva. Blocks of ice would be cut from its surface, and an altar and cross fashioned out of them. Accompanied by a suite of courtiers and ecclesiastics the tsar and the metropolitan would bless the waters, dipping a gold cross into them. The ceremony was rounded off by a salute fired by a battery facing the Winter Palace from the far bank of the Neva. In 1905 the salute was fired as usual—and shattered several palace windows, showering onlookers with broken glass. It appeared that one of the gunners had forgotten to exchange his shrapnel for blanks—a story not of conspiracy, but of a certain distinctly Russian kind of incompetence.[12] For official life in imperial Russia combined a remarkable degree of regimentation with elements of a hopelessness that prompted one British observer, Maurice Baring, to suggest that it was as if a complicated administrative machine had been set up in the heart of rural Ireland. Regimentation was reflected in some of the city's more eccentric regulations, such as the one that made it illegal to sell matches after 5:00 P.M. on Sundays, while it was only in April 1904 that ladies were permitted to ride on the top of the horse-drawn trams. There were city regulations of other kinds. When a pigeon fancier tried to get permission to import some birds from Finland he got caught in festoons of red tape that were exotic even by the standard of pre–World War One European bureaucracy. The objection to pigeons was that they could carry letters out of the country without risk of interception, bypassing the censorship to which any item of outgoing mail might be exposed. The pigeon fancier had to apply in turn to the police, the customs, the Ministry of the Interior, the Ministry of Finance, the War Ministry, and the Department of Engineers, since that department dealt with matters involving aviation. The request was finally turned down because he was considered to live too close to a military fortress whose secrets he, or his birds, might reveal.[13]

Yet despite such careful regulation St. Petersburg was a town in which things could go very wrong. Leaving aside such major disasters as Bloody Sunday in 1905, when troops fired on unarmed demonstrators bringing a petition to the tsar, things regularly failed on more modest levels, demonstrating the effect upon patterns of city life of generations of administrative incompetence. Take the following glimpse of St. Petersburg, January 21, 1905:

> The Egyptian Bridge collapsed yesterday. Fortunately no one was killed, and nobody drowned . . . along with the bridge part of a squadron of Horse Grenadiers fell into the Fontanka canal . . . The bridge should have been scrapped and replaced three years ago. Instead the municipal council allocated 575 roubles for repairs. But that sum only existed on paper. The contractor was given only 175 roubles, and obliged to sign a receipt for the whole sum. It is true though that no one required him to make any repairs whatsoever.[14]

By the time Rasputin was on his way there, the capital of Russia differed from other European cities in another remarkable respect. It enjoyed a degree of sexual openness, as opposed to licence, that by the standards of the age was extraordinary. Anyone leafing through the newspapers of the period will realise at once that he has entered a different world. Even the more distinguished dailies of the capital would carry between one and two-and-a-half pages of small ads. A reasonable proportion concerned accommodation and domestic help, but far and away the greater part consisted of advertisements offering various types of treatment for syphilis and gonorrhea. The treatments are classified by numbers–syphilis 606, or 914–alternatively they plug products such as Urital Galen, guaranteed to stop the most stubborn discharge in no time. That product was in hot competition with A. Ya. Akuliany's Armatin, advertised with equal generosity. The advertisements do not simply signify that there was more going on in St. Petersburg than elsewhere. That may or may not have been true. Essentially they testify to a relaxed and matter-of-fact attitude to certain uncomfortable facts of life, an attitude that fails to understand hypocrisy, and regards as fruitless attempts to pretend that certain conditions do not exist; in other words, they reflect an honesty and realistic openness that were among the most attractive characteristics of pre-revolutionary Russia. In the new Russia, of course, neither crime, prostitution, nor venereal disease exist.

Openness and frankness were reflected in a considerably greater degree of sexual freedom than that enjoyed in Edwardian England. Members of the older generation complained of the decadence of the 1900s, in both public and private life. Thus a bookseller complained that the works of radical politics that had constituted his staple for years had become difficult to move; readers had grown more interested in pornography and the wilder sides of religion and the occult. It was a time when people sought strong sensations, spiritual and physical, and when homosexuality ceased to be the love that dare not speak its name. Its climate is well reflected in the mediocre best sellers of M. P. Artsybashev. His best-known novel, *Sanin,* is a study of nihilistic, disruptive and sensual youth, with vulgarised versions of the characters of Nietzsche, Dostoevsky and Gide. They are free of all sexual taboos, and the book is a work of quite remarkable frankness. Characters are actually described having erections, and maidenheads fall at an amazing rate. The work makes out a case for immediate sensual enjoyment under the threat of nihilistic despair. The protagonists express no surprise when three of their number take their own lives for reasons that remain obscure but that smack of *tedium vitae.* The survivors continue to discuss life's meaning, or the lack of it, and bear witness to an unguided striving for spiritual fulfillment.

The first decade of the century was a time of spiritual discontent, reflected in certain St. Petersburg circles in an increasingly feverish search for God. Besides the ways of conventional Orthodoxy there was an ever-growing interest in other paths such as theosophy, table-tapping and séances, reflected in the proliferation of journals devoted to such matters.[15] In advanced literary circles there was to be found a strange blend of heterodox faith and sensuality, tinged with popular religion, as Nikolai Arsenev points out in his remarkable study *Russian Piety:*

> This religious hysteria . . . also had a profound influence on certain aspects of the literary and cultural life of the Russian intelligentsia on the eve of the First World War . . . What was being preached was excess, and an orgiastic philosophy, a mixture of paganism and the most sacred Christian mysteries, an ecstasy, a deliberate frenzy, both sensual and at the same time religious, or at least quasi-religious. A smell of decay, and exoticism and morbid emotionality, a quest for sensation, a profound lack of moral equilibrium, seemed to characterize the literature of . . . the first fifteen years of the twentieth century. These literary circles . . . were at the same time . . . connected with the underground currents of sexualism and pagan mysticism which animated the Russian ecstatic sects . . . This movement reflected a tendency that was much more closely related to the popular soul than one would have thought at first sight; related however to the morbid element of this soul, in its disease, to the sensual and sinister undercurrent which combined the sacred and the scabrous.[16]

Even in more conventional religious circles there was a shift of emphasis, a growing interest in popular and not always entirely Orthodox forms of religion, a turning towards the sects and holy men and women of the people. In the words of a devout Christian of the time:

> Religious Petersburg began to look for answers to its doubts and spiritual questions in new ways and entered the realm of

"popular" religion, that has no theological problems or contradictions, and was not committed to any body of dogma. It was all the easier to do so since there was no shortage of representatives of this kind of faith. And soon such representatives who had hitherto frequented the poorer parts of the city and the religiously inclined tradespeople of the city's markets, or visited the apartment of Archimandrite Theophanes, known to the whole city for his faith and currently Inspector of the Theological Academy, began to find their way into the drawing rooms and salons of high society.[17]

It was perfectly possible to witness the meeting of the world of primitive religion and the modern age upon the street. The thoroughfares of the capital abounded in sights such as the following:

> October 6, 1905
>
> I met a strange character this morning on the Nevsky Prospekt, wearing a cassock and with a tall staff in his hand. He was barefoot despite the snow and bare headed. He had a broad pleasant face covered with a thick beard . . . He was the pilgrim Vassily who always dresses like that however severe the frost, and collects money for the building of churches. They say that he is well known not just to the people but in the very highest circles.[18]

A few months later the author was travelling on a tram when Vassily got on and stood on the platform:

> His thinning hair was wet; he held his famous staff, with a cross on the top and a huge iron spike on the bottom . . . The holy gentleman's pockets were filled with brochures and copies of his life story. He hands them out and if he gets any money in return this immediately goes into a bag that hangs round his neck. Not so long ago a magistrate convicted him of causing a nuisance and brawling; the verger of the Kazan cathedral did not let him take his staff inside. He was offended and observed: "The Emperor Alexander III authorised me to take this staff everywhere, and now you want to stop me." He seized the verger. A struggle ensued and he was given a stiff fine.[19]

Vassily was a curious character well known in the capital. He was a peasant from the Kuban district, an illiterate soldier. His staff, weighing about fifty pounds, with a large silver cross, had frequently got him into trouble with priests who objected to his carrying it. Alexander III had indeed given him written authorisation to have it by him. He had been introduced into court circles by one of Nicholas's uncles, Sergei Alexandrovich, and it would seem that during the revolution of 1905 he offered Nicholas much advice about preventing revolutionary propaganda reaching the army and the maintenance of discipline. He would, when out of town, regularly send telegrams to the imperial couple, who were often known to reply. He fell from favour after a drunken brawl with a cab driver.[20]

To say that religious life was coloured by an enthusiasm verging on hysteria is not enough to convey the strange blend of ardent faith and superstition that reigned in the civilised Russia of those years. One can get some idea of the authority of superstition from the fact that during the Japanese war of 1904–1905 respectable newspapers would regularly carry stories of military miracles wrought by St. Nicholas on the Russian behalf. In the spring of 1912 in Novgorod there were persistent rumours that Antichrist had been born and the world was about to end. It was said that a baby had been born with iron teeth. As the priest christened the child he observed that it was a miracle. "This is no miracle," replied the baby, "the miracle is yet to come," and died. The reporter of the tale continues: "What kind of twentieth century is this? It has arrived on paper only, and we are really still in the depths of the 18th."[21]

It should be noted that in that year polite Novgorod society was very fond of bridge and passionately devoted to poker, at which everybody cheated as best they could.

In the capital one of the chief objects of religious enthusiasm was the priest John of Cronstadt (1829–1908). Since 1874 he had been the priest of the Andreevsky cathedral in Cronstadt, a naval base and suburb of St. Petersburg. He preached a popular brand of religion with a strong sectarian colouring, and was venerated by his flock of common people and aristocracy. He advocated absolutism and the need for the church to uphold the absolute authority of the Tsar Autocrat. He had the reputation of being a healer and a miracle worker, and to many seemed a likely candidate for sainthood, but it was a sainthood tinged with heresy. Hysterical women were known to interrupt his services calling out to him as "The Lord Sabaoth,"[22] an expression recalling the sectarian view of the Living God, and one which would also be applied to Rasputin by his more enthusiastic followers. John of Cronstadt also had a curious habit when eating with his admirers; he would take his soup, bless it, eat a spoonful and then pass it round as if it were a communion vessel from which each disciple would solemnly eat. This too was, as we shall see, a habit he shared with Rasputin. John's followers, the Joannites, were practically a sect in their own right. They were mostly hysterical mystics and beggars, persons from the lower orders, who from the 1890s onwards spread word of John's miracles, and described him as "the earthly incarnation of God," while his leading female follower was "the Mother of God." Because he had no time to hear the individual confessions of all those who wished to take communion, and in the Orthodox church communion must be preceded by confession, he established a kind of public confession in which everyone shouted their sins aloud simultaneously, making for a kind of clamour that would bewilder the most enthusiastic Southern Baptist, as the shrill voices of the women, who were usually in a majority, drowned the deeper tones of the men. John himself did not approve of his wilder followers, and would refuse his Joannites communion, understandably, since their attitude smacked strongly of heresy. Indeed, after John's death the official church took severe measures to stamp the Joannites out. This did not prevent the Russian Church in Exile from canonising John, proclaiming him a saint in 1964.

Archimandrite Theophanes (an archimandrite was a form of abbot), born V. D. Bystrov, was another of the capital's leading churchmen. He was associated with the Theological Academy, first as an inspector, later as its rector. Short, thin, reserved, with a dark beard and hair that seemed plastered to his skull, he was universally loved and respected as a churchman of outstanding faith, wisdom, and kindness. His prestige extended well beyond the academy, to St. Petersburg society and the court itself, for the emperor had recently chosen him as his spiritual advisor. As we shall see, for all his qualities he was not always a sound judge of character.

Although Theophanes was a more Orthodox churchman than John of Cronstadt he shared the latter's bias. He too believed that true faith was more easily to be found among the people, and liked to surround himself with wanderers, *startsy,* men of God, and *yurodivye.* The latter are yet another relic of an earlier age. The word is variously translated as fool in God, simpleton in Christ, holy fool. The type was regularly encountered in Holy Russia and was probably the survival of a notion, common enough in medieval Europe, that God had endowed the mad with a peculiar kind of sanctity. However, mental derangement as such was not necessary to become a *yurodiviy;* it could also happen that the search for God would lead a man to assume the role of a half-wit, as a form of humiliation and mortification of the intellect. Traditionally *yurodivye* were held to be spiritually pure, and were placed beyond the reach of human authority, whatever they might say in their half-witted stammerings. Thus one of the most famous simpletons of Russian history, Vassili the Blessed, had a spiritual authority that made even Ivan the Terrible tremble. He features in iron cap, hair shirt, and penitential chains in *The Boyar's Plot,* the first of Eisenstein's *Ivan the Terrible* films. In 1912 the town of Novgorod contained no less than seventeen *yurodivye* complete with penitential chains and caps of steel.

That Theophanes should hold wanderers and *yurodivye* in high regard may be greatly to his favour in some respects but it had some peculiar results, as in the case of Mitya Kolyaba:

> He was bow-legged, misshapen, almost mute, with a withered arm. He had to be led as his eyesight was very poor; his hearing too was deficient, and his speech consisted of a few horrible sounds, uttered in painful gasps. Whenever he was shaken by an epileptic attack and began to shriek his voice changed from an uncanny whisper into the sinister howling of an animal. Finally it would become an unnerving and fear-inspiring roaring and baying. The repulsive impressions thus created were enhanced by the insane flailings of his deformed arms. Indeed one had to have extremely strong nerves to endure the presence of this imbecile.[23]

Kolyaba was allegedly endowed with the power of prophecy. A sexton named Egorov claimed that when in a fit Kolyaba had the gift of tongues, and that he, Egorov, could interpret them. His reputation as a prophet and *yurodiviy* grew rapidly, and in 1902 he was brought to the capital where he made an excellent impression upon Theophanes, was introduced to various God-seeking members of the aristocracy and even taken to court. Indeed, in an extraordinary surge of heady God-seeking enthusiasm, a girl from the Smolny Institute, Russia's leading educational establishment for the daughters of the nobility, actually married him.[24] Prince Zhevakhov, a devout Christian of exasperating naivety, observed in his memoirs that St. Petersburg society did not accept Mitya blindly, but that it preferred to mistake a sinner for a saint than pass a saint by, failing to recognise him.[25] Although the religious circles of St. Petersburg may not have engaged in the pursuit of strange gods, they were certainly not averse to the cultivation of strange saints.

Late in the autumn of 1902 rumour of a new saint, prophet and miracle worker from Siberia began to reach the capital. A young and fanatical monk, Iliodor (his secular name was Sergei Trufanov), who was to become a prominent public figure and thorn in the flesh of church and state alike, first heard of the new man of God from Theophanes. The man of God was none other than Rasputin, news of his doings in Kazan having reached the Theological Academy of St. Petersburg. Theophanes observed to Iliodor that his existence was proof that:

> To this day our Holy Russia abounds in saints. God sends his consolation to His people from time to time in the guise of men of righteousness, and they are the mainstay of our Holy Russia.[26]

✧ ✧ ✧

Theophanes, always on the lookout for potential saints and persons of exceptional holiness, had heard of Rasputin from the bishop of Kazan; indeed, the bishop gave Rasputin a letter of introduction to Theophanes. Armed with this, and in the company of Archimandrite Chrisanthos, chief of the church's mission to Korea, Rasputin arrived in St. Petersburg in the spring of 1903 and lodged with Theophanes.

The Siberian man of God made a profound impression, and Theophanes soon introduced him to John of Cronstadt. The introduction, as described by his daughter, has a ring of family mythology about it. Rasputin is alleged to have entered John's church without any preliminary introduction, taking communion there among a crowd of peasants. It would seem that John immediately sensed his exceptional presence and gave him communion first. Later he blessed him solemnly, urging him to carry out the great things assigned him by the will of God. It may all have happened like that, although it seems more likely that the seventy-four-year-old priest had been briefed by Theophanes in advance. Nevertheless the incident as reported is significant as it represents the kind of thing that the admirers of Rasputin wanted to believe—one "saint" automatically recognising another.

A little later Theophanes introduced Rasputin to Iliodor. The latter's subsequent description of the meeting is coloured by extreme prejudice—an expression appropriate in view of the fact that Iliodor later tried to have Rasputin assassinated. A fanatic by nature, hysterical, and in later years a demagogue, Iliodor was initially one of Rasputin's greatest admirers, only to turn against him, concluding that he was the embodiment of hypocrisy and lust. If Iliodor describes him here as a suspect character, that suspicion is retrospective. One day Iliodor is greeted by Theophanes in the Academy; the inspector has "an unpleasant simpering peasant" at his side:

> "This is Father Gregory from Siberia," remarked Theophanes pointing to the peasant, who was treading with his feet on one spot as if on the point of darting off in a wild gallop. "Ah, ah, ah," I stammered in embarrassment, holding out my hand to the peasant. We kissed each other.
>
> Gregory was dressed in a cheap, greasy, gray coat the skirts of which bulged out in front like two leather mittens. His pockets were inflated like those of a beggar who deposits there any eatables that are given to him. His trousers, no less shabby than the coat, hung down over the coarse legs of his peasant boots evidently blacked with tar, and the seat of his trousers flapped like a torn old hammock. The hair on the saint's head

was roughly combed in one direction; his beard looked like a piece of sheepskin pasted to his face to complete its repulsive ugliness. His hands were pock marked and unclean and there was much dirt under his long and somewhat turned-in nails. His entire body emitted an indeterminate disagreeable smell.

Gregory, having kissed me, surveyed me with his eyes, then moved his thick blue sensual lips, from which his moustache protruded like two worn out brushes, slapped me on the shoulder with one hand keeping the fingers of the other in his mouth and, addressing Theophanes with a kind of ingratiating unnatural smile remarked: "He prays powerfully, very powerfully."[27]

Hindsight or not, much of this rings true, especially the physical description. Rasputin had something of the *yurodiviy* about him, with his restless jerky movements, his habit of blurting out strangely phrased intuitive judgments. "Powerfully" is a weak translation of the Russian *shibko,* a strange adverb to describe prayer, with a strong colouring of peasant idiom; "He prays mighty fierce" would be a better rendering. The encounter is peculiar in another respect. It took place, says Iliodor, on December 16, a date which had a peculiar significance in Rasputin's life. It would be on another December 16 eight years later that Iliodor, in the company of Bishop Hermogenes, a possible castrate, and the half-wit Mitya Kolyaba, would make a farcical attempt to kill Rasputin, and December 16 was also the date of his assassination. It is possible but unlikely that Iliodor falsified the date in retrospect, for he failed to draw attention to its significance. It is a strange coincidence that it should have been on that day of all days that Rasputin made the acquaintance of the man who would prove his bitterest enemy, do more than any other to attempt to discredit him, participate in a violent attack upon him, and mastermind at least one other assassination attempt that was nearly fatal.

For all Iliodor's subsequent reservations, Rasputin made a tremendous impression upon religious circles in the capital, gaining the admiration of churchmen and laymen alike. He was variously described as a *starets,* a *yurodiviy,* or a man of God, but all agreed that he was a potential saint. For devout and simple men such as Theophanes he fulfilled a particular need, the need to believe that Holy Russia could still bring forth persons of exceptional holiness, proof that God still favoured her and that her church was as strong as ever. As Zhevakhov puts it:

> [In those days] it was the best, not the worst who flocked to Rasputin, their only fault being ignorance in matters of religion, or a gullible belief in Rasputin's "sanctity." There were people who made the most extreme demands of themselves, who were quite incapable of compromising with their consciences, and who, suffering deeply in the worldly atmosphere of lies and falsehood, looked for a solution to persons who seemed capable of conquering sin and allaying the fears of troubled souls; the kind of people who felt themselves unable to fight a lone battle against lies, suffering and misery, and who needed the moral support of those who were strong in spirit.[28]

Rasputin, who now began to find his way into the salons of the religiously minded nobility, cut a figure so far removed from their limited experience of the peasantry that they were incapable of assessing him, while remaining willing to take him upon trust:

> Rasputin's success was aided by the fact that high society . . . was not conversant with religious matters, had little contact with the clergy, or, finding such contact unsatisfactory, was distinctly uncritical, accepting him as a *starets;* they did not dream of taking a critical view of his words and deeds.
>
> In fact they were scarcely in a position to do so, not only because Rasputin spoke in jerky unconnected phrases and cryptic hints, which it was impossible to make sense of, but because his reputation was based not on what he said, but upon the impression he made. The stiff necked world of Petersburg society was utterly bewildered by its encounter with a bold outspoken Russian peasant who was no respecter of persons of any kind, said "thou" to all and sundry, was quite oblivious to considerations of protocol or etiquette, and unimpressed by any setting in which he might find himself . . . He treated all comers with a gentle kindness, as "hungerers and thirsters after the truth."[29]

Rasputin, to the end, would dress and speak as a peasant. For all his eventual ambition and the fierceness with which he would defend his situation as the intimate friend of the empress, he never attempted to "better himself," alter his peasant manners and nature. It was as a peasant that he penetrated to the heart of the empire, and a peasant he was content to remain. In the days of pre-Petrine Muscovy the women of the Kremlin regularly received a stream of beggars, pilgrims, and holy men in their apartments, thereby maintaining a link between rulers and the people that Peter the Great severed. It took Rasputin to renew immediate contact between the court and the people, with consequences that would prove disastrous for all concerned.

Some of Rasputin's more extravagant biographers have suggested that his career was advanced by Freemasons and Jews; but they advance no evidence to substantiate their claims, nor could they. It has also been suggested that Rasputin owed his initial success in the capital to ultra-right-wing elements, who planned to place him close to the tsar, and use him as an advocate of their policies. There is no direct evidence to substantiate this claim either–however, it is the case that all of Rasputin's early protectors were associated with right-wing political or religious elements. This was true of Theophanes and of Bishop Hermogenes, another early ecclesiastical acquaintance, who was very close indeed to activist patriotic groups such as the Union of the Russian People. It was true too of the first society hostess to receive Rasputin in her salon.

Countess Ignatiev was the wife of Count N. P. Ignatiev, Alexander III's first minister of the interior, a stern reactionary who replaced a more liberally inclined predecessor. Although he had not held office for over twenty years, he was one of a number of "wise old men" to whom Nicholas II would turn occasionally for advice. In two years' time, when Russia was in revolutionary turmoil, he would advise the tsar to stick to his principles and not grant his country a constitution. The countess was a very devout woman, closely connected to some of the most distinguished families in the land. For years she had run the leading right-wing salon of the capital, and was held, by many, in the very highest regard. This was not an opinion shared by Sergei Witte, who thought her an ambitious and foolish old woman: "A very unbalanced personality of limited intelligence, who began to dabble in politics under the guise of an interest in the church."[30]

Nevertheless the Ignatiev salon was an important meeting place for government ministers, high-ranking ecclesiastics and aristocratic reactionaries. They met in an atmosphere of religious enthusiasm, celebration of the autocratic principle, and a not always very orthodox mysticism. In other words it was the perfect setting for Rasputin's launching into high society. The *starets* professed his own brand of popular faith, and combined it with his simple peasant's adoration of *Batyushka Tsar'*, the tsar and little father. He made a considerable impact, if we can judge by the appearance made by the recently canonised Serafim of Sarov, at a séance held chez Ignatiev. The saint manifested himself with his head ringed by a halo of fire, and announced: "A great prophet is among you."[31] It was generally agreed that the prophet was none other than Rasputin.

There can be no doubt that the *starets* derived enormous benefit from his admission to such exclusive circles. However, we should not assume that he was the only Holy Man of the people to be received by the countess; Mitya Kolyaba was also seen there, for example. Moreover we do not know how often he went there, or on what terms. Certainly to be received by the countess conferred a certain recognition upon him, but it does not appear that she continued to play a significant role in his subsequent advancement. In fact it could be said that a rather more significant role was played by an ordinary priest, Yaroslav Medved', who had frequently visited Tsarskoe Selo. He talked to Rasputin at great length of the extraordinary reception accorded Rasputin's own *starets* Makarii of Verkhoturye, confirming all the stories Rasputin had heard from him, of how he had been taken to Tsarskoe Selo and presented to Nicholas and Alexandra. Rasputin, who now decided, late in 1903, to leave the capital and winter in Pokrovskoe, must have set off highly content with his own reception in the capital, and possessed of the tantalising knowledge that there was still a long way he could go.

Although he may have departed trailing clouds of glory, there was a cloud of another kind low down on the horizon, the kind that was as yet "no bigger than a man's hand." A month or so after he left, in January 1904, Bishop Anthony of Volyn' paid a visit to the capital.

A distinguished theologian who had once been rector of the Theological Academy, he still took a great interest in its affairs, being considered a good friend to its younger students. He was enthusiastically informed of the remarkable impression made by Rasputin, but proved sceptical to the highest degree. Tales he had heard of Rasputin's behaviour in Kazan had convinced him that by no stretch of the imagination could he be taken for a saint. He said as much, denouncing him as an imposter, but Theophanes and Rasputin's admirers dismissed his warnings as idle talk, for Bishop Anthony was known to be an inveterate gossip. Nevertheless in certain circles it began to be whispered that "In Kazan Father Grigorii has been with women."

Theophanes's indignant rejection of these allegations is interesting because it sets a pattern. Over the years evidence of Rasputin's misbehaviour would accumulate steadily, only to be obstinately rejected by his admirers, because to accept it would prevent them from believing what they so desperately wanted to believe, that the extraordinary authority Rasputin asserted was proof that he was a man of God, with the power to remit sins. Rasputin offered such solace because he claimed to take the sins of others upon himself. Shorn of that power there was little he could offer the heavy-laden. The credulity which surrounded Rasputin is reminiscent of that displayed by the Germans who elected Hitler chancellor in Germany in 1933; his disciples wanted so badly to believe in Rasputin that he managed to persuade them, for a long time, that black was white—because that was the colour they needed it to be.

CHAPTER 6

RASPUTIN RETURNED to the capital, putting up at the Mount Athos monastic hostel. For all the rumours of his doings in Kazan, Theophanes and his friends gave him a warm welcome. They also helped him to extend his influence. It was at this time that he met a lady who was to become the most enthusiastic and most deranged of all his disciples. Mme. O. V. Lokhtina was a prosperous landowner married to an engineer in government service. She had been bedridden for years with neurasthenia, and doctors proved unable to help her. Rasputin, it would seem, managed a cure. A woman with a great capacity for enthusiasm, she became his unswerving lifelong admirer. She was his first intimate upper-class friend—he soon moved from his lodgings to stay with the family, and continued to live there for some years. It is highly probable that he became her lover, or at least applied sectarian arguments to test her capacity to conquer the temptations of the flesh.

Lokhtina is interesting in another respect; she was the only one of his society admirers overtly to profess sectarian attitudes—in this case well beyond the limits of mere eccentricity. For Lokhtina was overpowered by Rasputin, who may have cured her neurasthenia, but only at the cost of destroying her mental equilibrium forever. She came, literally, to worship him, would fall to her knees in front of him, kiss his hand and address him as the Living Christ or the Lord Sabaoth. To improve the quality of her worship she took to dressing entirely in white, in an echo of the sectarian aspiration to purity, with her dress bedecked with ribbons. Round her head she would wear a bandeau bearing the word "Alleluia," above which could often be seen a bonnet of wolf skin, made in Pokrovskoe, a gift from Rasputin. She became increasingly strange, displaying more than a tinge of sexual hysteria. Some years later she told Rasputin's daughter that Iliodor, who had by then turned against Rasputin, had attempted to rape her in his monastery cell. When other monks came running to her screams Iliodor convinced them that it was she who had tried to seduce him, whereupon they indignantly stripped her naked and tied her to the back of a horse, which they drove out into the snow. None of this seems likely, although Iliodor did know Lokhtina well enough at one stage to get hold of her diaries, which he used for his polemic against Rasputin. She eventually took her search for God to the extremes of *yurodstvo*. A photograph of her in 1914 portrays a woman in her forties, an aged Ophelia, with a strange and staring face beneath a beribboned hat, draped in a long white cloak. At the time she was living in a peasant's mud hut in the village of Morozovo searching for God.[1]

Lokhtina was the most extreme and longest lasting of Rasputin's lady disciples. We last see her before the investigating commission of 1917, making a brief and very dignified appearance. Her attitude toward Rasputin helps us to understand the kind of hold he could secure. To her he was a healer who had cured her of an admittedly nervous condition, which no doctor could help. He was also a great authority of a sectarian and popular cast, in whom spirituality and sexuality were inextricably confused. Thus he exerted a powerful influence on three interdependent fronts, health, sex and religion, with consequences that, at least for Lokhtina, were permanently unsettling.

In the spring of 1905 Theophanes and Yaroslav Medved' helped

Rasputin take his next and most important step, one which turned him from a Siberian guru into a historic personage. At Easter that year Theophanes introduced him to the highest circles, presenting him to Grand Duchess Militsa, who was married to one of the tsar's relatives, Grand Duke Peter Nikolaevich. The grand duchess and her sister Anastasia, Duchess of Leuchtenberg, were known as the Montenegrins (they were Montenegrin princesses, Negus by origin) or, more colloquially, as "the crows" because of their dark hair and colouring. The tsar's relatives disliked them, considering them overambitious and too conscious of their rank. They were notorious for insisting upon their right to follow immediately behind the emperor, empress and dowager empress on ceremonial occasions. As Grand Duchess Olga Alexandrovna put it: "The sisters were nicknamed Scylla and Charybdis, and nobody dared to make a move until the Montenegrin ladies were where they considered they should be."[2] To be fair, this was probably a case of one sister leading the other, for the two women were not alike. Anastasia was considered to be much the nicer of the pair, quiet, inward-looking, with a strong religious sense.[3] Militsa was very different; ambitious, domineering, full of envy and a born intriguer. She too was religious, but in a not very Orthodox way. She had made an extended study of patristics, and of Christian mysticism, and was also said to read Persian mystic texts in the original. However, her interests extended further still, embracing spiritualism, theosophy, table-tapping and every branch of the occult. In other words, she was just the sort of person to respond readily to Rasputin. She was impressed by his man-of-the-people manner, by his speech, which was frequently incomprehensible, and by his idiosyncratic commentaries upon the Scriptures, and was quite ready to believe that he possessed extraordinary powers of healing and divination. The high regard in which he was held by Theophanes and his circle confirmed her in her opinion, an opinion that had not inconsiderable consequences for Russian history, for Militsa, at this time, was very close to the tsar, and more especially the tsarina.

It is hard to imagine anyone less well equipped to steer imperial Russia into the twentieth century than Nicholas II. A family man first and foremost, a partner in one of the most loving marriages ever to come before the public eye, he would, as it has sometimes been said, have been perfect as the owner of a large estate in rural England; as an autocrat he was hopeless. He had not even had the benefit of proper preparation for his task. His education had essentially been that of a cavalry officer. According to a cousin, Grand Duke Aleksandr Mikhailovich, his principal tutor was a "dry unforthcoming general who impressed on his charge that the miraculous force of secret annointment during the coronation was sufficient to give the future autocrat of Russia all he needed to know."[4] Another highly critical account written before the revolution provides a more elaborate picture:

> Though masters in plenty came to instruct the tsarevich and his brothers and sisters they were nevertheless allowed to remain without that domestic training which alone gives to future sovereigns and people in high stations the knowledge to fulfill their duties in the proper way and to meet with dignity the responsibilities of their arduous position.
>
> Again, lessons, though they teach something, yet do not instruct those who receive them if they are not accompanied by an intelligent training, and of this the Imperial children had none. They were given elementary notions of languages and arts, but I doubt very much whether to the present day any of them, the Sovereign not excluded, could write a letter in French without mistakes. [Though it should be said that his written English was excellent.] The love of learning was not inculcated; reading serious books was never encouraged; the discoveries of science were only explained as things which existed, but not as things capable of further development. In a word the tsarevich received quite a middle class training, and though he was afterwards sent on a long voyage for the purpose of improving his mind and acquainting himself with the world, it is more than doubtful whether he derived any real benefit from it.[5]

Nicholas seems to have retained considerable naivete in matters scientific. Some time after he came to the throne, "an American succeeded in persuading the Emperor that he had discovered a way to defend the frontiers of a country as vast as Russia by the use of electric currents of such force that no enemy could possibly cross the line. This discovery was to do away with the need for an army. Naturally, he demanded certain pecuniary considerations in advance before revealing his secret. The emperor was greatly impressed, and it was only with a good deal of trouble that he was dissuaded from subsidising the ingenious inventor."[6]

Nicholas's personality did not help him overcome the limitations of his education. A short, neat figure of a man, five feet seven inches tall, he was timid, introverted and weak, in the sense that he was incapable of making up his mind and sticking to his decisions. However it must be said that he always commanded great love and loyalty in his immediate entourage, together with a considerable amount of respect. He had great charm and also a quiet, penetrating way of looking at a man that could make even the strong feel weak. Thus an ex-minister who knew him well and had no reason to love him wrote of "that delightful affability of his which captivates not only all who meet him for the first time, but even men who, like myself, know the exact worth of his gestures and phrases."[7]

Yet despite his considerable majesty of manner, as an emperor he lacked stature and that taste for power which is important for any politician, vital for an autocrat. His happiest years had been those spent as a junior guards officer. His favourite pastimes were physical, not intellectual. He loved riding, could walk any but the fittest courtier off his feet, enjoyed rowing, sailing, shooting and playing tennis; in his late forties he was still capable of giving the last Russian champion, left-handed Michael Sumarokov-Elston, a testing work-out. The pictures we have of him in the hands of the Bolsheviks, cutting wood or shovelling snow, are not icons of imperial humiliation, they show the tsar having a good time—with his coat off doing useful physical exercise.

The early years of his reign had passed under the "guidance" of his four massive uncles. As Grand Duke Aleksandr Mikhailovich put it:

> The well-built young man spent the first ten years of his reign sitting in his study behind a huge desk, listening with a feeling

> that went close to terror to the advice and directions of his uncles. He was afraid to be alone with them.[8]

As a ruler Nicholas never learnt how to use the advice of uncles, ministers or sages from Siberia:

> He was always timid, almost painfully so, and when by a strong effort of will he conquered that timidity, he came out with what he wanted to say in an almost brutal manner . . . He never had any opinion of his own . . . his want of mind making him always endorse the judgment of the last person he speaks to.[9]

Even if a minister had lost his confidence the tsar would receive him with the utmost courtesy and listen to him with great attention. He made it a point never to display emotion, although he might drum a little on the windowpane or smoke more cigarettes than usual. As A. A. Mossolov, for sixteen years head of the court Chancellery, put it:

> Nicholas was still perfectly able to give him a friendly reception, to thank him for his collaboration and to shake hands warmly with him when he left and then to send him a letter calling on him to resign.[10]

Yet weak though he may have been as a ruler, he possessed that peculiar dogged obstinacy that sometimes accompanies weak men in power. On the rare occasions on which he made his mind up definitely he was impossible to move; no argument, however convincing, could reach him. Take, for example, his reaction to a ministerial council that advised him to abolish some of the restrictions that Russia imposed upon her huge Jewish population:

> "Despite most convincing arguments in favour of adopting a positive decision in this matter, an inner voice keeps insisting more and more that I do not accept responsibility for it. So far my conscience has not deceived me. Therefore I intend in this case also to follow its dictates. I know that you too believe that 'the tsar's heart is in God's hands.' Let it be so. For all the laws

> I establish I bear a great responsibility before God, and am ready to answer for this decision at any time." So went his answer. None of the documents in my possession shows more clearly the tsar's mystical attitude towards the nature of his Imperial power.[11]

Those words were written by the last peacetime prime minister, V. N. Kokovtsov. Nicholas sincerely believed that he had received Russia from God, and was personally responsible for her well-being. This meant that he did not have the right to delegate or dilute his power in any way. It also meant that when he heard the voice of conscience advise a certain course nothing could dissuade him from taking it. Obstinacy, mysticism, and weakness combined to shape another and perhaps the most disastrous of all his characteristics: a deadly fatalism. We are all in the hands of God, and if it is his will that, for example, the Japanese annihilate the Russian fleet at Tsushima in 1905, there is nothing a tsar can do about it. Nicholas accepted the course of history passively. "Thy will be done" was his response, to the very end; and as he was always ready to point out, he was born on May 6, the day of Job.

The fatal calm that he displayed in such circumstances might be thought of as a version of the British stiff upper lip, but it was very different. Nicholas achieved his outward impassivity by withdrawing from the world, refusing to accept the significance, the existence even, of bad news. The display of calm was achieved at the price of a flight from reality, a secret and interior withdrawal reminiscent of a man who removes the telephone from his ear in order to reduce the sound of a nagging wife to a remote if petulant murmur. Nicholas, though by no means musical, was fond of Wagner, his favourite opera being *The Twilight of the Gods*.[12]

In one respect at least he was lucky, beyond the luck of many men, and certainly most heads of state. When the young Princess Alix of Hesse-Darmstadt came to Russia to attend the wedding of her sister Elizabeth to Nicholas's uncle, the grand duke Sergei, the princess and the tsarevich fell quickly and enduringly in love. In his diary for January 1891 he writes, "My dream is some day to marry Princess Alix H. I have loved her for a long while . . ." There were objections to the match; she was reluctant to leave her Protestant religion, especially since the service that would announce her conversion to Orthodoxy required her, literally, to spit upon her old faith. However, she eventually relented, and Nicholas was in raptures:

> Wonderful, unforgettable day in my life, the day of my engagement to my darling adorable Alix . . . Oh God what a mountain has rolled from my shoulders . . . The whole day I have been walking in a mist without realising what has happened to me . . . The whole world is changed for me; nature, mankind, everything; all seems to be good and lovable and happy.

Alexandra's reactions are similar. "Never," she was soon to write in what had become a joint diary, "did I believe that there could be such utter happiness in this world, such a feeling of unity between two mortal beings. I love you–those three words have my life in them."

A wise man once observed that all marriages, however disastrous, have had their peaks of glory, usually at the start. However "Nicky" and "Sunny" or "Sunshine" (Alexandra's childhood nickname) could lay claim to much more than that. In purely personal terms their marriage was an outstanding success. "Hubby" and "wifey" (it is singularly revealing of the domestic tone of their marriage that they should have chosen to refer to one another in the cosy language of upper-middle-class Victorian England) could lay claim to nearly twenty-five years of happiness. The letters the tsarina wrote her husband of twenty years' standing combine intimacy, tender love and suggestions of genuine physical passion, which makes them exceptional by any standards.

Alexandra was fortunate in the husband chosen for her, but otherwise there was little enough luck in her life. One of the younger daughters of the German grand duke of Hesse-Darmstadt, who had married Princess Alice of England, she was a granddaughter of Queen Victoria. After the death of her mother, when Alexandra was six, she moved to England and was brought up by her grandmother, in Kensington Palace, London. She was seventeen when she first met Nicholas–he was twenty-three–and was a striking girl with blue eyes, fair hair and a fine complexion. However, neither her Victorian upbringing nor her temperament had equipped her for her role as tsarina. This demanded qualities of tolerance and flexibility, a talent for being both firm and easy-going in intuitively apprehended doses, and above all the capacity to radiate warmth of spirit—none of which she was endowed with by nature or encouraged by her upbringing to adopt. Lack of charm is a handicap at the best of times; in the empress of Russia it was a disaster. Since the time of the second marriage of Peter the Great—to a Livonian peasant girl—it had been the custom for tsars and tsareviches to marry foreign princesses. However, these were usually accorded ample time to prepare themselves for the role of tsarina. In the case of Nicholas's own mother, Maria Fedorovna of Denmark, seventeen years passed between her betrothal to Alexander and her coronation. Alix had no such opportunity. Indeed, her betrothal virtually coincided with the death of her future father-in-law. She arrived in Russia a total stranger, scarcely able to speak the language—although she worked hard at it over the years and by 1914 was almost word-perfect, with the faintest touch of awkwardness and a slight English accent. She made a bad impression from the start: a certain Princess A. M. Baryatinskaya, who saw her when she arrived, was most struck by "her timidity and the exceedingly melancholy expression of her eyes not easily forgotten."[13] Others looked on her still less charitably, seeing her as cold, unyielding, charmless, and potentially domineering.[14] As a result the unavoidable gaffes of a newcomer went unforgiven:

> Far removed from the complicated interplay of court life, the young empress made mistakes that were insignificant in themselves, but which appeared heinous crimes to the eyes of Petersburg high society. This confused her and imparted to her that well known tension which informed her manner. This in turn sufficed to invite comparison between the dowager empress and the "cold snobbery" of the young tsarina. Nicholas II took these comparisons very much to heart and soon relations between the court and society grew very tense indeed.[15]

The young tsarina was sensitive enough to appreciate her lack of success with the nobility, a lack for which she held them alone responsible. Over the years the imperial family would steadily reduce their contact with society, dividing their time between official ceremonies and an intimate, almost recluse-like family life, while the tsarina demanded of all those close to her an undivided, uncritical, and unswerving loyalty. As a tutor would write a few years later:

> Exclusive as she was, she could not accept anyone who was not wholeheartedly hers. She only confided in friends whom she was sure to dominate; it was necessary to respond to her confidences by giving oneself to her totally.[16]

Anyone who showed signs of being critical was automatically dismissed as disloyal. Alexandra developed an uncompromising sense of "us" and "them"; "us" consisting of a handful of friends and the immediate family, while "they" were nothing less than the hundred million odd other inhabitants of the Russian Empire. A similarly uncompromising approach informed her attitude to government, and to her husband. In each case the attitude was one of autocratic domination, and tragically limited as a result. Pobedonostsev, one of the last great architects of reaction and the autocratic principle, allegedly described her as "More autocratic than Peter the Great and sterner than Ivan the Terrible. Her limited mentality makes her believe that she is gifted with great intelligence."[17]

Her insistence on absolute loyalty both in the empire and the imperial household–she once described herself to Nicholas in a letter in which she advised him on the running of the country as "wearing invisible trousers"–took its toll upon the tsar. Although it was not until the last years of his reign that she positively overwhelmed Nicholas with advice, the belief that her husband needed help of a very special kind can be traced to earlier years. In 1905, when the empire was in the grip of revolution, she observed that:

> You understand the crisis we are going through! It is most certainly a time of trial. My poor Nicky's cross is heavy, all the more so as he has nobody on whom he can thoroughly rely and who can be a real help to him. He has had so many bitter disappointments, but through it all he remains brave and full of faith in God's mercy. He tries so hard, works with such perseverance,

> but the lack of what I call "real" men is great. Of course, they must exist somewhere, but it is difficult to get at them. The bad are always close to hand, the others through false humility remain in the background. We shall try to see more people, but it is difficult. On my knees I pray to God to give me wisdom to help him in his heavy task. I wrack my brains to pieces to find a man and cannot; it is a despairing feeling.[18]

The empress would long hold the belief that her gentle, hardworking, desperately conscientious and devout "hubby" needed a real man or men to guide him and give him the strength he so badly needed. What was required was soul and integrity, not mere experience, which could so easily make a man false and ambitious. In due course she would find such a man in Rasputin.

Together with her narrow but strong character, Alexandra Fedorovna was, as may be deduced from the above, a woman of great piety. Although at first reluctant to leave the Protestant faith, she had embraced Orthodoxy eagerly on coming to Russia, and was profoundly absorbed by its emphasis on ritual, prayer and the cult of saints. She approached her new faith with the unbalanced eagerness of the convert. Her temperament, and a certain rigidity in her Protestant background, combined with her sense of personal rejection to make her commitment to Orthodoxy uncomfortably intense; it lacked that Russian equilibrium that is born of common sense, tolerance and resignation—all qualities which the empress quite definitely lacked. How Queen Victoria's granddaughter reacted to the openness and sexual frankness of St. Petersburg, incidentally, can easily be imagined.

Alexandra had a profound belief in the power of prayer, and looked to it both for practical guidance and for its capacity to heal. From an early age and long before she met Rasputin, she believed in miracles and in healing by faith. Like Nicholas she also believed in the power of saints and men of God to offer comfort and divinely inspired guidance.

No one could maintain that guidance of the highest quality was not needed. The unexpected death of Alexander III had cast its shadow over Alexandra's arrival, and left Nicholas ill-prepared to assume power. Next the imperial coronation turned to tragedy as it culminated in a disaster of a very Russian kind. Those familiar with the administration's incompetence had looked forward with trepidation to the week of official celebration that was to be held in Moscow. They felt that the strain imposed by the influx of foreign heads of state and other visitors, with all the concomitant problems of security and protocol, by the numerous official ceremonies, the huge crowds, and the manner in which the citizens of Moscow were prone to celebrate–getting drunk as quickly as possible–were likely to tax the collective competence of officialdom too testingly, particularly since the man in supreme charge of the proceedings was the tsar's uncle and governor-general of Moscow, Grand Duke Sergei Alexandrovich, whose ability to cope was very open to doubt.

Surprisingly, the official ceremonies went according to plan for the first two magnificent spring days, and we have a remarkable re-creation of them from the grand duchess Olga Alexandrovna, the last tsar's younger sister. She had no official duties, but on the morning of the coronation she went to the Cathedral of the Assumption, within the Kremlin walls:

> I was so excited that I could hardly sleep the night before. I was up long before anyone stirred. I suppose we had breakfast. I can't remember. Then Nana and a maid started dressing me. I wore a full-length court dress of silver tissue, and for the first time I had the wide red ribbon of St. Catherine's Order across my shoulder. They put a white *kokoshinik* [old Muscovite form of headdress], embroidered with silver, on my head. The dress had a mantle with a train falling down–pinned to the left shoulder. It was my first experience of wearing the "armour" as we called it, and I found it heavy and wearisome. I had a single string of pearls and no other jewelry. And it was such a hot day!

She rode in the procession in one of the gilded state coaches, which looked fine enough, but were miserable to ride in. The springing was terrible, and the passengers felt each one of the numerous bumps in the road all too well. Moreover, the coaches had not been aired before use, and were unbearably hot and stuffy. They moved slowly towards the Kremlin gates, through enormous cheering crowds, as peals of bells rang out from the city's 1,600 belfries.

The Cathedral of the Assumption is not large, and could only accommodate a relatively small number, in small special wooden stands built along its fresco-covered walls. Olga Alexandrovna was fortunate; she found a place close to a pillar against which she could lean during the five-hour service. For her, the most important moment came when the metropolitan of Moscow handed the emperor the crown, and he put it on his head:

> It looked a simple enough gesture, but from that very moment Nicky's responsibility was to God only. I admit that the very idea may sound unreal today, when the absolute power of sovereigns has been so discredited. Yet it will always retain a place in history. The coronation of a Tsar of Russia was a most solemn and binding contract between God and the sovereign, His servant . . . The ceremony ended with a very gentle and human climax. Alicky knelt before Nicky. I shall never forget how carefully he put the crown on her head, how tenderly he kissed her and helped her to rise. And then all of us began filing past them, and I had to leave my corner. I was just behind the Duke and Duchess of Connaught, who represented Queen Victoria. I swept a deep curtsey, raised my head, and saw Nicky's blue eyes looking at me with such affection that my heart glowed.
>
> That evening Moscow was lit up with illuminations and fireworks. Just before being tucked into bed, Nana let me have one last look from the big window at the distant scene. And for those fleeting seconds I was as absorbed in the spectacle as Napoleon must have been eighty years earlier when gazing, probably from the same window, at the burning of Moscow.[19]

On the third day it was the turn of the people of the city; they were to be entertained with food and drink and receive presents in the form of tin coronation mugs. The event was scheduled for noon on the field of Khodynka, about three miles northwest of Red Square. The crowds started to gather early on the preceding day, as trains coming into Moscow were so packed with expectant peasants that there was scarcely room to stand. Throughout the day the crowd gathered on the field, bringing supplies of food and drink with them, until by dawn on the morning of the ceremony there were, it is estimated, half a million people packed together so tightly that it was virtually impossible to move. A cossack who rode into the crowd in an attempt to break it up a little found that his horse was simply lifted off its feet, so tightly were they pressed together. Officials had seriously underestimated the size of the crowd, which had grown too large to control. It grew apprehensive and restless, fearing that there might not be a sufficient quantity of presents to go round. These were to be distributed from a line of booths at one end of the field.

Quite early in the morning the wishful thinking of the crowd interpreted the gesture of a workman close to them as an invitation to move forward and receive its gifts. As it moved forward slowly it transpired that a considerable number of persons in its midst had been dead for some time, and were simply supported by a crush so dense that no one could stir a hand. As the crowd went forward they fell to the ground and were trampled underfoot. The official inquiry recorded a total of 1,389 deaths. It found that the majority had died of suffocation; the preceding day had been very hot, registering 80 degrees Fahrenheit, and the heat had returned almost with the dawn. Moreover, onlookers claimed to have seen a thickish layer of vapour, carbon dioxide and vodka fumes, covering the crowd as it stood packed upon the field. Now the story of Khodynka, as it is usually told, suggests that its victims were trampled to death, in a series of trenches that crisscrossed the field, which had been used for military manoeuvres. In fact, it would seem that the trenches were in another part of the field altogether, and not one body was found in them.

Although the nature and scale of the disaster have been distorted subsequently, there was no denying the immediate sense of tragedy, or the fury of the survivors at inefficient authorities who had allowed it to happen. As carriages drove out to Khodynka field to witness the popular celebrations they were met with a procession of carts coming towards them. Pieces of tarpaulin were thrown carelessly across the corpses, which had been no less carelessly loaded, leaving many hands dangling over the side. As the carriages approached, the official party thought at first that people were waving to them.

Throughout the rest of that long day official celebrations were interrupted by long lines of carts bringing back the dead. Yet the aftermath did more damage still to the dynasty. That night the French ambassador was to give a ball for the newly crowned imperial couple. Nicholas decided, or was advised, that it was better to be seen dancing on the day of the tragedy than risk offending the French by declining to attend. The couple put in an admittedly brief appearance, their faces badly marked by the morning's events. Yet to have attended at all bore witness to an alarming lack of political judgment, a lack subsequently confirmed by the tsar's refusal to dismiss his uncle, Grand Duke Sergei, who was ultimately responsible for the thousand-odd deaths.

✧ ✧ ✧

Shortly after the marriage, in the spring of 1896, Nicholas brought Alexandra to the palace in Tsarskoe Selo, which would be their home for very nearly the rest of their lives. Tsarskoe Selo, The Tsar's Village, is today called Pushkin, after the famous poet who attended the Lyceum there. It was founded by the second wife of Peter the Great, and developed in the course of the eighteenth century. It was situated fifteen miles to the southwest of St. Petersburg, and set in the middle of a swamp. By the twentieth century the village had grown into a town of over thirty thousand inhabitants, and was connected to the capital by the oldest railway line in the country, opened in 1837. The journey took just half an hour from the centre of town to the tiny local station with its steeply sloping wooden roof. Close to the main line ran a second set of tracks, carefully patrolled by imperial gendarmes. As these reached the "village" they peeled off to the tsar's private station. It was considered too dangerous to run the imperial train on the public track. Sidney Gibbes, the tsarevich's English tutor, considered Tsarskoe Selo to be:

> A ruralised town in an urbanised wilderness. It contains a number of houses and barracks, for it is also a great military centre. But besides this there are many charming palaces set around with vast artificial parks; also expanses of water that have come to seem natural to the place. While that is Tsarskoe Selo itself, the country round it is still in pristine savagery, barren swamp.[20]

The railway station was connected to the imperial palaces by a wide boulevard with a double row of trees on each side. Along it were to be found the houses of the nobility, standing in their own grounds, each with its resplendent doorman, wearing a blue uniform and elaborately coloured sash and bandoleer. At the end of the boulevard was the magnificent eight-hundred-acre imperial park, ringed with an iron fence. It contained artificial lakes, follies, a pagoda, a Turkish bathhouse, monuments, triumphal arches, walks, and bridle paths. It was magnificently landscaped, heavily wooded in places, where shrubs planted by successive emperors had become small forests of lilacs. The park was open to the public from 10:00 A.M. to dusk, and had been so for many many years. It occupies a very special place in some of the greatest Russian poetry, and was a spot much loved by Pushkin himself, and by one of his greatest heirs, the twentieth-century poetess Anna Akhmatova. Public access to the imperial grounds was a worry to the security services, who did what they could by keeping a very tight control upon the residents of Tsarskoe Selo itself. Anyone taking up quarters there, for however short a time, was subject to careful vetting.

The two imperial palaces were also open to the public. The Old Palace had been built by the architect Rastrelli for Catherine the Great. It was a large building, now coloured blue and white, with over two hundred rooms. The second, so-called Alexander Palace, had been started in Catherine's reign, and designed by Quarenghi. It was completed in 1796, and was somewhat smaller, only a hundred rooms. It was situated some six hundred paces away from the Old Palace, beside a large artificial lake. The only tsars ever to like it were Nicholas I and Nicholas II.

Although the palace, much of which was destroyed in World War Two, during the siege of Leningrad, has been restored, it looked very different in the days of Nicholas II. Then its facade was overgrown with sweet-smelling lilac, which was inexplicably cut away by the Bolsheviks in 1920. Nicholas and Alexandra lived on a relatively modest scale in the west wing, which consisted of two stories. One entered the palace by a huge hemispherical hall, and turned right for the imperial apartments. The first room was an antechamber, full of portraits of earlier tsars, and, in later years, children's bicycles. Then came the library, and next the private apartments proper. First was Nicholas's public study, with comfortable leather armchairs, a mahogany desk, candelabra, a round table, and numerous photographs and paintings by nineteenth-century Russian artists. It opened onto an indoor pool on one side. Then came a dressing room and then his private study, which contained a billiard table and various personal memorabilia, including his old schoolbooks. On the other side of a central corridor were the empress's rooms. First a small room for her chief maid, then a dressing room and then the imperial bedroom. Nicholas and Alexandra always shared the same room, sleeping in twin iron-framed bedsteads. The room was generously hung with icons, and off it were a private chapel and the imperial bathroom. The next room was Alexandra's boudoir, the famous mauve room which she had furnished all by herself. Those who knew it were guarded in their opinions, but the general consensus was that it was very comfortable and also very ugly. It was a room of modest size with rather high ceilings, dominated by the colour mauve. The curtains and hangings were of mauve silk, and the armchairs had mauve covers. The woodwork was cream, however, and there were always large quantities of flowers, lilies and lilacs mostly. Strange though the colour scheme appeared to visitors, they found the furniture stranger still. Although the Romanovs had been acquiring fine furniture from Europe for the best part of two centuries, the tsarina wanted none of it. Driven by some memory of her Victorian childhood, which may also have accounted for her colour scheme, she insisted on buying her furniture from England, by mail order. She bought modern factory-produced furniture from a department store called Maples, still to be found to this day, and still catering to the tastes of a conservative middle class. Maples's furniture, incidentally, has defeated at least one Soviet scholar, A. N. Petrov. In a book published in 1969 about Tsarskoe Selo he describes the famous boudoir as being panelled in stained maple wood, "which was typical of the style fashionable at the turn of the century."

The second floor was turned over to the children. Nursery, schoolrooms, maids' quarters, and, in due course, three bedrooms, one for the tsarevich, one for the two elder grand duchesses, one for the younger pair. The children led a life of considerable austerity, sleeping on narrow, hard camp beds. It was the custom to deny imperial children comfortable personal accommodation until they came of age, although their apartments seemed luxurious enough to one of their cousins, the grand duchess Marie Pavlovna, who used to play there as a child:

> These rooms, light and spacious, were hung with flowered cretonne and furnished throughout with polished lemon-wood. The effect was luxurious yet peaceful and comfortable. Through the windows one could see the palace gardens and guard houses, and a little beyond, beyond the grill of a high iron gate, a street corner.[21]

This then was home for the imperial family for over twenty years. Except for trips to the Crimea, and Baltic cruises on the imperial yacht, it was there that they remained, in isolated domesticity. Nicholas worked hard. In the morning he would begin by dealing with his correspondence—he actually liked to open his own mail—and would see ministers and advisors. At eleven he might take a break and join his family for a stroll in the park, and then carry on working till lunch. This could be an elaborate affair, with up to twenty people at table, and four or five courses. Nicholas and Alexandra did not like rich food. The tsar never touched caviare, since he had upset his stomach by taking too much one day, and liked simple Russian dishes, such as cabbage soup—although he was very partial to suckling pig. After lunch he would work again for an hour or so before going for a ride in the park—his family preferred to be driven. They would meet again for tea, which was very much a family affair—Nicholas made a point of seeing the children then, since he often had to miss them in the morning. He would then work again till supper, receiving more visitors. After eating a simple meal at eight he might read to his family, or watch them doing needlework or sticking photographs into their albums. He would then retire to his study again for a little more work until his evening tea at eleven. He would then take his bath and write up his diary before turning in. The routine seldom varied, and the day-to-day life of the emperor and empress of all the Russias was essentially one of steady hard work and quiet domestic routine.

✧ ✧ ✧

The early years of Nicholas's reign had their fair share of unrest, assassination and terrorist activity. Already some of the more sensitive spirits in the empire were beginning to feel that it would come apart quite soon. The poet Alexander Blok could smell catastrophe on the wind. It was the unbridged and in his opinion unbridgeable gap between the people on the one hand, and the rulers and the intelligentsia on the other, that frightened him. Ironically it was the bridging of that gulf by Rasputin that did much to trigger the last act of the tragedy.

The rate of disintegration was accelerated by the war that Russia imprudently embarked upon with Japan, disregarding all the attempts of Japanese diplomats to preserve the peace. The Russians assumed that victory over the Asiatics would come to them as a matter of course, which was not the case. Although the men and their junior officers fought with courage and determination, the army was "outgeneralled" by the Japanese, and the general staff soon discovered that it was not possible to fight a successful war many thousands of miles away with inadequate lines of supply. The Russian land armies suffered heavy losses, and a series of crushing defeats. In January 1905 the stronghold of Port Arthur was surrendered, rather too quickly, it was felt by many independent military observers. In March, Russian armies were badly defeated at Mukden. Defeat on land was then compounded by shattering defeat on water, the destruction of the Baltic fleet in the Straits of Tsushima in May 1905. The fleet had been sent halfway round the world to engage the Japanese. On the way they shelled some English fishing boats off the Dogger Bank in the North Sea, mistakenly supposing them to be elements of the Japanese navy. The disaster, Russia's greatest military humiliation, was aggravated by the fact that it had been widely appreciated from the outset that the fleet's mission was a pointless gesture. Nicholas knew it too, and was strongly urged by some of his advisors to countermand the order to sail. He changed his mind several times before finally allowing the fleet to depart.[22]

Defeat after defeat made morale in the army drop steadily, and in the later stages of the war men began to turn against their officers—witness the following vignette of poor leadership and indiscipline described by Countess Kleinmichel. A colonel was travelling to the war by train with his wife and family, in the comfort of a private compartment. His senior NCO came to tell him that his command of 120 men had been crammed into a cattle truck intended for forty, they were short of water and so cramped that they could neither lie nor sit down. The colonel replied that he would be along shortly, and remained with his family. The NCO returned an hour later and observed to his officer that it might all be very well for him, but the men were being treated like cattle on the way to a slaughterhouse. The colonel placed him under arrest. Shortly afterwards he went to see him and was roundly cursed by the NCO, whereupon the colonel lost his temper, drew his sword and cut so deeply into the man's neck that he severed an artery. When the troops learnt what he had done they lost control, drenched their colonel in paraffin and set him alight, burning him alive in front of his wife and children.[23] As a contemporary diarist, A. K. Bogdanovich, put it: "It is a terrifying but interesting time that we are obliged to live through."[24] The same writer refers to our "immoral and unprincipled age."

An excellent example of that moral decay was the case of Evno Azef, one of the most celebrated double agents of Russian history. He was the son of a poor Jewish tailor, born in Grodno in 1869 and an engineer by trade. He was both a senior member of the tsarist secret police and a founder of the Socialist-Revolutionary party, and the leader of its terrorist section. He participated in a number of "expropriations," or bank robberies, and assassinations too. He helped to plan the assassination of Grand Duke Sergei, the governor-general of Moscow, but his greatest "triumph" had come a year earlier, in 1904, when he helped to plan the murder of his own boss, Plehve, the minister of the interior. While participating in acts of terrorism he continued to feed the secret police information of the highest quality. Although rumours that he might be a double agent were prevalent for some years in inner revolutionary circles, it was a long time before they were accepted, and caused the utmost dismay when it was finally recognised that Azef had indeed worked for both sides. Although he was condemned to death in his absence by a revolutionary court, he died a natural death in 1918. By the end of his career, it was suggested, he no longer knew himself whether he was a terrorist spying on the police or an agent spying on the terrorists. When the full Azef story became known to the general public it caused a major scandal, helping to set the mood of the latter years of imperial Russia, a kind of "post-Watergate" atmosphere that joined cynicism with paranoia. The mood would come to its climax in the autumn of 1916 with the widespread belief that the rot had reached the top and that the empress herself was working for a German victory.

✧ ✧ ✧

Military defeat and unrest in the cities and the countryside combined to bring about the series of events known as the 1905 revolution, often considered a dress rehearsal for 1917. There was no single dramatic moment that marked it, rather a steady rise of unrest and a weakening of the rule of law all over Russia. The revolution may be said to have begun in January 1905, with the so-called "Bloody Sunday" when a priest, Father Gapon, who had been closely involved with government-approved trades unions, led a huge crowd through the capital to the Winter Palace to petition the tsar for an eight-hour day, a minimum wage, and a constituent assembly. The tsar was not even in his palace at the time, although Gapon had given notice of his demonstration. Whether out of fear, malice or simple incompetence we cannot say, but at all events the palace guard were given orders to fire into the mob from close range, and a dreadful slaughter ensued, which has, properly, become an important feature of revolutionary history. Gapon, incidentally, went underground as a revolutionary hero, but a few years later was executed by revolutionaries as a government agent, less fortunate in this respect than Azef.

By the spring of that year there was widespread unrest all over Russia. The country was paralysed by strikes, revolutionary activity, and peasant violence. On one estate, the property of a Prince Orlov, who had a superb stable of thoroughbreds, the peasants soaked the horses' tails in petrol and set them alight, whereupon they rushed into the stables, which in turn caught fire.[25] There were also incidents full of a very Russian kind of black humour. One diarist records:

> Launitz told me that when they were taking some terrorists off to be shot, a priest was walking with them. It was very cold and

everyone was freezing, when the priest observed: "It's all very well for you, you're on a one way trip, but I'll have to go back."[26]

Military unrest spread from the army to the Black Sea fleet. Shortly after Tsushima, sailors on the battleship *Potemkin* mutinied, terrorising the coastline for a few days before sailing to Roumania, where they were interned. There were insurrections in the Baltic states, and in Poland, and, a little later, a general strike in Moscow and St. Petersburg. Neither Lenin nor Stalin played any part in these events, unlike Trotsky, who was active in the organisation of the St. Petersburg strike. By the autumn of 1905 the government could scarcely be said to be in control, and foreign governments were growing alarmed for their resident nationals. The British considered sending warships to remove their citizens, especial concern being displayed for the countless English governesses considered to be at risk in the capital. Although he managed to persuade them that it had not yet come to that, the British ambassador felt that Russia was moving, somewhat uncertainly it is true, toward revolution. He wrote that autumn:

> It is a fight in the dark, in the mud, with weapons which don't reach . . . On the one side autocracy, a little man with a snub nose, descendant of an alien and scarcely royal race, who is at the centre of this vast machine and the god of a hundred million. On the other—nothing at all—but just simply destruction.[27]

In the event Nicholas managed to defuse the unrest; after much hesitation and reflection, he was prevailed upon, on October 17, to grant a constitution, and signed a manifesto to that effect. He signed reluctantly, for he was betraying his coronation oath to rule as an autocrat, and however convinced he might have been of the practical necessity for concessions, he knew that he was breaking a sacred trust. It was not a universally popular measure. A graduate of the Smolny Institute recalls hearing the news. The entire school was summoned to assembly, and a lady-in-waiting, herself an old girl, appeared to address them with tears in her eyes, wearing the imperial insignia, or *chiffre*. She told them that, "Of course the Tsar-Emperor can do no wrong, *but* he has granted the nation a constitution."

Unrest did not die down at once. Indeed it was immediately afterwards that some of the sharpest street fighting broke out in Moscow, while in St. Petersburg there were massive street demonstrations with red flags waving, and not a policeman to be seen. The demonstrators obliged better-dressed members of the public to acknowledge their authority by taking their hats off to the red flags. However, the police had their own way of coping with the revolutionaries. They organised reprisals, persuading workers that students and Jews had triumphed over them, and would depose the tsar and govern themselves to the workers' disadvantage; the workers mounted savage attacks upon Jews and demonstrators as a result. The police had obligingly provided lists of Jewish residences.

However, the revolution was petering out. Virtually its last gasp came at Cronstadt, where the naval garrison mutinied, but were rapidly brought under control. The *Great Soviet Encyclopaedia* ascribes their failure to "The lack of clear leadership and plan of battle; the mutineers acted in a disorganised manner." The British ambassador observed at the time that:

> The mutiny at Cronstadt had been carefully prepared and only broke down because the mutineers all got hopelessly drunk in the first five minutes and were easy to capture.[28]

The mood of the year of revolution is captured beautifully by Mintslov. He recalled the prophecy of a nineteenth-century holy man in the reign of Nicholas I. The tsar asked him who would succeed his son Alexander. "Alexander," replied the holy man, astonishing Nicholas, whose eldest grandson was also named Nicholas. Was his grandson to die before he could succeed? "And after him?" "Another Nicholas." "And then?" The holy man fell silent, but the tsar urged him to speak. "Then will come a peasant with an axe in his hand!"

Mintslov, who had heard the prophecy in the reign of Alexander II, went on to observe: "Is this not the time of the peasant with the axe?"[29] He was wrong; it would take another twelve years for the peasant to arrive.

⟡ ⟡ ⟡

Nicholas, with his blend of obstinacy, weakness, and mystic resignation, and Alexandra, with her inflexibility, shyness, and exalté enthusiasm, were both devout Christians who shared an unhealthy and, in the final analysis, disastrous belief in the exceptional powers of saints and men of God, Orthodox and otherwise. They both believed that in their time, as in the time of the Apostles, there were persons specially favoured by God's grace, whose prayers accordingly had special power. The age of miracles was by no means past.

Nicholas, to be fair, was not the only tsar of recent times to have entertained extreme beliefs of this kind. The life and death of Tsar Alexander I has a web of legend woven around it, a web persisting to the present day. Alexander almost certainly condoned the assassination of his father, Paul, and, goes the legend, in the latter part of his reign grew increasingly aware of the need to expiate his guilt. Accordingly he faked his own death in the Crimean town of Taganrog. After a brief interregnum he was succeeded by his brother Nicholas, and vanished to become a *starets,* by the name of Fyedor Kuzmich, who wandered through Russia for many years, praying, healing, and working miracles. Alexander was well known for his inclination toward mysticism and the occult, and to this day Soviet scholars are not completely convinced that the story is untrue. One version of the legend suggests that he was later joined by his brother, the grand duke Konstantin Pavlovich, who also became a pilgrim and was still to be seen wandering the streets of St. Petersburg in the 1860s.[30] One of the strangest of all the rumours that circulated about Rasputin in the immediate aftermath of his assassination had it that he was the illegitimate son of Fyedor Kuzmich, and the real father of the Tsarevich Aleksey, who thus had more Russian blood in his veins than any Romanov since the age of Peter the Great.

Alexander is also alleged to have had a particularly interesting kind of contact with the sects. During his reign, the *khlysty* and castrates enjoyed a considerable freedom and popularity, even in the highest circles. It has been suggested that the leader of the castrates, one Selivanov, was advanced by a particular court faction as a possible "sincere" mediator between the tsar and, on the one hand, God, on the other, his people. If this was the case it is a most peculiar anticipation of the role to be played by Rasputin a century later. Nicholas's grandfather, the Tsar Liberator Alexander II, also took an interest in the occult, witness the presence at his court of a certain David Douglas-Home, a medium with great psychic powers, which were said to extend to levitation. Conan Doyle referred to him as the greatest psychic medium the world had ever seen, and Tsar Alexander was a sponsor at his wedding.[31]

The interest that Nicholas and Alexandra displayed in holy men of various kinds is reflected in one of the more curious statistics of their reign; the extraordinary number, relatively speaking, of canonisations that it saw. As a prerevolutionary British journalist wrote of Nicholas:

> In miracles and marvels he took a childish delight, and was as ready to believe messages from the invisible world . . . as in the wonders wrought by the relics of Orthodox monks whose names he himself added to the bead-roll of Russian saints. His predecessors were more chary of peopling heaven than of colonising Siberia. Nicholas I assented to the canonisation of Mitrophan of Voronezh (1832), whose body was found intact after it had laid over a century in the coffin, but that was the only beatification made during the reign. Alexander II allowed the Holy Synod to enrich the church with one saint, Tikhon Bishop of Voronezh (1864); his successor did not even add one.[32]

Nicholas beatified three saints in the early years of his reign—Theodosius of Chernigov (1896), Serafim of Sarov (1903), and Joseph of Belgorod (1911)—while in addition, the reign was to see three ceremonial exhumations, the last of which took place in 1916. On at least three of these occasions the action was the result of the emperor's personal initiative, a reflection of his need to believe that the age of saints was not past.

This was especially true of Serafim of Sarov. Father Serafim was a hermit who lived in the forest near Arzamas in the government of

Tambov. He had a reputation for saintliness and miraculous healing. On his way to Taganrog shortly before his "death" in 1825, Alexander I had spent a long time in conversation with him. When Serafim died in 1833 he left various manuscripts in his cell. They were all burnt on order of the Holy Synod, but a single piece of paper, dated 1831, escaped. This allegedly contained a prophecy to the effect that, shortly after his canonisation, which would take place in the presence of the tsar and his family, misfortune would come to Russia and torrents of blood would flow. Millions of Russians would be scattered over the face of the earth. This would be God's way of testing his people. A hundred years after his death Russia would grow great again and a new era would begin, in which Russia would be governed by church and state together. The prophecy seems to have come good in parts, although the new era in question coincides unhappily with the beginning of Stalin's purges, and the way in which church and state came together has done little for the Christian cause.

Nicholas insisted that Serafim be canonised, even though when his remains were uncovered it was discovered that he had failed the test of saintliness, since his body had decomposed. When Bishop Anthony of Tambov protested at the canonisation, Nicholas had him stripped of office and dispatched to Siberia. It was officially put forward that the preservation of hair, bones, and teeth were sufficient evidence of sainthood.[33] The decision was not well received and numerous anonymous letters were found in the capital suggesting that the only "worker of miracles" was Nicholas II himself.[34]

The elaborate ceremony of canonisation was indeed attended by the imperial family. In the course of the celebration Nicholas took time to consult a famous local peasant clairvoyant, Pasha of Sarov. Some years later Nicholas, describing the meeting to a very junior member of the Holy Synod, observed that "she deigned to see him," and made a profound impression upon him. She foretold the outcome of the Japanese war, and then evidently started to strike one of the many dolls she kept with her, calling it Sergei, in obvious reference to Nicholas's unfortunate uncle, the governor-general of Moscow, shortly to be blown to pieces by a terrorist bomb.[35]

The tsar and tsarina did not confine themselves to Orthodox saints and seers. They also took a great interest in spiritualism, the occult and table-turning. A few years later the tsar, looking very tired, would meet one of his aides one morning and observe with an apologetic smile that he had had rather a late night, since he "got somewhat carried away by spiritualism." Interest in less than orthodox religion accounts for the presence at the court of the last tsar of M. Philippe, occultist and clairvoyant. Had he not been eclipsed by his remarkable successor, M. Philippe would have played a much more prominent role in twentieth-century Russian history.

Philippe Nizier-Vachod, a Savoyard peasant, was born in 1849. At the age of thirteen he became an apprentice butcher in Lyons. He gradually discovered that he had exceptional powers, both of healing and clairvoyance, and aged twenty-three he set himself up as a fringe doctor and faith healer, which brought him into frequent and disagreeable contact with the orthodox medical practitioners of Lyons. However, this in no way affected the quantity or the quality of his clientele, for his consulting room in the Rue de la Tête d'Or was constantly filled with persons from every walk of life.

Monsieur Philippe, as he was known, was a "mild little man with a gentle manner and persuasive eyes."[36] Short, thickset, with a bushy moustache and brown hair that had a centre parting, he seemed an unremarkable man who took no trouble to conceal his peasant origins. However, like Rasputin, as soon as he began to speak, he quickly imposed his authority, by a combination of tone of voice, quiet authoritative smile, and remarkable eyes. One admittedly somewhat partisan description of these last says that "whereas they were usually chestnut he frequently appeared to various persons with eyes of a splendid blue." He is said to have possessed clairvoyant powers together with the ability to "read" people and assess their character:

> Often as he drew close to you he could tell you in a few words what was troubling you, and what you did not dare confess to him. On other occasions he would mention to one of the persons present something about their lives that only they could know, or something they had said in secret . . .[37]

The same account describes him as a faith healer with the most remarkable powers, and as a man who had a great sense that his power came from God, who worked through him.

Early in 1900 M. Philippe was consulted by two Russian ladies who were very impressed by his gifts of divination and his air of supernatural authority. At their insistence he accompanied them to Cannes, where he met the Russian grand duke Peter Nikolaevich, his wife the grand duchess Militsa, and her Montenegrin sister Anastasia.

At this time the Montenegrin sisters were the only members of the imperial family to have Alexandra's ear and affection. Her mother-in-law, the dowager empress, had never taken to her, and the coldness that grew up between them was not helped by the older woman's insistence that she take precedence over her daughter-in-law, or by her reluctance to pass down the imperial jewelry. Alexandra took such slights badly, and also took note of the fact that the Montenegrins were the only members of the family to treat her with the full respect to which, as empress, she felt entitled. Their attention extended beyond deference to the profession of admiration, and even affection. When Alexandra fell ill with a stomach disorder they dismissed her staff and looked after and nursed her personally. In the early years of the century their influence grew steadily as that of the dowager empress declined.

The Montenegrin circle was impressed by M. Philippe. He was invited to come and visit the sisters in Russia, and set off on December 29, 1900, from the Gare de l'Est in Paris. He spent two highly successful months in St. Petersburg and left with an impressive reputation behind him. It was now that the Montenegrins came to Nicholas and Alexandra with news of M. Philippe, introducing their "pet holy man" as later they would introduce Rasputin. In both instances their motives are open to question, in the sense that they sought to exploit the tremendous interest the imperial couple took in clairvoyants, hypnotizers, magicians and men of God. At the least they could expect their own situation at court to improve, as they could be seen both to feed and share the interests of Nicholas and Alexandra, acting, as it were, as suppliers of holy men to the court of the tsar. Moreover, it may well be that the Montenegrins and their circle hoped to exert influence upon the rulers by means of a holy man *en place,* who would follow the instructions of his sponsors.

In later years Prince Felix Yusupov, whose mind was admittedly more than open to the possibility that his country was the victim of a Satanic conspiracy on the part of Jews, bankers, and their unwitting instruments, the masons, expressed the belief that the latter had sent M. Philippe to Russia to attack the spiritual fabric of Holy Russia at its summit.[38] Although Russian masons do seem to have played a mysterious role in the February Revolution of 1917, one which is not as yet fully revealed, it does not seem likely that M. Philippe was one of their instruments.

Nicholas and Alexandra were to pay a visit to France that year, and ordered Grand Duchess Militsa to arrange to have M. Philippe presented to them. The meeting took place in September, in the palace of Compiègne and in the presence of the Montenegrins. M. Philippe created an impression that earned him an immediate invitation to Russia and the imperial palace at Tsarskoe Selo.

In a strange anticipation of the role Rasputin was to assume some years later, M. Philippe, peasant healer and clairvoyant, temporarily played the part of spiritual advisor to Nicholas, most powerful absolute ruler in the world. No decision of any importance was taken without consulting him, for was he not of these wise men especially chosen by God to guide anointed monarchs? The attitude was much encouraged by M. Philippe, who persuaded the tsarina that "if she submitted to the decrees of Providence and strove for spirituality she would always find teachers who strengthened her faith."[39] The monarchs consulted him on subjects of fundamental political importance: we learn from the tsarina's correspondence that "Our first Friend sent by God," encouraged their commitment to the principle of absolute rule, urging them on no account to grant their country a constitution.[40]

Philippe was not just an advisor and spiritual guide. Like Rasputin he had the reputation of a healer, and was said to have effected some miraculous cures at the imperial court. Indeed he so impressed the tsar with his natural curative powers that the tsar requested the French government to award M. Philippe a medical diploma, a request that caused much embarrassment. This was the first occasion on which the personal beliefs of Nicholas and Alexandra were reflected in their behaviour as emperor and empress of Russia.

The Frenchman's powers were held to extend beyond miraculous healing well into the realms of the paranormal. Maurice Paléologue, France's last ambassador to the tsar, maintains that M. Philippe, encouraging Nicholas's love of spiritualism and table-tapping, conducted regular séances where he raised the ghost of Nicholas's father, the redoubtable Alexander III, who gave his son advice on how to steer his country through the troubled years of the early twentieth century. We know from other sources that Nicholas was much given to such practices, and it is by no means implausible that he should have sought his late father's advice in this way. But other accounts of M. Philippe's activities place a considerable strain upon belief, since they would put him, as a practicing magician, on the same level as Shakespeare's Prospero. His biographer, who may be thought of as partisan well beyond the point of gullibility, claims that he possessed remarkable powers of weather control. On one occasion he calmed a stormy sea in order to smooth the passage of the imperial yacht. When asked to do something about a high wind that was threatening to spoil a military review, he could not abate the actual force of the wind, but proved able to prevent it from blowing at ground level and whipping up clouds of dust.[41] The same source endows him with powers of invisibility, which he exercised when riding with the empress in open carriages in order to avoid embarrassing her. One day in Yalta in the Crimea, Felix Yusupov's father recalled, he was going for a walk when he met the grand duchess Militsa driving with a stranger. He bowed, but to his astonishment she failed to respond. On meeting her a few days later he asked her why she had cut him, only to be told that he could not possibly have seen her, since she was with M. Philippe, "and when he wears a hat he is invisible and so are those who are with him."[42]

Inevitably M. Philippe made enemies. The imperial couple did not lead a conventional court life, preferring to confer the privilege of close acquaintance upon select members of the aristocracy and family, keeping almost everyone else at arm's length. M. Philippe came to enjoy a degree of intimacy that was quite inconsistent with his station, and that turned any frustrated would-be courtier against the

French peasant. That he should, rightly or wrongly, be regarded in his own country as an opportunistic charlatan, came to make his presence at court appear increasingly undesirable. It brought discredit on the tsar and tsarina and cast an unfavourable light upon their judgment. Moreover, Philippe managed to antagonise the Orthodox church, which not only rejected his heterodox teaching but, more important perhaps, resented his position as intimate spiritual advisor to the tsar and tsarina, a position that should by rights be held by a senior churchman.

Unlike Rasputin, who would prove able to take far fiercer opposition in his stride, M. Philippe was unable to counter the intrigues of his enemies. Besides, there was also a failure of a different kind. Since her marriage in 1894 Alexandra had given birth to four daughters, Olga, Tatyana, Maria, and Anastasia, the youngest of whom was born in 1901. For dynastic reasons it was vital that Alexandra should produce a male heir. M. Philippe claimed that he could ensure the birth of a son in the immediate future. Sure enough, in the spring of 1902 Alexandra declared herself pregnant and expected without fail to give birth to a son in due course—but fail she did.

The failure has been explained in two ways. The less charitable explanation, and hence the most attractive for that luckless woman's numerous critics, not to mention M. Philippe's scarcely less numerous enemies, was that she had suffered a false pregnancy, the consequence of hysteria and wishful thinking. However, it has also been claimed that Alexandra simply had a miscarriage, which was not an event that would have been given widespread publicity at that time. Although we cannot say which of the versions is the true one, the fact remains that M. Philippe's failure to assist in the birth of an heir marked a weakening in his position. In the meantime Nicholas was put under increasing pressure to let the Frenchman go. He had just received a most unflattering report of his activities in France from the head of the French section of his secret police, while Theophanes was also encouraging him to get rid of him. Late in 1902 M. Philippe finally returned to France, but returned in no disgrace. Not only did Nicholas part with him reluctantly, he sent him home with honours, having conferred upon him the title of inspector of port sanitary services, a post which gave him the rank of general, and more important, automatically made him a doctor of medicine. He also presented him with a magnificent motor car, a Serpollet, which a motor mechanic who worked on it subsequently described as "a presidential landau."[43]

It has been claimed that, before leaving Russia, M. Philippe made a prophecy to Nicholas and Alexandra. He is said to have comforted them with the assurance that one day he would be replaced: "Some day you will have another Friend, who will, like me, speak to you of God."[44] M. Philippe maintained his contact with Tsarskoe Selo on his return, carrying on a regular correspondence until his death in 1905, a death which he had prophesied to the very day.[45] For some time afterwards Anastasia attempted to keep up the goodwill that M. Philippe had created, seeking to maintain her influence over Nicholas and Alexandra with the suggestion that when the sage "relinquished the physical plane" his spirit had entered into her, so that she should be considered his effective reincarnation.[46]

M. Philippe was not the only French magician to get close to the court. A certain M. Encausse, better known under his *nom de guerre* Papus, was an occultist who enjoyed a considerable reputation in Parisian spiritualist and literary circles. He paid three visits to Russia, in 1900, 1903, and October 1905. On the last occasion he too visited Tsarskoe Selo. It was the time of the 1905 revolution. There was rioting in the streets of Moscow and the railways had gone on strike. The day after he arrived he too conjured up the spirit of Alexander III. Nicholas allegedly asked his father whether he should give way to the demands of the revolutionaries. The spirit replied that he was to resist revolution at all costs, but that it would return one day with a renewed violence which would be the direct consequence of his lack of severity in dealing with the present unrest. "No matter, take courage my son and do not abandon the struggle."[47] Papus then observed that he personally had the power to avert Alexander's prophecy as long as he should live, but no longer: he was to die on October 25, 1916, less than two months before Rasputin's assassination, while the dynasty was to fall some seventy days later.

He returned to France shortly after his interview with Nicholas, and for all his belief in the occult he seems to have been disturbed by the part it was allowed to play in the process of government. He observed to a friend that he could never have imagined that a monarch ruling over one hundred fifty million subjects would regularly look to table-turning and spiritual séances as a means of deciding political issues of the greatest importance.[48] Ironically, this reliance on spiritual guides is confirmed by a remark Nicholas made about Papus himself. Discussing one of the latter's books with his prime minister he observed that it contained insights, discoveries and revelations that might well put him in a position where he "would prove able to govern the country in person, altogether without any ministers of any kind."[49] It is true that he was smiling as he spoke, but there was nothing funny about his desire to rely on guides who possessed immediate intuitive access to "the truth" at the expense of political advisors of a more conventional kind.

Papus feared that the imperial couple would find themselves at the mercy of the first charlatan to try to take advantage of them. Like M. Philippe, he maintained a regular correspondence with them over the years, in the course of which he was to warn them repeatedly against the growing influence of Rasputin. Some months before he died he would write:

> Cabalistically speaking Rasputin is a vessel like Pandora's box, which contains all the vices, crimes and filth of the Russian people. Should the vessel be broken we will see its dreadful contents spill themselves across Russia.

For his part Rasputin did not greatly care for Papus and would observe that, since there was more sin to be found in the West than elsewhere, anything coming from Europe must needs be tainted; a very Russian point of view.

CHAPTER 7

Whatever may be said, the appearance at court of Gregory Rasputin, and the influence he exercised there mark the beginning of the decay of Russian society and the loss of prestige of the throne and of the person of the tsar himself.

RODZYANKO

"My son has so little luck with people."

NICHOLAS II'S MOTHER

It was the Montenegrins who had brought M. Philippe to Tsarskoe Selo. That they believed in his powers does not mean that they did not try to benefit from them. It is the ambition of the courtier to get as close as possible to the monarch; proximity confers prestige, influence, and possibilities of material advantage. Certainly the two sisters encouraged the spiritual and mystic penchants of the imperial couple, and to contemporary observers, their motives were anything but disinterested: "It would all be very funny if it were not so sad," A. A. Polovtsev, a member of the Imperial Council, wrote in his diary, adding, "When it comes to the Montenegrins and M. Philippe financial considerations feature very largely."[1] Nicholas's uncle, the grand duke Nicholas, had also played an important part in the promotion of M. Philippe. Now, late in 1905, the Montenegrins and the grand duke made a further effort to place a protégé close to the tsar.

The revolution of 1905 may in retrospect seem a mere curtain raiser to the revolutions of 1917, but it must have appeared somewhat different at the time, with widespread strikes, street fighting in Moscow and the capital, mutinous soldiers returning from the Far East, widespread looting and burning of landowners' estates in the provinces—not to mention the killing of the actual landowners. The imperial family were virtual prisoners at Tsarskoe Selo, not daring to enter their own capital and keeping a warship on constant standby with steam up ready to take them to safety. The attempt of the tsar to seek the advice of his late father gives some indication of the need he felt for reliable guidance; should he make concessions or should he continue to fight the revolution at every point?

It was apparently Grand Duke Nicholas who persuaded the tsar to sign the October Manifesto. Both he and the Montenegrins had been in constant contact with the palace for some time. In the course of the last three weeks of October there were only two days on which Anastasia did not visit the palace, while her sister dined there on at least seven occasions, such visits being backed up by innumerable telephone calls.[2] Nicholas and Alexandra did not normally see members of the family with anything approaching such regularity.

Anastasia Nicolaevna, who, it will be recalled, was married to the Duke of Leuchtenberg, grew increasingly close to Grand Duke Nicholas, a rapprochement both sensed and encouraged by Rasputin, who was an adept at providing his protectors with sayings that might encourage them in doing whatever they wanted to do. He observed that "the marriage of the brother and the sister will be the salvation of Russia"—Militsa, it will be remembered, was married to the grand duke's brother. The Montenegrins chose to regard this pronouncement as a prophecy suggesting that the grand duke and Anastasia must be brought together for the good of the empire. The marriage was also supported by Alexandra herself, and in due course it was indeed accomplished; divorce is rather easier in the Orthodox church, which also permits the celebration of second marriages.

Late in 1905 there was thus a certain conjunction of circumstances. The Montenegrins had grown very close to the grand duke, and collectively they had considerable influence over the tsar, greater perhaps than that of any other conventional pressure group at any other time in his reign. The group in question was distinctly susceptible to mystics and holy men, and not averse to making use of such persons to further their own ends. Rasputin's encouragement of Grand Duke Nicholas and Anastasia led them to suppose that, at the least, he might prove able to exert a useful influence on the tsar and tsarina; might indeed prove a suitable replacement for the defunct M. Philippe, enjoying as he did the support of Theophanes and the inner circle of ecclesiastics who had disapproved of the presence of a French occultist at Tsarskoe Selo. Besides, the tsar, whose protracted indecision had culminated in the indignity of the October Manifesto, was clearly in need of a spiritual guide to give him the kind of God-sent advice that he could never expect from mere politicians.

On October 31 Militsa, her husband, her sister and the grand duke dined with the imperial court and left very late. Next day the tsar and tsarina called on Militsa, a call recorded in the tsar's diary. It is one of those entries that mark history, although at the time the diarist is unaware that he is doing anything of the sort. It is the record of a casual encounter:

> We have made the acquaintance of a man of God named Grigorii from the government of Tobolsk.

That entry in the tsar's consistently unremarkable diary is the only account we have of Rasputin's first meeting with "Mama" and "Papa," as he would soon be calling the emperor and empress. Despite Nicholas's need for special guidance, Rasputin did not immediately impress him as such a person. True, he was no longer the filthy, unkempt Siberian wanderer. Although he still dressed as a peasant, he now wore good polished boots and expensive silk blouses. A true Russian peasant in this respect, he loved to have his achievements reflected in the luxurious quality of the clothes he carried on his back. Yet he had not, could not yet have developed his intuitive sense of courtier's statecraft. He was still tentative in his manner, ready to take refuge behind a mask of peasant naivety or even feign *yurodstvo* "simplicity in Christ."

Curiously, when he met the imperial couple on November 1, 1905, Rasputin realised an ambition that was very close to his love of peasant clothes made of expensive materials. Just as such clothes would show the world what he had become, so he could say, "See who I am, I am just a simple peasant, but grand dukes and duchesses like me, and I have been to Tsarskoe Selo and met the tsar and tsarina, and they like me too. That's the kind of man I am." To English ears it sounds like boasting, but a Russian finds nothing wrong with showing off as long as there is something genuine to show—and in its absence *vranye* or creative lying in the interests of self-glorification can also command respect. It is a simple act of self-affirmation, and if you neglect to perform it no one else will do so on your behalf. Rasputin would always feel the need to show others what he had become, pointing proudly to the quality of his acquaintance. He had a genuine need to be close to the high and the mighty, and not necessarily because he stood to gain materially from that proximity. It was in itself the measure of his achievement.

Yet there was more to the Rasputin of these years than mere courtier's ambition. He had, after all, impressed devout churchmen with his holiness, and it was to his spiritual qualities that he owed his success. He was not just a charlatan who could fool a lot of the people a lot of the time. Over the years he may have abused his talents, his insights, and his capacity to heal and to comfort, or to preach a simple but remarkably convincing brand of peasant religion based on love of the universal harmony of God's creation. Yet it is not unreasonable to ascribe to Rasputin's ambitions something beyond mere self-assertion. The man who would later insist with great urgency that he had some special significance for the dynasty, that "When I perish they will perish," and whom history in this respect would prove right, may well have felt that he had some special purpose to his life, and that this purpose was bound up with the last Romanovs. It would be preposterous to suggest that he was some kind of Siberian Joan of Arc, and yet an over-simplification to make out that he was nothing more than a confidence trickster, a Tartuffe or a Felix Krull. His character was an inextricable mixture of opportunism and a sense of destiny, charlatanry and genuine understanding, sensuality and spirituality. Moreover, his ego was sufficiently strong for him to be incapable of critical self-awareness; he was convinced that whatever he did was thereby right. He resolved contradictions by ignoring them, saying, "Contradictions, what of them, for you they are contradictions, but I am me, Grigorii Rasputin, and that's what matters;

look at me, see what I have become!" For all his insights, Rasputin lacked the kind of conceptual framework which might occasionally have made him feel at odds with himself. He was always ready to act on impulse, for it was through impulse and the immediate that he could both seize the truth and express his broad peasant nature.

His initial impression upon the imperial couple may have been a relatively modest one, yet it had curious repercussions. Some days later Nicholas II showed one of his household, Colonel Prince Putyatin, a letter. It was signed by the St. Petersburg priest, Yaroslav Medved', who had for some time been the spiritual counsellor of the Montenegrins. The letter begged the emperor to receive a certain *starets,* Grigorii Efimovich, who had come from Siberia bringing the tsar an icon of St. Simeon of Verkhoturye. The letter went on to observe that the *starets* was lodging in the house of its author. Nicholas told Putyatin that he would be delighted to receive the *starets,* especially since he had not had time to visit Verkhoturye on his Siberian tour.

It was obvious to Putyatin from the tsar's manner that Nicholas knew all about the letter in advance, and that the whole business was a put-up job. Indeed, when charged some years later with Rasputin's introduction to Tsarskoe Selo, the priest Medved' denied ever having written the letter in the first place—though of course anyone subsequently accused of introducing Rasputin to court might well be found to suffer from a lapse of memory.

At all events Putyatin duly went to Medved's house in the Peski district of the capital, collected the *starets* and brought him to the palace. He was received by the emperor and empress, to whom he presented an icon of St. Simeon thirty centimeters high and painted on wood. He was also presented to the family, the four daughters and the heir, the eighteen-month-old tsarevich Aleksey. Each child was given a small icon and a piece of consecrated bread such as one takes with one from an Orthodox church after receiving communion. Rasputin conversed for some time with Nicholas and Alexandra and had tea with them before he left.

The most striking thing about this reception is its domesticity, a quality that would set the pattern of Rasputin's visits for many years to come. Nothing could be further from the image of the emperor receiving a holy man from Siberia, who would lay an icon at the feet of the tsar and little father of his people. This was more like a married couple inviting a remarkable character to tea, to talk to him and because it might be good for the children. The tsar and tsarina always drew a sharp distinction between their public roles and their private lives, and their friends were very much part of the latter. Sadly, it was a distinction that was lost on the rest of Russia.

After Rasputin left, Nicholas asked Putyatin what he thought of him. The colonel prince was unimpressed. To him the man had seemed mentally disturbed and a hypocrite into the bargain. Putyatin's reaction was by no means untypical. Rasputin did not impress everybody on first acquaintance. There were many, men mostly, who rejected him from the start, finding his homespun religion and his staring eyes fundamentally false; his abrupt and jerky speech and movements signs not of holy simplicity but of mental derangement. However, the majority, including Nicholas and Alexandra, felt very differently on first acquaintance:

> In Rasputin's presence one immediately sensed the wisdom, gravity, deep comprehension of life and majesty of thought which he possessed to such a remarkable degree.[3]

The tsar's reaction to Putyatin's observations made his opinion very clear. He was obviously distressed, turning away and stroking his beard and moustache, which was a clear indication of displeasure second only to nervous smoking and drumming on the window pane—the ultimate point on the scale of imperial disapproval. Nicholas never mentioned Rasputin to Putyatin again. The colonel's views did not actually harm his career, although over the years he was treated with increasing coldness by the empress, who would not tolerate hostility of any kind towards her Friend.

However favourable the impression Rasputin may have created, his visit bore no immediate fruit. The Montenegrins, it is true, did all they could to advance his cause, as is shown by the following entry in the tsar's diary:

> Militsa and Stana dined with us; all evening they talked about Grigorii.[4]

However, despite their assiduities, Rasputin would see very little of the imperial family for the next eighteen months.

For Rasputin, 1906 was a quiet year, in the sense that he was not yet a public figure. True, he frequented aristocratic and even princely houses, but this was a time when mysticism and the quest for God, or strange gods, was much in vogue, and many great houses had their particular *starets* or holy fool to visit them and hold forth on matters spiritual. Rasputin was not invited to the palace that year but he did meet Nicholas and Alexandra occasionally in the Montenegrin residences. He cut a peculiar figure in that world, with his blue silk blouse and heavy boots, and attracted the attention of the security police, who found his appearance suspect but could find nothing to lay against him.

Rasputin spent most of 1906 in the capital, consolidating his position with ecclesiastics and the aristocracy. His reputation as a holy man grew fast and he soon gathered a following of disciples, women for the most part, who quite improperly conferred upon him the ecclesiastical title of Father Grigorii. Rasputin was sometimes bewildered by the extent of the veneration accorded him, but now, as always, would accept anything on offer, be it money or veneration, without question. However surprised he might be that some of his more enthusiastic followers eagerly assured him that he was a candidate for sainthood, he never showed it. He would enter a salon with a strangely tentative blend of confidence and uncertainty, looking around for potential enemies. He could smell these out almost immediately, and would make it his business to disarm them. He would do so by asking them a series of questions so personal–were they married, were they happy, did they love God, why did they not have more children–that he would gain ascendancy over them immediately, unless, as sometimes happened, he drove them off in disgust. He would then turn to "preach to the converted." He might cast his eyes around the richly furnished room, taking it as the basis for an impromptu sermon on the need for simplicity, humility and spiritual poverty, staring significantly into the eyes of the more attractive members of his entourage.

The most prominent member of his following was Olga Lokhtina, at whose invitation he gave up his hostel room to move into her house in the Peski district. Sadly, we have no details of his stay, and Lokhtina herself remains something of a caricature; lack of hard facts has made her pass into legend, becoming a part of the mythology of the "mad monk," and endowing her with the embarrassing capacity for exalté enthusiasm of Dostoevsky's sillier women. In a few years' time Rasputin himself would find her embarrassing, as she crawled at his feet and addressed him as the Lord God of Hosts, but at this early stage in his rise she was more than useful to him. When she took him out of his monastic lodgings and into her own house she did much to make him acceptable in the eyes of the world. It was one thing to have a peasant holy man call on you and hold forth in your salon, quite another to give him permanent house room; the implication was either that you had embarked upon a particularly taxing exercise in Christian self-humiliation, or that the peasant in question was house trained.

Olga Lokhtina also helped Rasputin in other important respects. Although he was not entirely illiterate he found writing and spelling more or less beyond him. He could never get beyond a painstaking scrawl, with letters wandering all over the page, while his spelling was a reflection of his Siberian dialect rather than a rendering of standard Russian. Accordingly he preferred to communicate by telegram, putting the onus of literacy upon the telegraphist. However, Olga Lokhtina now began to act as his secretary, copying out letters that he would sign with a spidery G.

That summer Olga Lokhtina blazed a trail that would be followed by numerous other ladies driven by curiosity, a desire to save their souls, and a thirst for strong sensation. She made the trip to Pokrovskoe and stayed in Rasputin's *izba,* living the simple village life. We may assume her stay followed the pattern of subsequent visits, which included mixed bathing and the sharing of Rasputin's bed in order to test the spirit against the flesh.

Rasputin was beginning to become something of a celebrity in the capital. In the words of General Spiridovich:

> The salons vied fiercely with one another to have Rasputin. The unbalanced ladies of Petersburg society could talk and think of

nothing else. They taught him how to dress, to groom himself, to wash, and much more besides.[5]

He learned about the use of expensive pomades to perfume his beard, and was taught how to look after his hands and fingernails, how to wash himself without going to steam in the bathhouse. However he could never be dissuaded from using the cheapest and strongest-smelling brands of soap, which he would favour to his dying day. Equally, his lady friends never succeeded in persuading him to abandon his peasant mode of dress, loose blouse and baggy trousers tucked into high boots. However, he was happy to wear the silk blouses they embroidered for him and the fine cloth trousers and red leather boots that they bought for him. But even though they managed to improve his appearance beyond measure, his new friends could do nothing for Rasputin's table manners. He obstinately refused to learn about knives and forks, continuing to eat as he had always eaten, with his fingers. By the end of a meal, moreover, it would be apparent that his beard also had its part to play; Rasputin was not fond of napkins either.

Although he had succeeded beyond the wildest dreams of any Siberian peasant, success had left Rasputin unaltered in many ways. He was content to remain himself in dress and behaviour. He had too much confidence to feel a need to adjust to his new surroundings. There is more to this than mere shrewdness and calculation, for there is much about his behaviour that could not be considered either calculating or shrewd. A more calculating social climber would have made the effort to restrain his appetites in order to sustain a reputation for holiness. Rasputin did nothing of the sort. In matters of sex he continued to live dangerously. He always would, and one cannot help admiring him for it. His urgent sexual drive was a vital part of his nature, whether he was concentrating his energies by trying to master it, or letting it rip regardless of the consequences. There was nothing cautious about his sensuality, much to the bewilderment of devout Christians who suddenly found themselves exposed to it. Mme. O., from the government of Volyn', was a good Christian, a long-time pupil of Theophanes, who used to stay with her, as did other members of the Theological Academy. It was from them that she had heard of Rasputin. In November 1906 Theophanes arranged for him to come and stay with her in the country. The visit got off to a strange start when she met his train, and he introduced himself by kissing her three times on her lips. Their subsequent conversations took peculiar turns, as Rasputin, nervously twisting his fingers through his beard, kept asking her whether there might not be something she had to tell him that she did not dare tell her confessor. When she replied with a smile that there was not he began to move nervously about the room, paused and suddenly said: "You know I know how to love really well."[6] Mme. O. pretended not to have heard, and when Rasputin became increasingly explicit she left the room. He subsequently invited her to become his "spiritual daughter," and when she pointed out that this could not be, since he was not a priest, and could not bless her, he replied that he possessed an inner excellence which was more important than any priestly rank; an attitude that smacks of sectarian heresy.

Rasputin did not stay long with Mme. O., and no actual scandal ensued, partly because she took the precaution of sending her young daughters and their Swiss governess away to stay with friends. Yet the interesting point about this brief episode is the unashamed nature of Rasputin's advances, and this despite Mme. O.'s reputation, and, more important, her contacts with the very person who sponsored Rasputin in the capital.

Perhaps Rasputin simply would not or could not restrain himself, and yet there may be more to the matter than that. Rasputin's sexual advances were immediately followed by the suggestion that Mme. O. become his disciple, implying that sex for Rasputin might, among other things, have been a way of achieving that absolute dominance a *starets* must have over his disciples; a serious attempt to achieve spirituality via the flesh. It would be wrong to compare Rasputin's behaviour to highly evolved Eastern cults such as Tantrism, which make specific use of sexuality, for this would be too ingenious by half. Nevertheless sexuality is an element in certain forms of Russian sectarianism to which Rasputin had been exposed. It also seems to have played an essential part in the way he addressed himself to his followers, one reason perhaps why he behaved so outrageously with potential adherents. Unequivocal sexuality was a means of establishing authority, not just the result of an unbearable itch.

Already in Kazan in 1903 Rasputin's behaviour had begun to cast a shadow over his reputation. Now, three years later, a number of his earlier supporters, such as Theophanes, were beginning to have serious doubts. Sexual escapades aside, men of God did not wear silk blouses and visit society women; fasting and asceticism play an important part in Orthodox conceptions of holiness. Yet it would be another four years before Theophanes would turn away from Rasputin for good, and it is curious that it should have taken so sincere and devout a churchman so long, just as it is curious that Rasputin should have retained the support of so many adherents for as long as he did.

There are a number of reasons why he "got away with things." In the first place Rasputin was himself undergoing a change. It took time for the unkempt pilgrim of 1903 in his greasy black coat and tar-stained boots to become the peasant dandy with a scented beard who was acceptable salon material; an outward change which reflected a change in the kind of company he kept. He spent less time now with priests and monks, more in palaces. The circles he moved in were exalté, enthusiastically religious and far removed from sceptical criticism. The very existence of men of Rasputin's supposed spirituality was a confirmation of their faith, and this made them reluctant to put him to the test. They believed that Rasputin was what they wanted him to be and were purblind to his shortcomings because they had no wish to see them. Thus one of the silliest of Christian enthusiasts, Prince Zhevakhov, who would subsequently attempt to alter the course of World War One by transporting to the front an unwieldy but very holy icon—he had been told to win the war that way in a vision—was well aware of Rasputin's shortcomings, but managed to explain them away. He realised that, as a rule, men of God remained within the walls of monasteries and did not frequent salons. He felt, however, that the quality of Rasputin's teaching, his ability to comfort and to cure, were undisputed, hence he was a holy man, and only persons indifferent or hostile to religion could possibly oppose him. This is more or less understandable, but Zhevakhov reaches the height of naivete when he attempts to explain away reports of Rasputin's more extravagant behaviour:

> With respect to actions which are apparently altogether at odds with morality or proper behaviour, these were considered a

form of "simplicity in Christ," in other words there was a deeply concealed purpose deliberately disguised by deceptive appearances. This is why when disquieting rumours of Rasputin's actions began to make their way into society, they were only believed with reluctance and were seen as a deliberate attempt to blacken the "saint."[7]

Rasputin was held to be a saint partly because people wanted to believe in his sanctity, but there were more tangible reasons too. Apart from his undisputed capacity to bring comfort, Rasputin's powers took two forms: clairvoyance and healing. As a clairvoyant he was unremarkable. He was capable of occasional flashes of prophetic insight of a generalised kind, for example his intuitive realisation that his own fate was bound up with the fate of the dynasty. Nonetheless, he was believed to be clairvoyant, for example by the Montenegrins, although he would insist to Nicholas himself that he had no such gift.[8] Still there are stories about his remarkable powers. Once a monk criticised him in his absence for being a charlatan and a womaniser. Shortly afterwards Rasputin came into the room, stared him down and said: "So you think I am a charlatan and a womaniser do you?"[9] Whether the story be true, false, or to be explained by a tip-off, it is typical of the kind of thing people at the time believed about Rasputin.

He was much more successful as a healer. Olga Lokhtina was a case in point. When interrogated by the Muravyev Commission in 1917 she maintained her faith in Rasputin as a *starets* and a healer with steadfast dignity, saying that he had cured her of a nervous stomach disorder that had kept her bedridden for the best part of five years. Spiridovich claims that he used the same techniques as M. Philippe, a combination of fervent prayer and hypnotic suggestion, which calmed the patient and made him believe that Rasputin was interceding with God on his behalf. There are remarkable instances of his working successful cures. Some can be dismissed as the wishful thinking of those who longed to believe in Rasputin, but this was by no means always the case. The tsarina's lady-in-waiting, Lili Dehn, has left a memoir that is in some respects partisan–defensive of Alexandra to the point of being more than fair to Rasputin–so that sceptics should regard the following account of a cure with some distrust. Nevertheless, it is unlikely that the entire episode was invented.

Her child is very ill and reluctantly she calls upon Rasputin to see if he can do anything:

> "Don't wake Titi," I whispered as we entered the nursery, for I was afraid that the sudden appearance of this strange peasant might frighten the child. Rasputin made no reply, but sat down by the bedside and looked long and intently at the sleeper. He then knelt and prayed. When he rose from his knees he bent over Titi.
>
> "Don't wake him," I repeated.
>
> "Silence. I *must.*"
>
> Rasputin placed a finger on either side of Titi's nose. The child instantly awoke, looked at the stranger unafraid and addressed him by the playful name which Russian children give to old people. Rasputin talked to him and Titi told him that his head ached "ever so much."
>
> "Never mind," said Rasputin, his steel eyes full of strange lights. Then, addressing me, "Tomorrow thy child will be well. Let me know if this is not so."[10]

The child fell immediately into a normal sleep; the fever had gone by morning and in a few days he was well again.

More remarkable still was Rasputin's capacity for healing from a distance. Again the following account comes from a slightly suspect source, E. F. Djaunumova, a lady who wished to make all she could of her meetings with Rasputin, and yet this was by no means the only occasion on which Rasputin proved capable of long-distance healing.

The lady in question was deeply upset to learn that her niece was dying. Rasputin noted her distress as soon as he saw her, and made her tell him all about it:

> Then something so strange happened that I cannot explain it . . . However hard I tried to understand there is nothing I could do. I don't know what happened, but I will describe it all in detail.
>
> He took my hand. His face changed and he looked like a corpse, yellowy, waxy and dreadfully still. He rolled his eyes till

> the whites alone were visible. He took my hand roughly and said in a dull voice, "She won't die, she won't die." Then he let my hand go and the blood flowed back into his cheeks again. He continued talking as if nothing had happened.

Some hours afterwards the lady got a telegram telling her that her niece had got better. She showed it to Rasputin:

> "Did you really help?"
>
> "I told you she would get better," he replied with conviction.
>
> "Will you do it again? Perhaps she will get quite well again."
>
> "You little fool, how could I? It was not from me that it came but from on high. And you cannot do it twice. But I said she would get better, so why are you worrying?"[11]

This is hardly conclusive evidence. Those who wish to believe in Rasputin's powers will accept it, sceptics dismiss it as worthless. Yet the fact remains that on one occasion at least Rasputin proved capable either of healing at a distance of some thousands of miles or of benefiting by a remarkable coincidence.[12] By the end of 1906 he had an established reputation as a healer, and not just of unbalanced women. He had a remarkable way with children too, as he once had with his father's horses; the same capacity to calm and inspire confidence in a patient. Indeed we have a brief child's eye view of him from this year. E. Judas, the niece of one of the tsar's doctors, M. I. Lebikov, met Rasputin as a child. They travelled east to Siberia in his company, which she found enthralling. He spent many hours talking with her, teaching her to "pray with most wonderful words," telling her never to pick flowers, "since it was cruel to take life by force." The man made a profound and positive impression upon her, one which subsequently inspired the fundamentally sympathetic book she wrote about him.

Of all the first-hand accounts of Rasputin, that of E. Judas inspires the most confidence, and it is surprising that it should be so little known. It is clearly favourable to him, but not hysterically so, and avoids all hint of sensationalism. There is nothing here about his supernatural powers, or his magnetic gaze that seemed to look deep into the heart. It places much more emphasis on quiet qualities;

gentleness, love of nature, respect for life, the qualities that made him good with children and animals, reminding us that whatever Rasputin's other talents might have been, perhaps the greatest talent of all was his ability to calm and comfort troubled souls.

CHAPTER 8

WITH OR WITHOUT the assistance of M. Philippe, the Empress had finally given birth to a son in June 1904, yet the happiness this brought Nicholas and Alexandra was short-lived. It was quickly discovered that the child suffered from haemophilia, the hereditary disease that had accounted for the deaths of four of Alexandra's immediate male relatives. It is curious, incidentally, that Nicholas should have been permitted to marry Alexandra in view of that flaw in her bloodline. From the point of view of the dynasty it can only be construed as a colossal oversight. On the other hand it has been suggested that the marriage was the outcome of fiendish and careful Prussian planning. It was allegedly engineered by Bismarck himself, with a view to the long-term debilitation of the house of Romanov. If so he was rather too successful, since the Russian revolution did a great deal to bring about the fall of the Prussian imperial house of Hohenzollern in November 1918. Haemophilia is transmitted by the female line, although it only affects males. Any mother of a haemophiliac, especially before the disease could be treated, was bound to experience a terrible sense of guilt at the mortal illness she had passed to her son. One can scarcely conceive of the degree of guilt experienced by Alexandra, who had failed to provide the empire with a suitable heir, and who saw her youngest child, her only son, under perpetual threat of death and often in terrible pain. Such pressures would be enough to test the strongest of women, and they proved too much for the shy, nervous and morbidly religious Alexandra. A cousin of the tsar's, Grand Duke Aleksandr Mikhailovich, described the imperial reaction:

> The emperor aged ten years overnight. He could not bear to think that doctors had sentenced his son to death or to life as an invalid.
>
> "Your Majesty should know," said one of the court surgeons, "that the tsarevich will never get well. Attacks of haemophilia will recur from time to time. It is vital to take the most severe measures to protect his highness from falls, cuts and scratches, because anything of the sort, be it ever so trivial, can be fatal for haemophiliacs." A huge sailor was ordered to look after Aleksey Nikolaevich's safety and carry him whenever the tsarevich had to remain on his feet for a long time.
>
> For his imperial parents life lost all its sense. We were afraid to smile in their presence. Visiting their majesties we behaved in the palace as if we were in a house in which there had been a death. The emperor tried to find relief in unremitting hard work, but the Empress was not prepared to submit to fate. She spoke constantly of the ignorance of doctors, and expressed an unconcealed preference for charlatans. She turned all her thoughts towards religion and her faith took on a hysterical character.[1]

In the words of Pierre Gilliard, one of Aleksey's future tutors:

> The empress knew only too well, that at any minute the smallest piece of carelessness which would have left anyone else perfectly safe could cause death. If he were to approach her twenty times a day she would give him a kiss on every occasion, as he came up or went away. I understand, for each time she left him she was afraid it could be the last.[2]

In such circumstances it is hardly surprising that Aleksey should have been hopelessly spoilt, wilful and, in some ways increasingly disagreeable as he grew older. Too much love, too much attention, made him consider love and attention as his unquestionable due, while the restrictions that his disease necessitated were doubly irksome to a child of his high-spirited energy and incapacity for concentrated mental effort. As he grew up there was more than one instance of his throwing his little tsarevich's weight about, requiring cabinet ministers to give him precedence, regiments to salute him, or sentries to march (a little way) out to sea. In later years his father was only half joking when he observed that he trembled for a Russia under the autocratic rule of his wilful little son and heir, whom he would sometimes refer to as Aleksey the Terrible.

The boy's illness remained a closely kept secret for some time. Although it seems to have revealed itself fairly soon after birth it would be a good five years before the handicap became common knowledge in court circles, and then the news only came out because the condition became more acute as time went by.

Granted her mysticism, her belief in holy men, and her healthy dislike of doctors, especially the kind of doctor who held out no hope for her son, it is understandable that Alexandra should have let the Montenegrins persuade her to turn to Rasputin to see if he could help.

He did. All we know of his first visit is that Rasputin came to the sick boy's bedside and prayed. Shortly afterwards the haemorrhage from which he was suffering at the time ceased. Rasputin then prophesied that the tsarevich would not die of the disease, which would disappear when he reached the age of twenty.[3]

The visit transformed Rasputin's situation. No longer a simple holy man, he had got through to the very core of the empire, well past the limits of the official court; henceforward he would be an integral part of the life of the imperial family. In itself this meant that he gained a degree of intimacy that he would share with a mere handful of others. The more successful he was at treating the tsarevich, the more directly dependent the emperor and empress of all the Russias would become upon Grigorii Efimovich Rasputin, native of Pokrovskoe.

We have no eyewitness account of his first treatment of Aleksey, but there is a hearsay version dating from the same year, from V. A. Telyakovsky, the director of the imperial theatres. He asks a friend in the know:

> "What sort of man is this Rasputin?"
>
> "He's a strange one. He was taken to the bedside of the tsarevich . . . The child looked at him and began to bubble with laughter. Rasputin laughed too. He laid his hand on the boy's leg and the bleeding stopped at once. 'There's a good boy,' said Rasputin. 'You'll be all right. But only God can tell what will happen tomorrow.' "[4]

There is not the slightest doubt that the tsarina believed in Rasputin's power to stop her son's bleeding. That is the single most important fact of the case. It gave him an immense hold over her, and, quite as important, convinced her of his holiness, his wisdom, and ultimately of the quality of his political judgment. Since he could work miracles he must be the second Friend sent by God to replace M. Philippe.

If Alexandra believed that he was able to arrest the bleeding it is reasonable to conclude that he did so. However gullible and prone to wishful thinking she may have been, credulity has its limits. We have to assume that Alexandra perceived a relationship between Rasputin's visits and the cessation of her son's attacks. Indeed, that Rasputin was able to exercise some measure of control over them is something that not even his most bitter enemies disputed. They preferred to find unattractive explanations for his success, suggesting that he had seduced Aleksey's nurse and persuaded her to feed him some special Tibetan brew to make him bleed. She would stop dosing him shortly after Rasputin called on the child and resume treatment later. The charge was preposterous, yet interesting, in that it acknowledged that Rasputin's visits did have an effect. In fact the imperial surgeon himself, Professor S. P. Fedorov, confirmed Rasputin's ability to check the bleeding. Having studied all the available research material on the disease he was convinced that medical science was helpless:

> And look, Rasputin would come in, walk up to the patient, look at him and spit. The bleeding would stop in no time . . . How could the empress not trust Rasputin after that?[5]

In fact bleeding cures are far from unknown to Russian folk medicine, which has a rich tradition of unorthodox kinds of healing, making much use of wise women, herbalists and "whisperers," or those who talk you to health. Some of these possessed the secret of arresting bleeding, which would be passed down from one generation to the next as a legacy. The author's own interest in Rasputin dates back to his childhood, when his Russian grandmother would talk about him. She considered him no more than a highly successful practitioner of folk medicine, observing that all over Russia there were persons who treated people, and especially animals, with a peculiar blend of folk medicine and sympathetic magic. To his more level-headed contemporaries there was nothing supernatural about his methods or his powers, he was just the most successful "whisperer" in the land.

Anyone who wants to find out about magic and folk medicine usually has to go to the accounts of anthropologists and ethnographers describing their field work, and such accounts are usually disappointing. The clinical eye of the trained observer, and the no less clinical style with which the observations are written out, tend to defuse the atmosphere of its magic. But we are fortunate enough to have an account of a "whisperer" written not by an ethnographer, but by one of the greatest poets of twentieth-century Russia. In *Doctor Zhivago* Boris Pasternak shows us a Siberian whisperer in action, and his description has all the uncanny folk poetry and magic of darkest peasant Russia built into it:

> The woman was saying:
>
> "Auntie Margesta, come and be our guest. Come on Wednesday, take away the pest, take away the spell, take away the scab. Ringworm leave the heifer's udder. Stand still Beauty, do your duty, don't upset the pail. Stand still as a hill, let milk run and rill. Terror terror, show your mettle, take the scurvy, take the scab, throw them in the nettles. Strong as a lord is the sorcerer's word.
>
> "You see, you have to know everything—bidding and forbidding, the word for escaping, and the word for safe keeping. You have to know what everything is. Now you, for example, you look over there and say to yourself: 'There's a forest.' But what

there is over there is the forces of evil fighting the angelic hosts . . .

"Now another thing. Suppose you take a fancy to someone, you just tell me. I'll make him pine for you, whoever he is . . . You think I'm boasting? Indeed I am not. Now look, I'll tell you. When the winter comes with blizzards, and whirlwind and snowspouts chasing each other in the fields, I will stick a knife into such a pillar of snow right up to the hilt, and when I take it out of the snow, it will be red with blood . . . that whirlwind isn't just wind and snow it's a werewolf, a changeling that's lost its little warlock child and is looking for it. That is why I struck with my knife, that is why there is blood on it. Now, with that knife I can cut away the footprint of any man, and I can sew it with a silk thread on to your skirt, and that man . . . will follow you step by step wherever you go. . . ."[6]

Despite the fact that Rasputin's visits had an undisputed beneficial effect upon the tsarevich, he could not combat the disease in any fundamental way. The nature of his treatment has been admirably summarised by Mr. George Katkov:

> There is nothing mysterious in his reputed ability to alleviate the sufferings of the tsarevich . . . No hypnosis could of course alter the composition of his blood to replace the deficiency which prevented it from coagulating normally. But it is well known that hypnotic influence can affect the vaso-motor system and cause a contraction of the vessels comparable to the effect of adrenalin and similar drugs. But to the empress the intervention of Rasputin seemed miraculous. . . .[7]

In addition Rasputin was very careful with the timing of his visits, arriving, whenever possible, when the attack was past its peak—if only, perhaps, because it would then be easier to induce the requisite contraction. However, Mr. Katkov's expression "hypnotic influence" begs certain questions. Rasputin did not practice hypnosis as such, did not put his subjects into hypnotic trances. A few years later he enrolled in a course on hypnotism, but little came of it, partly because the police had the hypnotist removed from the capital. Yet clearly he possessed the power to dominate, render his subject passive and relaxed, ready to surrender his will to the greater strength of Rasputin. If one chooses to term such a power hypnotism, in the broad sense of the word, then he was a hypnotist *par excellence*. However, the only person he ever put into a hypnotic trance was his future assassin, Prince Yusupov, who was capable of experiencing, or believing he had experienced, a wide range of sensations, and who was fond of acts of passive surrender to boot.

For Alexandra, then, Rasputin was much more than the source of unorthodox if effective medical treatment. If he could work miracles he must be a saint, if he were a saint he possessed, along with the power to cure, the power to guide and bless. Moreover, he was a man of the people, the people who "really loved" their tsar and tsarina, who made up the genuine Russia; the Russia that was cut off from them by the court and the over-sophisticated inhabitants of St. Petersburg and Moscow, with their malcontent revolutionaries conspiring to turn the people against their leaders. To the bitter end the emperor and empress retained this naive belief in the natural goodness of their subjects, never understanding that repressed head of violence which was in them, despite the "red cockerel" of arson and peasant revolt which had swept across the Russian land throughout the revolution of 1905. It was indeed the revolution that was largely responsible for their ignorance. From 1905 to 1910 the imperial family remained in virtual isolation in Tsarskoe Selo, never leaving it apart from holidays cruising in the Baltic or visiting their Crimean palace. Nicholas only resumed regular visits to his own capital in 1910. Such isolation is to be explained by fear of assassination, which was a serious danger. The tsar was the prime terrorist target, and in the course of those years the security forces scotched a considerable number of plots laid against him.

There were other, emotional reasons for the couple's isolation. The tragedy of her son's health had helped to render Alexandra emotionally unbalanced. She took to spending more and more time "resting" in a state of exhausted nervous tension, and became still further estranged from court and public life.

Curiously, the notion of the tsar's isolation played an important part in the ideology of autocracy. The tsar as father of his people, "Master of the Russian land" and the Lord's anointed, was at one with his subjects; if only they could get to know one another. But the tsar was cut off from his people by the so-called "*srednostenie,*" or dividing wall; bureaucracy, aristocracy, intelligentsia all came between him and his truly loyal subjects. Thus by definition all kinds of political experts, ministers, and advisors were essentially unwelcome; they mediated between the tsar and his people, preventing any possibility of immediate contact. Rasputin would provide the dynasty's first immediate contact in 250 years—with results that proved unfortunate for all concerned.

Rasputin succeeded in penetrating the *srednostenie* and was received in the palace as a friend—not simply brought in as a doctor when the tsarevich was ill. His visits were irregular and took place in the evening; when the emperor had finished working and listening to reports Rasputin would enter:

> They would kiss three times in the Russian fashion, and then would start to talk. He would speak to them of Siberia, of the needs of peasants, of his pilgrimages. Their Majesties would always discuss the health of the tsarevich and their current worries about him. When he withdrew after an hour's conversation with the Imperial Family he always left their Majesties cheerful, their souls filled with joyous hope. They believed the power of his prayers to the very end . . . No one could shake their faith in him.[8]

It would often happen that Nicholas and Alexandra would be accompanied by the rest of their family—the eldest of the four girls was then aged twelve.

Had they been in the habit of receiving strange visitors from the four corners of the empire, Rasputin's appearances at the palace would have been comprehensible, as the visits of their "token peasant." Yet this was anything but the case. Rasputin's visits, occasional though they might have been, came at a time when the tsar and tsarina were virtually without intimates of any kind. He was one of the very few persons who appeared before them at their personal invitation, and not in order to fulfill some aspect of imperial protocol.

The events of the last two years, from late 1906 to 1908, had changed Rasputin, altering his sense of purpose and accelerating a process that had already been working in him for many years. Ever since his early religious experiences he had been moving steadily away from conventional modes of God-seeking via the Orthodox church and the monastic path. Then came the first modest social successes of Kazan, when he saw the inside of a carpeted European-style house for the first time. Ever since then his life had moved increasingly in the direction of purely secular ambition. His piety, religious insight, and extraordinary powers seemed to have become a means to an end; not exactly the pursuit of material comfort, but of prestige, a place in the sun. Although he kept his peasant ways and, like the pilgrim mendicant he once had been, still gratefully accepted notes of any denomination that might be proffered him, his sense of purpose took a new turn. He began to feel he had a politico-historical mission, professing to have become convinced that somehow his destiny was linked to the destiny of the nation and the ruling house. The part he was to play was precisely that of the man of the people who penetrated the *srednostenie.* The tsar, he would frequently observe, was "surrounded by injustice and by lies," his advisors cut him off from his subjects. What was needed was a simple, devout man who would act in the interests of tsar and people alike.

Rasputin's new sense of mission and of his own importance coincides with his making a strangely uncharacteristic bid for, of all things, respectability. In 1907, we recall, he changed his name from Rasputin to Rasputin-Novykh. *Novykh* is a plural form of the Russian *noviy,* meaning new. His daughter Maria says that the name started as a nickname given him by the young tsarevich, who, whenever Rasputin came to visit him, would clap his little hands, bounce up and down with eyes gleaming, saying *noviy noviy*—the new one. The story has an improbable ring to it. Clearly Rasputin felt that his name, with its connotations of debauchery, lacked class, and made an attempt to make it look more respectable. That at least is the obvious inference, and yet one may wonder, in that case, why he retained the family name at all, since no addition could have eradicated its unfortunate connotations. Another more interesting explanation would be that the addition represents a change in Rasputin himself, with his new-found sense of political and historic mission as unofficial Friend, guide and advisor to the emperor.

✧ ✧ ✧

If it be true that a person's character is reflected in his choice of friends, the empress makes a lamentable showing. Two Russians would get close to her over the years; one was our Friend sent by God, a choice that, at least, indicates a total lack of political common sense on the part of a "Caesar's wife," the other, for all her Christian virtues, was an unctuous platitudinous mediocrity ill-equipped for the part that history would thrust on her. Anna Vyroubova's prominence can be seen as the reflection of a fundamentally limited, mediocre, petty bourgeois strain in the tsarina, the same cast of mind that inspired her to furnish her private apartments by mail order from Maples. Anna Vyroubova was her only close woman friend and the only Russian who liked, indeed adored, the empress for herself, with a blind, unqualified devotion.

Born in 1884, she was the daughter of A. S. Taneev, the emperor's chief of personal chancellery—a post that gave him the tsar's ear and hence tremendous influence and power. It had virtually become a hereditary office, having been held by Taneevs under five sovereigns. Taneev was the last of his line—he had two daughters but no sons. However he "placed" his children wisely. The younger married A. E. von Pistolkors, son of Princess Paley, the second wife of Grand Duke Paul Alexandrovich, who was an uncle of the tsar and father of one of Rasputin's future assassins. Anna, the elder daughter, did better still, being one of the chosen few who penetrated the *srednostenie* and won the friendship of the last tsarina. By the end of the reign she was playing a significant part in the government of the empire, as an intermediary between the tsarina and Rasputin. Taneev, a careful and ambitious man, was content to stay in the background, but he benefited enormously from his daughter's success and manipulated her situation to his own ends. Many of the ideas that Anna impressed upon the tsarina most certainly came from her father. However, he was at pains to maintain that his hands were clean, and whenever he was accused of sophisticated intrigue he would go pale with rage. Some felt he was prone to protest too much. However, to the end he had the skill to cover his tracks, and we cannot determine the scope of his influence. Certainly he had no interest in power for its own sake; his interest was restricted to personal advantage. He played no political role as such, but remains an obscure, slightly dubious figure content to remain in the shadows.

The story of Anna Vyroubova's success begins in 1902 with a severe attack of typhus. At death's door, her parents arranged for John of Cronstadt to come and pray over her; she recovered and the cure encouraged her to become increasingly ardent in her beliefs. She attracted the attention of the tsarina and her sister Elizaveta Fedorovna, and in 1903 became maid of honour to the empress. Romantic beyond the usual limits, Anna soon grew very attached to Alexandra. As Sergei Witte put it, she "regarded the Tsarina rapturously, everlastingly sighing Oh, oh!"[9] Alexandra returned her affection and singled her out for the altogether unusual honour of joining the family on their Baltic summer cruise. The tsarina began increasingly to confide in the young girl, because her faith in her loyalty was total; and loyalty, fierce, uncritical, unswerving, was the chief quality she demanded of a friend.

Anna Vyroubova was large and fair, with a slow, vacuous smile; an essentially loving character, she spoke slowly with a slight lisp, "as if she had a mouth full of porridge," the tsarina would say.[10] To a child she appeared "large with rosy cheeks, draped in furs; she looked at us children with an exaggerated kindness, warmth and we did not care for her much."[11] Contemporaries saw her differently: petite, with an innocent baby face and great appealing eyes, and so childish-looking that she seemed only fit for boarding school.[12] She was a remarkably limited person with little to offer beyond devotion. She was also susceptible to religious enthusiasm, and viewed the world in simplistic terms. As Pierre Gilliard wrote:

> With a sentimental and mystical nature Mme. Vyroubova conceived an unqualified adoration for the Empress, which was dangerous by virtue of its very intensity, which made for lack of clarity and sense of reality . . .
>
> Mme. Vyroubova had the mind of a child . . . and her judgment had not matured. Lacking intelligence and perspicacity she followed her instincts and for all this lack of consideration her opinions on people and things were never anything but absolute. A single impression was enough to make up her limited, child-

ish mind; she classified people according to first impression as "good" or "bad"–which simply meant "friends" or "enemies" . . .[13]

Gilliard goes on to observe that she was incapable of holding any political views herself, and that she was a tool in the hands of unscrupulous intriguers—by which he means her father. The intimate nature of her friendship with the empress, her inclusion as a member of the family on the Baltic cruise, struck the *amour-propre* of many people who found the favour she enjoyed inexplicable. It says much for the love of ingenious gossip in court circles—a love which would play a different part in the latter years of Rasputin's life—that an explanation was soon found. It was widely rumoured that the relationship between the tsarina and Anna exceeded the bounds of natural affection, in other words that they were lovers. Prewar Russia had a matter-of-fact readiness to accept unusual aspects of human behaviour that would never have been tolerated in London, New York, or even Paris. It was after all only ten years since the trial of Oscar Wilde, and yet the malicious glee with which the rumour was greeted is not pleasant. It was, moreover, widely believed in respectable circles. We have a guide to the gossip current in respectable circles in the shape of the diary of a general's wife, A. K. Bogdanovich. Her husband, E. V. Bogdanovich, born in 1839, and now blind, was nonetheless a person who was reputed to have huge influence in official circles, and was much sought after by leading political figures and court officials. He conducted the leading political salon of the capital, presided over by his wife, a quiet, very hospitable person, who was an excellent listener, but who seldom spoke. Instead she would record the gossip she heard in the diary she kept, largely for her husband's benefit. The diary reports that Anna and the tsarina kept up a lively amorous correspondence, and that on most nights, at 9:00 P.M. after dinner, when Nicholas left his family to work for two or sometimes three more hours, the two women would withdraw from the dining room, going through the mauve boudoir to the imperial bedroom.[14]

The rumours are preposterous; as preposterous as a later set which suggested that Vyroubova slept with Rasputin. Vyroubova had no interest in sex of any kind, and remained a virgin at least until 1918, when with great fortitude she submitted herself to a medical examination for the benefit of the Muravyev Commission, which duly established her virginity. Yet such rumours have a considerable interest. The fact that she was required to undergo such an examination suggests how convincing they appeared at the time. To anyone familiar with the source material such allegations of unnatural practices seem laughable, and yet they were believed. The imperial family were so remote, so little was known about them beyond a narrow circle of court officials and intimates, that people could believe the wildest rumours—that the tsar was an alcoholic, his wife a lesbian who later abandoned lesbianism to become Rasputin's lover and do her best to secure a German victory in World War One. The last tsar and tsarina made many mistakes; not the least of these was their belief that they could lead an ordinary family life, enjoying the same degree of privacy as any other quiet, happily married and well-to-do couple, and still be emperor and empress of Russia.

It may have been in order to stop tongues wagging that Alexandra Fedorovna decided that the time had come for Anna to get married, though it is hard to believe that the empress would have understood what it was that tongues were wagging about. More likely she was indulging an older woman's love of matchmaking. Anna's first choice was Orlov, a widowed cavalry commander and a friend of the imperial family. Nothing came of this, either from Orlov's reluctance or because he was considered too old for her. Instead a marriage was arranged with a naval lieutenant, Vyroubov, and in 1907 the ceremony took place, attended by the entire imperial family.

From the start the marriage proved hopeless. Vyroubov was a sullen, difficult man. It was said that he had been severely unhinged by news of the Russian fleet's annihilation at Tsushima, and had never recovered his balance. Whatever the accuracy of that analysis, the man was certainly violent, unstable, fond of the bottle and, at least when it came to Vyroubova, impotent. To make matters worse he found his wife's friendship with the empress hard to accept, and was prone to jealous scenes. Matters came to a head when he returned unexpectedly to their little house on the outskirts of Tsarskoe Selo. The empress and Orlov were visiting Anna, and the house was surrounded by security guards who failed to recognise Vyroubov and declined to let him in. A violent quarrel ensued, and the marriage was dissolved almost immediately afterwards. Of course it was rumoured that Vyroubov surprised Anna and the tsarina in bed together. The whole sorry business left a mark upon the wretched girl which drew her even closer to the tsarina, reinforcing the mutual need for sympathy and understanding.

It was Anna's curiosity about her marriage prospects that had first brought her into contact with Rasputin. A meeting had been arranged by Grand Duchess Militsa, who told her that in this world there were to be found persons living lives of such saintliness that they achieved clairvoyant powers. Such a person was Rasputin: his prayers were so powerful that they could secure anything he asked for. Vyroubova recollects the circumstances of that first encounter. Rasputin entered the room, kissed the grand duchess and was introduced:

> He was dressed in a simple black peasant's smock, and I was struck by his piercing, sunken deep-blue eyes. We all three began walking about the room. Rasputin asked me what I did, where I lived etc. I was very worried about my forthcoming marriage, as I scarcely knew my fiancé, so I asked him whether I should get married. Rasputin replied that he advised me to do so, but that the marriage would not be happy. The conversation took ten to fifteen minutes . . . I next met him a year later, and was overjoyed to see him. I wanted to visit him to discuss my unhappy circumstances and he gave me his address, he was staying with Olga Lokhtina. . . .[15]

Vyroubova, an essentially passive creature, credulous, affectionate, and enthusiastic, attached herself to the *starets* with unquestioning faith. To her he was a saint, and she continued to believe steadfastly in his saintliness to the end, never permitting evidence to the contrary, talk of drink, sexual excess and visits to the gypsies, to shake her devotion. Only when giving evidence to the investigating commission did she express reservations, appear detached from him and keep him at arm's length. But this was because the imperial family was still alive at the time and needed all the support she could provide. For all her silliness Anna Vyroubova remained loyal, and her performance before the commission was a magnificent display of phlegmatic stonewalling under pressure, a performance that deserves to be remembered.

Rasputin's attitude to his "Annushka" is curious. Although he would kiss and even caress her in public, he never made sexual advances to her, and was often heard to observe that Annushka was "not like that." Certainly he dominated her with his superior will and intelligence, but there was more than exploitation to the relationship. Curiously enough, they were alike in their modes of character assessment; they both relied on an immediate reading of personality. Rasputin seems to have understood that beneath Vyroubova's obtuseness and cloying sentimentality there was a pure, naive goodness. Utterly devoted to others, she sought nothing for herself. In the years to come he would lay great stress upon that quality, urging the tsarina, in troubled times, to turn to her. He praised not her judgment but her goodness, and she seems for Rasputin to have been one of the true inheritors of the earth, a worthy companion for the tsarina because of moral qualities that were more important than purely cerebral characteristics such as intelligence and judgment.

✧ ✧ ✧

Rasputin soon took possession of Vyroubova, applying his special brand of healing and comfort in the aftermath of her marriage. She in turn helped to give him an established situation in a small set of religiously inclined persons of society. Rasputin was now a welcome guest at Vyroubova's house in Tsarskoe Selo, and at her father's St. Petersburg residence, Number 4 Inzhenernaya Street. It was there that he established the hard core of his society following, devotees who would support him unswervingly to the end. The "inner circle" consisted of Vyroubova's sister and brother-in-law, the latter's aunt, Mme. Golovina, her daughter Munya and, curiously, ex-prime-minister Sergei Witte and his wife. Witte had been out of public life since 1905 but was still ambitious and eager to return. An intriguer by nature, he frequented the Taneev household for reasons of political ambition.

Rasputin began to move exclusively in this small world, leaving less exalted acquaintances behind him. He was content to be the centre of a tight circle of devout disciples. As yet, however, in 1908, his existence and the kind of company he kept were scarcely known; his was anything but a household name. We can indeed pinpoint the exact moment when his reputation begins to spread, from the following entry in the Bogdanovich diary, when its author first gets to hear of him. A friend had struck up acquaintance with Vyroubova's chambermaid, to whom he observed that her mistress was "a good and earnest woman":

> This made the girl laugh. She said she would show him photographs that would soon change his mind. It appears that Vyroubova is friends with some sort of peasant, and a monk to boot. And here she is photographed sitting beside him. [The friend] could not believe his eyes. The peasant has the stare of a wild animal, a repulsive, insolent appearance. Vyroubova does not display the picture, she keeps it in her Bible. Sadder still, the peasant is there when the empress calls on Vyroubova. Vyroubova has made him a blue silk shirt with her own hands. He often visits her in Tsarskoe Selo but has not yet been to the palace. [He had.][16]

Slowly but surely Rasputin was moving into the eye of a public for whom his existence as an intimate of Vyroubova, let alone the empress, was a scandal, a breach of etiquette so enormous that it posed a threat to the very fabric of the autocracy.

As Mme. Bogdanovich rightly anticipated, since Rasputin was close to Vyroubova he must soon grow close to the empress. Vyroubova would call upon her friend and protectress once or twice a day, and they would spend hours together in enthusiastic conversation, largely devoted to the remarkable qualities of Grigorii Rasputin. Moreover, the *starets* continued to enjoy the support of Theophanes, who was now a bishop, and had just been appointed personal confessor to the tsar and tsarina. At the latter's request Theophanes had even made a visit to Pokrovskoe to make further inquiries into Rasputin's background. It says more for the goodwill than the judgment of Theophanes, who would finally see through Rasputin in about eighteen months' time, that the report he submitted was altogether favourable. Once again it must have been a case of wanting Rasputin to be what he appeared—there was evidence enough of his sexual misdemeanours to be found in the capital without having to interrogate the village girls of Pokrovskoe into the bargain. Yet Theophanes preferred to ignore the evidence, since it might militate against Rasputin's potential sainthood. The capital was in need of someone to replace John of Cronstadt, the most celebrated holy man in Russia, who had died that year.

In the course of 1908 Rasputin saw more and more of the imperial family. By now he would exchange kisses with "Papa" and "Mama," as he referred to the emperor and empress, while they in turn addressed him as Grigorii. However, they would never actually kiss his hand; that is, would not quite treat him as an ecclesiastic of the highest rank.

Rasputin also spent a lot of time with the imperial children. The eldest, Olga, was twelve by now, and the girls must increasingly have welcomed anyone from the outside, who could talk to them of the world beyond the iron fence surrounding the imperial park.

Although by all accounts the imperial daughters were all very likable, they differed in character. Olga was of medium height, with a fair complexion, chestnut hair, and a nose that she referred to touchingly as "my humble snub." She was intelligent, but in later years disappointed her French tutor by her failure to apply herself to her studies. The second girl, Tatyana, eighteen months younger than Olga, was the tallest and most elegant of the quartet, with rich dark chestnut hair and deep blue eyes. She was proud, reserved, polite, but a little domineering. The younger children referred to her, teasingly, as "The Governess." Maria, the third daughter, was chubbier, lazier, less lively and a little more wilful than her sisters, with light brown hair. The other girls, who knew their Hans Andersen, would say that she had eyes "as big as saucers." Anastasia, the youngest, was the tomboy of the family. Lively as quicksilver, she was a splendid mimic, and capable of wreaking considerable mischief. She was just turned seventeen when the Bolsheviks shot her.

Nicholas and Alexandra encouraged Rasputin to visit the nursery and tell the children bedtime stories. He would speak to them of his own childhood, of the animals and people of Siberia, or the sights he had seen on his travels, and his conversation held them spellbound, making it virtually impossible to get the young tsarevich to bed, unless Rasputin took a hand in matters. The first time that the Grand Duchess Olga met Rasputin, it was in the children's quarters. Her brother the tsar had invited her up there to meet a Russian peasant. She found the four girls and their brother, all in white pajamas, being put to bed by their nurses, while, in the middle of the room, stood Rasputin:

> When I saw him I felt that gentleness and warmth radiated from him. All the children seemed to like him. They were completely at ease with him. I still remember their laughter as little Alexis, deciding he was a rabbit, jumped up and down the room. And then, quite suddenly, Rasputin caught the child's hand and led him to his bedroom, and we three followed. There was something like a hush as though we had found ourselves in church. In Alexis's bedroom no lamps were lit; the only light came from the candles burning in front of some beautiful icons. The child stood very still by the side of that giant, whose head was bowed. I knew he was praying. It was all most impressive. I also knew that my little nephew had joined him in prayer.

Yet although she was impressed the grand duchess took an instant dislike to Rasputin when, over the evening tea, he began to ply her with personal questions:

> Was I happy? Did I love my husband? Why didn't I have children? He had no right to ask such questions, nor did I answer them. I am afraid Nicky and Alicky looked rather uncomfortable. I do remember I was relieved at leaving the palace that evening and saying "Thank God he hasn't followed me to the station" as I boarded my private coach on the train for St. Petersburg.[17]

(Rasputin's questions may have been impolite, but they were very much to the point, since the grand duchess was miserably unhappy in a marriage that had been arranged for her, and would end in divorce in a few years' time.)

Whatever their aunt may have thought of him, Rasputin seems to have inspired very considerable affection in the other grand duchesses, if we are to judge from the remarkable letters they wrote to him around this time:

> My dearest friend,
>
> I often think of you, your visits and the way you talk about God. It is hard without you, there is no one to tell my troubles to . . . We often go to Anya's; every time I hope to meet you, my dear friend . . . Pray for me and bless me.
>
> Your loving Olga.

> My dear and true friend,
>
> When will you come? Are you going to be stuck in Pokrovskoe much longer? How are your children? . . . When we go to Anya's we all think of you. We would so like to go to Pokrovskoe. When shall we go? Please arrange it, you can do anything. God loves you so. And you say God is so good and kind that he will do anything you ask. So visit us soon, it is so dull without you. Mother is ill without you and it is so sad to see her ill. If you only knew how hard it is to see her ill. But you know because you know everything. I kiss your hand my dear friend I kiss your holy hand.
>
> God bless you, Tatyana.[18]

The tone of these letters is extraordinary in view of the fact that their authors were grand duchesses. They show us how Rasputin presented himself to them, and also indicate how dreadfully bored the girls were at Tsarskoe Selo. With his directness and lack of awe, Rasputin treated them as equals. He charmed, interested, and amused them. Stifled as they were by the claustrophobia of court and family, he brought them a breath of fresh air. They obviously liked him very much, and those who are disposed to find nothing but self-aggrandisement and evil in Rasputin should remember that he was good with horses too, and that animals and children are much harder to deceive than grown-up women or politicians.

CHAPTER 9

RASPUTIN did not always impress adults. When Prince Zhevakhov first met him in 1908 the initial impression he produced was lamentable. Rasputin seemed like a hunted hare, looking warily at his audience, who hung on his every word, however trivial, feeling it to be charged with inner significance, or nervously coming up to kiss his hand. Rasputin seemed uneasy, anxious not to say or do the wrong thing or otherwise alienate his admirers, whose actions and motives appeared to bewilder him. The admirers themselves were "convinced of Rasputin's holiness and for the most part they were a fine selection of the very highest circles, persons of the purest and noblest religious aspirations, whose only fault was that they knew nothing at all about what constituted a genuine *starets*."[1] However, this initial impression was rectified when Rasputin began to preach a sermon on the saving of one's soul, which Zhevakhov said he would recall to his dying day. As he started to preach Rasputin lost all his stuttering hesitancy, and spoke with a quiet authority. He began by observing that there was little of interest in the lives of saints as such;

more important was the way in which they achieved their sanctity, and how one might reconcile the quest for salvation with the secular life. The sermon, incidentally, was frequently interrupted by a hysterical Lokhtina howling protests of adoration, rather like the "Alleluia's" of vociferous Southern Baptists, which Rasputin choked off addressing her in the crudest language. He then continued:

> Salvation is in God. You can't take a step without God. And you will see God when you see nothing else about you. Evil and sin exist because everything hides God and you can't see him. The room you sit in, your affairs, your friends, all hide God from you, because you don't live or think according to Him. What then must you do to see God?
>
> After church pray and go out of town into the fields. Go on and on until Petersburg is out of sight and there is open horizon ahead. Then stop and think about yourself, how insignificant and helpless you are, and you will find the capital will shrink to an ant heap peopled by ants. What then becomes of your pride, power, riches and position? And you feel pitiful, unwanted, useless. Then you will look up and you will see God and feel with all your heart that the Lord God is your only father, that only God the Father needs your soul and only to Him will you surrender it. He alone will support and help you. Then you will know joy and that is the first step to God.
>
> You need go no further and return to the world, to the place you occupied before, cherishing what you have brought back with you like the pupil of your eye.
>
> The kingdom of Heaven is with you. Find God and live with Him and on every highday or Sunday, if only in your mind, leave your affairs and instead of paying calls or going to the theatre, go into the fields to God.

The author concludes:

> I have heard many sermons of great substance, but can remember none of them. The sermon Rasputin preached fifteen years ago I remember to this day. . . .[2]

The secret of Rasputin's power over his audiences resides in his talent for popularising God's truth, a talent that necessarily implies spiritual insight and experience. It is scarcely surprising that enthusiastic women such as Olga Lokhtina, prone to states of religious ecstasy, should have believed him to be a saint; a belief that Rasputin never did anything to discourage.

However actively Rasputin might urge his hearers to seek God he never turned his own back upon the life of the flesh. Social success did nothing to check his sexual activity, indeed this increased in sophistication at the top of the range–society ladies–and in frequency at the bottom, with visits to cheap prostitutes. He would regularly gather them up in the streets or places of entertainment, and wearing the heavy gold pectoral cross which the tsarina had given him, take them home or to public bathhouses. He also made advances to ladies of markedly higher degree, mingling religion and sexuality in his own version of the *khlyst* heresy. These ladies too he would take to the bathhouse, sometimes to teach them lessons of humility and self-control, sometimes for other reasons. He had two ways of reconciling sex with spirituality, both of them deriving from the sects.

> All Rasputin's disciples sincerely believed in his power, his teaching and its basic rule that without sin there can be no repentance; repentance is pleasing unto God; in order to repent you must sin in the first place.[3]

Such was a contemporary journalist's interpretation of Rasputin's behaviour; he described it as a form of mysticism that derived from an up-dated sectarian heresy. Akulina Laptinskaya, for many years Rasputin's servant, provides a glimpse of him in action:

> He would be surrounded by his admirers, with whom he also slept. He would do his thing with them quite openly and without shame. He would caress them . . . and when he or they felt like it he would simply take them into his study and do his business . . . I often heard his views, a mixture of religion and debauchery. He would sit there and give instructions to his female admirers.
>
> "Do you think that I degrade you? I don't degrade you, I purify you."

That was his basic idea. He also used the word "grace," meaning that by sleeping with him a woman came into the grace of God.[4]

✧ ✧ ✧

He clearly managed to persuade his lovers that they could achieve grace and purification through orgasm; an arrangement that appears to have been satisfactory to all parties.

Rasputin took care to keep news of his mystico-erotic practices from Vyroubova and the court; just as he would always bathe and put on fresh clothes before visiting Tsarskoe Selo, however drunk he had been the night before. He possessed remarkable powers of physical recuperation, and could always make a presentable showing however thick his head. Thus it was not news of his scandalous behaviour that set many officers of the court against him from the start. The empress knew how unpopular he was, which is why she tried to make her acquaintance with Rasputin known to at least one aide-de-camp, a certain Sablin, in a roundabout way. She began by observing that there were persons who acquired extraordinary powers by virtue of their ascetic way of life, going on to remark that funnily enough there was just such a person to be found in the Russia of the present day, and not so very far from Tsarskoe Selo . . .[5] Sablin was in fact one of the few courtiers who would have anything to do with Rasputin, and even then he acted from a sense of moral obligation toward the imperial family. All other officials were unremittingly hostile, their attitude being summed up by the head of the tsar's security service, General Dedyulin. When Nicholas asked him his opinion of the *starets,* he observed: "He is an artful peasant, dishonest, intelligent and with certain powers of suggestion that he knows how to exploit."[6] Nicholas replied that Dedyulin was wrong, that Rasputin "was just a good, religious, simple-minded Russian. When in trouble or assailed with doubts I like to have a talk with him, and invariably feel at peace with myself afterwards."[7]

General Spiridovich enumerated Rasputin's enemies at court, and could find only one enthusiastic partisan; Rasputin was never successful with men. Perhaps unconsciously sensing in him a sexual challenge of a highly irregular kind—that a peasant should constitute a threat or be considered a rival was of course preposterous—they preferred to dismiss him as a shallow charlatan.

Hostility toward Rasputin in court circles increased steadily, and proved damaging. Since Nicholas and Alexandra operated on the principle of "those loyal to us will be loyal to our friends," criticism of Rasputin increased the isolation of the couple. No one who criticised their Friend could be anything but an enemy. Spiridovich, incidentally, believed that the divisive effect of Rasputin's presence was much more damaging to the dynasty than any revolutionary activity. If ever a ruler needed regular contact with loyal supporters of judgment, ability, and a sophisticated political sense it was Nicholas II; fundamental differences of opinion on the increasingly important issue of Rasputin did much to deny him anything of the sort.

The hostility Rasputin inspired at court began to make his existence a public issue. To many eyes, that he should enjoy the imperial favour cast a slur upon the tsar and tsarina and brought the autocracy into disrepute long before anyone supposed that Rasputin possessed real power. It was sufficient that he should be known to be their intimate for their reputation to suffer gravely. As long as he continued to visit Tsarskoe Selo, Caesar and his wife could not be considered above suspicion, although it is hard to say of what they might have been suspected. From now on Rasputin was to arouse an ever-increasing and wide-spreading hostility, until to most Russians his very name became a synonym for the abomination of desolation.

Yet if we pause for a moment to consider the worst that Rasputin might be thought guilty of, at least in these prewar years before he and the tsarina were believed to be guilty of treason, the worst was not bad at all. He could be considered an adventurer, a womaniser who took advantage of the piety of others, also perhaps a false prophet. But this made him no worse than many other opportunists of the age, and a good deal better than some, such as Prince Andronnikov,[8] who made use of his private oratory to take advantage of young men in need of his protection.

Rasputin inspired indignation for two reasons. In the first place, as a peasant his success at court was considered a breach of protocol tantamount to sacrilege. Secondly, that he could behave as he pleased, and yet persuade people who should have known better that he was a saint, was an intolerable irritant to anyone who hated the sight of a charlatan getting away with it. The anger Rasputin aroused would always be out of proportion to his actions. Certainly he never did anything to warrant his assassination, not at least to Western eyes. However, it is significant that the Russian language has some very powerful expressions to cover notions of shame and disgrace, *pozor, styd, sram*—and to many educated Russians Rasputin constituted the ultimate disgrace of their age.

Now, late in 1908, Rasputin first came under scrutiny from various police forces. The tsar's personal security service soon decided that he was no security risk and hence no concern of theirs. It was decided that his relationship with the tsar and his family was a purely private affair. Nevertheless the security services decided, with splendid lack of consequence, that the capital would be better off without him. General Dedyulin ordered a detailed investigation into his St. Petersburg life. At the same time the prime minister and minister of the interior, P. A. Stolypin, ordered the Okhrana, or secret police, to look into his Siberian background: all this despite the fact that Rasputin was a private citizen with no official standing of any kind.

The two services came up with a mass of information about his private life that did little credit to him as a man of God. Stolypin compiled a lengthy report, the first of many, which he brought to the tsar. Nicholas, in the words of General Spiridovich, took the matter laughingly and promised to see no more of Rasputin. The minister tried to take matters further and had the police draw up a decree which banished Rasputin from the capital, exiled him to Pokrovskoe and forbade his return for a span of five years.

As is occasionally the case in Russian history, especially in matters involving the bureaucracy, we now ease briefly into the realm of farce. It was necessary that someone serve the decree upon Rasputin. The secret police planned to do so one day in St. Petersburg as he got off the Tsarskoe Selo train. However, Rasputin had been forewarned. As the train came in he jumped out of the still-moving carriage, bolted across the station, leapt into a waiting car and drew quickly away from the policemen who were running helplessly behind. He drove straight to the palace of the grand duchess Militsa and took sanctuary there. The police kept the palace under twenty-four-hour surveillance, which continued for three weeks. Their vigil was brought to an end by a telegram from the governor of Tobolsk announcing Rasputin's arrival in Pokrovskoe. The policeman in charge of the operation reported to Stolypin, asking for permission to travel to Pokrovskoe to serve the decree there. Stolypin felt that it was all becoming much too difficult and dismissed the officer with the resigned wave of a hand that Russians employ to signify that they have abandoned a struggle and are prepared to settle back and let things take their course.

✧ ✧ ✧

Although Rasputin remained capable of preaching and healing to the end, by 1909 the search for God and personal salvation was no longer the prime concern that it had been some years before. Social and material success had made him more interested in power than in spiritual perfection—his principal motive henceforward was to defend and extend his power base. He cannot be said to have made a sudden change of direction, it was rather a case of a steady shifting in emphasis over the years. He had always been ambitious, and would retain his particular brand of sensitivity, but from now on worldly interests manifestly took precedence over other concerns. Even though he might have had his share of hair shirts, chains, and mortification of the flesh in the past, by 1909 there was little of the ascetic about him. He enjoyed material comfort, luxury even, for its own sake and because it showed the world what he had achieved.

Conspicuous display began at home. Rasputin never turned his back on Pokrovskoe. He paid regular visits, once or twice a year, spring and autumn, and continued to do so to the end. His social success had made him a wealthy man, by peasant standards at least. In 1908 he gave the village five thousand roubles for a new church and had a magnificent new *izba* built overlooking the river, furnished handsomely with expensive rugs and good furniture. He also maintained a staff of three or four young servant girls. He needed a relatively comfortable and well-cared-for establishment, because increasingly he tended to invite women from the capital to spend time with him at his home. Although he could scarcely be called a family man, he never neglected his dependants. His relationship with his wife might best be described as an understanding–although she was known to drag peasant girls out of her house by their plaits.[9] She was on the whole tolerant of Rasputin's misdemeanours but was capable, as we shall see, of giving his St. Petersburg lady friends a hard time when they stayed in her house. He also took care of his children. His son, Dmitri, was an unremarkable young man of limited intelligence who remained content to be an uneducated peasant. His elder daughter, Maria, was different. She was intelligent and very teachable, and Rasputin arranged for her to have a private education, first in Kazan and then in a first-class St. Petersburg girls' school, the Steblin-Kamenskii Institute.

Pokrovskoe's most distinguished visitor in 1909 was Anna Vyroubova. She was sent there by the empress with two other ladies to report on Rasputin's home life and see whether he truly deserved the imperial confidence.[10] Rasputin's behaviour was not exactly exemplary. He paid crude court to one of his guests, and she returned with distinct misgivings as to his saintliness. Rasputin was never one to allow caution to interfere with short-term desires; he was incapable of self-restraint.

Lack of self-restraint is the keynote of one of the most complete of all accounts we have of his treatment of women. It comes from a Mme. Berlatskaya, a widow who also visited Pokrovskoe that year. The story begins with the easing of a soul. Mme. Berlatskaya was labouring under a massive sense of guilt, having recently left a faithless husband who had then committed suicide. Rasputin proved able to bring her comfort, relieving her of her guilt and enabling her to start going to church and receiving the sacraments again. He made her feel that she had been brought back from the dead, and she came to depend on him in the way that a patient depends upon her analyst, feeling herself in his power.

Power for Rasputin never went hand in glove with responsibility. He immediately began to abuse his hold over her. He persuaded her to accompany him to Pokrovskoe, and on the train to Tyumen he joined her in her sleeper and started to caress her intimately. At first she assumed that he was testing for powers of resistance but then, to use the distraught and exclamatory language of a silly but devout woman:

> Because he invited me to convince myself that it was as a man that he loved me, (Heavens, how can God help me to write all this down!), he obliged me to prepare myself as a woman, and began to do what a husband alone is permitted to do . . . having at the time what it is that men have when they are aroused . . . He forced me, caressed and kissed me and lay with me. He then did all he wanted, to the end. I suffered as never before, but prayed, giving myself entirely to God.

Afterwards she felt degraded, as she observed him making innumerable religious obeisances with a speed so unnatural that she found it impossible to pray. Next day he congratulated her on the way she had withstood his test, and purified herself of passion. He went on to say that it was his task in life to relieve everyone of their original sin.

> The next night he tested me again, becoming excited and obliging me to acknowledge his excitement. I had to conclude that I must be very dirty, impure and given over to passion since he clearly felt it necessary to subject me to perpetual testing.

When they reached Pokrovskoe Rasputin's wife was less than friendly. She bullied both the lady and the child who travelled with her, giving them little to eat. Rasputin continued to sleep with her on a mattress laid on the floor—until his wife removed it—and then on a thin floor covering, which he felt to be too uncomfortable for him to stay the entire night. However he persisted in making love to her, saying: "This is a heavy stone. I have never known one so heavy."

In Pokrovskoe he made another disciple wash his sexual organs in the bathhouse. "He was quite naked and ordered her in front of everyone and in their sight to wash the parts of his body that are covered up more than others." On the return journey Rasputin travelled second-class, while the woman and her daughter, who had exhausted their funds, were obliged to travel third. They went somewhat short of food, while he ate well and left them his scraps, which they shared.[11]

It is hard at first sight to reconcile such flagrant behaviour with the increasing prominence that Rasputin was beginning to enjoy, but in fact the behaviour is its direct reflection. As his position improved so did his self-confidence, the feeling that he could do as he pleased with anyone he pleased and get away with it. Such escapades became a personal index of his power and importance.

The autocratic tradition, most fully realised by Ivan the Terrible, Peter the Great, and Stalin, tends to be interpreted by less sophisticated Russians as the unrestrained exercise of the ruler's will; one man's right to do as he pleases. *Khochu mogu,* "If I want to I can; there is nothing to stop me," is the way that a Russian peasant, with lifelong experience of the arbitrary rule of those set above him, interprets notions of freedom won through power. Rasputin conceived of his situation as the licence to do what he wanted, and every time he got away with it his self-confidence was further reinforced.

The self-confidence was justified. Day by day Rasputin's hold over the empress was increasing. As Aleksey grew older his attacks became more severe and more frequent. Hitherto his condition had remained a secret, but now that the sickly six-year-old was so often bedridden or carried around by his massive sailor, his condition became more common knowledge. Increasingly Alexandra Fedorovna looked to Rasputin to relieve his suffering and provide her with comfort and advice, while she herself displayed signs of increasing eccentricity and neurosis in the form of extreme religious fervour. As Spiridovich put it, she suffered a *crise de prières* and took to visiting public churches, in the company of Vyroubova, trying to slip unnoticed into the crowd, which was not easy for an empress. She was driven by that most preposterous of Russian beliefs, that true faith resides only in the people, a cast of mind reflected in her increasing interest in Russian saints, pilgrims, people of God; an interest shared by Vyroubova and encouraged if not actually instigated by Rasputin. Persons in her entourage who could observe her closely talked guardedly of "neurasthenia" and the change of life.

CHAPTER 10

THANKS TO Rasputin's personal hold over the tsarina, and to a slightly lesser extent over the tsar, his career now moved into a new phase. No longer a mere friend of the imperial family, Rasputin became a political force. It is ironic that his first purely political action should have been in favour of a man who was to become one of his most dangerous enemies, the monk Iliodor.

Iliodor, in 1909, was much more of a public figure than Rasputin, and a more obvious threat to authority. A brilliant orator and a religious fanatic, he had built up a huge following with his fulminations. According to these the times were decadent, the church corrupted by complacency and good living, and the tsar betrayed, since Russia had passed into the hands of Jews, freemasons, and revolutionaries who were destroying both it and the Christian faith. The tsar was still great but he was surrounded by wicked men. Accordingly Iliodor preached a doctrine of resistance to authority as a first step in the fight against the forces of the revolution, corruption, and decadence, using a strange blend of monarchism and populism.

Iliodor had made his base in the southern town of Tsaritsyn (later Stalingrad, now Volgograd), where his disciples had built him a huge monastery, so crudely constructed that to one observer it seemed like a stage set.[1] From there he preached against the impending revolution, planned by Jews, supported by the intelligentsia and all civil servants, governors and ministers, led by Prime Minister Stolypin, who had sold their souls to its spirit. The monastery possessed an effigy of the revolution in question in the form of a gigantic dragon, the hydra of revolutions. Iliodor would end his sermons by decapitating it. There was also a portrait of Tolstoy which every passer-by was required to spit on.[2]

Iliodor was manifestly preaching sedition, yet the authorities found him strangely difficult to touch. They made various attempts to arrest or restrain him, but his hordes of supporters, and the underground passages with which his monastery was amply provided, appeared for some time to put him beyond the reach of the law. Indeed the farcical efforts of Stremoukhov, the governor of Saratov, to control or arrest him, efforts which made it clear that he was powerless unless he moved with several regiments of troops, provided disturbing evidence of the weakness of the tsarist government in its latter years and its inability to impose its rule.

After a particularly inflammatory sermon in 1909 the tsar himself intervened, ordering Iliodor to leave Tsaritsyn and proceed to the Siberian town of Minsk. Iliodor declined, but on this occasion was successfully evicted from his monastery. His reaction was to protest to the capital in the hope of getting the decree reversed; a perfectly sensible response. As we shall see, the personal nature of tsarist government, whereby the autocrat was unbounded by the rule of law, meant that he was free to override any decree, including his own. Law as such had no absolute authority; it was up to anyone who fell foul of it to persuade authority that his was a special case.

This is precisely what Iliodor now set out to do, and to this effect he visited his old acquaintance Rasputin. He had taken up new quarters in the capital in the apartment of a financial journalist, G. P. Sazonov, a close friend of Iliodor, and another acquaintance of markedly right-wing stamp. In fact Sazonov was a turncoat. He had originally been a radical, and a close friend of the assassin of Alexander

II, Zhelyabov. However, at some time in 1905 he had taken a sudden and violent turn to the right. This helped him materially. He secured a huge government subsidy for his weekly paper, *The Economist,* and he was also granted a licence to start a bank, which he sold at great profit. He did all he could to exploit his relationship with Rasputin, and would take him to smart houses and show him off there. He also tried to use him to help put through a series of financial deals connected with an attempt to break the liquor monopoly held by the state, but nothing came of this.

Rasputin received Iliodor with open arms, taking great care to show the monk how important he had become. He introduced him to Witte, the Taneevs, and to Vyroubova. After Anna had knelt at his feet and kissed his hand he turned to Iliodor and observed with a characteristically boastful ring: "See how important I am, and what do you think of me now?"[3] He also presented him to the tsarina, who encouraged Rasputin to talk to Nicholas and persuade him to reverse the decree. Here is Rasputin's account of the interview. He asked Nicholas to allow Iliodor to return to Tsaritsyn:

> "But how can I do this, since I have already given my consent to his transfer to Minsk? I even signed the order."
>
> "You are the tsar. Act like one. You have given your word and you can take it back. When you threw Iliodor to the dogs to be devoured you signed your name like this, from left to right. All you have to do is to sign it from right to left. Then you will have acted like a real tsar."[4]

This account rings true in one important respect. Rasputin's advice to Nicholas in future years would often begin with the reminder that he was a tsar, with the power to do whatever he pleased regardless of others' opinion–power was a simple matter of *khochu mogu.* Whatever the true facts may be, Iliodor attributed the subsequent reversal of the decree to Rasputin. He made no secret of this, and it rapidly became public knowledge that in church affairs at least Rasputin was able, as no other courtier or personal advisor, to get his own way with the tsar.

That autumn Rasputin, in the company of Bishop Hermogenes,

whom he had first met in the capital in 1904 and whose views were very close to those of Iliodor, came to visit the monk in Tsaritsyn. After Iliodor had explained to his followers that Rasputin was a man of God, a prophet, a miracle worker, free of passion, blessed with grace and powers of exorcism, who enjoyed the friendship of the tsar and tsarina, his enthusiastic and often hysterical devotees warmed to him and gave him a tremendous reception, receiving him, in Iliodor's words, "like an angel of God,"[5] bowing before him and kissing his feet. This was the first time that Rasputin had experienced anything on this scale, and he enjoyed himself enormously. He sent an enthusiastic telegram to the tsar and tsarina describing his reception and suggesting that it would be a good idea if Iliodor were to be made a bishop. He preached a sermon on the theme, "Have faith and conquer all inner devils, enemies and unbelievers," and then announced that he would receive women one by one in the corner of the church where confessions were heard. A queue formed rapidly, and he foretold the future to his clients, the first recorded instance of his practicing clairvoyance.

Yet once again Rasputin proved incapable of self-restraint. When he called on Iliodor's disciples he could not resist kissing the younger and prettier girls with remarkable enthusiasm, while thrusting older women impatiently away. He never seems to have had much time for older women, and would frequently observe to them, "Mother, your love is pleasing, but the spirit of the Lord does not come down to me," implying that the spirit descended via his sexual organs.[6] He also spent rather too long, four hours, praying alone at the bedside of a strikingly beautiful young nun said to be possessed of the devil.[7]

Rasputin stayed in Tsaritsyn for a fortnight before setting off by river for Pokrovskoe in the company of Iliodor. He left triumphantly. With a 160-rouble tea service, and holding bunches of flowers, he and Iliodor set off in a flower-bedecked monastic carriage, accompanied by large crowds of women singing patriotic songs, carrying banners and icons, driving to the jetty where a steamer was waiting to take them to Pokrovskoe. The river journey took a good nine days, which Rasputin devoted largely to talking to Iliodor about himself and boasting:

> The tsar thinks I'm Christ incarnate. The tsar and tsarina bow down to me, kneel to me, kiss my hands. The tsarina has sworn that if all turn their backs on Grisha she will not waver and still always consider him her friend.[8]

He went on to describe how he carried the imperial children on his back, kissed and confessed the tsarina. Most of these claims were exaggerated; Nicholas and Alexandra had too much natural dignity to behave in the manner described. Rasputin was indulging in a particular Russian habit, *vranye,* or creative lying designed to make the liar appear interesting and important. Rasputin in his latter years was much given to *vranye,* but because it is more exciting to accept gossip than reject it, too much of what he said was taken at face value. However, all good *vranye* has its elements of truth, and Rasputin's observations about the tsar and tsarina are no exception. Alexandra Fedorovna did indeed remain unswervingly loyal, in the teeth of bitter opposition and an overwhelming body of evidence illustrating Rasputin's loose living. However this may reflect on her political judgment, it says much for her loyalty to her friend.

Rasputin himself made a serious error of judgment on his way to Pokrovskoe with Iliodor. Prone as he was to boasting he did not normally confide in people; he had lovers and hangers-on, not friends. He seems to have thought that in Iliodor he had discovered either a friend or a kindred spirit; certainly an admirer who appeared uncritically impressed by everything he had to say. Perhaps this was enough to persuade him to unburden himself, for he turned the conversation toward sex, telling Iliodor what a lucky man he was, since he could have any woman he wanted, and recounting stories of his own exploits, while flirting openly with women they met on the boat. Iliodor grew increasingly disturbed by Rasputin, finding it impossible to reconcile his behaviour with holiness. He was more disturbed still by what he found at Pokrovskoe. For example, there were two "suspect" serving girls there who tried to share Iliodor's bed with him one night. He subsequently concluded that they were trying to make a *khlyst* of him. In the course of his stay Rasputin continued his boasting, telling Iliodor that he had visited the bathhouse with

Vyroubova and others; because, in his words, his penis did not function, he was free of passion. Iliodor was not so sure.

This kind of talk was dangerous enough, but Rasputin went further. He showed Iliodor a pile of letters that he had received from the tsarina and her daughters the year before–from which extracts have been cited above. More serious still, he was careless enough to give Iliodor the chance to remove some of them, thereby providing him with material for a major scandal. So convinced was he of Iliodor's loyalty that he was prepared to take terrible chances in his desire to impress him. The fact that Rasputin was anything but given to confiding and placing himself in another's hands suggests that he was drawn to Iliodor to an unusual degree.

He may well have felt the need for a friend at this time, for opposition toward him was increasing steadily as his situation became better known. For example, General Bogdanovich's wife was much better informed now than she had been eighteen months ago:

> I learnt a lot today that was interesting but also highly disturbing about Grigorii Efimovich Rasputin the famous *starets* who has penetrated into "impenetrable" places . . . I have heard that in Tsarskoe Selo everyone is shocked by Efimovich's insolence, but that he has the strong support of the tsarina. How can people be so blind? Three weeks ago Stolypin arrived with a report and waited for half an hour, for the "Master" [i.e., the tsar] was with his wife, in whose bedroom the scoundrel sat. When the Master's servant tried to tell him that he was a corrupt peasant he was told that he lacked faith, that he was blaspheming and so on. Despite his wife's foolishness the Master loves her and she influences him . . .
>
> The peasant has seduced a number of servants, one is pregnant and he has openly said that Annushka [i.e., Vyroubova] would look after the child. And such a person is received, is on intimate terms with the tsar and even gives him advice.
>
> And this is happening in the twentieth century! It makes you tremble. It is all the fault of the closed world that the tsar moves in.[9]

Rasputin's presence at court and his increasing influence now began to draw the attention of the press. A journalist, Novoselov, published an attack on him in a Moscow paper, *Golos Moskvy*. The official reaction to the piece confirmed Rasputin's status as an unofficial public figure. Although the attack was levelled at him alone, with no word of his association with the palace, the censor intervened, fining the paper heavily and confiscating all available copies of the issue; an inept move that drew widespread attention to the whole affair, as other papers carried the story of the censor's action.

All kinds of rumours began to circulate about Rasputin. One of the more extravagant made him a tool of the great world conspiracy of the Elders of Zion. According to their "Protocols" the elders make use of the Freemasons as unwitting tools in their battle against the Christian church. It was alleged that the masons, at a conference held in Brussels in 1905, had discussed the possibility of using Rasputin to help bring down the Romanov dynasty. The story seems most unlikely, although there is the tantalising fact that Vyroubova's father was himself a mason.

More serious than wild rumour and even newspaper criticism, Rasputin was losing support in certain quarters. He no longer enjoyed the favour of the Montenegrins. There had been a steady cooling in their relationship with the tsarina after Anastasia's marriage to Grand Duke Nicholas, while Rasputin had transferred his allegiance to Vyroubova and hence the tsarina. Though by now the Montenegrins were of little use as friends they could still be dangerous enemies. More important still, responsible churchmen such as Theophanes had turned from him. Theophanes had had his doubts for some time. He had long been aware of Rasputin's capacity for sexual misdemeanour and had repeatedly begged him to give up that kind of "healing," as Rasputin insisted on referring to it. He now became convinced that Rasputin was not the holy man he gave himself out to be, that he was indeed positively evil. He wrote to Iliodor, who still supported Rasputin, imploring him to defend him no longer, not to be taken in by his protestations, and to recognise him for what he was, a true disciple of the devil.

Theophanes was the first of many to attack Rasputin directly. When his attacks seemed to get him nowhere he asked the tsar to give him an interview. Nicholas declined. He would always do all he could to avoid confrontation of any kind on the issue of Rasputin, however overwhelming the evidence. His refusal to listen may be partly explained as the obstinacy of a weak man, but it is also the reaction of a man terrified of his wife. Besides, it would have taken a strong man indeed to listen to those who urged him to send away the only man in Russia who could alleviate the suffering of his son. Instead of receiving Theophanes, Nicholas arranged for him to see the tsarina and Vyroubova.

Theophanes spoke against Rasputin for over an hour, accusing him of being in a state of *prelest'*—having given way to spiritual temptation—an ascetic term used to describe one of the pitfalls that threatened Orthodox hermits and holy men. Alexandra countered his arguments with quotations from devotional works evidently prepared in advance. The interview got Theophanes nowhere. Anyone bold enough to criticise Rasputin to the tsarina's face could be sure that he would no longer retain the imperial favour. She was obviously fond of Theophanes, however, for in his case it was eighteen months before he was disgraced; reappointed to the bishopric of Taurida in Astrakhan—whose climate was not at all suited to the frail and potentially tubercular Theophanes.

Rasputin was well aware that he was making new enemies daily, and that it was his private life that had turned once loyal supporters against him. Unfortunately for anyone who would like to think of him as the embodiment of a certain Dostoevskian Russian stereotype, the Holy Sinner, Rasputin does not seem to have experienced, or at least expressed, remorse of any kind when considering his behaviour. The nearest he ever came to remorse was alcoholic depression. When acquaintances taxed him with stories of his disgraceful doings he no longer even bothered to deny them. "Half the tales are lies of course, but as for the rest, we are all human after all," was his usual response.[10] His dominant reaction was not remorse, but fear; the fear that he would no longer get away with doing as he pleased while remaining close to the imperial family. He once confided in Iliodor that he was terrified that news of his sexual activities might reach the tsarina. He dreaded to think what he would do if she "kicked him out" (*ot sebya shugnet*). Rasputin was confronted with a problem: how to reconcile what he wanted with what he ought to want. The problem was purely practical, conscience had no part to

BBC HULTON PICTURE LIBRARY

Grigorii Efimovich Rasputin.

COLLECTION VIOLLET

St. Petersburg: the Nevsky Prospekt.

COLLECTION VIOLLET

(LEFT TO RIGHT) *Captain von Lohman, of the Ismailovsky Regiment, Rasputin, and Colonel Prince Putyatin, Chamberlain of the Imperial palaces.*

MANSELL COLLECTION

Tsar Nicholas II in 1913.

MANSELL COLLECTION

Tsarina Alexandra in 1914

MANSELL COLLECTION
Nicholas II and the Tsarevich reviewing troops, 1916.

Russian officers arriving to repor for duty at the Winter Palace in St. Petersburg after the declaration of war.
BBC HULTON PICTURE LIBRA

COLLECTION VIOLLET

Rasputin surrounded by his admirers at tea, 1914. This photograph, accompanied by doggerel verses by V. M. Purishkevich and distributed widely to discredit Rasputin, suggesting he was an intimate of smart society women, caused bewilderment in St. Petersburg: with one exception (Mounya Golovina, seated fourth from left), the women were, in fact, all unknowns.

MANSELL COLLECTION

Tsarina Alexandra a short time after Rasputin's death. January 1917.

Prince Felix Yusupov, Rasputin's assassin.

COLLECTION VIOLLET

play. Anyone criticising or disapproving was by definition an enemy, to be done down by whatever means possible. In the meantime he would do all he could to keep his position secure while continuing to act as he pleased.

He still enjoyed the increasingly reluctant support of Iliodor, and, more important, of Bishop Hermogenes, Iliodor's chief protector. Hermogenes himself was something of a demagogue and a militant right-wing patriot, member of the Union of the Russian People and a virulent anti-Semite. A huge, fleshy man with delicate features and a high-pitched voice, it was rumoured that he was a secret castrate. Now, in 1910, he still maintained his support for Rasputin. "He is a servant of God, it is a sin to judge him and think critically of him," he observed to Prince Zhevakhov.[11] Rasputin, who needed all the help he could get, tried to turn this support to advantage in an attempt to give himself official status. One day Iliodor was asked to call on Hermogenes and there, in the bishop's study, he was amazed to find Rasputin wearing a cassock and a priest's pectoral cross—to neither of which he was entitled. He was, according to Iliodor, simpering horribly. It appeared that someone, almost certainly the tsarina, had suggested to Hermogenes that Rasputin should be prepared for the priesthood. The idea was initially Rasputin's: "They'll make me a priest and I'll become the tsar's confessor and I'll stay at court for ever,"[12] he had boasted. Now that Theophanes was in disgrace the way was indeed open for Rasputin to succeed him as the tsar's confessor. Accordingly Hermogenes ordered an allegedly reluctant Iliodor to prepare Rasputin for ordination; instruction was to begin at once. Unfortunately, it became clear almost immediately that Rasputin was incapable of any concentration. Unable to follow the text of the most basic prayers, consistently slipping in his own variants, his mind wandered and he soon began to daydream.

At the end of the second day of instruction it was obvious that Rasputin had no capacity for learning by heart—the first and most important requirement for the priesthood. This did not prevent him from having himself photographed as a priest, cassock, pectoral cross and all—although in later years he would deny that he, an illiterate peasant, had ever attempted to become anything of the sort.

He knew perfectly well that his escapades had come to the attention of Stolypin, and now made an attempt to convince that minister that he was harmless. He asked to see him, and it says much for his importance that the minister agreed to give him an audience, and took the trouble to ensure that the head of the tsar's security forces, Kurlov, attended the interview. Kurlov had never met Rasputin before. He saw:

> A thinnish peasant with a dark red wedge-shaped beard and intelligent piercing eyes. He sat by Stolypin at his big desk and started to point out that they were wrong to consider him a suspect character, for he was the most peaceful and innocuous of men. The minister said nothing, and it was only when Rasputin was about to leave that Stolypin observed that provided he behaved himself he could rest assured that the police would leave him alone. I then told the minister what my impressions were. I felt Rasputin was a certain kind of cunning Russian peasant, who knew what he was doing. He did not strike me as a charlatan. "All the same some day we'll have to reckon with him," observed Stolypin.[13]

Stolypin ordered a second report on his activities to be drawn up:

> It was largely concerned with his private life, a series of drunken and sometimes scandalous and riotous celebrations, a number of sexual liaisons and, recently, dealings with dubious entrepreneurs and backers trying to turn his influence to advantage. Against the advice of his inferiors Stolypin presented the report to the emperor who heard him without saying a word, and with characteristic obstinate calm suggested Stolypin proceed to the business of the day.[14]

Nicholas had too much dignity ever to show his feelings, and it is hard to say precisely what he thought of Rasputin at any time. As far as we can tell he began by having a very high opinion of him, which came to be qualified in the light of criticism and gossip. To the end he valued the calming effect he had upon the empress. "Better one Rasputin than ten fits of hysterics a day," he once observed in an unguarded moment. To the end, he would often act upon Rasputin's advice, as relayed by Vyroubova and the empress, and this only partly out of the fear of a hen-pecked husband and the resignation of a Job. Even now, though he began to realise that the *starets* was less than perfect, he treated unsolicited criticism such as Stolypin's report as a grave breach of etiquette, so grave that he could only pretend that it had not taken place; Rasputin was a personal friend of the family and beyond his minister's proper concern.

In the meantime the tsarina demonstrated that Rasputin still retained her confidence. Inquiring after his family she learnt that his wife and younger daughter were spending some time in the capital expressly to visit the elder girl, Maria, who was at school there. As a mark of her favour she arranged to have the girls presented to her, and to her own daughters, over tea. Maria Rasputina first heard of the plan when Anna Vyroubova telephoned the flat and coyly invited her and her sister to take tea with her, since a certain family was anxious to meet them. The two girls duly presented themselves at Anna's little house, and waited anxiously in her drawing room, with its elegant, delicate furniture. Suddenly the door opened and the empress came in, followed by her four daughters chattering gaily. It was clear from the way she moved that she was a regular visitor to the house. Nervously Maria started to drop a curtsey, head bowed in the manner appropriate to greeting royalty, but royalty swept up to her, took her by the hand, and raised her up to give her a resounding kiss. She then greeted her sister Varvara with an equal warmth, telling the girls how fond she was of their father and what a remarkable man he was. For all her two years of schooling in the capital, nothing had prepared Maria to deal with such situations. She froze, tongue-tied, and then, overcome by the need to say something, anything, blurted out: "Is it true, little Mother, that you have hundreds of servants?" The empress smiled at her inept question and replied, "Yes, my child . . . I have lots of servants of course, but I could do without them if it were necessary."[15]

Maria Rasputina's portrait of the empress is strangely convincing, and touching too. She appears kind, generous, enthusiastic and relaxed, doing her best to put the peasant girl at her ease. When the pressures of public worry and private grief were absent the tsarina could be warm, cheerful, and a good friend to the weak.

Soon the Rasputin girls found themselves talking easily with the grand duchesses. Maria was almost the exact contemporary of the eldest girl, Olga Nicolaevna, who quizzed her eagerly about life in the capital, and at Pokrovskoe. The girls seldom had the chance to meet anybody of their own age, other than suitable companions with comparable ways of life. The Rasputin girls were different:

> Strictly guarded as they were, more or less prisoners at Tsarskoe Selo, going out only on official occasions, the life of a girl of fourteen living in the town, who went to school with other children, and once a week went to the cinema, sometimes to the circus, seemed to them the rarest and most enviable of wonders.[16]

This must surely have been the most extraordinary tea party ever to have been held in Imperial Russia. Even the most relaxed interpretations of protocol would have found it totally unacceptable for peasant girls to take tea with imperial grand-duchesses and converse freely with them about the wonders of the weekly cinema. Yet, by all accounts, the occasion seems to have been a success, although as far as we know the experiment was not repeated.

Although he could sense storm clouds gathering, Rasputin continued to take appalling chances, possibly because the tsarina's marks of favour had convinced him he could not be touched. Alexandra Fedorovna had encouraged her daughters' nurse, M. J. Vishnyakova, to go to Pokrovskoe for a few weeks' rest, in the company of three other women including Olga Lokhtina. One night Rasputin forced his way into her room and seduced her. On her return she told the empress and also mentioned that on the journey Rasputin had slept with one of her travelling companions, Z. Manstadt. The empress simply refused to believe her, concluded that Rasputin's enemies had induced her to lay false charges against him, and sent her on indefinite leave of absence. The fight against Rasputin was then taken up by a second member of the imperial household, the children's governess, S. I. Tyutcheva, a daughter of the famous nineteenth-century poet. She had long resented the position Rasputin enjoyed with the imperial family and now tried to use the Vishnyakova incident to discredit him for good, protesting vociferously about his behaviour to all and sundry. She was an obstinate, self-important, and silly woman who had already made herself less than popular in the family by taking a hard line on discipline, insisting that certain types of conversation should not be held in front of her charges, and attempting to override parental views with which she disagreed. Her domineering nature had won her the reputation of "a man in skirts."[17] Curiously, Rasputin was not the first peasant that she had had dealings with. During the Japanese war she had worked as a bookkeeper in a welfare organisation run by the tsarina's sister. There she had befriended a peasant in the dispatch department, taken him into her office, and later got him the job of carrying an archbishop's mitre in religious processions. Such was her attachment to her protégé that eyebrows were raised when she was appointed governess to the imperial family.[18] It is perfectly possible that Rasputin may have antagonised her by not paying her the proper kind of court. In this case she overplayed her hand, offering a series of wildly exaggerated accounts of Rasputin's behaviour. She accused him of going unchaperoned into the bedrooms of the grand duchesses, and treating them with unforgivable familiarity which had distinctly sexual undertones. The tsar summoned her and heard her out:

> So you are another who does not believe in Grigorii Efimovich's holiness . . . And what would you say if I told you that through all these difficult years it is only thanks to his prayers that I have survived?[19]

Nicholas went on to observe that he did not believe a word of what she had to say, could only assume that she had been driven by malice and informed her that she was dismissed.

The next attack upon Rasputin was more serious; it happened by chance and came from a disinterested and unexpected source. Iliodor had returned to Tsaritsyn unrepentant, and continued to preach seditious sermons against the authorities, both secular and ecclesiastic. The Holy Synod ordered him to leave Tsaritsyn and take himself to the monastery of Novosil in the government of Tula in central Russia. Iliodor refused and called once again upon the support of the tsar.

Nicholas reacted weakly. He felt sympathy for Iliodor, and was unwilling to enforce the Synod's order. He was reluctant to intervene in church affairs, equally reluctant to let Iliodor do as he pleased. Accordingly he instructed one of his aides-de-camp, Mandryka, to proceed to Tsaritsyn and attempt to *talk* Iliodor into obeying the Synod's order.

Mandryka was received in Tsaritsyn with great ceremony, as crowds fell to their knees before him imploring him to allow Iliodor to remain among them. Eventually Mandryka persuaded Iliodor to proceed to Novosil. While in Tsaritsyn he called to see a relative, the mother superior of a local convent and an admirer of Rasputin. It transpired that she was in St. Petersburg at the time, but Mandryka was well received by the nuns, who told him all about Father Grigorii, the emperor's favourite. The discovery of Rasputin's existence came as a total shock to the aide-de-camp. He was shocked still further by a telegram they showed him from Rasputin to the mother superior. It had been sent from Pokrovskoe:

> A relative of yours is coming to Tsaritsyn on a mission that concerns us. Use your influence. Grigorii.

Although Mandryka moved in court circles he had never even heard of Rasputin before, and was most disturbed by what the nuns told him. He made further inquiries and discovered that the emperor's favourite was reputed to be a sectarian and a compulsive womaniser, who used a number of techniques, from exorcism to rape, to get what he wanted. Mandryka returned to St. Petersburg determined to tell the imperial couple everything, drawing up a long report of the holy man's misdeeds.

On Shrove Tuesday 1911 he delivered his report to Nicholas. It covered Rasputin's sexual activities, his probable sectarianism, his disgraceful character, and his attempt to influence Mandryka through the mother superior. Anyone of any decency could only be appalled at the position that Rasputin was permitted to enjoy, and of course Mandryka could only assume that news of his true nature had been kept from the tsar. "It is even rumoured," he concluded, "that this man enjoys the favour of Your Majesty." At this point Mandryka, who was a highly strung person, broke down and sobbed. The tsar fetched him a glass of water, thanked him and permitted him to withdraw.

Some days later the mother superior sent for Mandryka and drily observed that he had ruined his career. Rasputin had not been invited to the palace since his report. Not only had Mandryka slandered a good man, he had made an implacable enemy. In the event Mandryka did not ruin his career; he was made governor of Novgorod in 1914, but whereas he used to lunch regularly with the imperial family, he was never invited to eat with them again.

Rasputin's daughter suggests that yet another scandal took place at this time. Her father had, she reports, made the acquaintance of a Finnish dancer. One evening he spent some hours in a restaurant with her before returning to her house for a party, which rapidly turned into an orgy. Rasputin, falling down drunk, had his photograph taken surrounded by naked women.[20] Shortly afterwards he was given a set of prints and told that he must either leave town or have them shown to the tsar. Rasputin allegedly gave the matter a lot of thought and decided there was only one thing he could do. He took the prints to Tsarskoe Selo and asked to see the tsar. He showed him the photographs and explained that he was being blackmailed. Nicholas inspected them carefully and then observed with a sigh that Rasputin had been foolish, yielded to temptation, and allowed himself to be exploited by subversives and revolutionaries who would stop at nothing to discredit the monarchy. In the circumstances it would indeed be best if he were to leave the capital for a time.

There is no intrinsic reason to doubt Rasputin's daughter, unless it be that the photographs were never actually used to discredit Rasputin, even though he did not stay away for long. If Nicholas did see such pictures he could no longer have been in any doubt as to Rasputin's frailties, and the fact that he continued to enjoy the imperial favour can only suggest that the hold he had over Nicholas and Alexandra was very strong indeed, that they were almost literally in his power. One also has to assume that the photographic techniques of the age were able to do justice to a late-night orgy–either by use of flash powder or by ensuring that Rasputin and his bevy of lovelies kept still long enough to permit a protracted time exposure.

CHAPTER 11

By early 1911 Rasputin's stock was low. The evidence against him had accumulated steadily over the past year, and while Nicholas might have been able to dismiss Tyutcheva's charges as wild exaggerations, he was bound to take the tearful Mandryka much more seriously. According to Spiridovich he ordered Rasputin to appear no more at Tsarskoe Selo, or, as his daughter would have it, advised him to make himself inconspicuous for a while.

Rasputin decided to make a pilgrimage to the Holy Land. The idea was probably suggested by Taneev, in order to give the appearance that he was seeking to expiate his misdeeds. This is not to say that the pilgrimage was all a sham. Rasputin was capable of reconciling attitudes and values that the Western mind might consider incompatible. He would not have left the capital unless he had had to. He did not feel an overwhelming sense of remorse. Yet since he had to go, and a visit to the Holy Land appeared well advised, why not allow the ritual of pilgrimage to do its work upon his inner being? In other words, there was no necessary contradiction between the purely political motives for his journey and the pilgrim's cast of mind which he adopted on it. There is nothing to say that someone who enters a church to escape a thunderstorm may not pray devoutly once inside.

Such an interpretation of his attitudes is speculative, yet all one knows of the man suggests that there was more to him than hypocrisy and opportunism. The contradictions of his behaviour stem less from hypocrisy than from solipsism, the belief that he alone in the universe was really real. He had a tremendous sense of ego; anything he might do was right by definition simply because he wanted to do it; he was incapable of being at odds with himself. This is a trait of character that he shares with political demagogues, martyrs, fanatics, and founders of religions, a trait that can make great men or warped eccentrics. Rasputin was no warped eccentric, but the increasingly trivial nature of his ambition, which became reduced to that of a politically minded courtier with powerful appetites, ensured that he fell well short of any kind of greatness; the man has been overshadowed by his myth.

Rasputin's pilgrimage invites such consideration of his motives because it gave rise to his only "book": "My thoughts and reflections; a short description of my journey to the Holy Places and the meditations on religious matters to which they gave rise." The work consists of some twenty thousand words of travel notes and pious reflections, which are designed to convey a sense of Rasputin the simple man of God, moved by sun, sea, and the Holy Places, to profess a naive and natural piety. The book could never have been written by Rasputin, who was incapable of producing anything longer than a scrawled postcard. It consists of impressions that he dictated subsequently to Olga Lokhtina, and which must have been carefully edited. They were initially intended to impress the tsar and tsarina, and to suggest that his pilgrimage had reformed him. Since he was capable of such sincere religious experience, rumours of his scandalous behaviour could safely be discounted. The notes had their desired effect upon Alexandra. In the last year of Rasputin's life, when criticism of him was at its fiercest, the notes were published, in a deluxe edition and at the tsarina's instigation, in an attempt to prove that Rasputin was not the monster that rumour would have him be.

We seldom hear Rasputin's own voice in these notes. They have a stilted literary style that lacks all the rich, idiomatic flavour of his speech, or the obscurantism of his cabled spiritual exhortations. Yet although the dominant tone is a somewhat self-conscious and unctuous display of piety they occasionally strike the kind of simple note that so impressed Prince Zhevakhov when he heard Rasputin preach:

> The sea brings comfort with the utmost ease; when you get up in the morning and the waves talk, dance and delight. And the sun shines on the sea, as if it were rising oh so gently, and then your soul forgets all mankind and looks at the light of the sun, and joy lights up in your heart, and the soul senses the book of life and the wisdom of life–beauty indescribable! The sea wakes you from the dream of life's worries, you think a lot, of your own accord, without effort.[1]

There are flashes of humour too. He condemns the high-ranking Orthodox ecclesiastics because they lack spiritual poverty, which is the only quality respected by the masses. He also points out that many monks had grown fat on high living in their monasteries:

> Of course for God all things are possible. There *are* monks that are born fat; health is a gift of God, and some of them are bearers of the divine spark–that I do not deny.[2]

The writings preach a faith based on naivete, simplicity, and universal love–an essentially popular faith that emphasises the quality of human feeling, love being more important than intelligence or ritual, since only through universal love could man attain faith:

> If you love you will never kill; all commandments are subservient to love, it contains all wisdom, greater than Solomon's, and love alone is real, all the rest is scattered fragments, through love alone can heaven be reached.[3]

The writing possesses one quality characteristic of Rasputin. It is highly immediate, and has no sense of overall plan; it picks up one point or topic after another, always dwelling on the particular and lacking in perspective. Immediately after the passage just quoted he points out that better arrangements should be made for poor pilgrims travelling to the Holy Land. Precisely the same concern for ordinary people, together with a tendency to concentrate on the trees at the expense of the wood, would characterise the advice he was to give the tsarina on the conduct of the Great War. As for the religious content of the notes, they manage to project a powerful image of faith founded in simplicity and love. Whatever Rasputin's motives may have been in compiling the notes, he must have possessed a certain degree of spiritual insight to have been able to concoct them. Even if he were a charlatan, he had the ability to produce an uncanny imitation of the real thing.

✧ ✧ ✧

Rasputin left Russia at the end of February and did not return till the last week of June. He kept in touch with the imperial family, and with Iliodor, largely by telegram. Iliodor had challenged authority yet again. He had escaped from the Novosil monastery, and eluding elaborate attempts to apprehend him, had shut himself up in his Tsaritsyn stronghold, in defiance of Governor Stremoukhov, who had laid siege to the place. There was not much else Stremoukhov could do; he recognised that to capture Iliodor would require a full-scale military action which would have grave consequences for the stability of the province and might well prove unsuccessful in the end. The monk, who had been joined by Hermogenes, was defended, in the words of the governor, "By a fanatical mob of howling, hysterical women, and men, tough barefoot peasants, who shook their fists and swore to kill anybody who tried to touch him."[4] Their loyalty was in part to be explained by a widespread belief, which Iliodor did not discourage, that he was the illegitimate brother of Nicholas II by a father of the purest Russian blood. It had been 150 years since a tsar had had a drop of Russian blood in him. A despairing Stremoukhov felt his was a world in which anything could happen: "Who can guess at all the possibilities in our country, of possibility unlimited?"[5]

The governor, having reached the limit of his authority, went to the capital to consult Stolypin. There he discovered that Iliodor and Hermogenes still enjoyed the obstinate support of the tsar, who believed in Iliodor's character without altogether approving of his actions. Stolypin's response to the breakdown of law in Tsaritsyn was extraordinary, demonstrating the frailty of the administrative machine, a frailty that began at the top. He suggested that, in the interests of law and order, Stremoukhov should proffer the tsar his resignation in an attempt to bring him to his senses. Stremoukhov agreed, and said he would use the opportunity to tell Nicholas the truth about Iliodor, Hermogenes, and also Rasputin; he produced a photograph of the three of them sitting together. Stolypin agreed.

Next morning Stremoukhov received a telephone call in his hotel room. The caller did not identify himself, but the voice was clearly Stolypin's. It told him not to talk about "the third man" in the photograph when he was at Tsarskoe Selo. The caller then hung up. Nothing can give a clearer indication of Rasputin's prestige. He had no position of any kind, was abroad and under a cloud, and yet the prime minister and minister of the interior felt bound to advise a junior not to discuss Rasputin with the tsar, giving his instructions anonymously and not even daring to mention Rasputin by name.

Nicholas paid no attention to Stremoukhov, other than to reject his resignation; this was largely because Rasputin had been in touch, urging that Iliodor be allowed to remain. Shortly afterwards the Holy Synod sent a telegram to Iliodor: "In consideration of the petitions submitted by the people the tsar condescends to permit the priest Iliodor to return from Novosil to Tsaritsyn."[6] Nicholas had relented. It was a triumph for the forces of disorder.

Rasputin made his way back through Russia in the summer of 1911, arriving in Tsaritsyn late in June. According to Iliodor he was no longer given a spectacular welcome by admiring crowds. He was annoyed to see copies of a photograph he had had taken with Iliodor and Hermogenes—the one that the governor had wanted to show the tsar—which had been mutilated to cut him out. According again to Iliodor, when he left he insisted on being given an elaborate send-off and expensive presents. From Tsaritsyn he travelled on to Saratov to call on Hermogenes, and there too he was not received with any remarkable warmth.

It was as if Rasputin, by calling on Iliodor and Hermogenes, was trying to drum up ecclesiastical support. This would also account for his championing of Iliodor over the last two years. He was not usually prone to fighting other people's battles, not, at least, to fighting unrewarded. However, now even these eccentric and unreliable churchmen were turning against him.

Rasputin had courted their support on his way to the capital, uncertain of the reception he would get there. He need not have worried. As Stolypin had already understood, scandals or no scandals, he had become a force that politicians had to reckon with. His return from the Holy Land marked the moment when he began to acquire a measure of real political influence.

By the middle of 1911 Stolypin had lost the support of Nicholas, partly, it has been suggested, because of his continuing opposition to Rasputin. Matters had come to a head when he failed to get through an administrative reform establishing elements of local government in the western provinces. Stolypin offered his resignation, but insisted that the tsar suspend the chamber and enact the legislation by decree. This was duly done, but Stolypin no longer enjoyed the imperial confidence. He could tell from various marks of disfavour—no place on the imperial train on a journey south to Kiev, for example—that politically speaking he was doomed.

The tasr made or dismissed ministers at his discretion, and especially in later years appointments were determined by increasingly peculiar criteria; less concern was displayed for administrative competence and political experience, and more, too much in fact, for that nebulous concept known as "character," which may have a proper part to play in a headmaster's choice of school captain, but which should not be used to determine the right persons to administer the Russian Empire. Rasputin benefited enormously from this bias; of administration and politics he knew nothing, but he and his piercing eyes could read character second to none. Now for the first time, Nicholas actually called upon these gifts. In his search for a new minister of the interior he invited Rasputin to proceed to the town of Nizhny Novgorod and "look into the soul" of its governor, A. N. Khvostov, a young man whose ambitions outstripped his abilities.

Rasputin duly proceeded to Nizhny in the company of Sazonov, and asked Khvostov for an interview. The governor, understandably bewildered by the intense and self-confident peasant, gave him short shrift despite Rasputin's declaration that he had been sent by the tsar to weigh him up for a new and responsible position. It was only after Rasputin left that the terrible possibility dawned upon Khvostov that this Gogolian Government Inspector might have been the real thing. Knowing his Gogol well enough to remember that it was the postmaster's reading of the mail that revealed Khlestakov to be an imposter, he ran an immediate check on all outgoing letters and telegrams, only to discover that Rasputin had indeed wired Tsarskoe Selo: "He is smart (*shustyer*) but still very young," it read. A few weeks later he was summoned to Nicholas's presence and given a cool reception.

It was not thanks to Rasputin alone that Khvostov failed to get the job. Stolypin's replacement as prime minister, Kokovtsov, had told Nicholas that to make Khvostov a minister would be tantamount to jumping off a cliff—which would not prevent Nicholas from appointing him some four years later. Yet that Nicholas should have made such use of Rasputin in the first place almost defies belief. It can only be explained by a mystic faith on the part of the tsar in Rasputin as a person of exceptional intuitive judgment, someone who could tell at a glance whether a man was "good" or "bad," plumbing the depths of his soul and detecting those qualities which an adroit politician could always conceal from the scrutiny of a tsar, to whom no one told the truth. Rasputin would be Nicholas's "eyes" and help him spy out what would otherwise remain hidden.

Soon afterwards Rasputin displayed visionary power of a different kind. From Nizhny he had gone to Pokrovskoe for a short stay, to be joined there by Vyroubova, and from Pokrovskoe had travelled on to Kiev, where the tsar and tsarina were to celebrate the inauguration of local government in southwest Russia.

It was arranged that Rasputin would stay with the leader of the local branch of a moderate monarchist organisation—"moderate" meant that, unlike the Union of the Russian People, it did not take its defence of the autocracy to the point of lynching Jews. The prospect of Rasputin's stay made the leader nervous; for, as he put it, he was a married man. He was pleasantly surprised to find him a simple, agreeable guest who behaved himself perfectly. Next day Rasputin joined with members of the organisation to watch the tsar parade through the city. The leader had trained his men to produce a "Hurrah" of quite exceptional volume with which to attract the imperial attention. Sure enough the empress turned to them as she passed and they shouted; she noticed Rasputin, who promptly gave her his blessing. Stolypin was riding in the next carriage and when Rasputin saw him he suddenly went pale, crying out, "Death rides behind him, behind Peter. Don't you see him? There he is!"

All that night Rasputin tossed and turned, calling out that something terrible was about to happen, that death was near and that he could do nothing about it.[7]

That night at the Kiev opera house Stolypin was shot down by Bugaev, a terrorist and police spy who was suspected of involvement in an assassination attempt, and who had been admitted to the theatre by official invitation. The circumstances of his admission have never been satisfactorily explained, but it is unlikely that it was the result of conspiracy.

Stolypin died of his wound a few days later, but Rasputin was quick to comfort the tsar and tsarina, assuring them that Stolypin's usefulness was at an end anyway and that the new prime minister, Kokovtsov, was an excellent choice. There is a tantalising possibility that there is more in his remark about Stolypin than meets the eye, that it was indeed an act of something tantamount to clairvoyance on the part of Rasputin. The autopsy revealed Stolypin to be a very sick man, with a matter of months to live.* As far as we know, no one was aware of his condition, least of all Stolypin. Only Rasputin understood that his usefulness was truly at an end.

* I am grateful to Kyril Fitzlyon for telling me this little-known fact.

CHAPTER 12

RASPUTIN FURTHER CONSOLIDATED his position as a secret or, rather, not immediately apparent influence on public life by securing the appointment of V. K. Sabler to the over-procuratorship of the Holy Synod, making him minister for church affairs, a post he would hold until 1915. The mechanics of the process remain unclear and unrecorded, in the sense that we do not know just what it was that Rasputin said to the tsar and tsarina to get Sabler the job, although from future and better documented recommendations we may infer that he told the tsarina that Sabler was a good man, a man of character, whose loyalty to the imperial couple was beyond question. At all events informed gossip attributed his appointment directly to Rasputin,[1] and certainly from this moment on he seems to have had a hold over ecclesiastical appointments that he would maintain until the end. With the support of Sabler and various lesser synodal officials, who also owed him their places, Rasputin was now in a position to make or break whichever churchmen he pleased, and had suddenly become a very dangerous man to challenge, as Iliodor and Hermogenes would soon find out.

Rasputin had lost their support for good. Iliodor in particular had turned against him, partly out of disapproval, largely out of jealousy. He found Rasputin's immorality and his success with women impossible to stomach. In December of that year, 1911, Iliodor and Hermogenes both found themselves in the capital for various reasons. They decided, allegedly appalled by rumours that Rasputin was now boasting that he was the tsarina's lover—something he never was, incidentally—that the time had come to make him mend his ways. They proposed to confront him with the chronicle of his misdeeds and call upon him to repent or suffer dire consequences. The confrontation was to take place before witnesses—a journalist, Rodionov, a merchant, two priests, an academician and the half-witted cripple and fool in Christ Mitya Kolyaba.

Rasputin had just returned from Yalta, where he had been staying close to the imperial palace. Iliodor collected Rasputin from his lodgings and ostensibly took him to call on Hermogenes. There was an uneasy delay while the rest of the witnesses were being assembled, and Rasputin started to look suspiciously about him, pacing up and down and growing agitated, but in due course the witnesses arrived, whereupon the whole solemn affair collapsed into one of those comic and embarrassing scandals that Dostoevsky is so fond of.

The proceedings started with an address from Mitya, who could not be restrained. Mewling and spitting horribly, he approached Rasputin, waving his withered hand and accusing him of ungodliness and sexual transgressions. With his other hand, the good one, he began to beat and punch Rasputin, then suddenly grabbed him by the penis, which he attempted to pull off. Rasputin bent double in an understandable effort to shake Mitya free, whereupon the corpulent Hermogenes, also calling on him to repent, started to belabour him with a heavy cross. There was hysteria and violence aplenty in the air, and it was as well for Rasputin that he managed to tear free of Mitya, avoid Hermogenes, and make his escape, for there was no knowing where the violence might have ended; he could easily have been killed.

This was the first known attempt to harm Rasputin physically, and curiously enough it took place on December 16, the anniversary of his first meeting with Iliodor and the day of his death at the hands of Yusupov five years later.

Rasputin and his supporters in the synod responded to the onslaught with stunning speed and strength. Hermogenes, himself a synod member, was ordered to leave the capital while the synod was in session, an unheard-of sanction. When he refused he was exiled to the Jirovitsky monastery in the government of Vladimir, where he would remain in the most wretched circumstances until 1917, subsequently dying a martyr's death at the hands of the Bolsheviks. Strangely, he retained a measure of admiration for Rasputin to the end. Looking back on the whole sorry business he wrote:

> We, the representatives of the senior clergy, are more than all others to blame for having advanced him . . . It was we who pushed him forward . . . But to my thinking at the outset the divine fire glowed in Rasputin's soul. He was imbued with a certain inner sensibility and I confess freely that I felt his influence upon me. He more than once responded to my grief, and in that way won me over, and, in the beginning of his career won over others.[2]

Iliodor was arrested and imprisoned in the Florishchev monastery, but unlike Hermogenes he would not stay confined for long.

The satisfaction that Rasputin, a vindictive man, must have felt at the discomfiture of his enemies was short-lived. Indeed, his revenge did him more harm than their physical onslaught. Overnight he had secured the disgrace of an eminent and popular member of the Holy Synod and a religious rabble-rouser who had hitherto appeared beyond the reach of the law. There could be no more public indication of the extent of Rasputin's influence. Where previously he had been the subject of gossip and head-shaking for a handful of persons in the know, the scandal of his influence now became the major political issue of the day.

Numerous stories about him appeared in the press, including a boastful interview he had given to Rodionov, the journalist who attended his "assault," describing how he took jewel-bedecked society ladies to bathe with him in Pokrovskoe to give them lessons in humility. The government, viewing criticism of Rasputin as a covert attack upon the dynasty, reacted by forbidding the press to mention his name, which simply confirmed that he was as close to the tsar and tsarina as suspected. Matters were not improved by the refusal of the government to give any reason for its decision to censor the press. More serious still, Iliodor had entrusted Rodionov with the letters he had stolen a year earlier in Pokrovskoe. These were now copied and circulated. The grand duchesses' little communications were compromising enough, but there was worse to come, in the shape of a letter of the tsarina's that was open to serious misinterpretation:

> My much loved never to be forgotten teacher, saviour and instructor, I am so wretched without you. My soul is only rested and at ease when you, my teacher, are near me, I kiss your hands and lay my head upon your blessed shoulders. I feel so joyful then. Then all I want is to sleep, sleep for ever on your shoulder, in your embrace. It is such happiness to feel your presence close to me. Where are you, where have you run off to? . . . Come back soon. I await you and yearn for you. I ask you for your holy blessing and kiss your blessed hands. Your eternally loving Mama.[3]

The tone of the letter is startling enough for one to question its authenticity, appearing as it does for the first time in its entirety in a Soviet journal. Yet in view of the fact that non-Soviet sources quote extracts from it, which correspond closely to the full text (e.g., Milyukov, p. 100), it would appear to be authentic, and a major source of embarrassment to the tsarina and to Rasputin.

Rasputin was unnerved enough by the campaign he had unleashed to secure an audience with the prime minister, Kokovtsov. The latter gives an embellished account of the interview in which he claims stoutly to have resisted a determined attempt to hypnotise him. He told Rasputin that he was doing grave damage to the tsar, and that he should leave the capital at once. The reaction was hostile and ironic: "Very well, I'll leave, but if I am that bad and bad for the tsar they had better not try to get me back."[4] His words suggest that he knew the extent of his hold over the family. Next day Nicholas anxiously asked Kokovtsov if he had exiled Rasputin, and was most relieved to learn that he had not. He went on disingenuously to deny acquaintance with him, saying that he had only met him very occasionally. Kokovtsov was surprised to discover that Nicholas already knew the gist of his talk with the *starets*.

Although he had not actually been exiled, Rasputin nonetheless felt it prudent to leave the capital, and returned to Pokrovskoe in the middle of January 1912. He left with his tail very much between his legs. A Siberian member of the Duma, A. Sukhanov, who first met him at the time in Pokrovskoe, recalled that he was terrified of the consequences of the scandal and was an object of derision in the village. His stock would not rise again at home until a certain "miraculous" cure that he was to perform just over a year later.[5] Indeed, his departure did nothing to abate the scandal. The issue was gleefully taken up by anti-dynastic elements of the Imperial Duma, who were delighted by the Rasputin affair. The attack was led by A. I. Guchkov, who proposed to ask a highly critical question in the house. It may well have been Guchkov, incidentally, who circulated the tsarina's letter. However, the president of the Duma, Rodzyanko, described by the tsar to his son as the "biggest and fattest man in Russia," but a person of lesser spirit than he was of stature, managed to dissuade him. With an uncomfortable degree of insight he saw the issue of Rasputin as a threat to the monarchy itself, describing it as the Russian version of the "queen's necklace," the scandal that did much to destroy the reputation of Marie Antoinette.

The sense of outrage felt in the capital is captured in the following entry from the diary of A. K. Bogdanovich:

> February 18.
> I take up my pen feeling crushed and wretched. I have never known a more disgraceful time. It is not the tsar but the upstart Rasputin who governs Russia, and he states openly that the tsar needs him even more than the tsarina; and then there is that letter to Rasputin in which the tsarina writes that she only knows peace with her head on his shoulder . . . The tsar has lost all respect and the tsarina declares that it is only thanks to Raspu-

> tin's prayers that the tsar and their son are alive and well; and this is the twentieth century![6]

Rodzyanko may have persuaded Guchkov to exercise some restraint, but he was not prepared to let matters rest and miss the chance to put pressure on the tsar. He compiled a dossier that he felt would suffice to destroy Rasputin. He first showed it to Nicholas's mother, the dowager-empress, who observed sadly that her daughter-in-law appeared to lack political judgment of any kind. Rodzyanko then took it to the tsar, and made a verbal report on its contents.

He described Rasputin's presence at court as more damaging to the dynasty than any revolutionary action, and supplied details of Rasputin's immoral behaviour, going on to suggest that he was almost certainly a *khlyst*. The president was impressed by the tsar's response. Nicholas was visibly saddened and distressed, grew very quiet, and finally thanked him for doing his duty as a loyal subject. Yet Nicholas's character was such that the interview probably did more harm than good. Even now Nicholas defended Rasputin to Kokovtsov, or rather maintained that the matter was a purely private affair:

> Rasputin is a simple peasant who can relieve the sufferings of my son by a strange power. The empress's reliance upon him is a matter for the family, and I will allow no one to meddle in my family affairs.[7]

Nicholas was nevertheless disturbed by the report, much of which was new to him, and asked Rodzyanko to obtain from the Holy Synod a secret dossier on Rasputin that it held. It was delivered by M. Damansky, the over-procurator's assistant and a supporter of Rasputin, who attempted to defend him. The next day Damansky reappeared asking for the return of the dossier, but Rodzyanko, on learning that the request came not from the tsar but the tsarina, refused. When she heard of his action Alexandra Fedorovna grew hysterical and observed that such persons as Rodzyanko and Guchkov were fit only to be hanged.

On the strength of the additional material available to him, pertaining largely to Rasputin's early days in Pokrovskoe, Rodzyanko prepared a second report and requested another interview with the emperor, convinced that he could persuade him to get rid of Rasputin once and for all. To his astonishment the request was refused. Nicholas had evidently decided that the issue of Rasputin was not to be a political concern.

To the tsar, with his lack of political sense and obstinate adherence to the principles of autocracy, Rodzyanko's "loyal address" seemed to be an unpardonable intrusion tantamount to *lèse-majesté*. If Rodzyanko had got his facts right, this made his action still worse. It suggested that the empress's judgment was at fault, and this called for an even greater degree of support for her; the more Nicholas heard, the more necessary such support would become. Facts were dreadfully hurtful, but they could not make him change—not only would that have constituted a betrayal, but the prospect of telling Alexandra that the Friend must go would have daunted a more determined man than Nicholas. All he could do was absorb the bitter news of Rasputin's behaviour, suffer and endure in silence.

When looking back on the period preceding a revolution it is too easy to find critical moments, turning points and the like, which take on disproportionate significance in the light of subsequent events. Nicholas's reign abounds in them. Yet the tsar's response to the first outright public attack upon Rasputin was more of a turning point than most, if less obviously so than many others. Just for a moment Nicholas encouraged Rodzyanko, who was not disloyal, to build the strongest possible case against Rasputin. However, partly due to pressure from his wife, he then decided that an attack upon Rasputin from parliamentary circles was necessarily an attack on the dynasty itself. Criticism of any kind, *however justified,* must needs be a disloyal act. The autocratic Nicholas was incapable of understanding that his relationship with the nation's representatives must involve some measure of give and take, and the attitude of the Duma toward Rasputin alienated him still further. He concluded that, as a body, it was hostile and anti-dynastic, and should therefore be ignored whenever possible. As Kokovtsov wrote:

> In the emperor's intimate circle the concept of a government, of its significance, dwindled, and in its place emerged with increas-

> ing force and clarity the purely personal nature of the emperor's rule, while the government increasingly came to be considered as a wall cutting the ruler off from his people.[8]

It was an attitude that steadily alienated support for the autocratic principle, until by January 1917 it was supported by practically nobody except for a lunatic fringe of fanatical ultras, some but by no means all the army commanders, and most but not all of the imperial family.

For all the damage Rasputin did to the dynasty and the relish with which the Duma's left exploited his name, there is nothing to suggest that he was ever used directly by revolutionaries to discredit the monarchy–with one very curious exception. Rasputin's alleged sectarianism was a major factor in the criticism now levelled against him. As early as 1910 Novoselov had accused him of being a *khlyst,* and his piece in Guchkov's paper, *Golos Moskvy,* was now republished as a pamphlet. Had his heterodoxy been confirmed it could easily have destroyed him once and for all. A middle-of-the-road faction of the Duma, the Octobrists, Guchkov's party, commissioned an expert on the sects to establish the nature of Rasputin's faith. The conclusions were published in the March edition of a journal called *The Contemporary.* The expert had had a series of protracted discussions with Rasputin and had been fully convinced of his Orthodoxy. As evidence this is valueless; it simply established that Rasputin was able to make a convincing showing as an Orthodox believer–just as he had done many years before in Pokrovskoe. Yet, to an uncritical eye at least, it seemed to give Rasputin a clean bill of health.

The investigation was the work of V. D. Bonch-Bruevich, who happened also to be a close friend and collaborator of Lenin. Moreover, it was a whitewash; Bonch-Bruevich omitted to observe that for all his "Orthodoxy" Rasputin revealed to him sectarian habits of speech and thought. Furthermore, Guchkov suggests in his memoirs that Bonch-Bruevich wrote him a letter in which he described Rasputin as a scoundrel and a practitioner of his own break-away brand of sectarianism, though he was not, strictly speaking, a *khlyst.*[9] In his article Bonch-Bruevich had denied the very existence of the *khlysty,* describing the designation as a term of opprobrium invented by Orthodox anti-sectarians.[10] It would be going too far to suggest that had Rasputin not existed the revolutionaries would have invented him—he was beyond any inventive powers known to man—but since he did exist it would have been a major tactical blunder to have him discredited for good, and as any Soviet historian will tell us, when it came to revolutionary tactics, V. I. Lenin was infallible.

Rasputin conducted a spirited defence by telegram from Pokrovskoe, bombarding the tsar and tsarina with communications such as the following:

> Dearest father and mother! See how the devil gains in strength, the evil one. The Duma serves him, it is full of lutionaries [i.e. revolutionaries] and Jews.* And what is it that they want? To get rid of the Lord's anointed as soon as they can. And Guchkov is their ringleader, he spreads slander, and kindles rebellion. Father, the Duma is yours, do as you want with it. What are these questions about Grigorii? It is the devil's doing. No questions should be asked.
>
> Grigorii.[11]

Other cables urged the tsar and tsarina to ensure that the "Cur Iliodor" be properly shut away and well guarded. Olga Lokhtina, who was friendly with both Rasputin and Iliodor, attempted to bring the two men together again, only to receive a note in Rasputin's appalling handwriting, subsequently reproduced in *Iskry*, an illustrated journal, to the effect that, "If the dog Serezhka [Iliodor] is forgiven then the dog will devour us all."[12]

* Despite this remark Rasputin was not an anti-Semite. In later years he would have a Jewish secretary, and during the war did a lot to assist Jews seeking permission to reside in the capital—albeit for a consideration. When a merchant's wife once asked him why he did not use his power to get rid of all the Jews in Russia, since they were putting her husband out of business, he replied: "Are you not ashamed to talk like that, they are people just like you and me, and I expect we all know at least one good Jew, if only our dentist." Indeed in the war years Rasputin had an increasing number of Jewish friends and acquaintances, becoming positively pro-Semitic.

Having managed to convince both her husband and herself that any criticism of Rasputin was an attack upon the dynasty, Alexandra Fedorovna proceeded to recall Rasputin. He returned to the capital on March 13, 1912, and went at once to Tsarskoe Selo to meet the tsarina in Vyroubova's house. This small white single-story building, three minutes' walk from the palace, its telephone connected directly to the palace switchboard, would henceforth be the setting for virtually all Rasputin's meetings with Alexandra.

In the course of the next few days, Rasputin's closest adherents, Anna and her family, notably her father, and also ex-prime-minister Witte, who was hoping to use Rasputin for a political comeback, could be seen displaying open signs of triumph.[13] Their protégé had weathered the worst storm he had so far had to face. It was a storm that had taken its toll of Nicholas. Whatever his shortcomings, his weakness of will and poor judgment, he was the most decent of men. He had been severely pained by the scandal of recent months, especially sò since much of it concerned his wife. He described himself as "suffocating in this atmosphere of gossip, lies and malice,"[14] and it must have been with a sigh of relief that he set off with his family for a spring holiday in their Crimean palace. They travelled in the imperial train, an elaborate affair with eight coaches painted blue and bearing the imperial coat of arms. These trips were expensive, costing 100,000 roubles (at 1914 values 10,800 pounds or 51,250 dollars) each way for security alone;[15] a major factor being the need to dispatch two identical trains—it was never made known which one contained the imperial family, thereby halving the chances of a successful terrorist attack.

We tend to think of Russia in terms of ice and snow, and it comes as a shock to realise that along the Black Sea the climate is close to that of the Mediterranean. The Crimean town of Yalta, with its spectacular backdrop of mountains, had palm trees and cypresses growing in the streets. With a population of thirty thousand, it was Russia's most popular and expensive resort, while the surrounding area was famous for its vineyards. Many wealthy families would have a place in or near Yalta, along with their country estates and their accommodation in the capital. To Russians used to their severe North Continental climate the Crimea, with its sun, its semitropical vegetation and wildlife, the fruit, the smells, and the sound of the cicadas buzzing like katydids in the heat of the day, appeared an unreal paradise. Even the place names were strange. The Crimea had long been inhabited and ruled by Tartars who owed allegiance to the Ottoman Empire, and even after it came under Russian rule in the late eighteenth century, both the Tartar names and the Muslim Tartar population remained–until, that is, the latter were deported *en masse* by Stalin, who thought he would feel safer if they were removed from their homeland and shipped east into Asia.

The imperial family had long been in the habit of taking spring or autumn vacations on their estate, Livadia, two and a quarter miles to the southwest of Yalta. They used to stay in a modest but airy two-story wooden house, overgrown with vine and honeysuckle, in a slightly wild informal garden. It was there that Nicholas's father, Alexander III, had died in October 1894. However, the house became too small for Nicholas and his family. They built a new palace, or rather palazzo, a larger building of white granite in the Florentine style, which was completed in 1911. It too was furnished by Maples, with a colour scheme of the tsarina's choice in which, as usual, mauve predominated. It was in Livadia that the imperial grand duchesses had their first taste of social life, at tea parties and later dances, to which suitable young officers from the Black Sea fleet were invited. It was in the palazzo that Churchill, Stalin, and Roosevelt met for plenary sessions of the Yalta conference in 1945.

Life in Livadia was pleasant and informal. The tsar loved to walk, and prided himself on his ability to exhaust his companions. Even the security forces could reduce their vigilance and devote themselves to more frivolous forms of imperial service, such as their action when Nicholas lost a cap, which was blown over the cliff side. The intrepid policemen brought up a squad of dogs, which they lowered down the cliff face. After retrieving several petticoats, a pair of man's trousers and numerous straw hats they finally came up with the imperial headgear, which was duly restored to its owner; the episode was accorded a special display in the imperial police museum.[16]

The family set off on March 16, and with them went Rasputin; the empress had smuggled him aboard their train. However, he did not stay for long: on learning of his presence Nicholas put him off between St. Petersburg and Moscow, leaving him to follow independently. He arrived in Yalta on the twenty-first, three days after the imperial train. The local paper, *The Russian Riviera,* announced that he was staying at the Hôtel de Russie, one of the best hotels in town. There ensued a *contretemps* that casts a curious light upon his status. The news of his arrival came as a surprise to the minister of the interior, who had arrived in Yalta that day; he had been assured that Rasputin had gone back to Pokrovskoe. The minister then learnt that the local governor knew nothing of Rasputin's presence, since the chief of police had received strict orders from the court to tell no one that he had followed the train south. There ensued an abortive attempt to prosecute the paper for publishing false information, since Rasputin's presence was a court secret. The attempt was abandoned and the police contented themselves with removing his name from the hotel register. He only remained in Yalta for a few days before going back to Pokrovskoe.

It is easy to understand why the court should have wanted to keep Rasputin's presence a secret, although it is startling to see the tsar and tsarina actually deceiving their own minister. However, there is a possibility that they had wind of a plot to murder Rasputin. Some time earlier the leader of a right-wing clique had suggested to the mayor of Yalta, a fiery and excitable Georgian patriot named I. A. Dumbadze, that many Russians hoped that "my dear, inimitable Ivan Antonovich would drown the dirty adventurer in the Black Sea."[17] Dumbadze took the advice to heart but was reluctant to act on his own initiative. He sent a "for your eyes only" telegram to the head of the secret police, requesting permission to do away with Rasputin on the ferry between Sebastopol and Yalta. The police chief showed the telegram to the minister of the interior, who ordered him to do nothing. He subsequently learned that Dumbadze's plan was, in his words, "hazy."[18] There was a vague idea of luring Rasputin to the top of a cliff, robbing him and throwing him over, giving the impression that he had been attacked by bandits. Dumbadze waited in vain for an official order to proceed with his assassination.

Russian public life in those days was not without its contradictions. While some government servants sent telegrams proposing Rasputin's assassination, others devoted themselves to protecting his life. He had, as General Spiridovich puts it, achieved a semi-official status. Although he had no formal office, the police understood that as a person close to the imperial family he should be protected. From now on he would seldom travel without some kind of plain-clothes escort. There was surveillance as well as protection; the prime minister was anxious to learn all he could about Rasputin, and had his police chief, Stepan Beletsky, place him under observation. He set a team of "experienced undercover surveillance agents" (*konspirativnykh filerov*) on him to keep a record of his doings.[19]

In the capital their task had been relatively simple, but surveillance in Pokrovskoe was harder. Beletsky had installed a permanent agent there, but he had his problems; Rasputin was very popular in the village. Moreover, there was another difficulty. As Beletsky, a prolific and virtually unreadable memoirist, puts it, in a bureaucratic style that is beyond parody, Rasputin had befriended the "civil service element" (*sluzhebniy element*) in Pokrovskoe, which, he said, consisted of the local postmaster. This meant that Beletsky's man could not wire his reports from there and had to take long, uncomfortable trips to the next telegraph office.[20]

Rasputin passed the rest of the summer and early autumn in Siberia, while in European Russia the tsar and tsarina were occupied with the commemoration of Napoleon's defeat a century before. This culminated in a celebration on September 8 upon the battlefield of Borodino. From there the family travelled west for a shooting holiday on their Polish estates of Belovezhe and Spala. Belovezhe was the finest shoot in Europe, a splendid forest with a remarkable head of game: elk, wild boar, deer, and above all a magnificent herd of European bison, sixteen hundred strong. Spala was a more modest affair, a quiet hunting lodge in a forest with less variety of game. The shoot was not without its ceremonials. The guns were woken at 7:00 A.M. by a hunting horn, while a military band played to them at lunch. Only stags of ten points or more were shot. Nicholas had shot twenty-six pointers, but these could only be killed when the rut was on. The evenings were largely informal affairs, but there were traditions: anyone shooting a stag on the first or last day of the shoot was required to consume a bottle of champagne, drunk out of a strange horn vessel.[21] Nicholas, though a good shot, was no sufferer from blind blood lust. He would often let driven stags go by him, and could never bring himself to shoot hares.

Shortly after they arrived at Belovezhe the tsarevich had an accident. He was playing about in his bathroom, and as he jumped into his large sunken tub he knocked his knee against a ledge.[22] A few moments later he fainted and was carried to his bed. His mother and the house physician, Botkin, treated him, while the lunchtime concerts were cancelled to give him a chance to rest. Fortunately he responded to treatment and he and the rest of the family duly travelled on to Spala. As he left Belovezhe the tsar observed that he was looking forward to next year's shoot; the guest of honour was to have been the kaiser, who had invited himself, but he had put him off to 1914.

Although Aleksey had improved he was still unable to walk, and was carried everywhere by his sailor, Derevenko. But now came a second disaster. In the course of a rather bumpy drive with his mother Aleksey had a relapse. The inner bleeding started again and caused a large tumour to form in his groin. It was very painful and dangerous, threatening blood poisoning and peritonitis. At first the boy kept screaming with pain, but as he weakened the screams turned into an increasingly hoarse wail. He knew that he was likely to die, and asked his mother whether death would make the pain stop. He also asked her for a little headstone over his grave, begging her to have him buried "in the light," under a blue sky. For the first time his mother understood that the eight-year-old could appreciate that he might be dying.

Two surgeons, Fedorov and Rauchfuss, were summoned from the capital, but after examining the child they said that there was nothing they could do. Fedorov refused to open the tumour, since his patient might easily bleed to death. For the first time bulletins were issued about the tsarevich's condition, and guarded though they were they grew increasingly pessimistic until the evening when Rauchfuss and Fedorov concocted a text which would be a suitable preliminary to the announcement of his death. Only a miracle, said Fedorov, could save him now; by which he meant the spontaneous reabsorption of the tumour. In the meantime Aleksey was given the last sacraments.

In her despair Alexandra Fedorovna turned to Rasputin. Anna

Vyroubova sent a telegram to him in Pokrovskoe telling him that the tsarevich was dying. According to his daughter, Rasputin received it during lunch, which he interrupted to pray hard before his favourite icon, the Virgin of Kazan. He prayed for a long time and when he had finished and had crossed himself a final time his face was grey and streaked with sweat. He went to the telegraph office and sent the following telegram to the tsarina: "The illness is not serious, don't let the doctors tire him." He later sent a second one saying that God had heard his prayers and Aleksey would recover.

Next morning the tsarevich was better, and soon the doctors said he was out of danger. Immense care was taken by General D. T. Hesketh, the commandant of the Western Railways and the son of a Lancashire Hesketh who had become a Russian citizen in the middle of the last century, to ensure that the train rode smoothly. The brakes were not used once on the entire journey. Once back in Tsarskoe Selo, the tsarevich completed his recovery, although a contraction of the leg muscles made him lame for a year.

Rasputin had proved capable of healing at a distance before. He was known to soothe the tsarevich and talk his headaches away over the telephone from St. Petersburg to Tsarskoe Selo. But the Spala incident was different, different indeed from any reliable account of his previous cures. These had all come from people who believed in Rasputin and his powers and whose testimony can neither be cross-checked nor taken on trust. There can be no doubt about the events described above; they have been confirmed by too many independent observers, not all of them sympathetic to Rasputin. (The only discrepancy in their accounts concerns the initial accident. Some memoirists write of the tsarevich damaging his knee in a rowing-boat.) Aleksey was believed to be dying; the doctors gave him up; Rasputin was asked to help; he sent a telegram; Aleksey got better. In fairness it should be said that Professor Fedorov had observed that there was one medical option left, a desperate card he dared not play; he probably meant surgery, but it is just possible that he played it and kept quiet about it afterwards. If this unlikely contingency is abandoned, we are faced with the alternative explanations of coincidence or a power of prayer and healing that knew no distance.

Whichever choice the reader may make, he may rest assured that the empress did not believe it was coincidence. Her faith in Rasputin's intercessionary powers was confirmed once and for all. Henceforward his position would be unassailable.

CHAPTER 13

Leningrad is exceptionally suited to catastrophes, said Anna Akhmatova, that cold river, which always has heavy clouds over it, those threatening sunsets, that frightening moon. The black water with yellow reflections—it's all terrifying. I can't imagine how disasters and catastrophes look in Moscow; there is nothing like that there.

LIDYA CHUKOVSKAYA,
Conversations with Akhmatova

ACCOUNTS OF LIFE in prewar St. Petersburg emphasise moral decay and a sense of impending doom—and not all the descriptions have the benefit of hindsight. Alexander Blok had long known that his country would fall apart, and when the revolution came he was ready for it, had been preparing himself for it for years. Blok's sensitivity to his age was so acute that it was tantamount to the power of prophecy. But one did not require his nose for disaster to experience the sense of an ending.

By 1913 the notion that the time was out of joint had become a cliché of popular journalism. Early that year the painter Repin had exhibited a huge, and to some eyes even today, bad painting of Ivan the Terrible, having inadvertently killed his son, with a lot of blood about. When it was slashed by a vandal, the editor of *Vechernee Vremya,* a St. Petersburg evening paper, observed: "This disgraceful and incomprehensible action, this piece of savagery is not an isolated instance; it is a genuine sign of the times, when there are no values, no education, a total absence of moral sense."[1]

A fortnight later the same paper ran a piece on contemporary theatre, which began: "Without doubt we are living through a tragic period in the history of Russia and perhaps of the world." After a fatuous attempt to account for this by a change in the earth's axis, the author continued, "No matter why, we are living through tragic times. The tragedy of morality, the family, society, individuals, nations." The grave tone of the article was marred by its position next to a photograph of Peter Alupkin, a talking cat, black and white with a white face, black ears and head, currently appearing at the Pallas Theatre.

The press reflected a sense of decline in other ways. A new method for treating sexual neurasthenia was featured on the front page: "A characteristic of our neurotic age, there are always many people who suffer in secret from sexual neurasthenia as well as from the other kind."[2]

It is easy enough to caricature a society by its press, yet the sense that an old order had ended extended well beyond the newspapers. In 1913 a critic of the regime writing under the name of "P. Vassili" observed that St. Petersburg society had given itself over entirely to pleasure-seeking, choosing to ignore the rising tide of anarchism and revolution. There was a widespread atmosphere of cynical indifference, a lack of loyalty to the monarch. The one driving force was a feverish urge to get rich quick:

> It is a kind of frenzy that has seized people on every hand, and that frenzy perhaps, unknown even to those that are attacked by it, may be the expression of a feverish haste to get the most they can out of a state of affairs that cannot last for much longer.[3]

The sense of doom manifests itself in another way, in the remarkable epidemic of suicides over these years. Suicide had become fashionable, as a course of action to be adopted by jilted lovers and young persons down on their luck or bored to despair. Reports of adolescent suicides of this kind are a regular feature of the press: a random sampling of the *Petersburg Gazette* for the first ten days of April 1913 produces twenty-two suicide reports, including ten cases on the sixth. Only two of the victims were over twenty-five, and twenty of them were girls.

This was the city to which Rasputin now returned in triumph. He no longer lodged with friends. From 1912 onward he had rented an apartment of his own, moving twice before finally finding what he wanted: flat number 20 at 63-64 Gorokhavaya Street, Tel: 646-46. He would live there, visits to Pokrovskoe apart, for the remainder of his life. It was not a particularly smart address. Gorokhavaya Street, today Dzerzhinsky Street, lies in the western part of the city, running north-south from the Admiralteistvo (Decembrist Square) to the Zagorodniy Prospekt. It was conveniently close to the train station for Tsarskoe Selo, and the house itself was opposite police headquarters. Indeed, the kind of overcoat favoured by plain-clothes men was known as a Gorokhovoyo coat. In *The Idiot,* it is on that street that Dostoevsky locates the dark house of the Rogozhin family, the scene of the murder that is the climax of the book. Rasputin had a third-floor flat overlooking a courtyard. Its great attraction was a set of back stairs that enabled him to come and go as he pleased, escaping the eye of the doorman or *dvornik,* the equivalent of the Parisian *concierge,* who, like his French counterpart, could be expected to be a police informer. The flat had a large antechamber, to the right of which was a dining room, followed by Rasputin's bedroom and a bathroom, which he never used, preferring to go to the public steam baths. On the other side was a large room he used for his receptions, with a series of chairs arranged around the walls, in which a samovar was kept lit, providing hot water all day. The flat was furnished simply, with plain practical furniture, and a number of icons, the decorations consisting of vases of cut flowers and bowls of fresh fruit. It was here that Rasputin held court in the final and most influential period of his life. He was a public figure now. The mere fact that he had survived the scandals of the spring was a further index of his prestige. As one of the tsarina's ladies-in-waiting put it:

> When he returned to the capital his clientèle increased. Professional political intriguers, unscrupulous senior officials, who hoped that he might casually mention their names to the authorities, junior officials who hoped he might speak of them to their

chiefs, all came to his flat. Society women as well as many of his own class came to him, some from curiosity, others with the hope that it might bring them into contact with the court.[4]

✧ ✧ ✧

To understand why Rasputin was beginning to attract such a following one has to appreciate the role played in tsarist Russia by the petition. The country was of course governed by laws, but beyond mere law there always existed the personal will of the tsar. Since he was all-powerful he could override his own laws—and was constantly being requested to do so. The head of his personal chancellery handled over seventy thousand petitions a year. They were broken down into forty different categories, from "Exceptions to the rules governing the registration of births, marriages and deaths of Old Believers" to "Petitions senseless and anonymous" [sic]. In most cases the petitioner asked the tsar to make an exception for reasons of natural justice, hardship, or the personal qualities of the petitioner.[5] They regularly began with the expression: "Had it been permissible under the law I should never have taken it upon myself to trouble His Imperial Majesty . . ."[6] In other words, seventy thousand times a year the tsar was asked to go against his own laws. In a manner reminiscent of procedures in France of the *ancien régime,* the law might be the law, but there was always a good chance that it could be overridden in a special instance. The principle of special instance operated from the highest levels of the administrative machine to the lowest—where a five-rouble note might persuade a local court official to adjust matters in the donor's favour. Since Rasputin clearly had immediate and effective access to the tsar and tsarina, he could be of immense service to any one of the seventy thousand clients who felt theirs to be a special case.

It was this irregular nature of Russian public life, the personal quality imparted to it from the very top, that made Rasputin a political force. As yet the petitioners who came to him were relatively few—it would take the war to establish him as an unofficial *maître des requêtes* and the last resort of anyone requiring the impossible. By the end, according to one eyewitness, himself a client:

> Three to four hundred people would call on Rasputin daily . . . one day it was seven hundred . . . I saw uniformed generals, students, school girls asking for financial support. There were officers' wives asking for favours for their husbands, parents asking for military exemption for their sons.[7]

✧ ✧ ✧

In these prewar years Rasputin never had three hundred callers a day —a figure which must itself be open to some doubt, while seven hundred would have created a queue stretching half a city block. Yet even now the number of people turning to him was significant, and a direct reflection of his supposed influence, the belief that he was closer to the tsar than any minister or official.

Rasputin's attitude to his supplicants is revealing. He did not exploit his position outrageously; that is to say, he seems to have been modest in his demand for bribes. Certainly he did not go short of presents and was prepared to ask for money from those in a position to give it, but in all the criticism, informed and otherwise, levelled against him there is little to suggest that he was greedy, or that his principal motive was financial gain. This is all the more remarkable since the bribe had always been an integral feature of Russian public life and was recognised as such. It was not until the eighteenth century that provincial administrators received a salary; up to that time they were appointed to their posts *na kormlenie,* for nourishment: in other words they were expected to live by extortion. The assumption that public servants needed to "have their hands warmed" was as true in the early twentieth century as it is today, when whisky, jeans and long-playing records can open doors that would otherwise remain closed. Admittedly, in the latter years of the old regime a little delicacy was often welcome. An English businessman who needed the goodwill of a senior civil servant in 1912 appeared in his office one blazing July day carrying an umbrella. When asked why, he bet the official a substantial sum that it would rain within ten minutes. They waited, he lost his bet, and paid up on the spot; his request was granted without further ado.

Rasputin did not exploit his position to amass a fortune. He took little interest in money as such, lacking the abstract turn that takes a cerebral delight in the accumulation of wealth. By nature he was a sensualist, not a banker. He enjoyed spending money and also enjoyed giving it away. Far from exploiting his humbler supplicants, he often appears to have helped them, witness the following account by an ex-police chief based on agents' reports:

> Almost one half of the visitors who called on Rasputin consisted of poor people who hoped to get some material assistance from him. They were never disappointed, for Rasputin never once refused to help anyone who needed money. Whenever a well-to-do caller left a pile of money behind him Rasputin distributed some of it to the next poor petitioners waiting to see him . . .
>
> Very often too it happened that simple country people would call on him for no reason other than curiosity, and because they wanted very much to talk with the man who, though an ordinary peasant, had found access to the court. Rasputin generally saw such visitors and made these doubly welcome . . . and it was especially such visitors from the country who could be sure of leaving with a present.[8]

Although it is hard to believe that Rasputin passed every rouble he received to the deserving poor, he did indeed keep his pockets stuffed with bank-notes, which he would distribute with conspicuous generosity.[9] This is not to say that he was disinterested, far from it, yet his behaviour tells us a lot about what motivated him–a particular kind of peasant ambition. He wanted not money, but consideration, and the money he took, or distributed, was material proof of the situation he had created for himself. That people from all walks of life should come to him for help was another demonstration of his importance. In like manner he was not interested in power for its own sake, except in so far as he needed to keep his position secure. It was enough that his advice be heard, that his recommendations be considered, for the world to see that Grigorii Efimovich had arrived. Money and influence had symbolic significance as an index of success, like a mink coat worn on a summer's day.

This is not to say that he did not exploit his situation, any more than he was a disinterested healer and easer of souls. Just as he abused his spiritual authority to have sex with his patients, he exploited his new-found power over his petitioners, who were frequently called upon for payment in kind. A surveillance report filed by an agent called Terekhov a few years later recorded:

> 3rd November
>
> A woman wishing to have her sick officer husband transferred to the capital calls on Rasputin.
>
> When she left the flat she told the porter what a strange man he was.
>
> "Some girl let me in and took me into a reception room: then Rasputin came out to me and said, 'Take your coat off and come in here' . . . He did not really listen to my request, but started to stroke my face and breasts saying, 'Kiss me, I have come to like you.' Then he scrawled some note and approached me again. 'Kiss me, kiss me, I like you.' He kept the note saying, 'I am cross with you, come back tomorrow.'" The agent asked her if she would return and she replied:
>
> "No, if I come back I'll have to give him what he wants, I can't do that so I must not return."[10]

The lady was fortunate compared to another petitioner who wanted her husband returned from administrative exile in Siberia, and who asked Rasputin to help. He said he would if she would sleep with him.

> Neither her tears, her entreaties, her talk of her children had any effect, and taking advantage of her distraught condition and regardless of the fact that there were people in the next room, he took her by force, and then visited her several times in her hotel, constantly promising that he would arrange matters, and take a petition to the tsar from her . . . She was eventually persuaded to return home. Rasputin did nothing about the petition because, as he put it, "she was insolent." The room in Rasputin's flat next to the dining room, where the bed was, and to which no one was admitted when he was not alone there, could tell many similar tales. The surveillance also reports cases when dishevelled petitioners of the lower classes ran from the room screaming, cursing and spitting, while attempts were made to pacify them and get them out of the flat.[11]

There are plenty of well-attested tales of such sexual exploitation, but they do not mean that Rasputin necessarily had to rely on blackmail and force to have his way. They suggest that he was sexually aroused by power, by subjecting women to his will. Although he would sometimes indeed resort to blackmail, or something close to physical force, his strength of character and emotional indifference to the consequences of a rebuff were usually enough. As one observer wrote of his hold over women, shortly after his death: "His strength derived from the power of his personality, and his ability immediately to assume an attitude of the most extreme familiarity towards any person of the opposite sex who came into contact with him."[12]

He unsettled women meeting him for the first time by his unnerving manner, while his disjointed conversation might have led one to believe one was dealing with a half-wit, had it not been for his disturbingly concentrated stare:

> Rasputin arrived shortly after eight. He entered Varvara Petrovna's salon for the first time, with a free easy gait, and striding across the carpet mounted an attack on his hostess with his opening words.
>
> "What have you hung on your walls, little mother? It's a real museum, you could feed five villages with what hangs on your walls, see how you live while peasants starve."
>
> Varvara Ivanovna began to introduce Rasputin to her guests. Immediately he would ask each one if she were married, and where her husband was, why she had come alone.
>
> "If you'd come together I could see what kind of a life you have together . . ."
>
> He carried on a merry conversation, joking and clowning. Above all I noticed his eyes; with a fixed steady gaze his eyes blazed with a kind of phosphorescent flame. It was as if he were feeling out his listeners with his eyes, and sometimes he spoke more and more slowly, dwelling on his words, getting muddled, as if his mind were elsewhere. Suddenly he would pull himself together again, grow embarrassed, try to change the subject. I noticed that his stare had an extraordinary effect, especially on women, who found it dreadfully embarrassing, would grow disturbed and begin to look at him timidly, and were often drawn

to come up and start talking or listening to him. After staring at someone like that he would begin to talk to somebody else, and then suddenly turn back to the one he had stared at twenty minutes before, and breaking off his conversation would say:

"It's bad, mother, bad, yes, you cannot live like that, look, try to make amends, it's a business, love, yes . . . well."

Changing the subject again he would start moving round the room while people would whisper that he had divined something, spoken the truth, that he had second sight, and a nervous *exalté* mood would descend, the kind of mood you find in the proximity of holy men in monasteries.[13]

Rasputin's following of enthusiastic ladies in search of God, the *rasputinki,* as they were derisively known to unbelievers, now gathered regularly in Rasputin's flat, where they met for meals. Although the flat would be decorated with expensive flowers, and there were also large baskets of fruit, the food was basically plain peasant fare: fish soup, which Rasputin adored, fish, black bread, eggs, dessert. Rasputin never ate meat of any kind. There would be plenty to drink, however. Rasputin scarcely touched spirits but liked red wine and was excessively fond of Madeira. Russian Madeira is a strange and wonderful thing. It is a domestic fortified wine that can have remarkable properties. In Gogol's *Government Inspector,* the mayor of a provincial town boasts: "We have some local Madeira that does not look much, but it can still fell an elephant." It was that kind, and not the delicate product of the Islands, that Rasputin drank, and often enough it felled him.

The meals had their rituals: Rasputin, who dispensed with knives and forks and thought that a man with a beard had little enough need of napkins, would sit at the head of the table and use food as a means of teaching his followers humility. He would spoon mountains of sugar into his admirers' tea, which was considered a form of grace, or would bite into a pickled cucumber, and then offer the remains to a disciple to finish. Alternatively, he would solemnly distribute hard-boiled eggs, which were duly eaten, while the shells would be preserved as precious relics of the meal.[14] Sometimes Rasputin would take the process of humiliation further. After dipping his fingers into a dish of jam he would turn to a woman and say: "'Humble yourself, lick it clean, lick it clean.' Whereupon the lady in question would duly suck his fingers free of jam in public."[15]

He preached that salvation could be achieved through humiliation and the annihilation of pride, and rejection of his advances was considered an act of pride. The teaching is strangely reminiscent of the French erotic masterpiece *The Story of O,* the account of a search for liberation and transcendence through sexual humiliation. Perhaps Rasputin's activities should be thought of in terms of a spiritual eroticism as opposed to mere animal appetite. Certainly he accompanied his dining-room rituals with garbled preaching. One of his petitioners recalls a first visit. Rasputin suddenly handed her paper and pencil and ordered her to record his words:

> I began to write: "Rejoice in simplicity, woe to the rebellious and the wicked, the sun warms them not . . . Forgive me Lord, I am a sinner, I am worldly, and my love is a worldly love. Lord, work miracles, humble us. We are thine. Great is Thy Love for us, do not be angry with us. Send obedience to my soul and the joy of Your Love and Grace. Save and help me O Lord.
>
> "Take that and read, read with your heart," he said.[16]

On such occasions he would pass out typewritten copies of poems he had written, in the style of the *Song of Songs*. They were largely incomprehensible, save for the occasional phrase such as "Fair and high are the mountains but my love is higher and fairer still, because love is God,"[17] an equation of sacred love and profane passion that is the cornerstone of Rasputin's special version of the sectarian heresy.

He went on to preach the need for humility, saying that his "young ladies" were deceitful, full of guile, for he could see into their hearts. Then they all went into the next room, where there was a piano:

> "Play *Along the High Road,*" he said suddenly and without relation to what had passed before. A lady sat down and started to play. He got up, began to rock in time, moving and stamping his feet. He danced unexpectedly gracefully and well, moving

across the room light as a feather, squatting and shooting out his legs, approaching the ladies and luring first one and then another out to partner him. One came out with a kerchief, and moved up to meet him. No one was surprised. It seemed that dancing in broad daylight like that was the most natural thing in the world.[18]

Rasputin could be startlingly rude and abrupt, complaining to his maids about the behaviour of his guests, for example. He constantly infringed on all codes of social behaviour, but never appeared to be acting out of a desire to be clever or provocative. He had little rational understanding of the impact of his actions, and gave the impression that he did not consider them to be unusual. He was his own man and did as he pleased, and that was that.[19]

The mature Rasputin had little sense of inner contradiction. He delighted in every manifestation of his "broad peasant nature," and one of the most important of these was his passionate love of drink, music, and the dance. He was the kind of Russian who felt, usually after a glass or two, that although he might be having a good time, that good time was still incomplete, too quiet and inactive. The supreme good time required music and the controlled release of energy combined with a surrender to ecstasy that could only be found, as Rasputin puts it, by setting off into dance, *pustit'sya v plyas.* When it was suggested to Rasputin that dancing was incompatible with the dignity of a *starets,* he defended himself with vigour: "But one prays to God as well in dancing as in a monastery. One praises Him in the joy that, in His goodness, He has created. David danced before the Ark of the Lord."[20]

St. Petersburg night life had changed a lot in the past decade. There had never been a shortage of restaurants and other places of entertainment, but until the early years of the century these had been reserved for men and lady-professionals only. No respectable woman could be seen eating out. From 1906 onward, as part of the general loosening of moral standards that followed the Japanese war and the revolution, society women began to be seen in the smart restaurants of the capital, Cubat, Donan, Contant, Ernest, The Bear. In an effort to preserve their morals the chief of police ordered that the bolts be removed from the doors of the private dining rooms with which such establishments were generously provided to ensure privacy at intimate dinner parties.

Rasputin loved night life, and in the latter years it became his main amusement. He was especially fond of the Villa Rhode, an establishment on the outskirts of the city on the right bank of the Neva, and a little more easygoing than some. He loved to sit the night through there, often drinking himself into a stupor, a process that required an alarming number of bottles of Madeira, in the company of hangers-on, prostitutes, or society ladies. He loved to fill his coat pockets with ladies' trinkets, scent, silks, and bon-bons, which the singers from the chorus would rifle as he cried out delightedly, "The gypsies are robbing me." He was also to be seen in more respectable establishments, such as the restaurant of the Astoria Hotel, which still exists, more or less, to this day. The headwaiter in 1914 was Joseph Vecchi, an Italian, who in the thirties and forties became a familiar feature of London's night life. He managed a restaurant, Hungaria, staffed almost entirely by White Russians that he passed off as Magyars. He had vivid and not entirely pleasant recollections of Rasputin, who was not the kind of guest to gladden a headwaiter's heart. He recalled that his favourite dish was *solyanka d'esturgeon,* characteristically a typical Russian dish, fish and vegetable soup, but made with the most expensive ingredients. Vecchi did not care for the way Rasputin ate, observing that he "grabbled" [sic] his food.[21]

After dinner it was the fashion to visit a nightclub, the best-known being the Aquarium, an establishment with glass walls behind which there were tanks of brightly coloured fish. After the nightclub Rasputin loved to go on to the gypsies. Fond as he was of Russian song and dance, if Rasputin ever loved anything with steady passion it was gypsy music. The gypsies lived in families on the city outskirts. In the capital they were to be found in Novaya Derevnya—new village—in a district known as The Islands, where every extravagant evening out would end. Gypsies from Moscow were deemed to be vastly superior, more authentic, better singers than any others, and the greatest of all the gypsy singers was Varya Panina:

> Even when she was well on in years this very ugly woman always dressed in black, cast a spell over her audience with her

dark pathetic voice. At the end of her life she married an army cadet of eighteen. On her deathbed she asked her brother to accompany her on the guitar while she sang one of her greatest successes, "The Swan Song," and she breathed her last on the final note.[22]

You can see gypsies in Moscow to this day, in the gypsy theatre on the Leningrad Prospekt, next to the Sovetskaya Hotel, once Moscow's most famous restaurant, Yar, and one of the great gypsy locations. The gypsies look quite different from Russians, with dark skins and black or hennaed hair. They favour bright-coloured clothes–red, violet, purple. The men wear baggy trousers tucked into high boots, and wide-brimmed black hats, the women long gathered skirts, shawls, and scarves. Even today they are evidently a race apart. Yet neither their performances nor even their weddings which are still held in the old Yar restaurant, begin to recreate the old and magical impact of "the gypsies."

Although their women were often strikingly beautiful, the gypsies were never prostitutes. There was only one way an infatuated young man could possess a gypsy, however rich or wellborn he might be, and that was marriage and a colossal gift to the family. Indeed, many of the oldest families in Russia have gypsy blood. The gypsies were essentially entertainers, or rather enchanters. A party would make an appointment to visit a family at one or two in the morning. They would be shown into a big, brightly lit room with a long table and some wicker chairs. Opposite sat the gypsy women, their men standing behind them with their guitars. The oldest woman would be seated in the middle of the line. Then they would start to sing: "They could transcend the barest walls, warm the coldest most calculating hearts with their wizardry. They were sheer hypnosis."[23]

The best account of their impact comes from a Scotsman, Robert Bruce Lockhart, who was assistant British consul in Moscow before and during World War One, and whose *Memoirs of a Secret Agent* is a minor classic in its evocation of Russia before and during revolution. Here, he is recalling a Moscow singer:

Maria Nicolaevna's . . . art . . . was on a far higher plane than the singing of mere drinking songs. When she sang alone her voice, now passionate, now appealing, then sinking to an infinite sadness, my heart melted. This gypsy music is in fact more intoxicating, more dangerous than opium, or women, or drink, and, although champagne is a necessary adjunct to the enjoyment there is a plaintiveness in its appeal which to the Slav and Celtic races is almost irresistible. Far better than words it expresses the pent-up and stifled desires of mankind. It induces a delicious melancholy which is half lyrical, half sensuous . . . It breaks down all reserves of restraint. It will drive a man to money lenders and even to crime. Doubtless it is the most primitive of all forms of music, somewhat similar in its appeal (may the spirit of Maria Nicolaevna forgive me for the sacrilegious comparison) to the negro spirituals. And it is very costly. It has been responsible for the bulk of my debts. Yet tomorrow if I had thousands and the desire to squander them, there is no entertainment in New York, Paris, Berlin or London or indeed anywhere in the world, which I should choose in preference to a gypsy evening at Strelnya in Moscow or the Villa Rhode in St. Petersburg.[24]

One of the author's most precious possessions, which miraculously accompanied his mother's family out of Russia, is an old worn-out record of Varya Panina singing two gypsy romances. Through years of wear you can still hear her rich, deep, contralto voice, a strange blend of melancholy and extraordinary power, sounding like an infinitely enriched and melodious Edith Piaf, conveying a profound melancholy of expression, the great artist's capacity to make one feel that her song has captured the whole of life's all too intermittent richness.

CHAPTER 14

It is tempting to try to label Rasputin, to define and contain him. With his love of drink, dance, gypsy music, his belief in ecstasy and the search for God through passion, he might be thought of as the essential Dionysiac. Certainly he trusted his impulses, preferred action to contemplation, and was anything but a quietist. Yet such labels are misleading, if only because they imply an element of intellectual choice; they encourage one to forget that for all his power Rasputin had the tastes, ideas and appetites of a peasant who found himself in a unique position, able to do more or less what he wanted. His behaviour is an ironic comment on the ideas of those nineteenth-century thinkers–Herzen, Tolstoy, Dostoevsky–who supposed that Russia's salvation was to come from the heart of its uneducated masses.

The Dionysiac label is the more misleading since Rasputin was not simply some primitive incarnation of the spirit of ecstasy. In the later prewar years it was generally supposed that he was a significant political force, that he could make or break politicians. The belief was correct in one sense. Because he was close to the tsarina, jealous of his influence, and highly vindictive, no one, not even a minister, could afford to cross him. Yet his "political" influence was of an essentially personal kind, concerning itself with the granting of favours and the making of appointments. He was a courtier, not a politician, and his political views were limited, naive, and had little impact:

> Such views as he had were simple enough. He was nothing more than a plain Russian patriot and genuine monarchist. Monarchy meant for him a kind of religion . . . The subtleties of so-called higher politics went far beyond his horizon, and he was quite unable to comprehend what various parties or groups in the Duma, or the newspapers were ultimately aiming at. His fundamental principle in politics consisted simply in the *pacification* . . . of the enemies of the tsar.[1]

There are only two instances of his attempting to affect policy in the prewar years. He tried, without success, to persuade the prime minister, Kokovtsov, to abolish the government monopoly on the sale of liquor. We can only guess at the motive, but he was probably acting on behalf of some of the financiers who had begun to try to exploit his influence. His second political intervention was more successful and more interesting. As the chief of the secret police wrote:

> However artless he was in politics he took a very great interest in all that appeared to him to be of practical importance and value for the people. Even in St. Petersburg drawing-rooms he still remained enough of a peasant to be able to sympathise with the peasants and to understand their needs.[2]

For him the most important need of all was peace. Rasputin was utterly opposed to war, which he viewed as an affair in which a great many peasants were taken from their land to be maimed and killed. His pacifism emerged clearly in 1913, when his country all but became involved in a war between Southern Slavs and Turks in the Balkans. Jingoistic patriots demanded that Holy Russia come to the aid of her co-religionists, and Rasputin did all he could to avert what he believed would be a disaster. In a newspaper interview he attacked the militant patriots, decrying war as anti-Christian:

> Let the Turks and the foreigners devour each other. They are blind and that is their misfortune. They will gain nothing and simply advance the hour of their death. While we, leading a peaceful harmonious life, will once more rise above all others.[8]

Rasputin's advocacy of peace went beyond newspaper articles. He approached the tsar directly, going on his knees and imploring him to keep Russia out of the war. It is impossible to determine the extent to which Rasputin may have influenced Nicholas. Certainly he was more disposed to listen to Rasputin than to many conventional advisors. Nor can one dispute the fact that on this occasion Rasputin's political judgment was sounder than that of the moustachioed chauvinists who urged the tsar to sweep through the Balkans and fly the flag of Orthodoxy from the Hagia Sophia in what had once been Constantinople—1913 was a bad time to start a crusade. At all events, whether or not Rasputin was personally responsible for keeping Russia out of the war, he always believed that it was essentially his doing.

1913 was also the tricentenary year of the Romanov dynasty. The event was commemorated by the striking of a special one-rouble coin depicting Nicholas II in the foreground, while behind him loomed the bearded profile of his ancestor Mikhail Romanov, the founder of the dynasty. To uncharitable eyes the latter bore an unfortunate resemblance to Rasputin. The celebration included such events as an imperial progress to the Ipatiev convent at Kostroma where Tsar Mikhail had received a deputation of boyars begging him to ascend the throne. (By an uncanny coincidence, the house in Ekaterinburg in which the last tsar and his family were murdered by the Bolsheviks was called the Ipatiev house.) There was also a gala performance of Glinka's *A Life for the Tsar*. The most patriotic of all Russian operas, it tells the story of Ivan Susanin, who laid down his life for Tsar Mikhail Fedorovich, done to death by treacherous Poles. Foreign dignitaries seeing the piece for the first time found it hard to follow, and with reason. For fear of offending Polish sensibilities, Poland having since become a reluctant member of the Russian Empire, the climactic scene depicting Susanin's murder was omitted, and to unfamiliar eyes the opera seemed to end a bit flatly. At another ceremony, a thanksgiving service in the Kazan cathedral on the Nevsky Prospekt, now the museum of atheism, Rasputin ran afoul of one of his archenemies, Rodzyanko.

As president of the Duma, Rodzyanko had a weak man's touchiness. He had taken careful steps to ensure that "his" members were situated as prominently as possible for the service and was outraged to discover that Rasputin had taken a place in front of the block of places he had had reserved for them:

> He was dressed in a magnificent Russian tunic of crimson silk, patent-leather top-boots, black cloth full trousers and a peasant's coat. Over his dress he wore a pectoral cross on a finely wrought gold chain.[4]

Rodzyanko indignantly asked him what he was doing there, and disregarding the official invitation card which Rasputin produced, he threatened to have him thrown out by the serjeants-at-arms unless he left at once.

> With a heavy groan and a murmured: "Oh Lord forgive him such a sin!" Rasputin rose slowly to his feet and shooting a hasty look of anger at me slunk away . . . a Court Cossack helped him on with his magnificent sable-lined coat and placed him in a car. Rasputin drove away.[5]

In itself the incident is trivial, but it is revealing of the irregular quality of public life. Rodzyanko considered Rasputin's prominent position to be a slight to the dignity of the Duma. Disregarding the fact that Rasputin was there by official invitation from, as he put it, "persons more highly placed than you," Rodzyanko resorted to the threat of force in order to get what he wanted, an objective more important to him than protocol or ultimately the rule of law itself. Small wonder that it had proved necessary to screw down the desk lids in the Imperial Duma to prevent deputies from making constant use of them for purposes of banging.

Rasputin was growing increasingly aware of the hostility towards him. His attitude to his enemies was identical to that of his most fervent supporters, Vyroubova and the tsarina. It was a simple matter of the confrontation of good and evil, a point that emerges in a characteristically garbled telegram he sent shortly after the clash with Rodzyanko. It was addressed to Major General V. N. Voyeikov, the palace commandant. The translation is accurate and no more confused than the original.

> Look my dear fellow, not even porridge tastes good unless you are used to it; now there are millions of wasps so believe that in matters of the soul we must all be trusted friends, a small group perhaps but of one mind while they are many but scattered and their rage shall have no power but the spirit of truth is with us look at Annushka's face it is your greatest comfort.
>
> Grigorii.[6]

The most vicious wasp of all was the monk Iliodor. Unstable at the best of times and dreadfully ambitious, he was now even more convinced of Rasputin's evil, since he rightly held him responsible for his disgrace. The authorities had finally succeeded in shutting down his Tsaritsyn establishment, but even in his confinement in the Florishchev monastery Iliodor continued the fight against "the holy devil," as he called him. He sent a series of letters to the synod and to Vyroubova, giving details of Rasputin's sexual misdemeanours, and cursing Over-Procurator Sabler for supporting him:

> You have bowed down before the licentious *khlyst* Grisha Rasputin as if he were the devil. You are a traitor and an apostate. Your corrupt hands are unworthy to hold the most holy tiller of God's church, the bride of Christ. They should be shining the devil's boots in hell. I say this from a sense of priestly duty . . .[7]

He called on the synod to unfrock him:

> Either indict Rasputin for his horrible crimes, committed on religious grounds, or unfrock me. I cannot reconcile myself to the

> fact that the synod, the bearer of the blessing of the Holy Ghost, should shield the holy devil who desecrates the Church of Christ. Know that I am willing to rot in a dungeon, but that I shall not reconcile myself to the desecration of God's name.[8]

Rasputin conducted a vigorous epistolary defence from Pokrovskoe:

> Dearest Papa and Mama,
> Iliodor has allied himself with demons. He is rebellious. They used to flog monks like him. Yes, tsars had them flogged. Now bring him to heel. Have no mercy . . . Grigorii.

When he heard of Iliodor's proposed renunciation of his habit he wrote:

> Dear Papa and Mama,
> What kind of a devil is this Iliodor? He is a renegade. Damned. He is mad. He needs a doctor or it will get worse. He will end up singing with the devil.
>
> G.[9]

The Holy Synod, in the person of Sabler, who was fundamentally sympathetic to Rasputin, expelled Iliodor from holy orders before he could resign them. He resumed his secular name, Sergei Trufanov, and was sent under house arrest to his native village in southern Russia. Trufanov took matters a stage further and voluntarily left the Orthodox church. On his way home he filled in the space in a hotel register reserved for the visitor's religious faith with the expression "My own, Iliodorian."[10]

This ultimate disgrace caused a further stir; it was seen as yet another manifestation of Rasputin's influence. To many eyes Trufanov began to appear something of a martyr, a view confirmed when, one after another, all the seven ecclesiastical members of the synod who had unfrocked him were granted tokens of the imperial favor.[11] Rasputin was delighted by his enemy's fall, but in another letter to Papa and Mama urged them to have the police keep a close eye upon him. He was still frightened of the man, and with cause.

Trufanov was a dangerous fanatic who had a following of no less fanatical devotees, many of whom were women who had been "wronged" by Rasputin. Early in 1913, and with Trufanov's active encouragement, some of them had conspired to entice Rasputin with the promise of sex and put an end to his wrongdoing by castrating him. However, Rasputin got wind of their plan and it came to nothing.

He spent the spring of 1914 in Yalta, following the imperial family there. He stayed at a smart hotel and clearly enjoyed the protection of the palace. It was made clear that any official, from the fiery Dumbadze down, who criticised Rasputin in any way would suffer immediate disgrace. This encouraged the *starets* to behave worse than ever. He struck up an intimate acquaintance with two young women hotel guests who lived on the same floor. Still worse to contemporary eyes, he brought the tsar and tsarina into disrepute by spending much of his time in the company of the hotel staff boasting of his intimate acquaintance with the family. The boasts were confirmed by the numerous calls that Vyroubova paid him; her carriage could be seen waiting outside the hotel for hours at a time.[12] Shops selling guides of Yalta also did a brisk trade in photographs of Rasputin.

The gossip mounted and Nicholas made one of his occasional attempts to allay it. He ordered Rasputin to return to St. Petersburg early, collect his family—his wife had come to join his daughter in the capital, where he had rented a separate apartment for three months—and return to Pokrovskoe until further notice. The order was halfway between a punishment and a prudent measure.

Meanwhile, in the capital Rasputin's daughter was enjoying the attentions of an anonymous admirer. He telephoned her to tell her that he had been following her for days, entranced by her beauty, and called back repeatedly. He eventually asked to see her, only to learn that she was returning home to Siberia with her father. The Rasputin family took the train to Tyumen and travelled on by steamer. On board Maria was approached, as she put it, "by a dark gentleman whose appearance she did not much care for"—in other words a Jew—who introduced himself as a journalist, Davidson, and revealed that he was her secret admirer, determined to follow her home.

Davidson came from Vilna, and had been writing for some time for the not entirely reputable daily *Birzhevye Vedomosti.* His interest in Mlle. Rasputina was strictly professional; he was party to a plot which he hoped would give him the story of a lifetime.

One of the women who had conspired to mutilate Rasputin the year before was a certain Chionya Gusyeva, a once good-looking ex-prostitute now seriously disfigured by syphilis. She was an ardent follower of Trufanov and had moved to his village in order to share his exile. There she grew convinced that it was her sacred duty to destroy Rasputin and asked Trufanov for a blessing which he accorded her with alacrity, telling her to follow the man until she killed him. Realising that he would be held responsible for the murder, Trufanov decided that it was time to leave. Disguising himself as a woman–he had shaved off his beard on leaving the church–he gave his guards the slip and, in the company of his sister, travelled north by steamer. He eventually crossed the border into Finland, going on to Sweden.

In the meantime Gusyeva had gone south to Yalta, but found that Rasputin had already left. She proceeded directly to Pokrovskoe disguised as a beggar and waited there at the riverside for his steamer to arrive. A day or so after he got home the postman delivered a telegram to the house, which was accepted by one of Rasputin's relatives. On learning that she had failed to tip the man, whose support he valued greatly, Rasputin hurried out to catch him. On his way he was met by a beggar woman, her face hidden by a shawl, who asked him for money. As he put a hand in his pocket she pulled out a knife and stabbed him in the stomach, driving the blade up to the rib cage and wounding him badly. Yet as she pulled the knife back for a second blow Rasputin had strength enough left to hold her off with his stick until an angry crowd grabbed her and allowed the *starets* to collapse.

It was a bad wound; there was a high risk of infection and the nearest doctor, Vladimirsky, was in Tyumen. It took him six hours to reach his patient, and he was obliged to perform an emergency cleaning and patching operation on the spot. Rasputin refused an anaesthetic but soon fainted. Vladimirsky considered it vital to get him to a hospital immediately, even though it meant a six-hour drive over hard-baked and rutted summer roads. That he should have chosen to move his patient in such circumstances is either a serious reflection on his judgment or an indication of the gravity of Rasputin's condition. If this was indeed so critical, it is a remarkable testimony to the man's physical strength that he survived the journey, and soon began a slow and painful recovery, although he was obliged to remain in the hospital until well into August. In due course the doctor received a gold watch from the empress as his reward for saving Rasputin's life.

While Rasputin was still lying in Pokrovskoe, Davidson appeared at the door and asked to speak to Maria. She immediately realised that she had been deceived, and that he was almost certainly a party to the conspiracy. Although she got rid of him immediately, this did not prevent him from filing his sensational story, which he attempted to follow up with a series of unsigned and unflattering articles about Rasputin's activities, while continuing to pester his daughter for more information.

Davidson was attended to soon enough. Rasputin had wired the tsarina, who was cruising in the Baltic, about the attempt on his life. The press was immediately forbidden to print anything about him, while Vyroubova asked the assistant chief of police, S. P. Beletsky, to silence Davidson and recover any notes he might have pertaining to the case. Beletsky, who had done Davidson favours in the past, was able to stop him from doing any more damage, and recovered his notes, which proved harmless. Davidson later spent a little time in custody before going to work for the censor's office.

Gusyeva was arrested, after narrowly escaping a lynching. She announced that she had tried to kill Rasputin for abusing his so-called sainthood, for his heresies, and for raping a nun. The authorities felt it would be a mistake to put her on trial. After a short imprisonment she was conveniently declared insane and put in an asylum in Tomsk. Her relatives made repeated efforts to get her out, on the grounds that she had "got better," but the doctor in charge insisted that she continued to display symptoms of "psychological disturbance and exalted religiosity."[13] She did not get out until after the February Revolution, after which no more is heard of her.

Anyone who believes that the First World War was the result of an elaborate conspiracy would do well to consider the timing of Gusyeva's attack on Rasputin. For it took place within hours of another, successful assassination: Gavrilo Princip's murder of Archduke Ferdinand thousands of miles to the west in Sarajevo. Although it has usually been accepted that Princip was a member of a Serbian patriotic organisation, perhaps an offshoot of the Black Hand, it is curious that during his show trial in Moscow, in 1937, the Bolshevik Karl Radek should have hinted mysteriously that there was more to the Princip assassination than met the eye. Conspiracy theory thrives on such enigmatic asides. It is just conceivable that Iliodor, through the Union of the Russian People, might have been in touch with Serbian patriots who agreed to synchronize assassination attempts, but all in all it seems hardly likely. Besides, anyone considering the causes of the First World War would do well to recall A. J. P. Taylor's reminder that among the persons responsible was the archduke's chauffeur, who took the wrong turning, which permitted Princip to get his shot in. Be that as it may, Rasputin would always remain convinced that had he been well he could have kept Russia out of the war.

In the critical weeks of July 1914, as Europe began to mobilise, the tsarina turned to Rasputin for guidance. She sent a steady stream of telegrams to Tyumen, all to the effect that the prospect of war was terrifying, that Rasputin should pray for them and support them with his advice. The replies were somewhat mixed; at first they described Alexandra Fedorovna's fears as exaggerated:

> Do not worry too much about war, when the time comes you will have to declare it, but not yet, there will be an end to your troubles.
>
> 16 July
>
> My dears, my precious ones, do not despair.
>
> 19 July
>
> I believe in, I hope for peace, they are doing wicked things, we are no part of it, I know how you suffer, it is very hard to be apart from one another.
>
> 19 July[14]

However, as the telegrams took an increasingly urgent turn, Rasputin began to implore Nicholas to stay out of the war, wiring to Vyroubova that, "The war must be stopped—war must *not* be declared; it will be the finish of all things."[15] He followed the telegram up with an urgent letter to the tsar in which he foresaw, with a clarity unclouded by war fever, that her involvement would bring about the end of imperial Russia. The letter is not precisely a prophecy, but the result of an overpowering sense that war could bring only disaster. It is written in a shaky scrawl, and abounds in spelling mistakes —he even misspells Russia. Its tone is very disturbing:

> Dear friend,
>
> Again I say a terrible storm cloud hangs over Russia, Disaster, grief, murky darkness and no light. A whole ocean of tears, there is no counting them, and so much blood. What can I say? I can find no words to describe the horror. I know they all want you to go to war, the most loyal, and they do not know that they will destruction. Heavy is God's punishment; when he takes away men's understanding it is the beginning of the end. You are the tsar, the father of your people, don't let the lunatics triumph and destroy you and the people, and if we conquer Germany, what in truth will happen to Russia? When you consider it like that there has never been such a martyrdom. We all drown in blood. The disaster is great the misery infinite.
>
> Grigorii.[16]

Nicholas did not listen. Afterwards Rasputin would always maintain that, had he been able to see the tsar in person, he could have kept Russia out of the war. Having missed his chance, however, he accepted that Russia must fight on to victory:

> Had I been there, there would have been no war. I would not have permitted it because we must not spill our blood before we are ready, but since we are at war we must see it through to the end, because if you are going to fight then fight to the finish, half measures are useless, because you will only have to fight again.[17]

Rasputin was not alone in the belief that he could have kept Russia out of the war. It was a view shared by one of the keenest political intelligences in the country. Admittedly, Sergei Witte was pro-German, had substantial holdings in German banks, and rightly considered that a war with Germany could not be won. Moreover, he was using Rasputin in his attempt to make a political comeback. Yet the assessment he made of Rasputin to one of the grand dukes on July 2, 1914, is remarkable nevertheless. He saw him as the only man who could save Russia and resolve the complicated political deadlock between the pro- and anti-war factions, adding:

> You do not know just how intelligent this remarkable person is. He better than anybody knows Russia, her spirit, moods and direction. He knows it all by some kind of sixth sense.[18]

CHAPTER 15

The gift of organisation is not in the Russian nature.
"B.W."

SHORTLY BEFORE Russia mobilised, the war minister, Sukhomlinov, who before long would find himself in prison on charges of treason, published a newspaper article announcing that, should it come to a war, the imperial army was ready. It is true that humiliating defeat at the hands of the Japanese had brought about some much needed changes. There had been a huge improvement in the quality of instruction at the staff colleges, producing a whole generation of keen and well-trained young staff officers. Yet by no stretch of the imagination could the army be considered ready for war. It was drastically short of supplies, rifles, and notably ammunition, and would remain so until the final months of the regime. Yet its lack of readiness was not just a question of supplies, but also one of attitude, upon almost every level of the ramshackle civil and military machine. In peacetime, and under no great strain, the machine ticked along, more or less. Incompetence, corruption, stupidity, and inadequate distribution systems made for a lack of efficiency that was notorious but still tolerable. When the demands of war required the machine to operate at full speed, its inefficiency rapidly became critical, and at every level it began to break down.

Neither the Imperial Guard nor the army had been properly prepared for a modern war, witness the pattern of the Guard's summer manoeuvres. These were essentially a social event and a source of great expense to the officers, who had a colossal baggage train, including a large marquee that was set up every night. In it there would be served a four-course dinner with immaculate table linen and four wine glasses a head; in the meantime, exercises in the setting of defensive pickets would be conducted on the camp perimeter. The manoeuvres themselves followed a well-tried pattern, ending with the opposing sides advancing upon one another while the tsar waited in the middle. Just on the point of being overrun he would have the retreat sounded, and serve a cold lunch to fifteen hundred officers—the postmortems were often somewhat confused. In 1913 there had been a small change made in the battle plan, to the rage of one general who complained that he had followed the same line of advance for fifteen years, "and now some whippersnapper is ordering me to do God knows what."[1]

> The atmosphere in the line regiments was worse: There was very little order in the old tsarist army. Discipline was weak. Soldiers, and officers in particular got away unpunished with behaviour which would have seen them court martialled and probably shot in any other European army. On the other hand in no other army was human life held in such low regard.[2]

Armies, especially the imperial armies of the early twentieth century, were not renowned for their intelligence or their gentleness, yet the Russian military machine managed to combine a blend of stupidity, inefficiency, and brutality that was special, even by the standards of the day. Two particular instances from Sukhomlinov's memoirs stick in the mind. Shortly before the war there were problems in the army medical school. The students resented military discipline, were unorthodox in their dress, and slack about saluting both their senior officers and one another, to the anger of the aforementioned officers. Sukhomlinov continues: "The rage of the officers reached the point at which one of their numbers was obliged to draw his sword and cut a piece off a student's skull."[3] The action is gross enough, but grosser still is the total absence of any comment from Sukhomlinov about the nature of the officer's "obligation."

The second instance illustrates a certain kind of administrative callousness and inefficiency. On a tour of the military districts of the Far East Sukhomlinov discovered that a district commander had hit on an elegant way of distinguishing his Chinese residents from the itinerant workers who crossed the frontier daily: a taxing problem, since he found that they all tended to look much alike. He distinguished the residents by means of a cord twisted round the wrist and sealed with a lead seal. Unfortunately the cord used to contract when its wearer got his hands wet, cutting into the flesh and causing considerable distress. It was not until Peking responded by putting cords round the *necks* of its Russian residents that the practice was suspended.[4]

The summer manoeuvres of 1914 had been a tense affair, at which the Austrian military attachés were visibly unhappy and kept themselves to themselves. There were plenty of rumours attributed to informed diplomatic sources, and the atmosphere was uneasy as the Guards regiments advanced upon one another, and upon Nicholas, for the last time. The tsar was his usual unperturbed and fatalistic self. The capital was tense too; there was a lot of industrial unrest, sabotage, and street violence, with small mobs smashing trams and street lamps.[5] Even the weather seemed to reflect the tension. It was close and thundery, while the city was ringed with fires and dark clouds of smoke from the peat bogs that surrounded it, which had been smouldering all summer long; the smell of burning was inescapable.[6]

When Russia finally declared war on the Central Powers it brought the most extraordinary manifestation of national solidarity and patriotic fervour that the nation had known for decades, as the people, apparently to a man, rallied to a just war and to their tsar. As one of the grand dukes put it: "Never in all Nicky's twenty years of luckless reign had he heard so many spontaneous hurrahs."[7] In like manner the people of Prussia joined with their kaiser to welcome, as he put it, "A bright and joyous war," while the English and the French were excited, too.

The mood in Moscow was no less enthusiastic, as Robert Bruce Lockhart remembers:

> My recollections of those first war months in Moscow are remarkably vivid, although today they seem more like a strange dream. I have to shut my eyes to recall the enthusiasm of those early days. There in the patchwork of my memory I see again those moving scenes at the station; the troops, grey with dust and closely packed in cattle trucks; the vast crowds on the platform to wish them God speed; grave bearded fathers, wives and mothers, smiling bravely through their tears and bringing gifts of flowers and cigarettes; fat priests to bless the happy warriors. The crowd sways forward for a last handshake and a last embrace. There is a shrill whistle from the engine. Then, with many false starts, the overloaded train, as though reluctant to depart, crawls slowly out of the station and disappears into the grey twilight of the Moscow night. Silent and bare-headed, the crowd remains motionless until the last faint echo of the song of the men who are never to return has faded into nothing. Then, shepherded by the gendarmes, it files out quietly into the streets.
>
> I come away with a hopefulness which overrides my better judgment. Here was a Russia which I had never known–a Russia inspired by a patriotism which seemed to have its roots deep down in the soil.[8]

Patriotism and war fever took various forms, some of them less welcome than others. At the opera and ballet, which continued to function in full splendour through the hungriest years of war, right up to the revolution, the orchestra would begin by playing the national anthem of every one of the allies, while the audience stood to attention. As Bruce Lockhart put it:

> By the time the number of allied hymns assumed the dimensions of a cricket score, the fervour evaporated, and the heavy-paunched Moscovites groaned audibly at an ordeal which lasted over half an hour.[9]

The initial enthusiasm was more than skin deep. The Duma, which had hitherto satisfactorily fulfilled the role of thorn in the imperial flesh, declared its solidarity with Nicholas and the war effort. There were other ways in which the nation responded to the challenge—for instance, its acceptance of a government ban on the sale of liquor. This had various consequences. Not only did the troops go sober to the front, but the city lost one of its familiar features with the disappearance of drunks from the streets. There was also a marked increase in personal savings and an equally marked falling off in the crime rate. In some circles, such as the General Staff, the ban caused considerable hardship, as officers were obliged to turn to tea:

> The effect of prohibition has been to make some of the older officers require increasing quantities of sugar, and I well remember a general whose tower of sugar always overtopped the tea in his glass.[10]

In fact the ban did not hold for long. It was soon possible to get all the vodka you wanted in a restaurant—through the simple expedient of ordering it by the teapot.

This book does not claim to tell the story of Russia in the Great War; the sorry tale has been told often enough elsewhere. Yet there are points that cannot be made too often. In the first weeks of the war the Russian armies under Samsonov advanced further into Germany than they would for over thirty years, only to be surrounded and virtually annihilated at the battle of Tannenberg, after which Samsonov shot himself. The advance was precipitous and injudicious, the lines of communication too long, and supply was rendered difficult by the inadequate railway system. The army betrayed its movements by sending wireless messages *en clair*—supposing it safe enough to send by night when no one could be expected to be listening. Individual units fought with extraordinary bravery, meeting machine-gun fire with the bayonet and little else, but brave soldiers and good junior officers were let down by their high command. To students of Russian history the story has a familiar ring. In Solzhenitsyn's summary of the action in *August 1914* he concludes that, "Russia must needs be governed by fools, there is no other way."[11]

Yet incompetent, precipitate, unwise though that advance may have been, it had a kind of idiotic sublimity. Russia advanced despite her unreadiness, at the urgent request of her allies, notably the French, in a desperate effort to put enough pressure on the Germans to save Paris. They succeeded. The Germans were obliged to transfer a significant number of troops to the Eastern front, together with their finest commanders, Hindenburg and Ludendorff. It was the Russian sacrifice and not a handful of Parisian taxis that created the "miracle on the Marne." Russia stood to gain nothing by sacrificing her armies as she did; her General Staff acted out of a sense of honourable obligation to distant allies, displaying a kind of disinterest that has not subsequently been seen in the history of the twentieth century—except in 1916 when another, successful Russian offensive against the Austrians on the southern front helped to save Verdun.

Rasputin's recovery was slow. He returned to St. Petersburg at the end of August, but the wound kept him virtually bedridden for another month and he was never to be completely well again. It continued to hurt a lot, and the combination of shock and pain marked a turn for the worse in his personal life. He had always liked to drink a lot, without being a habitual drunkard in single-minded search of oblivion. Now he looked increasingly to alcohol as a pain reliever, beginning to drink vodka again for the first time in many years, as the quickest way of getting where he wanted to be. Even his daughter, his most loyal supporter, conceded that from now on he drank steadily and was often found intoxicated at unusual times of day. Also for the first time he became subject to prolonged and morose fits of drunkard's depression, while there was a corresponding waning in his spiritual powers. His daughter states that he found it increasingly difficult to pray, and turned more and more to sex and drink out of despair at what she terms the dark night of his soul. Certainly in those later years there was an increasing urgency in Rasputin's drinking and womanising, which suggests a shift in balance between the spirit and the flesh.

His political position had also deteriorated, in that his power base seemed compromised. Anna Vyroubova had had a serious falling-out with the tsarina. She had become over-familiar with her friend, arousing her jealousy and even venturing to criticise her to her husband; nothing enraged Alexandra more than suspicion of disloyalty. She later referred in a letter to Nicholas to Anna's "hideous behaviour" throughout 1914,[12] a time when the two friends were hardly speaking. However, it would seem that this coldness did not extend to Rasputin. Alexandra continued to seek his guidance, and from the early stages of the war she turned to him for advice upon its conduct, as reflected in letters such as the following, concerning a change of appointment he had encouraged her to suggest:

> 25 October 1914
> Our Friend wishes me quickly to speak to Maklakov [minister of internal affairs], as he says one must not waste time till you return. So I shall send for him, pardon me for mixing in what does not concern me.[13]

Alexandra was foolish to let Nicholas see that she was acting on the advice of their Friend, for Nicholas at the time was far from well disposed towards him. The tsar's attitude to Rasputin veered regularly from trust, through resigned acceptance, to attempts to be rid of the man or at least send him away for a time, whenever the disgrace became too much to bear. The confidence Nicholas had experienced at the outbreak of war, the feeling that he was the leader of a nation united behind him, and the joy he took in leading a soldier's life in the healthy, manly atmosphere of the front, all encouraged him to make another attempt to shake off Rasputin. It has been suggested that his hostility was fuelled by Rasputin's opposition to the war and, more plausibly, by an extremely unflattering report on him from the chief of police, General Djunkovsky. At all events Rasputin himself acknowledged that at that time "Papa was very angry with him."[14]

It might not have needed a miracle to restore Rasputin and Vyroubova to favour, but it was indeed a miracle that did so. On January 2, 1915, Anna Vyroubova was on a train from Tsarskoe Selo to Petrograd, as the capital had been rechristened. There was an accident, and Vyroubova was badly hurt; a radiator in her carriage came loose and shattered both her legs. It took several hours to clear the line and get her, still unconscious, to the Tsarskoe Selo hospital. Her condition was grave enough for her to be given the last rites. Although unconscious she kept muttering requests for Rasputin to pray for her.

Her mother did not want Rasputin to go to her daughter, and he only learned of the accident on the following day. He had some difficulty in getting hold of a car, and the journey to Tsarskoe Selo on a bitter day in snow and a heavy frost was a slow one. When he arrived he went into Vyroubova's room unannounced, to find Nicholas and Alexandra together with the imperial surgeon, Princess Gedroitz, who had given her patient up for dead. (Women doctors were not unusual in Russia. As early as 1893 there were 546 woman doctors in the empire—as opposed to 2,500 in the United States and 186 in Great Britain. They played an increasingly important role during the Great War.) Without saying a word Rasputin went straight to Vyroubova, took her hand and said, "Annushka, wake up, look at me!" To the general amazement she came to. "Grigorii, is that you, thank God!" He then turned to the others and said: "She'll recover but will always be a cripple." Rasputin proceeded to stagger into the next room, where he fainted. When he came round he felt very weak and had broken out into a heavy sweat.

This is Rasputin's last attested major act of healing. He himself would always say that he had "raised Annushka from the dead," and it may be an indication of how weak his powers had become that his action took such a visible toll on him. There are no other examples of his being weakened in this way. It is reasonable to suppose that Anna's plight would have made him summon all the strength left in him, for he had always held her in the highest regard, considering her the embodiment of simple goodness. Henceforward she was, as he put it, "dearer to him than anybody."[15]

As with his cure of Aleksey in Spala, the facts are beyond dispute. Anna was pronounced to be dying; Rasputin appeared, called on her to come to; she did so. Moreover, she recovered, but was indeed obliged to use first crutches, then sticks for the rest of her life. Of course Rasputin's arrival may have coincided with a turning point, but once again the weight of probability favours the conclusion that he really did possess a healing power, while it should also be remembered that no one had a greater faith in Rasputin than Anna Vyroubova.

Rasputin followed up his initial treatment with regular visits and therapeutic telegrams:

> 10 i 5
> Although I could not be with you in body, I send you joy with my spirit. My feeling is a divine feeling. I send an angel to console and comfort you, call the doctor.[16]

If a non-partisan biographer, across the space of more than 60 years, feels obliged to concede that there was something unusual about Rasputin's restoration of Vyroubova it is easy to imagine its impact upon an impressionable couple who believed in holy men and miracles as a proof of holiness, and who had actually been at Vyroubova's bedside at the time. Not only did the miracle bring Anna back to favour, it confirmed the tsarina's faith in Rasputin and restored that of the tsar to a sufficient degree to make his disgrace unthinkable.

CHAPTER 16

RASPUTIN'S CLOSENESS to the imperial family had already done serious damage to the dynasty. At the least, Alexandra Fedorovna's association with Rasputin was unwise. No public figure can afford the view that his private life is of no concern to others, still less the consort of an absolute ruler a few years after a revolution that had nearly succeeded, with public opinion largely hostile to the autocratic principle. Still worse was the fundamental failure to appreciate that criticism could be constructive. To Alexandra, anyone offering the slightest criticism of Rasputin, and hence of her behaviour, became an enemy. Rasputin too was incapable of learning from his critics; anyone criticising him was simply a threat.

Over the years a void had formed about the imperial couple, who had driven away anyone with the sense and courage to offer constructive advice. It was a void that they could not afford. The failure of Nicholas and Alexandra to keep open house for the nobility, to lead a court life, made for resentment, but still worse, for ignorance. The intimate private world of Tsarskoe Selo was innocent in the extreme, but because innocence was not seen to be done, because Rasputin could come and go as he pleased for all his deplorable reputation, it was easy to believe the worst, namely that he was the tsarina's lover.

It is the case throughout Rasputin's life, and indeed beyond it, that the myth was more important than the man. It was what people believed about him, far more than what he actually did, that mattered, and contributed to the destruction of imperial Russia.

Historians in the West are rightly quick to remind us that it was the war, not Lenin, that brought about that destruction. Indeed, as late as December 1916 Lenin believed that no revolution would be seen in his lifetime. It was military defeat and its consequences that were primarily responsible for the February Revolution. However, it is also the case that the war made for an increase in the power of Rasputin, the increase being amplified by rumour until he came to embody disgrace, corruption, and even treason, a dark poison infecting the nation at its fountainhead.

While the Russian armies were regularly successful against the Austrians along their southern front, their record against the Germans, at least for the first fifteen months of the war, was disastrous. The Russian commanders revealed total lack of tactical sophistication or concern for human life. One vignette of a failed operation in 1914 sticks in the mind as defining the quality of Russian tactics and the spirit of the old Russian army. An officer recalls a night attack on the southern front by a Guards battalion. They moved forward without reconnoitering, simply advancing in two lines with a fifty-yard interval between—not easy at night over strange ground. The second line caught up with the first as they went in, and the battalion suffered eighty percent casualties. Next morning the corpses could be seen where they fell, in rows, as if lying at attention. The attack, intended as a surprise, was no surprise at all, since its objective, a burning warehouse, clearly illuminated the attackers.[1] The essentially nonchalant attitude to casualties is even reflected in the press. One account of a Russian defeat begins:

> How they die when they have to! . . . These men know how to die with honour, giving their enemy a worthy example of courage and inflexible steadfastness.[2]

It was not for nothing that the imperial Russian army had been nicknamed "the great silent one" (*velikaya molchal'nitsa*).[3] The last awestruck comment on the Russian casualties come from an enemy, the German commander Paul von Hindenburg:

> In the ledger of the Great War the page on which the Russian losses were written has been torn out. No one knows the figures. Five or eight million? We, too, have no idea. All we know is that sometimes in our battles with the Russians we had to remove the mounds of enemy corpses from before our trenches in order to get a clear field of fire against fresh assaulting waves. Imagination may try to reconstruct the figure of their losses, but an accurate calculation will remain forever a vain thing.

The French and British and American losses, which the respective nations have taken so much to heart, are as nothing compared to those of the imperial Russian army in the Great War, and yet whether they were five or eight millions one would still be obliged to observe to the war's survivors, who had a civil war, Stalin's purges and World War Two to look forward to, that when it came to losses the Russian nation had as yet seen nothing.

Despite Sukhomlinov's confident assertion that the army was ready, it was nothing of the sort. Not only had the number of men Russia would put in the field been severely underestimated (by mid-1916 she was calling up her thirteenth million), but there were more serious miscalculations about the duration of the war and the rate at which ammunition would be expended. By the time the war was six weeks old, Russian factories were producing thirty-five thousand shells a month, Russian guns firing forty-five thousand a day. Small wonder that the batteries soon fell silent or were restricted to four or five rounds per gun per day. There was also a serious shortage of rifles; it is perfectly true that troops were sent into action unarmed, ordered to glean what weapons they could from the battlefield. "We don't want to die with sticks in our hands," the men complained.[4] The army was also deficient in other respects. When gas was first used against them, on June 1, 1915, the press said that the troops had had time to take "the necessary measures"–these consisted of men peeing on handkerchiefs which they then knotted round their heads. There were, in fact, gas masks in plenty, but owing to an administrative blunder they were thought to be unnecessary, and they did not reach the front in time. Although, curiously, at the outbreak of war Russia possessed more aircraft than any other power, there was only one antiaircraft battery, which was kept to defend the imperial palace at Tsarskoe Selo.

Another striking and characteristic example of incompetence combined with callousness and, in this case, paranoia, was the treatment of the Jewish population in the forward areas of the southwest front, Galicia and Bukovina. The military, anti-Semitic by tradition, concluded that they might be pro-German, and decided to deport the entire population, wholesale. Complete villages would be ordered to move out, lock, stock, and barrel, at a few hours' notice. Quite apart from the distress that such instructions created, no provision was made by the military to look after the streams of refugees once they quit the forward area. They were left to their own devices, to wander off and find food and shelter as best they could:

> People have been thrown out of their homesteads with only a few hours to prepare for their departure and have been chased into the unknown. Whatever supplies they had, and sometimes even their homes were set ablaze before their eyes . . . All this confused, exasperated exhausted crowd fills all the roads in a continuous stream, impeding troop movements and throwing life in the rear of the army into utter chaos. Everywhere slow-moving carts with household goods and cattle dragging their feet . . . people dying in hundreds from cold, hunger and disease . . . child mortality reaching terrific dimensions . . . unburied corpses by the roadside, and so on and so on.[5]

The war casts a startling new light upon Rasputin's relationship with the tsarina. To date this could only be inferred from hearsay. From now on Nicholas would spend so much of his time at the front that the imperial couple had to maintain a regular and extensive correspondence, in English, in which, increasingly, Alexandra would tell her husband what to do.

When we read the tsarina's letters, see how she regarded Rasputin, and the hold he had over her, it comes as a shock. However prepared one may be by descriptions of her as devout, mystically minded, superstitious, it is still unnerving to see a member of a European ruling house accept without question that a peasant should be an emissary of God sent to provide personal guidance to the dynasty. That Siberian peasants going into action in 1914 should have taken German aeroplanes to be a sign that God was fighting for the enemy is strange enough. Since the tsarina truly believed that God had sent Rasputin to guide them, she, on the contrary, must have concluded that the Almighty was fighting for Russia.

The way in which Alexandra's letters refer to Rasputin is curiously revealing. She never uses his last name; he is always "Gregory," or "Our Friend." It is as if by using the form Rasputin, with its connotations of sexual licence, she would be obliged to face up to his unsavoury reputation, whereas she wished to see him in an altogether different light. Looking back on her life with Nicholas, on the anniversary of their betrothal, she observed how fortunate they had been to have had "Two Friends sent us by God,"[6] the other one being M. Philippe. The expression is anything but a mere figure of speech, and the letter abounds in lines such as:

> No, hearken to our Friend, beleive [sic] him. He has yr. interest and Russia's at heart–it is not for nothing that God sent him to us–only we must pay more attention to what he says. His words are not lightly spoken and the gravity of having not only His prayers but His advice is great.[7]

The next day she follows up:

> I am haunted by our Friend's wish and *know* it will be fatal for us and the country if it is not fulfilled. He means what He says when He speaks so seriously.[8]

The letters are increasingly full of references to "Our Friend and His wonderful God-sent wisdom."[9] They continually stress the need to follow his advice:

> Had you been here, I think God would have helped me and you could have remembered our Friend's words. When He says not to do a thing and one does not listen, one sees one's fault always afterwards.[10]

The belief that Rasputin was the messenger of God comes out in her attitude to his critics—who are simply going against the light:

> I entreat you, at the first talk with S [i.e., Samarin, over-procurator of the synod] and when you see him, to speak very firmly—do my Love for Russia's sake, Russia will not be blessed if her Sovereign lets a man of God's sent to help him be persecuted. I am sure.
>
> Tell him severely, with a strong and decided voice, that you forbid any intrigues against our Friend, or talks about Him, or the slightest persecution, otherwise you will not help him.[11]

We can gather from the letters that Rasputin was now in almost constant contact with the tsarina. He would take the train to Tsarskoe Selo, or, later, travel in a chauffeur-driven car put at his disposal by the War Ministry, and meet her discreetly in Anna Vyroubova's little house. He seldom went to the palace itself, but was frequently to be seen proceeding to and from the capital. An eyewitness recalls seeing him leave the train at Tsarskoe Selo in the early months of the war:

> He was dressed as a peasant, with a cap such as is worn by the lower orders pulled down over his eyes: he was dirty and unkempt in appearance but he wore a handsome and costly fur coat. His face was thin and pale, but his eyes were his most extraordinary feature—they were very large and deep set, and so penetrating that they seemed to pierce through and through whoever met his gaze.[12]

Rasputin made various kinds of contribution to the war effort, some spiritual, others practical in their intent. He sent Nicholas icons and one of his sticks, which Alexandra advised the tsar to keep in his office "near the one Mr. Philippe touched."[13] He also sent icons to some of the tsar's commanders, who were less appreciative. He prayed, too, for purely practical results:

> Our Friend is always praying and thinking of the war. He says we are to tell him at once if there is anything particular. So she [i.e., Vyroubova] did about the fogg (sic), and he scolded for not having said it at once, says no more foggs will disturb.[14]

Some of the more practical advice was frankly ludicrous. Grand Duke Aleksandr Mikhailovich (Sandro), in charge of aviation, was desperate for aeroplane engines:

> Anya told our friend what I said about Sandro's despair, and he was very much put out about it. He had a long talk with Sekretev on the subject and he says he has heaps of things one could perfectly well use for the machinery of the aeroplanes.[15]

We also find him trying to take a direct hand in matters of the state at the highest level; here submitting the draft of an encouraging telegram for Nicholas to send:

> (Our Friend) begs you very much to send a telegram to the king of Serbia, as he is very anxious that the Bulgarians will finish them off. So I enclose the paper again for you to use for your telegram–the sense in yr. words and shorter of course.[16]

Rasputin also offered strategic advice:

> Now, before I forget, I must give you a message from our Friend, prompted by what he saw in the night, he begs you to order that one should advance near Riga, says it is necessary, otherwise the Germans will settle down so firmly through all the winter that it will cost endless bloodshed and trouble to make them move; now it will take them so aback that we shall succeed in making them retrace their steps. He says this is now the most essential thing and begs you seriously to order ours to advance. He says we can and we must, and I was to write to you at once.[17]

Although Rasputin's military advice was sometimes strange, it never achieved such heights of absurdity as the following tactic proposed by an armchair general:

> With much skill Knyazevich finds the losses might be less, as when heavy fighting goes on, one must go quickly under their range (i.e., the guns) as they are for heavy distances and cannot change quickly.[18]

In many respects the advice Rasputin offered was sound. In his blinkered, intuitive way he was a person of great penetration and intelligence, and one who could see the war from the viewpoint of the common man. Unlike most of the generals in that war, he understood that it was pointless to sacrifice thousands of lives for a few yards of territory:

> He finds better that one shld. not advance too obstinately as the losses will be too great–one can be patient without forcing things, as ultimately it will be ours; one can go on madly and finish the war in two months but then thousands of lives will be sacrificed–and by patience the end will also be gained and one will spare much blood.[19]

Advice of this kind was offered quite frequently, always with the emphasis on avoidance of needless bloodshed:

> Our Friend sends his blessing to the whole Orthodox army. He begs one should not yet strongly advance in the north, because he says if our successes continue being good in the south they will themselves retreat there, or advance and then their losses will be very great, if we begin there our losses will be very heavy. He says this is an advice.[20]

The final sentence calls for comment. In so far as we can judge from Alexandra's letters, Rasputin distinguished between two kinds of counsel, "advice" and "things seen in the night." Presumably the former was the product of his conscious meditations, the latter the result of flashes of insight acquired at other times, when asleep, daydreaming, and so on. The tsarina sometimes characterises an observation of his as deriving from one or the other source.

There were plenty of other occasions when Rasputin tried to discourage needless loss of life. He displays a similar concern for ordinary people, notably the peasantry, in his attitude towards the call-up. He begged Nicholas to delay calling up reserves for as long as possible, reminding him that the men were needed to work in the fields. However, not all his practical advice stems from this "worm's eye view" of war. He could display shrewdness of a different kind. When early in the war Russia captured a couple of Austrian towns, Lvov and Czernowitz, Nicholas paid them a victory visit, much against Rasputin's advice. He felt that were the towns to be recaptured the tsar would look somewhat foolish; they were recaptured, rendering Nicholas's victory visit distinctly premature.

He was also quick to recognize that massive conscription, coupled with Russia's inadequate railway system, had created most serious problems with respect to food production and distribution. Food was scarce and grew immensely expensive. Rasputin frequently spoke at length to the tsarina on the subject, which he considered to be a matter of the gravest urgency. He came up with elaborate and ambitious proposals, suggesting the suspension of all other rail traffic for four days to let through trains carrying flour, butter, and sugar. He also tried to bring about an improvement in the distribution of bread in the shops, reducing queues by having shopkeepers cut the bread up and measure it out in advance.[21] He was much concerned with overcharging for basic foodstuffs, and also tried to check an increase in the cost of public transport, which he pointed out hit the poor but not the rich:

> Our Friend begs you should give the order that one should not augment the prices of going in town in trains; instead of four kopecks now one must pay ten kopecks and that's not fair on the poor people; let the rich be taxed but not the others who daily have often more than once to go by train.[22]

In short, his guiding principles were sound. He understood more clearly than any conventional advisor the hardship caused by shortages and rising prices—the cost of living for the working classes doubled over the war years. These were indeed the immediate causes of the unrest that turned into the February Revolution; the urgency of his representations suggests that he understood that here lay a genuine threat to the dynasty. The official attitude was that nothing could be done about shortages, at home or on the front. Ministers reacted to complaints from the army with the splendid instruction to "eat less," horses were to be given ten as opposed to twenty measures of oats a day and go without hay altogether if necessary.[23] The suggestions made by Rasputin, however elaborate, always focus on detail, they are the work of a mind that thinks in close-up. Yet at least he understood that Petrograd and Moscow were being strangled by the supply problem. Whether the problem could have been solved is another matter, for the machinery of tsarist government was simply unequal to the task.

It is hard to know how much attention the tsar paid Rasputin. It is extremely unlikely that he took his military advice seriously. In this area his "power" was almost certainly negligible. Nevertheless, that he was known to be close to the tsarina made him a force of sorts. Certainly he had his say in certain ministerial appointments. When Beletsky became deputy minister for internal affairs, and hence in charge of the surveillance of Rasputin, he discovered, in his own words, that he was a "colossal figure."

However, it is important to realise that there was a tendency on the part of his critical contemporaries to want to consider Rasputin all-powerful, a tendency he did little to discourage. His own boasts as to the extent of his influence may well have been colored by elements of wishful thinking and *vranye,* or creative exaggeration. We cannot say for sure just how much influence he wielded over Nicholas. Certainly ministers who came out against him were frequently dismissed. Certainly he had considerable say in ecclesiastical appointments. Certainly some ministerial appointments accorded with his recommendations. However, this was not invariably the case. For example, in April 1915 he tried to oppose the appointment of Samarin as over-procurator, and failed, although Samarin, it is true, did not last long. He failed to get other appointments through; the failures include V. S. Tatishchev as minister of finance in December

1915, and General N. I. Ivanov as minister of war in January 1916. At the very least it should be recognised that although certain appointments to ministerial office appear to tally with his recommendations it was certainly not the case that the tsar greeted his every suggestion with a resigned and uncritical acceptance.

When it came to petitions, however, Rasputin had become the most powerful man in Russia after the tsar. His flat was now crowded with people from every walk of life who wanted rules bent in their favour. Petitioners ranged from those in search of commercial concessions or appointments to those seeking exemption from front-line service or the suspension of sentences of prison or exile. Rasputin would send some of the petitioners on to Alexandra, who would bring their cases to the attention of the tsar. More often he would hand his client a note, to be given to a particular minister or government official, which took the form of an illiterate scrawl: "My dear, please do it, G." There were so many of these in circulation that they might well have become a form of currency.

Rasputin would also call on ministers, especially newly appointed ones, to establish himself with them. The minister of trade and industry, Prince Shakhovskoy, received a visit from Rasputin shortly after taking up his post in late February 1915. He evokes his staring eyes, and jerky, almost incomprehensible speech. Rasputin finished his visit by unloading a heap of petitions onto his desk, ending subsequent calls in the same way. He never bothered to follow the petitions through and see if they were executed. Shakhovskoy did not pay them any attention, and Rasputin was not in the least concerned. His object was to be accorded respect; only those who received him rudely or not at all became his enemies. If an official was sufficiently in awe to carry out his requests, well and good; if not, no matter. Rasputin, in other words, relied for his success on a degree of bluff, while taking little interest in the fate of particular cases. Indeed, he was known to confuse petitions hopelessly, to the point of recommending two rival candidates for the same post.[24]

Rasputin's private life had acquired a new and urgent tempo. As he drank more and more heavily, there was a decline in his spirituality, awakening in him a sense of loss that could only be alleviated by further drinking. Although his remarkable powers of recovery still enabled him to appear at Tsarskoe Selo the morning after a very late night in reasonable shape, even the tsarina grew aware that he liked a drink or two. She observed in one letter to Nicholas that their Friend was very merry, "but not tipsy!" A few extracts from his surveillance reports give us an idea of the nature of his pleasure-seeking:

12 February
Rasputin and an unknown woman went to house 15/17 on Troitskaya Street . . . at 4:30 in the morning he came back with six drunken men and a guitar. They remained till six, singing and dancing. Rasputin saw no one that morning, he slept.

March 10
A certain Evgenya Karlovna Ezhova came to Rasputin to ask him to help her secure a 1 million rouble contract to supply linen to the forces. Just before 1:00 A.M. 7 or 8 men and women called on Rasputin and stayed till three. Everybody was shouting, singing, dancing, and they all left with Rasputin, drunk, and set off somewhere.

11 March
At 10:15 A.M. Rasputin was seen on Gorokohovaya Street and followed to No. 8 Pushkin Street, home of the prostitute Tregubova, from there he went to the bathhouse.

14 May
At 5:00 P.M. he drove to No. 15 Malaya Dvoryanskaya St. At 10:00 P.M. one of the windows in the flat was unlit, but one of the detectives could see a woman leave the lighted room to look into the dark one, she quickly ran back. Then Rasputin could be seen running out of the dark room, he grabbed his hat and coat and ran out onto the street with two men chasing him. They just ran out, called out, "There he goes" and went back inside. Rasputin jumped into a cab at a run and went down Liteiny Prospekt looking anxiously over his shoulder.[25]

This was a fairly acceptable level of scandalous behaviour, confined as it was to private houses. The police did make efforts, however, to prevent him from disgracing himself in public, even encouraging his favourite restaurant, the Villa Rhode, to keep a special and exceptionally remote private room reserved for his exclusive use.[26]

Yet it was impossible to keep the man out of trouble. In March 1915 he went to Moscow to pray at a particular tomb in fulfillment of a vow made in hospital the year before. After a day of devotion he went on to Yar to spend the evening there with a group of hangers-on and journalists, taking a large private room. The party started to drink heavily and in due course called for a chorus of gypsies. Rasputin, very drunk indeed, began to boast openly and loudly of his relationship with the tsarina; he pointed to an embroidered blouse he was wearing and said that "the old woman" had made it for him. He continued to hold forth in a way that brought the tsarina into disrepute. Matters grew worse when one of the company challenged him to prove that he really was Rasputin. He found an original way of establishing his identity, by unbuttoning his fly and waving his penis at the public. He then proceeded to hand out a series of notes to the singers with slogans such as "Love unselfishly," and rewarded the gypsies, who were growing uncomfortable, with large sums of money.

News of Rasputin's behaviour soon got out, and public opinion was scandalised by the image of him boasting about the tsarina in a state of undress. However, the governor of Moscow, General Adrianov, made a report to the minister of internal affairs, N. A. Maklakov, and his assistant Djunkovsky, which played the incident down. The minister submitted a still milder report to the tsar, who promised to read it, but apparently did nothing of the sort. Matters rested there for a few months, until Maklakov was succeeded by Prince Shcherbatov, who was much more hostile to Rasputin. He ordered Djunkovsky to reinvestigate the scandal and make a proper report. Not only did Djunkovsky draw up a much fuller account of the evening, he went further into the story of Rasputin's way of life, producing a comprehensive and unflattering account that he submitted to the tsar. Nicholas listened carefully and thanked him for being so frank. He sent for Rasputin at once, and was angry with him as never before. Rasputin did not seek to deny his behaviour, simply observing that he was as human and as much a sinner as the next man. Nicholas ordered him away to Pokrovskoe, and Rasputin set off, feeling subdued and depressed. He observed to one of the agents escorting him that life could sometimes be very hard for seekers after truth and righteousness.

The report was also shown to Alexandra by the palace commandant, Major-General Voyeikov, and, as he later mentioned to Spiridovich, at the sight of it she burst into tears. This is the only record we have of her reaction to news of Rasputin's misdeeds. Distressed though she may have been, her loyalty and faith remained unshaken. She immediately wrote a series of letters to Nicholas attacking Djunkovsky:

> If we let our Friend be persecuted we and our country shall suffer for it . . . I am so weary such heartache and pain fr. all this—the idea of dirt being spread about one we venerate is more than horrible.
>
> Ah my Love when at *last* will you thump with your hand upon the table and scream at Djunkovsky and others when they act wrongly—one does not fear you—and one *must*—they must be frightened of you otherwise all sit upon us . . . .[27]

Alexandra does not question the accuracy of the charges, she simply takes the view that anyone attacking Rasputin is attacking the dynasty and hence must be wrong by definition. The letter worked; Nicholas did thump with his hand. Soon afterward he wrote Shcherbatov a note insisting on Djunkovsky's immediate dismissal—thereby losing yet another loyal and able servant.

Matters did not rest there. The press under Maklakov had been subject to the strictest censorship with regard to Rasputin. Now Shcherbatov, in another attempt to discredit him, permitted the publication of some savage attacks. One article in *Vechernee Vremya* on August 17, 1915, suggested that Rasputin was opposed to the war and working for the "German Party," the start of one of the most enduring and damaging untruths, while the most virulent piece of all appeared in *Birzhevye Vedomosti,* which considered his very existence as a reflection upon the whole rotten regime.

> How could it happen?
>
> How could a dark *parvenu* make a mockery of Russia for so long? Even if the Senate, the church, the ministers, the Duma it-

self and the Imperial Council could tolerate such a mockery, how could Russia herself put up with it? The mere fact that they could tolerate such a miserable joke constitutes the core of evil, the most conclusive condemnation of a regime whose treachery and vacillations have become common gossip.

Not even the appearance of a Rasputin seemed too exceptional, too implausible and out of the ordinary. It accords with the style in which we live, and does not stand out against the background. It is a style of "all things are possible, all things permitted" where double agents are rehabilitated in triumph and members of the secret police regularly take part in terrorist expropriations. In such a world not even Rasputin seemed unusual. We are so accustomed to scandal that not even this scandal has disturbed us much. Authority and society have been corrupted for decades by these exceptional circumstances, the absence of the most elementary rule of law.

We have reached the point where nothing surprises us any more, not even Rasputin. No one even realised the disgrace. Simply an effort was made to silence the press, while much that appeared abroad was exaggerated. Yet what was there to exaggerate when the naked truth was worse than any lie?[28]

The piece is signed "Lukian." Whatever such articles might have done to public opinion, they were no immediate threat to Rasputin. They merely secured the dismissal of Shcherbatov after three months in office. His successor, A. N. Khvostov, would hold office for six clear months, a time that saw intrigue, corruption, and disgrace reach surprising new heights.

On his way back to Pokrovskoe, Rasputin got into further trouble. He boarded the steamer at Tyumen on August 9, and began to drink. When other passengers declined to drink with him, he struck up with a group of soldiers, bought them vodka, gave them money and began to sing with them. He then invited them to a second-class saloon for a meal, but the captain refused to allow them to be served. He quarrelled with the captain, and then publicly accused a steward of stealing a considerable sum of money. The steward denied the theft and asked for a police investigation. Rasputin then quarrelled violently with two other passengers and returned to his cabin, where he could be seen through a window dead drunk. He spent the last two hours of the journey on the floor in a stupor and had to be carried ashore at Pokrovskoe, where his daughters met him and drove him home. Next morning, with all the remorse of a drinking amnesiac, he was horrified to hear the details of his escapade. This threatened to have serious consequences, since the steward, A. Rylov, wished to take him to court. It was some time before the new minister of internal affairs and his deputy Beletsky could be confident that the affair had been satisfactorily buried.

Rasputin had family business in Pokrovskoe. Much to his consternation his son Dmitri had been called up. Alexandra's letters to Nicholas made much of the hardship this would cause, while Rasputin referred to himself as Abraham sacrificing Isaac. In the event no sacrifice proved necessary; judicious string-pulling secured Dmitri a place as a medical orderly on a hospital train. This same visit also provided the only glimpse we have of Rasputin's relations with his father. An agent reported a savage quarrel between the two of them, in the course of which Rasputin, in Karamazov-like rage, hurled his father to the ground and beat him. His father continued to curse him, saying, "All he knows is how to grab his servant Dunya 'by the soft parts of her body.'" Father and son were both drunk. When his father died the following year Rasputin did not go home for the funeral, wear mourning, or give up drinking for a single day.[29]

CHAPTER 17

Truly the Russia of 1916 could still provide scenes and characters for the pen of a Gogol.

SIR SAMUEL HOARE

THE WAR had brought Rasputin into contact with a number of persons of doubtful reputation, who were out to benefit as much as they could from hostilities. There was, for example, the banker D. L. Rubinstein, whose acquaintance dated from 1914. The director of a Kharkov bank, he had become financial manager of the estate of Grand Duke Andrey Vladimirovich. This in turn enabled him to become managing director of the Private Commercial Bank of St. Petersburg. He became prominent in financial circles, a director of other banks, of mines and insurance companies; the list of his positions took up seventeen lines of the Petrograd *Who's Who*. He had known Vyroubova since 1908, and in April 1914 he secured a hold over her, when she unwisely accepted approximately ten thousand pounds (or fifty thousand dollars) for unspecified charities. Subsequently he helped Rasputin financially, occasionally paying the rent on his apartment. He grew close to him over the war years, and the closeness paid off. When he was arrested in 1916, and imprisoned on suspicion of treason dealing with German and Austrian banks, it was thanks to the personal efforts of the tsarina on his behalf that he was released a few months later. Rubinstein used Rasputin for protection and to help him with his dealings; he had no interest in politics as such, unlike the most unsavoury of all the persons to attach themselves to Rasputin, Prince M. M. Andronnikov.

For many years Andronnikov had been playing a part remarkably similar to Rasputin's as a political fixer, helping petitioners get what they wanted. When interrogated by the investigatory committee, the "*aide-de-camp* to the Lord Almighty," as he termed himself, described his profession as "visiting ministers," while he was simply "a citizen who wishes to be as great a help as possible." Bearing a striking resemblance to a Gogolian conman, he had made it his business, for years, to ingratiate himself with ministers on their appointment. He would congratulate them in terms of embarrassing extravagance, and give them and their wives expensive presents. He was never to be seen without a bulging briefcase—usually stuffed with nothing more important than old newspapers. However, when his flat was searched on his arrest after the revolution it revealed two carloads of impeccably filed documents, relating to his dealings with various ministers. Unlike Rasputin, Andronnikov was unashamedly out to take as much money from his clients as he could, and lived very well indeed. Since religion was *à la mode* he was conspicuously, unctuously religious, and one corner of his bedroom was fitted out as a chapel. He was notorious for his fondness for young men, whom he would seduce in the same bedroom, in return for promises of protection that were seldom fulfilled. Cadets of the leading military academy were expressly forbidden to visit him.

One of the most remarkable of all instances of rule-bending concerned his Petrograd flat. He rented this from a Countess Tolstoy, who, on hearing of his sexual escapades late in 1915, decided to evict him. He complained to the minister of internal affairs, A. N. Khvostov, but was told that, the law being the law, he would have to go. However, the deputy minister, Beletsky, came up with an answer of considerable elegance. He proposed a change in rent regulations for the entire capital; all tenancies contracted before the war were to be guaranteed for its duration—the measure was ostensibly to prevent landlords from breaking leases and charging exorbitant wartime rents, but in fact the sole purpose of the change was to secure the well-being of Prince Andronnikov![1]

The prince used to entertain Rasputin to meals of his favourite fish soup and Madeira. He also helped him develop his contacts, introducing him, for instance, to Shakhovskoy, the minister of trade and industry. Andronnikov had considerable power, including the power to make or break ministers. He and Rasputin together were at least in part responsible for the disgrace of the minister of war, Sukhomlinov, who was subsequently imprisoned on suspicion of high treason.

The story of Sukhomlinov's dismissal is complex and unlovely, and did terrible damage to the authority of the regime, helping create widespread belief in the existence of so-called "dark forces," a pro-German party at the centre of the government, headed by the German tsarina. The military disasters of the first winter of the war had encouraged a search for traitors and scapegoats, generating a degree of spy fever quite without parallel. Everyone was on the lookout for the enemy within. The country was flooded with rumours of treason; there were stories of Russian munitions factories making shells for German guns, taxi drivers would confidently maintain that at least ten generals were working for the other side, and at the front it was widely believed that traitors were responsible for the shortage of rifles, shells and ammunition.[2] Students in the Baltic provinces were arrested for speaking German, while it was rumoured that local Baltic barons were converting their tennis courts into gun emplacements. The newspapers provided another instance of paranoia when they accused some millers of German descent near the front of communicating with the enemy, using their windmills, which had hitherto "stood suspiciously still," as semaphores of generous proportion to signal Russian troop movements to the advancing enemy.[3] One of the consequences of this climate of chaos and suspected treason was the enormous number of deserters; by 1915 there were up to two million wandering in armed bands far behind the lines, and they posed such a menace that the minister of the interior stated that he was unable to guarantee the safety of Tsarskoe Selo.[4]

When the Russian Tenth Army was badly beaten in January 1915, and its Twentieth Corps wiped out, it came as a comfort to learn that there was a scapegoat: a certain Colonel Myasoedov was suspected of espionage. A protégé of Sukhomlinov's, he had already, in 1912, been accused of spying for Austria, and had fought a duel with Guchkov in an attempt to clear his name. Now, on evidence flimsy enough to be virtually nonexistent, he was arrested and court-martialled for espionage and looting. The loot consisted of two small terra-cotta figures; the basis for the accusation of espionage, that he had asked a trivial question about local troop movements on a visit to the front line. He was convicted, sentenced to death and executed with disgraceful speed, a miscarriage of justice of the worst kind.

Myasoedov's "treason" led to a smear campaign against Sukhomlinov, and Andronnikov, a personal enemy, was responsible for much of the smearing—by word of mouth and a series of scurrilous pamphlets. Nicholas eventually felt that he had to dismiss his minister, while assuring him that he never doubted his loyalty—which did not prevent Sukhomlinov's arrest on suspicion of treason. As the British foreign secretary, Sir Edward Grey, observed to a Russian parliamentary delegation, their government must be confident indeed if it felt able to treat a minister of war in such a manner. Curiously enough Rasputin agreed. Although he had been a sworn enemy of Sukhomlinov's and had added his weight to Andronnikov's campaign, he disapproved of the imprisonment. When Andronnikov expressed surprise at his change of heart he replied that it was a bad time to divide the ranks: "There must be no quarrelling with anybody, it is a time to live in peace with all and sundry."[5]

Rasputin had introduced Andronnikov to Vyroubova, and he succeeded in impressing that foolish woman enormously, notably by his boundless praise for Rasputin. Andronnikov had also befriended Beletsky, ex-deputy police chief and now a senator, telling him to expect significant ministerial changes in the near future. He intended to get rid of the minister of internal affairs, Shcherbatov, whom he hated, and who was conveniently hostile to Rasputin, replacing him with A. N. Khvostov, whom Rasputin had "interviewed" when he was governor of Nizhny Novgorod. Khvostov, who had once described himself as a person lacking "centres of restraint," was quite unworthy of office. Utterly without principle, he was a political adventurer who conducted government business in a style, as Spiridovich put it, of "jovial banditry." He was a fool, impulsive to a degree, and quite devoid of political sense. His approach to politics was that of a fun-lover; he came to it with a fatalistic but astoundingly cheerful fecklessness. Nevertheless Andronnikov satisfied Vyroubova that he would make a suitable minister. He convinced her of his loyalty to Rasputin and made her feel that he would be energetic in his defence—a defence that, since this was the time of the Yar scandal, was greatly needed. Alexandra took his cause up with Nicholas, describing Khvostov as: "A very fat young man of much experience . . . his body is colossal but the soul high and clean."[6] She justified her political activity by maintaining that she was surrounding her "poor weak hubby" with good men and true, who would keep the Duma and all the forces of opposition and mischief in order:

> Some are afraid I am meddling in state affairs, (the ministers) and others look on me as the one to help as you are not here (Andronnikov, Khvostov, Varnava [see below, p. 263] and some others). That shows who is devoted to you in the *real* sense of the word— they will seek me out and the others will avoid me—is it not true sweetheart?[7]

In addition to recommending Khvostov, Alexandra put forward the name of Beletsky as the minister's deputy, in place of Djunkovsky. He too had convinced Vyroubova of his devotion to Rasputin, and the tsarina managed to secure his appointment together with that of Khvostov.

As far as we can tell Nicholas did not resent his wife's participation in affairs of state. On the contrary, he seems to have welcomed it, if we can judge by letters such as the following:

> Think, my Wifey, will you not come to the assistance of your hubby now that he is absent? What a pity you have not been fulfilling this duty for a long time . . . I know of no more pleasant feeling than to be proud of you, as I have been all these past months, when you urged me on with untiring importunity, exhorting me to be firm and stick to my opinions.[8]

It was largely thanks to their support of Rasputin that Andronnikov, Beletsky, and Khvostov had got what they wanted. They realised that their first task in office was to come to terms with him. They met him secretly the day after his return to the capital, and were all three struck by the change in his manner. He had grown confident to the point of arrogance, and had a poise that they had never known in him before. It was hardly surprising; he had, after all, survived yet another threat of permanent disgrace, only to see his enemies dismissed from office and persons entirely dependent upon his goodwill put in their place. The "friends" felt it incumbent upon them to convince him forthwith of their good intentions, and via Andronnikov immediately passed him a considerable sum of money from one of the minister's secret funds.

Rasputin now became an official personage, since the new minister fully recognised that his goodwill was essential if he wished to stay in office. Andronnikov took a special "conspiratorial" flat where he and Rasputin could meet discreetly. It was there that Andronnikov handed government money over to him and entertained him generously. A ministerial car was also put at his disposal. Partly in order to keep control over him, the minister increased the number of detectives responsible for his protection and surveillance. This became somewhat limited in its scope, because the agents had no car and were thus unable to follow Rasputin when he drove off into the night. However, a regular round-the-clock guard was mounted outside his flat, involving some thirty agents in all. The agents nicknamed him *tyemniy*, "the dark one." They enjoyed their surveillance and were regularly invited in and entertained. Rasputin was glad of their presence, for he had come increasingly to fear assassination. Khvostov in the meantime did all he could to keep on good terms with the *starets*, even to the point, on one occasion, of joining in the singing of a gypsy choir performing to Rasputin at the Villa Rhode. However, on the whole he tried to keep his acquaintanceship a secret.

In order both to control Rasputin and to keep him at one remove, Beletsky found Rasputin a personal bodyguard, a colonel of police named Komissarov. He was a rough and disreputable figure, one of the very few agents of the tsarist secret police to go on and work for its Bolshevik successor, the Cheka. A coarse, down-to-earth, and fun-loving man, a heavy drinker to boot, he delighted Rasputin from the start. When first introduced to him, Rasputin put up an elaborate smoke-screen of unctuousness and pious talk. Komissarov listened for only a few minutes before blowing it away once and for all, interrupting the holy man brutally by saying: "Stop the holiness, talk sense and have a drink."[9]

Rasputin always respected the direct approach, and had more than a little scorn for anyone fool enough to be taken in by him. He accepted Komissarov immediately. Henceforward it was he who paid Rasputin his monthly government allowance, together with an additional sum "for good works." None of the participants in the arrangement, incidentally, ever made it plain in their testimony to the Muravyev Commission quite why it was that Rasputin should have received government money. One presumes that they felt that if they were not to pay him, something bad could easily happen to them, and since there were funds that did not have to be accounted for, and since the tsarina wanted Rasputin to be happy, they might as well use the funds to secure that happiness.

The traffic was not one-way. Each morning Komissarov would call on Rasputin, collect the current batch of petitions and requests, and listen in on his daily telephone calls to Vyroubova and the palace. Thus the "conspiratorial flat" became an unofficial clearinghouse between the government and Tsarskoe Selo, a place where the views of each party could be communicated to the other without recourse to official channels. Komissarov discovered that it was important to conclude business by the end of the morning, for Rasputin could not be relied upon to be coherent after lunch. In the evenings Komissarov would usually take him out to dinner, picking up the bill, and Rasputin too if necessary. He reported regularly to his minister, telling him how, as he put it, with more than a hint of *vranye,* "He and Rasputin decided matters of state and discussed possible changes in the government."[10]

Komissarov often had to keep him out of the most serious kind of trouble, as on the occasion when they were on a train in Tsarskoe Selo station and Rasputin was very drunk. He wanted to stroll, or stagger, along the platform before the train left. Komissarov dissuaded him, saying that if he were to be seen drunk in public, the empress might get to hear of it, which would upset her. Rasputin's reaction was that of a drunk who kicks against authority because when sober he has to address that authority with deference. He began to curse the empress in such hair-raising language that even Komissarov was disturbed. He shook him severely and observed that if he ever heard Rasputin talk like that again he would choke the life out of him.

Rasputin's ability to make and break public figures was considerable, especially in the realm of church affairs. In a little over two months he brought down the over-procurators Sabler and Samarin; Alexandra's letters to Nicholas make it clear that it was almost entirely his doing. He was also responsible for some extraordinary appointments. He secured the archbishopric of Tobolsk for a protégé of the most dubious qualifications. Varnava, born Vasili Nakropin in 1859, an illiterate gardener's son who never completed any kind of formal education, had become a monk in 1899. An ambitious and intelligent opportunist who preached a simple form of popular religion with the normal Orthodox anti-Semitic bias, his ecclesiastical career had been remarkably successful. When he met Rasputin in 1910 he was already head of the monastery of Novogolubinsk in the diocese of Moscow.

Said to be a man of powerful sensual appetites and an intimate of Andronnikov's, he also had eccentric tastes in other respects. He enjoyed being photographed in his archiepiscopal robes laid out in a sumptuous coffin.[11] Although he never believed in Rasputin's holiness he recognised that he would make a useful ally. It was thanks to Rasputin that Nicholas insisted on his appointment to the archbishopric, going in the teeth of his over-procurator, who felt the appointment would be a disaster. Varnava went to great lengths to sustain his popularity with the imperial couple, emulating Rasputin by sending them encouraging telegrams. On one occasion he tried to touch the empress's heart with the announcement of a miracle. He sent a telegram announcing that a cross had appeared in the sky above a village church, and remained there for a quarter of an hour:

> I felicitate you with this vision and believe that God has sent you this sign in order to uphold visibly with love his devoted ones.

The tsarina was not so sure that this was the case, writing nervously to Nicholas: "God grant it may be a good sign. Crosses are not always."[12]

Varnava went on to create something of a national scandal. Anxious to increase his own importance and his popularity with Nicholas and Alexandra, he proceeded, in open defiance of the Holy Synod, with the ceremonial uncovering of the remains of a local holy man, John of Tobolsk, rightly confident that he had the imperial approval, and that the couple would support him in his challenge to their own ecclesiastical authorities. The ceremony was to be the last event of its kind in imperial Russia. Varnava's open disobedience of the synod caused widespread dismay, for it was regarded as a serious challenge to authority. Grand Duke Andrey Vladimirovich, for example, saw in it a sign of a terrifying surge of sedition: "The whole of Russia is talking about it. Priests everywhere are preaching to the people the kind of thing I would not dare to whisper in my sleep."[13]

Another of Rasputin's ecclesiastical protégés was Pitirim. Well known for his homosexual practices and suspected of embezzling ecclesiastical property, he had, as bishop of Kursk, given open support to a group of sectarian *khlysty* who believed in his sanctity and claimed that his head was ringed by a halo. It may be his sectarian sympathies that initially won Rasputin's support for him. At all events it was Rasputin, with the help of Khvostov and Vyroubova, who secured his promotion and had him made first exarch (a sort of ecclesiastical viceroy) of Georgia and then archbishop of Petrograd, the senior archbishopric of the Russian church. The appointment caused an uproar. Not only was he unworthy of the office, his promotion was obviously the work of Rasputin. It has been described as the most disgraceful episode in the history of the Russian church, and it made him the most hated ecclesiastic in the land.

Initially Pitirim was supported by Khvostov, who recognised that since Nicholas had appointed him in the face of such fierce opposition he must have a great deal of influence at court. Indeed, as Beletsky observed, Pitirim enjoyed the confidence of Nicholas, Alexandra, and Vyroubova to a greater extent than anybody else except for Rasputin. Like Khvostov, Pitirim was reluctant to let it be known that he was a protégé of Rasputin's and did all he could to keep his association with him secret. He too had an intermediary in his secretary Osipenko, variously said to be either his lover or his natural son. Osipenko visited Rasputin daily, passing on and receiving commissions. Alas for the archbishop, he failed to keep his acquaintanceship secret. Rasputin had no reason to conceal their closeness and caused Pitirim great embarrassment by boasting about it in public. Out of a sense of delicacy Khvostov had till then pretended to be ignorant of Pitirim's acquaintance with Rasputin. But when the archbishop failed to support him on a matter of policy, Russia's minister for internal affairs found the time to play him a practical joke. He instructed Komissarov to collect Rasputin and go with him to call upon Pitirim at a time when he, Khvostov, would be with the archbishop. Rasputin walked in unannounced and without knocking, making it perfectly clear that he and Pitirim were on the most intimate terms, much to the latter's pain and embarrassment. Khvostov was delighted by the whole affair.

Khvostov, Beletsky, and Andronnikov had hoped to contain Rasputin. By recognising his position and paying him generously they expected him to keep to "official channels," work through Komissarov alone, put their case to Vyroubova and the palace, and otherwise stay out of trouble and remain in the background. Beletsky himself went to great lengths to clean up after Rasputin, avoid scandal, and keep him out of trouble. On one occasion, for example, he learned that someone had obtained the draft of a letter of his to the tsarina recommending a change of prime minister, and was hoping to publish it. Beletsky managed to buy it back for a little over a thousand pounds sterling. He did not want the vendor to know that he was selling it to the government, so he used one of his agents, whom he described as an expert in disguise and widely travelled, to buy the letter from its owner, masquerading as a British journalist.[14] The trick worked and the letter was duly destroyed.

Khvostov's policy of containment did not work for long. Discretion was not in Rasputin's nature, he got no satisfaction from operating behind the scenes, and his impulsive temperament was not suited to a low profile. Moreover, he found Khvostov's desire to conceal their association insulting. He wanted consideration, not sums of money passed furtively in a "conspiratorial flat." Understanding what was happening soon enough, Rasputin declined to play. He continued to address himself to other ministers, and started to bypass Komissarov. Still worse, he began to make playful use of the telephone. He would make drunken calls to the wives of Khvostov and Beletsky, asking to speak to their husbands, whom he referred to by their first names. Since both Khvostov and Beletsky were so ashamed of their association with Rasputin that they had kept it from their families, the telephone calls, which were incidentally made in front of Rasputin's friends, were not well received.

Feeling that the *starets* was beginning to escape their control, Khvostov and Beletsky decided that it was time for him to take a trip. They planned to persuade him to make a tour of the holy places of Siberia in the company of an abbot, who had agreed subject to his being promoted to archimandrite, and who was to travel with a more than generous supply of Madeira. At first Rasputin agreed to go; the matter of his shipboard scandal had not been settled and he was afraid that news of it would reach the tsar. However, as soon as Beletsky arranged for this case to be buried once and for all, Rasputin blandly announced that he had no intention of leaving the capital. It was probably as well, since it seems to have been Khvostov's intention for him to have had an accident *en route*.

A few months in office had persuaded the minister that he no longer needed Rasputin, while his failure to contain the man meant that at any moment news of their association might become public knowledge. Moreover, he had reason to suspect that Rasputin was intriguing against him. He was hoping to be made prime minister as well as minister of internal affairs, but in the event the post went to B. V. Sturmer. Although Khvostov's agents found it hard enough to keep track of Rasputin now he had a car, they did manage to find out that he had been seeing a lot of Sturmer recently. Rasputin favoured Sturmer's appointment because he felt that it would be easy to control him; he was heard to dismiss the future prime minister as an elderly marionette, "an old man on a string."[15]

True to his character as a person "without restraining centres," Khvostov decided that the thing to do was to have Rasputin assassinated, and that the persons best placed to carry out the job were the officers charged with his security. He started to have roundabout chats with Beletsky about the danger Rasputin posed, not just to the dynasty, but to Khvostov and Beletsky too. It takes time to put across the idea that you want a man killed, if only to make sure, before you declare yourself, that your listener is sympathetic–which Beletsky certainly appeared to be.

Beletsky discussed Khvostov's proposal with Komissarov, who quickly seized the minister's point. His testimony to the investigatory commission makes splendid reading. Where Beletsky hides his roguery behind clouds of dreadful bureaucratic jargon, and occasionally breaks down in tears at the thought of "all the filth" he waded through, Komissarov is cheerful, brutal, and to the point. He had a racy turn of phrase, and was not the kind of man to talk of "terminating with extreme prejudice" when his boss wanted a man hit (*ubrat'*). However, he warned Beletsky against doing Khvostov's dirty work, while the minister kept his hands clean, and this set Beletsky thinking. If, as he put it, despite his in-built repugnance, he were to plan the murder and see it through in the interests of "higher order," would he really benefit, could he trust Khvostov to keep his promise?[16] He concluded that he could not, and decided therefore not to go against his "conscience." Beletsky fails to win our admiration for deciding to spare Rasputin.

He chose to humour Khvostov, and appeared to go along with him when the minister suggested various plans. They would send a car for Rasputin to take him to meet an anonymous admirer. The car would slow down in an alley and Komissarov's agents in disguise would jump in, put a cloth over Rasputin's head and a noose round his neck, strangle him, and dump him in the river. Beletsky was dubious. It would mean removing the normal surveillance, which would make Rasputin suspicious, and too many agents would be needed to carry out the plot. When Beletsky failed to come up with anything better Khvostov began to get impatient; brandishing his pocket Browning he would threaten to do the job himself. To keep him happy Beletsky suggested having Rasputin beaten up as an interim measure. Khvostov agreed and it was proposed to have him invited to a certain house one night; Komissarov's men would set on him when he left. News that something was afoot reached Rasputin, who told a journalist on the evening in question that there was a minister who had once kissed his hand but who now wished to kill him.[17] That night Rasputin stayed at home. The failure angered Khvostov and made him look foolish, for he had indicated to a number of people that something nasty would happen to Rasputin that evening.

The minister was fast losing confidence in Beletsky. He now approached Komissarov directly, offering him two hundred thousand roubles of government money—a colossal sum, one could live like a rich man on three thousand roubles a month—if he would do the job. Khvostov suggested he try poison, and in the hope of involving a sworn enemy of the minister's, the banker Rubinstein, proposed that Rasputin be sent a crate of Madeira, ostensibly from Rubinstein, which would be poisoned. Komissarov pointed out that the plan would fail if Rasputin were to thank Rubinstein before taking a drink. Nevertheless he undertook to procure some poison.

In order to do so he went to Saratov, where he had been stationed, and where he had some business of his own to do, and presumably the appropriate criminal contacts. He returned with a wide selection of phials containing assorted poisons, and impressed Khvostov with his account of their effects. Incredibly, he had tried them out on a number of cats belonging to Rasputin that lived in the "conspiratorial flat." The cats had reacted violently and died in great pain, mewing horribly. By now Komissarov was playing a double game, for he assured Beletsky that the poisons were not poisons at all but various kinds of coloured water. Beletsky believed him, or claimed he did, which was a mistake. The cats really had been poisoned, and Rasputin, who had had a falling-out with Andronnikov, was convinced that it was the prince's doing when he entered his conspiratorial apartment and found it littered with dead cats. He construed it as an act of petty malice, rather than a rehearsal for his own dispatch.

Khvostov in the meantime decided to go it alone. He charged one Rzhevsky, a dubious journalist, with the organisation of the killing, suggesting he use Rasputin's old enemy Iliodor. The monk, who was living in Norway at the time, was as hostile to Rasputin as ever. He had written a book attacking him, *Rasputin the Holy Devil,* and had plans to drop thousands of copies over the front line from an aeroplane. Khvostov sent Rzhevsky to make contact with him in Norway, and he apparently agreed to organise a plot. However, Rzhevsky's journey did not go unnoticed. Beletsky, having finally decided that it would be imprudent to side with Khvostov, was having Rzhevsky watched. At the Finnish frontier he arranged for an incident to be staged by a gendarme officer, who jostled Rzhevsky and caused a scene. Rzhevsky was detained and official note was taken both of his incognito and of certain papers in his possession. Despite his protestations that he was on a secret mission on behalf of Khvostov he was told that a report of the incident would go to Beletsky. The latter had in the meantime done some research and discovered that Rzhevsky was guilty of fraud; he had been misdirecting certain Red Cross funds for which he was responsible in the general direction of his mistress. On his return from Norway he had an uncomfortable interview with Beletsky, who had no trouble forcing him into revealing the assassination plan.

News of the incident had also reached Rasputin via a dubious associate of Rzhevsky's, Heine, who had leaked the story to Rasputin's secretary. Rasputin had an immediate conference with Vyroubova and Alexandra. He was in a panic, which was not helped when Komissarov told him that he had orders to remove his bodyguards. General Spiridovich found him a very frightened man in a conversation with him in which Rasputin tugged nervously at his beard and complained that *Tolstopuz,* "Fat-belly," as he had nicknamed Khvostov, was out to kill him.

Beletsky had finally committed himself to the defence of Rasputin and the betrayal of his minister. He had Rzhevsky arrested, and a search of his flat produced a letter that linked Khvostov directly to the assassination plan. In the middle of this mess of intrigue Nicholas returned from the front for a brief visit. While Alexandra urged him to secure Rasputin's safety, his palace commandant, General Voyeikov, or "Eneral Faveika" as Rasputin would refer to him, gave him an unflattering report on the whole affair, which concluded with the recommendation that Rasputin be sent home for good to avoid further scandal. As usual Nicholas listened calmly, nodded, and did nothing, while Voyeikov earned the tsarina's undying hatred.

Alexandra tried to give Rasputin all the support and the sympathy that she could, even to the extent of having him take communion with the family at Easter. She found the experience very moving. As the Gospels were read out they made her think "so vividly of Gregory and his persecution for Christ and our sakes."[18] When news of the joint communion got out, it caused a scandal, and was duly distorted by rumour to suggest that the service had included strange sectarian rituals, providing yet another source of delighted gossip.

Khvostov and Beletsky were now at daggers drawn. The minister put the blame for the murder plan upon his assistant, at the same time trying to get rid of him by making him governor of the far-flung Siberian province of Irkutsk. When Beletsky learnt of his appointment he burst into tears—he always cried easily, often breaking down and sobbing during his interrogation by the Muravyev Commission—and when he asked Khvostov why he had been sent into a kind of exile the good-natured minister burst out laughing and said that none of this would have happened if only they had killed Rasputin. However, Beletsky fought back. He went to see Vyroubova and told her the story from the beginning, making it clear that Khvostov had long been planning to do away with Rasputin. Khvostov in the meantime attempted to defend his own position. He gave a long and bizarre interview to two distinguished newspaper editors, which was largely devoted to blackening Rasputin's name, associating him with the pro-German party and observing that he was undoubtedly an agent of "world espionage," whatever that might mean. When asked to substantiate his charge, Khvostov of course had nothing to say. Yet in a wartime Russia that lived on paranoia, half-truth, and rumour, such accusations coming from a minister did untold damage. They fed the positive need felt by patriots who found Russian reverses inexplicable to believe in treason in high places. The absence of any proof was no more an obstacle to belief that it had been in the case of the luckless Myasoedov.

Rasputin grew more and more afraid of assassination. He rejected a suggestion of the prime minister, Sturmer, that he return to Pokrovskoe, because he was terrified of being killed *en route*. Indeed, when one reflects that the minister for internal affairs was plotting actively to have him murdered, it is hardly surprising that he felt insecure. In an agitated conversation with Spiridovich he prophesied the imminent downfall of Khvostov, boasting that Nicholas had already asked him to look around for a replacement. Then, checking his hysterical expressions of panic, he suddenly grew calm and looked Spiridovich in the eye:

> They are certainly going to kill me, my dear. And you are all going to die too. And they will kill Papa and Mama as well.[19]

One did not have to be a prophet to sense something of the kind by now. Those who knew what was happening were secretly resigned to disaster. As Major-General V. N. Voyeikov, the palace commandant, observed, commenting on the Khvostov affair, "What does it matter. We are all going to die anyway."[20] It was in that same spring of 1916 that Alexander Blok sensed that it was all over. It was not the Khvostov affair that convinced him, however, but a little street scene that caught his eye and told him that the old world was finished. On Easter night, shortly after Rasputin had taken communion with the tsarina, Blok went to look at the celebrations outside St. Isaac's cathedral. The crowd was a small one.

> There were scarcely any illuminations. No solemnity whatsoever, though neither was there the gloom and blackness of former years. All over Falconet's statue [the equestrian statue of Peter the Great, symbol of St. Petersburg] swarmed a crowd of little boys, hanging on to the tail, sitting on the serpent, smoking under the horse's belly. Total demoralization. Petersburg finis.[21]

Khvostov was duly dismissed, which did not prevent him from continuing to gossip, and Beletsky made matters worse by giving an extended interview in his own defence to *Birzhevye Vedomosti,* for which he lost his governorship. Khvostov's own summary of the whole affair is characteristic and charming. "I cannot deny that there was a certain negligence on my part," he observed.[22]

It was a question of much more than negligence. Even by Russian standards it was a grotesque political scandal that brought discredit upon all concerned. As Spiridovich put it, Khvostov "dealt the tsarina and the prestige of the monarch one of the most powerful and damaging blows of all."[23] The scandal also represented a potential turning point. Alexandra was all too aware that she had put forward Khvostov's name on Rasputin's recommendation.

> Am so wretched that we, through Gregory, recommended Khvostov to you–it leaves me not peace–you were against it and I let myself be imposed on by them.[24]

The disastrous nature of the appointment might conceivably have brought Alexandra to her senses and made her reassess the value of Rasputin's advice. Her failure to learn from the experience is a sad illustration of the axiom that the gods first drive mad those whom they wish to destroy.

CHAPTER 18

The situation is always going from worse to worst.

THE RUSSIAN DIARY OF AN ENGLISHMAN

THE AMOUNT OF attention paid to Rasputin, ranging from bribery to projects of assassination, gives an idea of the extent of his importance. Although this was largely restricted to petitions and appointments, it did not quite stop there. When Nicholas, in the summer of 1915, was considering the possibility of taking over supreme command of his armies, much against the advice of his ministers, Alexandra encouraged him to do so. In order to make her point more emphatically she recalled Rasputin from Pokrovskoe, where he had been keeping a low profile in the aftermath of the Yar affair. He returned to the capital for five days, from July 31 to August 4, and talked to Nicholas, urging him to do as he saw fit and assume command regardless of his ministers. He had earlier bombarded him with telegrams confirming him in his autocracy, reminding him that he was an anointed monarch who should do as he thought best.[1] He also provided a more tangible kind of help. When Nicholas was about to face his ministers and inform them that his mind was made up, he received a letter from his wife reminding him to prepare himself by looking at Rasputin's photograph and combing his hair with Rasputin's comb. However, it must be said that in no sense was the advice of Rasputin decisive. Nicholas had made up his mind, comb or no comb.

Although it is arguable that there was nothing obviously wrong about Nicholas's decision to assume supreme command, that indeed there was much to be said for it, the decision was nonetheless disastrous. One wonders whether Rasputin did not encourage it precisely because it would keep Nicholas from the capital. The tsar himself had often observed that he preferred the healthy atmosphere of GHQ to the intrique and scandal of Tsarskoe Selo and Petrograd. Yet it was in the capital and not with the army that the real problems were to be found, and Nicholas turned his back on them, just as he turned his back on reports of Rasputin's doings "after hours." More serious still, by leaving the capital Nicholas allowed Alexandra to assume an increasingly important role, with terrible consequences. No one believed that a Russian tsar wanted a separate peace, but a German tsarina was a horse of a different colour. Had she not been allowed to take a more prominent role in her husband's absence, had she remained the tense, shy, and domestic lady withdrawn from public life, the slanderous aspersions upon the "German woman's" loyalty could never have been so damaging, Rasputin's hold over her could never have grown so much a matter of public concern.

His influence was by no means exclusively pernicious. At one time in 1915 the tsar used to make a habit of visiting hospitals in Petrograd and the surrounding provinces. For some reason he abandoned the practice, a change of policy which Beletsky and Khvostov felt to be a mistake. They mentioned the fact to Rasputin, who spoke to the empress, and sure enough the tsar immediately renewed his visits.

Rasputin did not often involve himself with politics. He was hostile to the Duma simply because it was hostile to him, and only interested in those of its proceedings that affected him personally. However, he did play a political role upon one occasion. In February 1916, for the only time in its history, Nicholas attended an opening of the Duma. It was intended as a conciliatory gesture, an attempt to bridge the ever-growing gap between the government and the country's elected representatives. It was Rasputin's boast that it was he who was responsible for the gesture. One morning, suffering from a severe hangover, he had invited his detectives in for tea and a glass or two. In the course of their conversation he told them that he had been asked what should be done about the Duma and had decided he should "send the boss there himself, let him open it and no one will dare do anything."[2] Rasputin would boast regularly that he could get Nicholas to do whatever he wanted, feeling himself to be the stronger personality for, as he observed to one journalist, "the tsar can change his mind from one minute to the next, he's a sad man, he lacks guts."[3] It was apparently Sturmer who proposed to get the tsar to the Duma. A protégé of his, a journalist named Manasevich-Manuilov, suggested Rasputin try to persuade him, and he agreed, sending Sturmer a message to the effect that "Papa will visit the Duma."[4] Visit it he most certainly did, though whether as a result of Rasputin's urging we cannot say.

Rasputin tried to keep as tight a hold over Nicholas as possible. This depended, to a considerable degree, on the tsar's paying frequent visits to Tsarskoe Selo. At headquarters he was beyond the reach of Rasputin, who never succeeded in getting permission to go to the front. The first time he had suggested it was to the previous commander-in-chief, Grand Duke Nicholas, who observed laconically that were Rasputin to appear at headquarters he would hang him. The tsar was no more anxious to have him at the front than his cousin. Not only was he out of reach of Rasputin there, he was also out of contact with his wife, who was taking an increasingly active interest in the business of government. Like Rasputin she kept urging Nicholas to be a strong tsar, to ignore his ministers and advisors and ensure he preserve the absolute authority of the throne for the sake of "Baby," since baby's temperament was such that he could never succeed as a constitutional monarch. On the other hand Alexandra, the wearer it will be recalled of "invisible trousers," also devoted much energy to telling her husband what to do. Nicholas felt lonely at headquarters, and his only comfort, as he put it, was the company of his son. Accordingly Aleksey was beginning to spend more and more time at the front. This eventually began to cause distress to Alexandra, who rightly felt that his education was suffering. It also displeased Rasputin, for a different reason. When Nicholas was alone he would make frequent visits to Tsarskoe Selo out of concern for his son's health, and was thus more easily to be got at.

Rasputin joined Alexandra and Vyroubova in urging Nicholas to leave the boy behind, and on one occasion grew so insistent that Nicholas became very angry. Observing that he would do as he pleased, he took Aleksey with him. Whether Rasputin had had some premonition we cannot say, but the fact remains that on the train journey to HQ the tsarevich knocked his nose against a window and the bleeding could not be stopped. The imperial train turned back, riding as gently as possible: that night Rasputin was telephoned and asked to come to the boy's bedside at once. For the one and only time on record he refused, merely giving some instructions as to treatment over the wire. He only appeared late the next day and stopped the bleeding at once. Of course he was triumphant and observed that the tsar would be more likely to listen to him in the future. It was a long time before the tsarevich visited the front again.[5]

Whatever Rasputin's influence might have been, it was rumour, not the fact, that counted. Despite scandals such as the Khvostov affair, little was known about him outside the inner circle, and what was known proved a mere point of departure for extraordinary speculation.

Wartime always breeds rumours, the Great War more than most, perhaps. There was, for example, the classic British rumour that suggested a Russian army had passed through England in the night, on their way to fight on the Western Front. Evidence of their passing was the snow they had shaken from their boots and left behind them in the railway carriages that had carried them across the country. Yet when it came to extravagant and improbable rumour, Petrograd was in a class by itself. Rigid censorship made for an absence of reliable hard news, and this left too much room for communication of half-truths by word of mouth. The situation was made worse by official attitudes. Government sources went to great lengths to conceal enemy advances and communicate good news only. In fairness it must be said that in this respect they were outdone by Stalin's regime. In the early phases of World War Two, when the Germans were driving into Russia, one Red Army general was nearly shot for marking fresh German advances in on his map—whether for spreading alarm and despondency or for "negative thinking" it is hard to say. At all events imperial Russian officials went out of their way to hide bad news. As the British military attaché, Sir Alfred Knox, wrote:

> The secretiveness of many responsible Russian officials and their suicidal desire to present the situation in a falsely favourable light made it at all times exceedingly difficult for allied representatives to keep their Governments posted with timely and accurate information.[6]

This combination of factors made for an extraordinary nightmare atmosphere, in which, as one British observer, C. Hanbury Williams, put it, there was "an utter absence of any method in which what is true is separated from what is false."[7] The last U.S. ambassador, J. P. Marye, found the miasma of rumour enveloping the capital utterly bewildering:

> Russia is a land of irresponsible *on dit,* and it takes time to find out what among the things you hear is true and what is not.[8]

One of the most sensitive accounts of the atmosphere of wartime Petrograd was the diary kept by Zinaida Gippius. The wife of the novelist, poet, and critic Dmitri Merezhkovsky, she was one of the most distinguished poets of the age in her own right. A striking woman, tall, with red hair, her talent, her intellect, and her style of life made her a blend of notoriety and distinction that anticipated some of the extravagances of London's Bloomsbury set by a quarter of a century. As Simon Karlinsky writes in an introduction to a recent study, in which he gives her talent the recognition that it deserves:

> Gippius was also a remarkable early theoretician and practitioner of androgyny and psychological unisex, who rejected the traditional male/female roles as early as the 1890's.[9]

Her diary portrays the capital as a place of destruction and of death, a place she rechristens Chertograd, Devil-town. It is not an expression that she uses lightly. She may not have believed in God, but she certainly believed in the Devil. "The Devil was for her a real being, one of the most important . . . in her cast of characters." It was he who had taken over her city, setting the mood that characterises the last winter Rasputin would spend on this earth:

> There is no firewood in Petersburg, and not much to eat. The streets are filled with rubbish. The most frightening and crude rumours are disturbing the masses. It is a charged, neurotic atmosphere. You can almost hear the laments of the refugees in the air. Each day is drenched in catastrophes. What is going to happen? It is intolerable. "Things cannot go on like this" an old cab-driver says.[10]

A newspaper article develops her sense that the city is a place of rumour and pending catastrophe:

> Petrograd has turned very tense in the last month. The political mood is white hot, and even the apolitical are beginning to think, and discuss what's going on, as our nation's history grows sombre and incomprehensible and a mad squall of rumour blows with special strength, and the rumour has a very special ring to it.[11]

Liberal circles were becoming convinced of the existence of a "Black Bloc" that wished to make a separate peace with Germany. The bloc was believed to include pro-German courtiers, the prime minister, the minister of internal affairs, and the entire right wing of the Duma. Its object was to gain control of the tsar, create a weak government and stifle the voice of genuine patriotism. The bloc was believed to welcome Nicholas's assumption of supreme command, since continuing military failure, which was considered inevitable, would incline him to sue for peace.[12] In the meantime at the front soldiers said that it was unlucky to receive a decoration from the hands of the tsarina; anyone so doing was bound to stop a bullet.[13] There were also widespread rumours among the common soldiers that the Germans had given ministers a billion roubles in return for their promise to starve to death as many peasants as possible, while the minister of the court, Count Fredericks, was believed, thanks to his Germanic name, to have sold western Russia to the enemy for personal gain.[14]

One of the best comments on such allegations of treason was offered by D. S. Shuvaev, a person of no ability who much to his surprise was made minister of war in 1916 (the incumbent, Polivanov, allegedly lost his post because he deprived Rasputin of the three military cars that had been placed at his disposal).[15] When accused of working for the other side he made the classic retort: "I may be a fool but I am not a traitor."[16]

Belief in the existence of the bloc was widespread at home and at the front. It is quite without foundation, as historians such as Melgunov and Katkov have shown—although a separate peace might well have saved Russia from revolution. The rumours may have had their origin in historical precedent. During the Seven Years' War, 1756–63, there was a powerful pro-Prussian party in Russia, which was at war with Prussia at the time, headed by the tsarevich Paul, who was married to a German princess, the future Catherine the Great. When he succeeded to the throne he immediately signed a separate peace treaty with Prussia, altering the direction of the war and arousing great hostility and a sense of shame among patriotic Russians.

To many eyes Alexandra's association with Rasputin was a confirmation of her treachery. Not only was it widely supposed that he was her lover, it was also believed that he was in the pay of the Germans, receiving large sums from them via the Swedish embassy, according to Rodzyanko, the leader of the Duma. In May 1916 the Constitutional Democrats had planned to publish a free newspaper abroad to secure foreign support for their opposition to the regime. A secret police report from a Colonel Martynov stated that its most serious intention would be to expose the treacherous part played by Rasputin in Russian political life and court circles.[17]

Incredible rumours circulated about Rasputin. Some members of the Duma actually believed that the Germans had introduced a double, to behave especially badly in public in order to discredit him still further. There was also paranoid talk of a certain "black car" that Rasputin was said to drive through the capital late at night, crossing the *Champ de Mars* and disappearing mysteriously over the Palace Bridge, firing shots at random, killing and wounding for pleasure.[18] Rasputin had so much become the topic of dinner party gossip that some hostesses put up signs in their dining rooms that read, "We do not talk about Rasputin here."[19] The sister of one of Rasputin's eventual assassins characterises the mood of that autumn:

> It was about this time that I first heard people speaking of the emperor and empress with open animosity and contempt. The word revolution was uttered more openly and more often; soon it could be heard everywhere. The war seemed to recede to the background. All attention was riveted on interior events, Rasputin, Rasputin, Rasputin, it was like a refrain: his mistakes, his shocking personal conduct, his mysterious power. This power was tremendous; it was like dusk enveloping all our world eclipsing the sun. How could so pitiful a wretch throw so vast a shadow? It was inexplicable, maddening, almost incredible.[20]

A journalist sums the situation up:

> And over Petrograd, in place of the imperial standard, floated Rasputin's undergarment, in anticipation of the approaching Soviet of workers and peasants, a symbol of impending rule by the scum of the earth.[21]

The sense of paranoia and nightmare emerges in little details as observers watched the situation deteriorate:

> They have just arrested Alvin Juin for spying, the regime is finished. [Juin was the owner of the best restaurant in town.] If the spy hunt has been taken to the kitchens of the Maxim's of Russia and an innocent French patriot taken for a German spy then anything is possible.[22]

Far and away the most obvious sign of demoralisation was the speed with which Nicholas changed his ministers. The last two years of the regime saw no fewer than forty ministers hold the thirteen cabinet posts, including four prime ministers, four ministers of war and six ministers of internal affairs. There are parallels to be drawn between the latter stages of the Russian Empire and the last years of France's *ancien régime*. It was felt in both cases that the country could be saved by ministerial changes, with a correspondingly rapid rate of reshuffling. Alexandra seems to have believed that ministerial change was an adequate substitute for good government. Prince Shakhovskoy, who was minister of trade from February 1915 to the end, says about the period: the only word to describe those two years is "nightmare."[23]

As we have seen, Rasputin was and remained a major factor behind the various changes. Ministers such as Sukhomlinov and Khvostov lost their positions because of him, new ones were appointed upon his recommendations of their loyalty, ability, and largeness of soul; though after the Khvostov debacle Nicholas did grow more cautious. Nicholas's changes earned the name of "ministerial leapfrog," and as one anti-tsarist Moscow politician observed, decades of propaganda could not have done what the leapfrog did "to destroy the ultimate support of the regime and reveal its essence to the most unenlightened and apathetic bourgeois."[24] A satirical poem on the subject, which was popular at the time, begins, "In lack of system there's a system,"[25] a lack which came to appeal to the "sporting instinct" of ministers and potential ministerial candidates alike.[26]

We can appreciate something of the impact of these changes on public opinion from a secret police report submitted early in 1916. It places special emphasis on the damage done by an embittered exminister, Samarin, whom Rasputin had had dismissed from his post of over-procurator of the Holy Synod:

> In the present instance we must speak of even more than the decline in the prestige of the supreme power: the symptoms are at present of an anti-dynastic movement which has already begun and is steadily developing . . . After mingling with diverse sections of society, we are pained to report that, should we respond to every instance of brazen and overt insults to His Majesty the Emperor . . . the number of trials . . . would reach an unprec-

> edented figure. And this is as much the mood of the middle and higher bourgeoisie . . . as it is of the lower classes . . .
>
> Perhaps no one, not even the most unrestrained revolutionaries, has caused so much harm, has furthered to such a terrible degree the decline in the prestige of the supreme authority by blackening the person of the monarch, as has Samarin . . . The details of the role played in public life at this present moment by the notorious *Starets* Rasputin were heavy blows and insults, not only to His Majesty the Emperor, but especially to Her Majesty the Empress Alexandra Fedorovna . . . the filthy gossip about the tsar's family has now become the property of the street.
>
> We must also note together with this feeling of extreme disrespect for the person of Her Majesty the Empress Alexandra Fedorovna the widespread feeling against her as a "German." Her Majesty the Empress is regarded, even in intellectual circles, as the inspirer and leader of the campaign for a separate peace with Germany.[27]

The chopping and changing that lay at the heart of much of this gossip and discontent are partly at least the result of the frighteningly poor quality of Alexandra's judgment. Although she fought like a tigress for her "hubby," she must be considered to have been foolish and naive to the point of tragedy. Eighteen secluded years in Tsarskoe Selo had done nothing to develop her political sense. She was inflexible and single-minded in her political aim: to preserve the autocracy for her son:

> For Baby's sake we must be firm as otherwise his inheritance will be awful, as with his character he won't bow down to others but be his own master, as one *must* in Russia, while people are so uneducated. Mr. Philippe and Gregory said so too.[28]

Nicholas, in the meantime, tragically underestimated the extent of hostility to the dynasty. He believed it to be limited to Petrograd and Moscow, supposing the real Russia to be behind him. Too many years spent witnessing enthusiastic demonstrations of loyalty from bearded peasants falling to their knees and blessing him, or townspeople greeting him with bread and salt, had given him a false sense of security as father of his people. This encouraged him to dismiss articulate criticism of his policies as the opinion of a hostile and unrepresentative minority uncharacteristic of the masses. He forgot that it was those very masses who had sent out the two great rebel leaders of modern Russian history, Stenka Razin in the seventeenth century and Pugachev in the eighteenth, and who had also let loose the red cockerel of violence and arson that had run across the face of the Russian land in 1905.

Recent events, a real and reasonable fear of imminent death, and the increasingly taxing pace of his drinking and womanising had taken a heavy toll of Rasputin. A woman who met him in the spring of 1916, having last seen him the previous summer, was struck by the change. He had aged, grown thinner, more lined and drawn.[29] He was also having presentiments of his own death and the end of the dynasty. Although the Khvostov affair was over, the presentiments were still with him. Maurice Paléologue, the French ambassador, attributes the following to him in his diary entry for April 26, 1916. Rasputin is talking to a friend:

> Do you know that soon I shall die in terrible pain? But what can I do? God has sent me to be sacrificed to save our dear sovereign and holy Russia. Despite my terrible sins I am a Christ in miniature.

Although Rasputin was capable of unctuous cant, this could often be mingled with perceptive glimpses into the future. On another occasion, passing the fortress of St. Peter and St. Paul, he claimed to have a vision:

> I see many people tortured there; not individuals but whole crowds; masses, clouds of bodies, several grand dukes and hundreds of counts. The Neva will be red with blood.[30]

Rasputin was not the only one to have such visions; a courtier put his view of the future more idiomatically: "There's going to be a revolution and we are all going to hang. Who cares which lamppost we dangle from?"[31]

Despite Rasputin's misreading of Khvostov and the signs of panic he had displayed in recent months, Alexandra's faith in him remained unshaken. Hearing the Gospel read at Easter had made her "think so vividly of Gregory and his persecution for Christ and our sakes."[32] She urged Nicholas always to keep his photograph nearby in order that he should benefit from its powers.[33] She remained confident in his clairvoyance: "He sees far ahead and therefore his judgment can be relied on."[34]

She declared her confidence in him once more when he set off for his regular summer visit to Pokrovskoe. She sent Vyroubova and a lady-in-waiting, Lili Dehn, to accompany him, making a pilgrimage on her behalf to the shrine of Varnava's new holy man, John of Tobolsk. Rasputin kept in touch with her by means of his usual cryptically worded telegrams:

> A bad tree will fall whatever the axe that cuts it. St. Nicholas is with you—by his miraculous appearance he always works wonders.[35]

Even the tsarina was beginning to get a sense of impending collapse, but this simply strengthened her attachment to Rasputin. His advice, she felt, was invaluable to her in her determined efforts to preserve the monarchy for "Baby," and his influence in matters of personnel selection was still considerable. It was recognised by one of the more exotic figures on the fringes of Russian political life, who now sought to exploit it in a manner somewhat reminiscent of Andronnikov. Unlike that unlovely prince, Peter Aleksandrovich Badmaev was not a venal scoundrel, although he was widely and improperly held to be a quack. Badmaev was a Siberian Asian, a Buryat. After studying Oriental languages in his youth he first served in the Office of Foreign Affairs and then studied medicine in a military medical academy. He abandoned an orthodox medical career when he grew interested in the medical lore of Tibet, which is very evolved. Their doctors:

> Observe the actions of plants and certain products from animals upon people, preserve Tibetan medicines and cures and study

> anatomy very carefully but without making use of vivisection and the scalpel. They are skillful bone-setters, masseurs and great connoisseurs of hypnotism and animal magnetism.[36]

European Russia rejected such practices as charlatanism in those days, and it is only now that Tibetan medicine is being accorded serious recognition in the Soviet Union.

By 1916 Badmaev was a white-haired old man who stressed his Asian background by wearing rich silk caftans and Asian-style boots. He had come to the capital early in this century and built up a successful practice. A godson of Alexander III, he was well connected and his patients ranged from Sergei Witte to the *yurodiviy* Mitya Kolyaba and his wife. He also had politico-commercial ambitions and had presented to Nicholas elaborate plans for the development of Russia's far east. Before the war he had been close to Iliodor and also to Rodzyanko, who had come to him for support in his campaign against Rasputin. In past years he had unsuccessfully sought permission to treat the tsarevich, but Aleksey's European doctors would not allow it. This may account for a curious legend, according to which he and Rasputin conspired to treat the boy with a secret potion administered by Vyroubova. The story is quite untrue; for one thing the two healers were enemies at the time. However, early in the war Badmaev made his peace with Rasputin, who would call on him in private, though without ever giving him his confidence. Rasputin was not a man to trust repentant enemies. "That Chinaman will betray you for a kopeck," he once observed, in one of his succinct summaries of character.[37]

It was in Badmaev's flat in the winter of 1915 that Rasputin was introduced to A. D. Protopopov, ex-deputy president of the Duma and a long-time friend and patient of Badmaev. Together with Kurlov, an ex-chief of police, Protopopov would meet Rasputin to discuss the course of the war, and, in particular, problems of rising prices and food supply. One day Badmaev told him that "it had occurred" to Rasputin that he would make an excellent minister. In fact it was Badmaev who had first proposed that Rasputin should secure appointments for Protopopov and Kurlov, suggesting that it would benefit Rasputin and the tsar. Protopopov would enjoy the support both of the Duma and of the banking and commercial communities, and was well qualified to deal with the economics crisis, while there was indeed support for his candidacy in parliamentary circles. When Protopopov first heard the suggestion he was incredulous, but Rasputin assured him "with much giggling and simpering"[38] that he would get him a portfolio. He duly put the case to the tsarina.

Alexandra was quickly convinced of his suitability, and wrote repeatedly to Nicholas to that effect:

> Gregory begs you earnestly to name Protopopov there. You know him and had such a good impression of him—happens to be of the Duma and is not left and so will know how to be with them . . . I think you could not do better than name him.[39]

Alexandra was not alone in considering that Protopopov might form a bridge between the tsar and the Duma. Rodzyanko also supported his candidacy for that very reason. Nicholas was unconvinced at first and had the temerity to question Rasputin's judgment. Protopopov's background did not appear to qualify him for the Ministry of Internal Affairs:

> Thank you with all my heart for your dear, long letter, in which you pass on our Friend's instructions. It seems to me that this Protopopov is a good man, but he has much to do with factories etc. . . . I must consider this question, as it has taken me completely by surprise. Our Friend's opinions of people are sometimes very strange, as you yourself know—therefore one must be careful, especially with appointments to high offices.[40]

Nevertheless, within a week Protopopov had the job. Even by standards current at that time the appointment was a disaster. Far from building bridges between the Duma and the government, Protopopov turned his back on his old associates, discovering in himself a capacity for devotion to the monarchical principle that bordered on idolatry. He displayed a blind loyalty that may have endeared him to the tsarina, but which further alienated parliamentary circles and added to the isolation of the imperial couple.

The new minister had regular meetings both with Badmaev and

with Rasputin—whom he would call on at night. Rasputin had arranged for his surveillance to be suspended at 10:00 P.M. to assist his comings and goings. To ensure his support Protopopov paid him a salary of one thousand roubles a month out of his own pocket, beyond the government sums, and more important, gave every appearance of taking the *starets* seriously, professing a belief in his historic mission and in his sanctity, an attitude that both flattered Rasputin and won the sympathy of the tsarina. It would be kind to assume that Protopopov was play-acting, and perhaps he was, but this was not necessarily the case. His subsequent behaviour suggests he was capable of any eccentricity. After Rasputin's death he tried hard to convince the tsarina that Grigorii's spirit had literally entered into him. His subsequent denial of that charge to the investigating commission reveals the extent to which his mind was unhinged. He breaks away from a line of interrogation and apropos of nothing observes, "Besides, Mr. President, I imagine you have heard those absurd rumours put about in the Duma alleging that I tried to make persons in Tsarskoe Selo believe that the spirit of Rasputin had entered into me." He refutes the charge by observing that he did not attend the funeral and did not even know where the man was buried.[41] In the last months of the regime his total lack of judgment and failure to understand the mood of the capital made a considerable contribution to the final collapse.

Rasputin was not entirely convinced by Protopopov. "His honour stretches like a piece of elastic," he once observed.[42] Yet the new appointment was a further confirmation of his influence, and moreover the minister appeared to take Rasputin seriously. They had long discussions about the nation's problems and sought together for ways to reduce the length of the queues stretching outside the capital's bread shops. The minister's attitude convinced Rasputin that he was more powerful than ever; that, in his own words, "he held Russia in the palm of his hand."[43]

Rasputin's hold over the tsarina, and her unqualified trust in his judgment involved her and the tsar in certain not very savoury affairs of which they should have stayed clear at all costs. The first of these was the case of the banker Rubinstein. It will be recalled that he had been arrested on suspicion of high treason. Now, in the autumn of

1916, Rasputin set about securing his release—probably having taken a substantial bribe from the banker's wife. At his instigation the tsarina wrote a series of letters to her husband asking that he be taken from his prison in Pskov and banished to Siberia. She conceded that he might have been involved in dubious deals but observed that he was not alone in that. He had moreover been arrested in the hope of finding material to be used against Rasputin. The latter also sent Nicholas telegrams urging the man's release. Once again Nicholas was worn down by such persistence and eventually ordered that Rubinstein be set free—thus feeding the myth that Alexandra was working for the enemy, for no one supposed Rubinstein to be innocent of treason. It would have been the height of folly at the best of times for a tsarina to involve herself in the case of a man who by her own admission was of the most doubtful financial reputation, and these times were any but the best.

Alexandra made the same mistake again in the case of Sukhomlinov. Once more she urged Nicholas to release him, on the advice of Rasputin, who had taken a liking to his fourth wife, a young woman of expensive tastes. The tsarina even sent Nicholas the form of the telegram he was to send to the prime minister ordering the case to be dropped.[44] Once again she was prompted less by the voice of natural justice than by the voice of Rasputin, and once again her intervention was unwise, giving the appearance that she was lending her support to a traitor. Feeling herself surrounded by enemies, the tsarina became increasingly strident and authoritarian in her approaches to her husband. She was convinced that she and Rasputin were giving him the strength that he lacked, supporting a weak man for Russia's good:

> I don't see why the bad should always fight for their cause and the good complain, but sit calmly with folded hands . . . I have more energy than the whole lot put together and can't sit calmly by . . . I am therefore disliked, because one feels . . . I stand up for yr. cause, Baby's and Russia's. Yes, I am more Russian than many another and I won't keep quiet.
>
> . . . all my trust lies in our Friend who only thinks of you, Baby and Russia. And guided by him we shall get through this

heavy time, but a Man of God's is near to guide yr. boat safely through the reefs.[45]

Sweety mine, you must back me up, for your and Baby's sake. Had we not got him all wld. long have been finished . . . We are living through the hardest times, but God will help us through, I have no fear. *Let* they (sic) scream.[46]

Be the emperor, be Peter the Great, John the Terrible, the emperor Paul, crush them all under you, don't laugh you naughty one. It is *war* and at such a time *interior* war is *high treason.*

To which the tsar of all the Russias replied:

Tender thanks for the severe written scolding. Your poor little weak-willed hubby.[47]

The situation in autumn 1916, as it appears to contemporary eyes, is succinctly summed up by Sir Bernard Pares, professor of Russian at Liverpool University; he knew the country well and spent the war years there:

The initiative comes from above; and there–above–we are faced with the strangest of human triangles, the complicated and abnormal relations of three persons, Rasputin, the empress and the emperor; set in ascending order of authority and a descending order of influence.[48]

CHAPTER 19

There were so many Achilles' heels, such hopelessness in the way the country was run. Everything lay in ruins.
N. A. MAKLAKOV
MINISTER OF THE INTERIOR, 1912–15. EXECUTED 1918.

THE AUTUMN OF 1916, which saw the thirteenth million called to the colours, was cold and wet; winter set in early and was extraordinarily severe. At one stage no fewer than twelve hundred locomotives had burst their frozen pipes and were immobilised, increasing the problems of food supply. Life in the capital had become very hard. Everywhere one could see long, grey queues standing outside food shops, and even the upper classes were beginning to suffer. Not only had the war created a staff problem—the English and French embassies shared a single dining-room servant—but even for the British Military Mission food had grown hard to come by and exorbitantly expensive. Almost worse than the actual shortages were the uncertainties created by inefficient distribution. The difficulties have a familiar ring to anyone acquainted with life in Russia today. While there was virtually no meat to be had in any of the main cities, railway depots and warehouses were filled with rotting carcasses, which had eventually to be turned into glue, or simply thrown away, because of the authorities' inability to organise their distribution to re-tail outlets. Shortages were reflected in soaring prices for such essential items as bread, sugar (when obtainable), and firewood. The efforts of the authorities to control prices made for greater confusion still:

> Often . . . when supplies should have been available, the shops became mysteriously empty, and some necessary commodity, flour or butter for example, totally unobtainable. These were the occasions when an incompetent bureaucracy was attempting to control prices without the power to ensure supplies. In due course the unworkable restrictions would be withdrawn . . . and immediately, as if by a magician's wand, flour and butter would again appear in the shop windows.[1]

Some things remained unaltered despite the misery. The Petrograd ballet was as brilliant as ever, featuring the famous *prima ballerina assoluta* M. F. Kseshinskaya, once the mistress of Nicholas, when he was tsarevich, and the future Princess Romanovsky-Krassinsky. Rumoured to use her influence to speculate in the black market, she certainly did not suffer unduly from wartime shortages, and ensured that throughout the war her household had a liberal supply of coal—which may explain why Lenin made her house his headquarters when he returned to Russia in 1917. The war had not put a stop to race meetings either. Racing had gone on at the hippodrome, with eight-race cards every week. Still the mood of "Chertograd" was growing increasingly desperate, as can be seen from the following entries in the diary of Zinaida Gippius:

> Oct., 1916
>
> People are dying like flies, blown away like gossamer. Young, old, children, all the same. Stupid ones, clever ones—all are stupid. Honest men, thieves, all are thieves—or else they are mad.
>
> Nov., 1916
>
> Russia is a very large lunatic asylum. If you visit an asylum on an open day you may not realise you are in one. It looks normal enough but the inmates are all mad.[2]

Curiously the war news was far from bad. Russian armies under General Brussilov had been remarkably successful on the southern front, and now that many of the supply problems had been solved the purely military prospects were better than ever before. However, there had been a serious breakdown in communication between GHQ and the government, since the army no longer trusted its political leaders, and acted entirely independently of them*—to the extent that the War Ministry had to rely on its intelligence reports of enemy troop movements to ascertain what its own armies were doing.[4] To military eyes the capital was corrupt, full of treachery and defeatism. Indeed, its atmosphere was unhealthy:

> Here in Petrograd everyone thrived on empty rumour and vile gossip. It actually became the fashion to attack the government in public and utter bitter criticism of Tsarskoe Selo, passing on a series of false and improbable facts about the emperor and his family.
>
> Coming home one would see guards officers, close friends, politicians and civil servants, and what they had to say was astounding . . . All they talked of was the irresponsible influence of dark forces at court, of Rasputin, of Vyroubova, Protopopov and even of contacts between Tsarskoe Selo and the kaiser's family . . .[5]

The main subject of gossip was Rasputin. By late 1916, a memoirist observes, he was "the most talked-of figure in Russia."[6] It had taken a long time for the legend to assert itself, but now, at a moment of high unreality, when anyone was prepared to believe anything, the Rasputin "Myth," the whole accumulation of rumour, scandal, and supposition of political power, magic, and heresy really came into its

* Sometimes their actions were independent to the point of farce and beyond; thus the minister of finance, Bark, in March 1915 received a communication from the chief of staff, General Yanushkevich, to the effect that he would have to pay American interests four-hundred million roubles in gold by the end of the year in payment for ammunition. The army had blithely signed the contracts, with sublime disregard for the fact that they were thereby signing away a third of their nation's total gold reserves.[3]

own. Rasputin did much to feed the myth himself. He seems to have had his own inkling of an impending crack-up, a sense that Russian history, and his own life with it, were getting out of hand. A journalist describes her impression of him that autumn:

> Some kind of power was sweeping him along in some direction, he tried to control it. In those days when I used to meet him it was as if he had been taken off his feet and was borne by the whirlwind, the tornado, had lost himself. He would repeat certain words in a fever. "God, prayer, wine," mixing everything up, confusing things, could not understand himself, tortured himself, had convulsions, threw himself into the dance despairingly, with a cry on his lips, as if he were plunging into a burning house. . . .[7]

For some time his way of life had begun to make him experience occasional spasms of guilt. In the autumn of 1916 he had even told Vyroubova that he would only continue in public life for another five years, by which time Aleksey would be cured; then he would devote the rest of his life to wandering and saving his soul.[8] However, for the moment he drank more and more heavily, and appeared so often in public drunk and in dubious company that Badmaev literally went on his knees to him to beg him to be more discreet.[9] It was as if Rasputin were being defiant. "They think I'm a scandal, well I'll show them how scandalous I can be, and still the tsarina needs me." He boasted regularly of his closeness to the tsarina and of his power, boasts that took a dangerous turn. He was heard to suggest that Nicholas was too weak to rule, that Alexandra should become regent and reign as a second Catherine the Great. Rasputin allegedly encouraged her, "since Papa understands nothing and cannot cope."[10] An English officer observed, on hearing the suggestion, "Catherine was a wonderful ruler of Russia, but these are not the days of Catherine."[11]

The sense of demoralisation and loss of confidence in the capital was brought to a head on November 1 when P. Milyukov, leader of the Constitutional Democrats, made a speech in the Duma that has been described as the first revolutionary act in Russia. He began by stating that all confidence in the government's capacity to win the war had long vanished, and then, with a vulgar but effective piece of oratory, he began to criticise one governmental action after another, rounding off each criticism with the rhetorical question, "Is this stupidity or is it treason?" He inclined to the view that, great though the stupidity might have been, the scale of the disaster implied treason, and in the highest places. He advanced absolutely no evidence, but the nation was so willing to believe in a German conspiracy that the charges, including the most serious charge of all, were accepted without a murmur. Milyukov, quoting an Austrian paper, suggested that "a pro-German party had gathered around the young empress," a phrase which he improperly uttered in German—only Russian could be spoken in the Duma. This open assault upon the tsarina, the tsar, and the government might have done untold damage to the dynasty, but it did greater damage still to Rasputin.

CHAPTER 20

> The women believed in him, whereas the officers had to get rid of him if they were ever again to believe in themselves.
>
> GÜNTER GRASS ON RASPUTIN

> It has always seemed to me, in going back over past history, that the death of Rasputin, however desirable it was on moral and other grounds, was the factor leading to the final debacle of the Romanoffs.
>
> HANBURY WILLIAMS

> What's the point, we're all doomed anyway.
>
> MAJOR-GENERAL VOYEIKOV

In his speech Milyukov had cited an article in a Swiss paper, *Die Berner Tagwacht,* in which Rasputin, together with Andronnikov, Pitirim and Rubinstein, were named as the powers behind recent ministerial appointments. By the kind of innuendo that had come to pass for logic in the latter days of the war, this was considered proof enough of Rasputin's treachery. Although Milyukov had never concealed his bitter hostility to autocracy, his speech had repercussions far beyond his own supporters. It made a profound impression on the eldest surviving son of one of the wealthiest and most powerful families in Russia, who had long had his own suspicions about Rasputin and whose mother was a bitter enemy of the tsarina—Prince Felix Yusupov.

Count Sumarokov Elston's mother, the princess Zinaida, was the sole surviving child of Prince Nicholas Yusupov. She married Count Sumarokov Elston of the Chevalier Guards and the tsar allowed the Yusupov title to pass to her husband upon the death of her father. Felix, who was thirty in 1916, had grown up on the most intimate terms with the imperial family. One of his childhood friends was Grand Duke Dmitri Pavlovich, son of Grand Duke Paul Alexandrovich, an uncle of the tsar. The grand duke's summer palace, Ilinskoe, outside Moscow, was close to the Yusupov estate of Archangelskoe, which had once belonged to Ivan the Terrible, and the Yusupov children used to play with Dmitri Pavlovich and his sister Marie Pavlovna. In later years, in the capital, the Yusupovs often gave dances for young people in their palace on the Fontanka, a massive building, the work of the architect Quarenghi. It contained three ballrooms, a theatre and an art gallery, which house the finest private collection in Russia. This included five Tiepolos, a superb Rubens, a Velásquez, and two late Rembrandts. There were also numerous works by French painters of the seventeenth and eighteenth centuries–Claude, Watteau, Boucher, Fragonard, David. There was even an equestrian portrait of Felix's great-grandfather in Tartar dress, by Gros. Along with a collection of gold and enamelled snuff boxes, and a rock crystal chandelier that once had belonged to Marie Antoinette, there was a superb pearl, the Peregrine, "so round that it always rolled off a flat surface."[1] Visitors to the Yusupov drawing-rooms would be struck by their table decorations: crystal bowls crammed with uncut sapphires, emeralds, and opals. Small wonder that even Olga Alexandrovna, the tsar's sister, believed the rumour that the Yusupovs were much wealthier than the Romanovs. The Fontanka Palace was not their only town residence. They also had a slightly smaller palace on the Moika canal, where Felix first made the acquaintance of the Taneev family, including their fat daughter Anna, and where, some years later, he would assassinate Rasputin.

As he grew up Felix provoked a certain disquiet in his father, a rough, not to say brutal, military man, and his ambitious, authoritarian mother. It was not just that he was ardent in his pursuit of expensive pleasures, such as gypsy music, and fundamentally unserious to boot. If anyone in Russia could afford expensive tastes it was Felix. He adored gypsy music, and was himself a very reasonable performer of their songs, which he sang to a small guitar. He was also fond of the theatre and amateur theatricals, and he loved to dress up.

The problem was that he preferred to dress as a woman. As an adolescent he regularly indulged in transvestite escapades, appearing, for example, as a French singer at the Aquarium. There was one unfortunate occasion when he broke the string of one of his mother's necklaces and the pearls scattered across the nightclub floor.

From his own life story and the memories of those who knew him in later years, Yusupov emerges as a person of great charm and considerable selfishness. He loved scenes and dramas, had an extravagant personality, was capable of flamboyant, queenlike behaviour, with a tendency to get into trouble and a distinct lack of mature judgment. He was also capable of idealistic enthusiasm, which seldom amounted to much, since he had little staying power. Yet it would be wrong to suppose that Yusupov lacked an inner life. He was capable of fits of mystic exaltation and was very interested in the occult and in spiritualism. He had the politics of his rank, being a devoted monarchist, and, as an adolescent, had kept pictures of Louis XVI and Marie Antoinette in his room, with a vase of fresh flowers in front of them. His homosexuality did not always sit lightly upon him, and he made various attempts to "cure" himself, turning to yoga and a little later to marriage.

Yusupov had met Rasputin in 1909, when the *starets* was first becoming fashionable. He was introduced by one of the most devoted of his disciples, Mounya Golovina. According to Yusupov's memoirs Rasputin made a strong but unfavourable impression; he appeared crafty and sensual, a man of power rather than a man of God, who muttered incoherently as he took possession of you with his gaze. That was the last Yusupov saw of him for some time, because he left Russia to spend two years at University College, Oxford—where for the first time in his life he knew real cold as he walked across the damp carpet of his bedroom to wash his face in the rapidly cooling water of his hand basin.

One suspects that an Oxford education was yet another attempt to "cure" Felix, or at least to prevent him from causing trouble at home, but Oxford was scarcely an obvious choice for someone trying to lose the homosexual habit. He had charm, personality and flamboyance enough to influence others and scandalise their connections. He was very close to his childhood friend, the grand duke Dmitri Pavlovich, who was three years his junior. The tone of their correspondence is one of, at the least, *amitié amoureuse,* and at one time before the war the tsarina forbade Dmitri to see Felix, who himself began to be watched over by the secret police.[2]

The tsarina did not often intervene in this way, but Dmitri Pavlovich was an exception. On the whole the tsar and tsarina did not feel great love for those beyond their immediate circle; their attitude to more distant relatives was one of formal affection. However, they felt real tenderness toward their cousin Dmitri.[3] He was a person of great charm, warmth, and vivacity, with clean-cut good looks. Felix himself describes him as "extremely attractive," tall, elegant, and well-bred, with deep thoughtful eyes;[4] he was also a talented entertainer, and was able to make the tsar and his daughters rock with laughter at his stories.[5] He was one of the few outsiders to enjoy the intimacy of their family circle. Indeed in 1912 there were rumours that he was engaged to the tsar's eldest daughter, Olga Nicolaevna.[6] Alexandra took a maternal interest in him and her letters to Nicholas mention him often, frequently expressing the fear that Dmitri, who was easily led, had "got in with a bad set,"[7] and it is true the grand duke was often to be seen driving wildly about the capital in a brand new hundred-horsepower automobile. Before the war he served in the Horse Guards, his father's regiment, and was then appointed the tsar's aide-de-camp.

In the event it was Felix himself, and not the tsarina, who put an end to his intimate friendship with Dmitri. In another attempt at getting straight he turned to marriage. The object of his choice, Irina Alexandrovna, a member of the imperial family, was a granddaughter of the dowager empress, a cousin of Dmitri, and daughter of Grand Duchess Xenia, Nicholas's sister. Despite certain misgivings about Yusupov's reputation the marriage gained the imperial approval and was celebrated in February 1914 in the Annichkov Palace. It was a magnificent affair. The bride, in a lace veil that had belonged to Marie Antoinette and a tiara of rock crystal and diamonds, drove up in a coach with four white horses to be given away by the tsar himself. The young couple started their married life in the ground floor of the left wing of Felix's parents' house on the Moika. The marriage put a considerable strain upon Yusupov's friendship with Dmitri, since he too had been in love with his cousin—which may perhaps explain in part her attraction for Felix.

At the outbreak of war Felix's father was governor-general of Moscow. He lost the post quite soon, largely as the result of his inept handling of the anti-German rioting that broke out early in 1915 as crowds sacked and looted German properties or those with German names. It should not be thought, incidentally, that the Muscovites were the only ones to behave in this way. There were plenty of instances both in Paris and in London of stores with German names being stoned, while all over France courageous men and women were known to do their bit for victory by bravely kicking dachshunds in the ribs, regardless of any possible retaliation. Yusupov began by allowing the Moscow looters and rioters a free hand, and then seems to have changed his mind, sending in the police, who behaved with a characteristically Muscovite callousness. For example, they bricked up the exits to a number of German wine shops, which still contained large numbers of looters within, dead-drunk, who at the end of the war, claimed an English observer, "will be found like brandy cherries."[8]

The dismissal of her husband had done much to turn Princess Zinaida against the tsarina, and over the war years the letters she wrote to her son grew increasingly critical of the role she was playing. Felix replied in kind, writing of the pernicious influence of Rasputin, who, he slowly came to feel, was a unique embodiment of power and of evil.

He had renewed his acquaintance with the *starets* in the early autumn of 1916. His mother's letters, which were so critical of the tsarina, and the increasingly extravagant stories circulating about Rasputin, were beginning to work on him, making him feel that Rasputin was the most serious obstacle standing in the way of a Russian victory. In his unstable way Yusupov seems to have begun to feel that he had a historic mission, that he would save Russia by his own *podvig,* or glorious action, which might entail martyrdom. It was with some such intention in mind that he had allowed Mounya Golovina to arrange another meeting with Rasputin.

He found him changed; he dressed much more richly and his face had been markedly coarsened by high living. Yet to Felix his conversation seemed just as rambling, while admiring disciples of the opposite sex listened as carefully as ever. Curiously, Yusupov did not dismiss him as a charlatan. He felt that Rasputin had colossal inner strength, but lacked the intellect and judgment to make proper use of it; in other words he seemed to him a remarkable embodiment of power without responsibility, which is by no means a foolish assessment of Rasputin's nature.

By his own account Yusupov paid Rasputin a second visit in his effort to understand him and his historical role; in effect to decide what was to be done with him. He concluded that he was a cynical, ignorant peasant whose influence over the tsarina was boundless, whose private life was irregular, and who was altogether lacking in conscience.

Yusupov paid several fruitless visits to Rasputin, who had undertaken to "treat" him—presumably for instability and possibly for homosexuality. According to Yusupov treatment consisted of a form of hypnosis. He lay on a bed and Rasputin bent over him:

> I felt a power enter into me sending a warm current through my body. At the same time I was overcome by a general lethargy; my body grew stiff. I tried to talk but my tongue no longer obeyed me and I gradually passed into a kind of sleep, as if I had been given a powerful narcotic. I would only see Rasputin's eyes shining before me, sending forth two phosphorescent rays which melted into a great luminous circle that drew closer and then fell back again. . . .[9]

The account continues with his faint efforts to resist Rasputin's hypnotic power, only to find himself completely under his command.

Yusupov's experience is puzzling, for it is the only account we have of Rasputin's exercising hypnosis. Felix is not always a reliable witness, and this description of him lying helpless and immobile in the thrall of a powerful and evil man sounds more like the erotic fantasy of a passive homosexual than an accurate account of what really happened. Even more preposterous is the allegation that Felix saw a number of German spies in Rasputin's apartment, persons that Rasputin described as "*zelyeninkie*" (little green men), which Yusupov took to be an idiomatic term for foreign agents or their associates.

This appears at best to be a misunderstanding. Rasputin, who took a positive delight in inventive turns of speech, was always fond of creating nicknames for friends and associates, and this expression has an authentic ring to it. He may well have been referring to associates of a financier and journalist called Manus, who wrote in the newspaper *Grazhdanin* under the name *Zeleniy,* "The green one."[10] Yusupov could not possibly have seen a lobby full of German agents at number 64 Gorokhavaya; imagination and wishful thinking were always among his stronger suits. Yet whatever or whoever he did see sufficed to confirm his worst suspicions and made him all the more responsive to Milyukov's speech of November 1. It was this that convinced him that the time had come to act.

His first step was to pay a call upon a Duma member, the jurist Maklakov, a member of the kadet party who was most surprised to see him. They had never met before and moved in very different circles, both socially and politically. Yusupov informed him that he had the greatest admiration for his public criticism of the conduct of the war. However, ignorant as he was of life at court, Maklakov could not know that the key was Rasputin–not a symptom but the true cause of Russia's problems. Yusupov enlarged upon Rasputin's hold over the empress, even suggesting that Nicholas was known to hide from the man to avoid granting his requests. He went on to observe that there were only two solutions left–either to buy Rasputin off or to kill him. Maklakov did not take the enthusiastic prince overseriously, and told him as much, whereupon Yusupov replied, "If you will not or cannot bribe him there is no choice. He must be killed and that is precisely what I have just decided to do."

Maklakov got the impression that he had so decided at that very moment. He observed that the killing would be pointless, since someone else would immediately take his place. Not so, replied Yusupov; Rasputin was irreplaceable:

> You say that because you do not believe in his supernatural powers. But I know about such matters and I assure you Rasputin possesses a power that you meet only once in centuries . . . If he were killed today the empress would go to a home for nervous disorders within a fortnight and Nicholas would become a constitutional monarch.[11]

Maklakov was still at a loss to know why Yusupov had approached him, but it soon became clear. Felix went on to say that he could not do the deed himself, since he was practically a member of the imperial family. "If I were to become a killer it would be tantamount to revolution"—even Yusupov had bouts of clarity. He went on to suggest that Maklakov find a terrorist to do it, and suddenly the politician understood. In his political naivete, Yusupov had come to a spokesman of the parliamentary opposition expecting him to be in touch with revolutionary terrorists, failing to appreciate that there was a difference between parliamentary opposition and revolutionary activism. Maklakov still refused to take Yusupov seriously and matters rested there. However, the prince soon found another figure to support him.

V. M. Purishkevich had long been the most notorious and exotic figure in tsarist parliamentary politics. He was known as being "so right-wing that the only thing further right was the wall." An ardent supporter of the Union of the Russian People, he was essentially an unstable demagogue; as early as 1907 he had the reputation of being short of ballast: "He has no lead in his legs," one old politician observed.[12] He was "a short, bald and extremely animated man who could not stay a single moment in one place," in the words of a former prime minister.[13] He well understood how to exploit the theatrical side of electoral politics, and was known to use the most extravagant electoral techniques—such as composing humorous verses about his opponents, which he printed and circulated in thousands of copies.[14] He used the same publicity techniques to attack Rasputin, accompanying doggerel verses with photographs of him at tea surrounded by his admirers—he had many thousands printed. The photographs, reproduced in this book, caused great bewilderment when they came out. Rasputin appears to be surrounded by smart society women, and yet this is not the case. I spoke to a very old lady who had moved in the highest circles of wartime Petrograd, and who remembers the astonishment the photographs caused when they first appeared. Who were these people? Nobody could recognise them. With the exception of Mounya Golovina, who can be seen sitting close to Rasputin, with her young, open, almost boyish face and somewhat demented smile, the women were all unknowns. However chic their appearance, Rasputin's admirers, as photographed, were definitely not members of the smart set.

Purishkevich took his flair for showmanship into the Duma. He had been known to throw water at leading members of the opposition[15] and would sometimes make his view of the left wing apparent by appearing with a red flower in his fly. His behaviour made him the best known, if not the best-loved parliamentarian in Russia; his picture was sold on street corners; toys would be named after him, and his latest extravagance was always a source of delighted gossip. He was a showman rather than a solid politician, impulsive, inconsequent, and lacking in judgment. He was, however, an ardent patriot and had devoted much time and money during the war to running a hospital train and providing comforts for the troops.

By 1916 even Purishkevich had turned against the dynasty. On November 19 he delivered a powerful attack in the Duma on the conduct of the war, his diminutive figure, bald with a thick, half-trimmed beard, moustache, and pince-nez, dwarfed by the gigantic President Rodzyanko, who kept calling that he was out of order and trying in vain to silence him. Purishkevich began by saying that his love for his native land obliged him to speak out, and that he could see all too clearly what and who were harming Russia and denying her victory:

> The disorganisation of our rear is undoubtedly being carried out by the enemy, and it is being done by a strong, relentless, and resolute hand. We have a single system, the system of devastation in the rear . . . .
>
> I take the liberty to say here . . . that all this evil comes from those dark forces, from those influences which push this or that individual into position and which force up into high posts people who are not capable of filling them, from those influences headed by Grishka Rasputin . . . It is necessary that the legislative body, being the voice of the entire country, and now united in spirit on the question of victory, finally raise its voice about this, Russia's greatest evil, which is corrupting Russian public life. These past nights I couldn't sleep, I give you my word of honour. I lie with my eye open and imagine a series of telegrams, reports, notes which this illiterate peasant writes now

to one minister, then to another, and most frequently of all, it is said, to Alexander Dmitrievich Protopopov, and which he requests them to act upon. And we know there were instances when the failure to fulfill these demands entailed the fall of strong and powerful men . . . If you are loyal to your sovereign, if the glory of Russia, her power, her future, intimately and inseparably bound up with the grandeur and the splendour of the tsar's name, are dear to you, go to Imperial Headquarters, throw yourself at the tsar's feet, and beg permission to open his eyes to the dreadful reality, beg him to deliver Russia from Rasputin and the Rasputinites big and small . . . and you (turning to the ministers) . . . go to headquarters and plead with the sovereign that Grishka Rasputin be not the leader of Russian internal public life. (Loud and prolonged applause from Center, Left and Right; voices: "Bravo!")[16]

Yusupov was present at the speech, which he found tremendously impressive, for it summed up his own sense of imminent catastrophe. Next day he wrote to his mother:

I don't know how it will all end. We seem to be living on the slopes of a volcano and the same thoughts lurk in all our heads.[17]

Anti-dynastic feeling was indeed on the increase. The secret police were picking up widespread rumours of an impending palace coup.[18] There were other sinister signs; one politician noticed a growing interest in books about the assassination of Emperor Paul I, while the general in charge of the Inzhenetskii palace, where the killing happened, reported a sudden increase in the number of persons wishing to visit the murder room.[19] In the meantime, throughout the late autumn and early winter of the year, Nicholas received a series of letters and visits from members of his family imploring him to get rid of Rasputin and persuade his wife to play a less active political role before it was too late, all of which did nothing but harden Nicholas in his resolve.

Yusupov now persuaded his old friend Dmitri Pavlovich to join him in his conspiracy. As Nicholas's aide the young grand duke had spent much of the war carrying out official duties on the tsar's behalf. There are, for example, photographs of him distributing decorations in the tsar's name. Alexandra's correspondence mentions him more than once, usually urging Nicholas to find him plenty to do because when idle he found it all too easy to "get in with the wrong set." He too had independently arrived at the conclusion that Rasputin was fatal to Russia. He believed that he had some kind of drug which he administered to the tsar, paralysing his will, so that his physical and mental condition were such that he was unable to get rid of him. Dmitri concluded, moreover, that by ridding Nicholas of the turbulent *starets* he would free him from the no less pernicious influence of his wife–not to mention those will-sapping drugs.

It appears that Dmitri was by no means the only young nobleman to be approached by Yusupov. His intentions were widely known in his immediate circle. At least one Guards officer rather younger than Felix was anxious to join him in his conspiracy–but had to hold back when he discovered that he could not get the necessary leave. Many years later, on his deathbed, this officer was still tortured by the knowledge that he might have prevented the killing and hence perhaps averted the fall of the dynasty. "I could have told him, I could have told him," he kept repeating, the inference being, according to his family, that he had missed an opportunity to warn Nicholas what was afoot.

It was about this time that the author's grandmother had occasion to observe Yusupov in a hotel in Yalta. She remembers that he was part of a group of junior Guards officers that was behaving in a strangely secretive and conspiratorial manner. When she heard of the killing of Rasputin she concluded that at least part of the conspiracy had been planned in the hotel, and this too would suggest that knowledge of the plot was not confined to the handful of actual participants.

Yusupov, recognizing a kindred spirit in Purishkevich, went to see him two days after hearing him speak and invited him to join the plot. The fiery politician accepted with alacrity, and the conspirators met immediately to make a plan. Yusupov was greatly taken by Purishkevich from the start. In a letter he wrote a week before the killing he described him as "an amazingly kind and decent fellow."[20]

The outlines of their plan were quickly formed. They proposed to entice Rasputin with the lure of Yusupov's hospitality. It was decided to invite Rasputin to Felix's palace on the Moika, ostensibly to introduce him to his wife, Irina, who would in reality be in Yalta, and to poison him there. They would be joined by two other assassins, a young officer named Sukhotin and Doctor Lazovert from Purishkevich's medical train. With more enthusiasm than discretion, Yusupov sent a letter to his mother and his wife full of cryptic hints about the blow he was going to strike for Russia. His wife wrote back by return:

> Dear Felix,
>
> Thank you for your insane letter. I could not understand the half of it. I realise that you are about to do something wild. Please take care and do not get mixed up in any shady business.[21]

The letter goes on to order him to be sensible, exercise restraint and do nothing without her.

The conspirators met again the following night in Purishkevich's train, and Yusupov produced some potassium cyanide with which to do the job. They then tried to fix a date for the assassination, which was not easy, since Dmitri Pavlovich's engagement book was full for the next fortnight. They eventually decided on December 16.

Felix was not the only one to be indiscreet. A few days later Purishkevich buttonholed Maklakov in a corridor of the Duma building. He said that he knew all about the conversation he had had with Yusupov, that the killing was on and set for the sixteenth. Would Maklakov change his mind and join them, since they would not after all be using hired assassins? Unfortunately, Maklakov could not; he conveniently remembered that that night he was to address the Moscow Society of Jurisprudence, and felt obliged to refuse. However, the next time Yusupov came to see him he took the young man more seriously. In Maklakov's own words, he did not wish to help him, but neither did he wish to stop him. Since he had little confidence in Purishkevich's judgment or discretion he felt obliged to offer the conspirators what advice he could to ensure that their action succeeded.

He discussed their murder plan in some detail, offering advice on the problem of body disposal. They should not, he said, take the corpse to the front by train and dump it on a battlefield as planned. Rasputin would have to be found if the killing was to have real effect. Maklakov agreed with Yusupov that the identity of the killers must not be known, since that might indeed set off a revolution–in other words, rather than saying, "Don't do it in case there's a revolution," he said, "Don't get *found out* in case . . ." Yusupov kept trying to persuade the deputy to put his speech off and join in, observing that it was not every day that Rasputin was assassinated. Maklakov continued to refuse, however, and eventually Dmitri Pavlovich persuaded Felix that it was as well not to include a member of the opposition, since this might give the killing the wrong sort of public image.[22]

However, Maklakov did make a contribution to the killing. He advised Yusupov that it should be a silent affair, and that silence was best assured by hitting Rasputin upon the head and then running a car over his corpse. He went on to suggest that they use something like his own life-preserver or blackjack, which he proudly produced for the prince's inspection: he had acquired it abroad before the war. Yusupov begged him for the loan of it, and Maklakov only complied with the utmost reluctance; not because he had scruples, but because it could not be replaced in wartime Russia.[23]

Purishkevich did not confine his indiscretions to Maklakov. In the press room of the Duma he boasted openly that Rasputin was to be killed in the Yusupov palace and that Dmitri Pavlovich was to be one of the assassins. He even named the day to a colleague, V. V. Shulgin, and told Sir Samuel Hoare that he and some friends were about to "liquidate" (his word) the *starets*.[24] It had been decided that the corpse was to be dumped into the Neva, and accordingly Purishkevich and his wife went shopping and bought some heavy chains to wrap round the body. For the time being they kept them hidden on their train.

Rasputin, in the meantime, was having further premonitions of disaster. When the tsar, who had spent a week at home, set off for the front again, he asked Rasputin for his usual blessing. "This time it is you who should bless me," he said, and kissed the tsar's hand, for the last time.[25] Others recall that in the first two weeks of December he seemed depressed. On the thirteenth, he had his secretary, Simanovich, help him put various affairs in order, depositing a large sum of money in the bank in his daughter Maria's name, and burning quantities of documents and papers.[26] It must be said, however, that accounts of Rasputin's premonitions have to be treated with circumspection, since it would help his legend to suggest that he had a feeling of impending death. Indeed, his failure to anticipate and ward off assassination, and the naive alacrity with which he accepted Yusupov's invitation would soon cause many of his admirers to lose faith in his powers.

However, we know from the tsarina's letters that Rasputin at this time was a very frightened man. He had given up appearing in public, given up going to restaurants, and stayed at home. "He never goes out in ages except to come here."[27] Moreover, he does indeed seem to have had a sense of impending and all-embracing disaster, according to a curious document published by Simanovich. He reproduces the manuscript and there is no reason to doubt its authenticity:

> My dears my precious ones,
>
> A threat hangs over us. A great misfortune is coming. The face of the merciful Mother of God has grown dark. The spirit has entered the silence of the night and there is no consolation. The anger will be terrible and there is no place to run to. It is written "Stay watchful for you can know neither the night nor the hour." The time has come for our land. The blood runs chill with fear. There is so much blood, so many cries of pain. The night of dreadful suffering is dark, I cannot see. My hour will soon come. I have no fear but you must know that the hour will be bitter. I will suffer a great martyrdom. I will forgive my torturers and will inherit the kingdom. You will take pity on me. The young ones will see much. You need not pray long for God to give you strength, you will all be saved. I grieve for you and for our lives. God knows the way of your suffering. People without number will be destroyed. Many martyrs will die. Brother will die at the hand of brother. There will be a great misfortune. The earth will tremble. Hunger famine and drought will come and there will be signs seen all over the world. Pray

that that will be for your salvation, and by the Grace of the Saviour and the protection of the Holy Mother joy will come to you again.

Grigorii.[28]

On December 12, Rasputin dined at Tsarskoe Selo with Vyroubova and the empress for the last time. He told the tsarina to tell Nicholas to "be firm, have faith in Our Friend, follow my advice, that is his advice, and trust us in everything."

According to another report Rasputin had grown increasingly thoughtful in the early days of December. He would often look at his family and ask them how they would manage without him. When his son left for Pokrovskoe he observed that if he were to survive to Christmas well and good, he would live a long time, but that in the meantime his soul was suffering without respite.[29]

Rasputin had become strangely fond of Yusupov, "the little one" as he nicknamed him. Partly he was flattered by his attentions; after all, Yusupov was practically a member of the imperial family, and more important, the first nobleman of the highest rank to pay him such attention. Tsarskoe Selo excepted, Rasputin was most emphatically not received in the best circles. But also he liked the man, loved to listen to him singing his gypsy songs, and constantly urged him to visit the gypsies with him—and this at a time when he had virtually given up going out for fear of his life. He was disappointed by the prince's repeated refusals but was overjoyed when Yusupov telephoned him and suggested he come to his palace on the Moika on the night of December 16 to make the acquaintance of his wife, the emperor's niece. Rasputin accepted on condition that Yusupov call for him in person. He asked him to arrive late and come up the back stairs, hoping in that way to leave unnoticed. Why he should have wished to escape attention remains a mystery. It may even have been out of consideration for Yusupov, whom he did not wish to compromise. At all events Rasputin was sufficiently dazzled by Yusupov's position, sufficiently flattered by the prospect of being introduced to his wife, for him to trust the man completely. Social ambition had allayed his natural mistrust, so that it may be said in a very real sense to have destroyed him.

The conspirators had decided to kill Rasputin with poison administered by Yusupov *en tête à tête*. He would conduct his victim to the assassination chamber, where they would wait, ostensibly for the end of a party going on in another part of the palace. The conspirators had decided to dispose of the body by throwing it into the water. They had found a suitable spot on the Petrovsky bridge over the Malaya Neva, between the Petrovsky and Krestovsky islands—not far from the spot where Svidrigaylov, the evil genius of *Crime and Punishment,* committed suicide. Maklakov asked them to send him a telegram in Moscow when the deed was done.

Dr. Lazovert spent December 15 working on the car they were going to use, one of those attached to Purishkevich's hospital service. Not only did he need to make sure that it was in good order, he had to paint out the red-lettered legend *Semper Idem* that all the hospital cars had emblazoned on them.

CHAPTER 21

It was carried out in the manner of a scenario designed for people of bad taste.

TROTSKY ON RASPUTIN'S MURDER

THE MORNING OF Friday December 16th was cold, ten degrees of frost with, as Alexandra put it, "wee pink clouds."[1] Later in the morning it began to snow heavily, and the snow only stopped in the early hours of the next morning. Rasputin woke cheerfully enough. He went to church and on to the bathhouse heavily guarded, returning about 11:00 A.M. to hold court. Shortly afterwards an elderly woman rang the bell of his flat. She was a writer interested in the occult, and an ardent patriot, who had decided to attempt to bring Rasputin to his senses and make him understand the harm he was doing his country. She was shown into a room in which a number of well-to-do women were sitting. When Rasputin appeared they flocked to him, some trying to kiss his hands, others contenting themselves with the hem of his garment. Rasputin pushed them impatiently aside to go straight to his new visitor and ask her what it was that she wanted. Saying nothing she simply met his eyes and stared at him until, for once, it was Rasputin who turned away. She went on to ask him if he appreciated the damage he was doing, whether he knew anything of his nation's history and whether he loved the tsar.

> In truth I've read no history–I'm just a plain ignorant peasant, I can only just read, and as for writing, I often cannot read my own. But as a peasant I truly love the tsar, although I am guilty of much against him and his family; but I swear to you little mother that I did not mean to . . . Little mother I feel my end is near. They'll kill me, and then the throne won't last three months. I thank you for coming, I know you listened to your heart. I feel good with you, and also afraid. . . .[2]

The woman continued to talk with him, asking him why his disciples treated him like a holy man, calling him father. His reply was most revealing: "Ask those fools for yourself," he said. If they were prepared to take him for what he was not, he was not the man to discourage them. He then asked his visitor for her blessing, saying that his soul was very heavy.

The rest of the morning Rasputin remained depressed. The depression was not eased by an anonymous telephone call informing him that he was about to be assassinated. He took a great deal of wine at lunch, and got too drunk to handle a telephone call from Tobolsk. He slept for a long time in the afternoon and sobered up by the time Vyroubova called in the early evening. She had a present with her from the empress, an icon Alexandra had acquired in Novgorod; she and the children had signed their names on the back. Rasputin told Vyroubova and Mounya Golovina, who had been there since noon, that he was going out that night to the Yusupov palace to meet Irina, who, it would seem, needed "treatment." Vyroubova was surprised that he should have been invited to call after midnight. She urged him not to go, saying that if Felix and Irina were too ashamed to receive him openly he would only humiliate himself by accepting their invitation. Rasputin appeared to agree and promised to stay at home.[3]

An hour or so after Vyroubova left Rasputin received Protopopov's evening visit. He always arrived late, after the surveillance had been called off. He warned Rasputin that there was a plot against his life and told him that, whatever he might do, he should not go out that night. Rasputin agreed, Protopopov left, and he began to get ready. He bathed and washed with great care and then got dressed, putting on baggy velvet trousers, new boots, and a magnificent silk shirt embroidered with corn flowers and girded with a crimson sash. He had some trouble fastening the collar and got his maid-servant, Ekaterina Ivanovna Potyemkina, to fasten it for him. He then lay down to rest, fully clothed, and when she asked why he told her that he was going out later to see "the little one."

First thing that morning Yusupov had gone to pray for a long time in the Kazan cathedral[4]–he did, after all, regard himself as carrying out a holy mission against the forces of evil. He went on to his military academy, the Corps des Pages, to do some work–for he was proposing to sit an exam the next day. He then went back to his palace on the Moika embankment to make a final inspection of the room in which he proposed to poison Rasputin.

In order to convince his guest that Irina was at home, Yusupov had decided not to use an upstairs reception room but a basement specially converted for the murder. As he brought him in, a gramophone playing at the top of the stairs would create the illusion that there was a party going on in another part of the palace. When Felix arrived that morning his workmen were still busy transforming a naked basement into an opulent bachelor's "den," laying carpet and even fitting new doors. In the daylight the space seemed dark, with grey stone walls and floors and a low, vaulted ceiling. There were two small windows looking out onto the embankment. Arches divided the area into two rooms, one a kind of dining room, the other containing a spiral staircase that led first to a door opening on to the courtyard, and then up to Yusupov's study.

The rooms had been furnished from the vast family store, with porcelain vases, chests, tables, and carved wooden chairs. The dining room, with its red granite mantelpiece decorated with gilt cups and majolica plates, had a Persian carpet and a splendid inlaid chest of drawers, upon which there was a seventeenth-century Italian bronze and crystal crucifix. In front of this was spread a magnificent bearskin, and as Yusupov put it so delicately, a table "where Rasputin was to take his last cup of tea."[5] He ordered his major-domo, Buzhinsky, to buy some biscuits and some cream cakes, and get wine up from the cellar. He would be entertaining that evening and the staff were to keep to their quarters until he rang for them.

Purishkevich stayed at home for most of the day, and in the evening, to kill time, went to attend a session of the Duma. However, when he got there he found the chamber unlit; not enough deputies had turned up for there to be a quorum. Instead, he went into a Duma office, writing letters and making telephone calls to pass the time. In due course Dr. Lazovert came for him by car and they set off together for Yusupov's palace a little after eleven. Purishkevich was armed with a blackjack and, as he put it, "a magnificent revolver."[6]

By eleven o'clock everything in the palace was ready. A fire was burning, the red velvet curtains had been drawn, and the rooms looked much less gloomy by artificial light. They felt warm and cut off from the outside world. Dmitri Pavlovich arrived at the same time as the others, and together they inspected the premises and made the final preparations. Yusupov went across to the inlaid chest and took out a box containing the poison. He then placed three cream and three chocolate cakes upon the table. Dr. Lazovert put on his rubber gloves, reduced the potassium cyanide crystals to a fine powder, took the tops off the cakes and filled them up. Just then the fire began to smoke badly and it was a good ten minutes before they could get it to draw again. They then went into the next room, intending to pour liquid potassium cyanide into two of the four wine glasses there. However, they decided to do it later, twenty minutes after Yusupov set off to collect Rasputin, for fear that the poison might evaporate. At all events Lazovert said, there was enough cyanide in the cakes alone to kill Rasputin many times over.

The doctor then put on a chauffeur's coat and hat and Yusupov a magnificent coat of reindeer skin, and together they set off for Gorokhavaya Street. As he left, Yusupov reminded the others to put some dance music on the gramophone as they returned. They arrived at Number 64 some time after midnight and rang the bell. Rasputin answered it himself, saying, "There is no one up, the children are asleep, come in, little one."[7] His maid, however, overheard him, and peering out from the kitchen could see that his visitor was Yusupov.

Felix was very struck by Rasputin's dress and appearance. He had never seen him so well turned out. He had combed his beard and hair very carefully and smelt strongly of cheap soap. Clearly he set great store by his invitation. As he put on his fur coat and beaverskin hat he asked Yusupov anxiously whether they would be alone. Felix reassured him and they set off together.

When he arrived at the palace Rasputin heard a gramophone playing "Yankee Doodle" and Yusupov told him that Irina was entertaining a few friends. Until they left he suggested they go downstairs to have some tea, cakes, and a glass of wine.

After they sat down they started a somewhat halting conversation. Yusupov nervously offered Rasputin a biscuit, which was not poisoned, and only afterwards passed him the cake stand. To his horror Rasputin refused. As his daughter has pointed out, Rasputin never ate cakes, finding them too sweet for his taste. Eventually he agreed to accept first one and then another, and Yusupov watched him carefully, only to find that the poison took no visible effect. He then suggested he try a glass of their own wine from the Crimea. Again Rasputin refused, making him more anxious still, but he poured wine into the two unpoisoned glasses and they drank together. Rasputin appreciated the wine but asked for Madeira, holding out his glass. The prince tried to persuade him to accept a fresh one, but Rasputin insisted that the first would do. Felix took it from him to fill it up, managed to drop it, and at last contrived to give him one of the glasses with the poison in it. Rasputin drank; again Yusupov watched and waited, and again nothing happened. To his horror the poison was taking no effect and Rasputin began to seem invulnerable, protected by the forces of evil.

Rasputin's resistance to cyanide is one of the most potent elements in his legend, and it has not yet been satisfactorily explained. There can be no doubt that he took something other than normal food and drink. The autopsy revealed the presence of a greyish-brown substance in his stomach. Nor can there be any doubt that the assassins were expecting to poison their man. Poisoning is a splendid method for a would-be killer in cold blood who is also his victim's host. At no stage does he actually have to reveal that he is about to commit murder, he simply watches and waits. He thereby avoids the terrible moment of naked embarrassment when both parties know what is about to happen and look one another in the eye. Yusupov would have gone to any length to avoid catching Rasputin's stare in such circumstances. Yet we do not have to credit Rasputin with superhuman physique to account for his resistance. The poison itself may have been ineffective. It had not been tried out, and the fact that Rasputin neither smelt nor tasted anything strange suggests that it may have been weaker than supposed. Indeed, this was not the first occasion on which cakes poisoned with cyanide had failed to take effect. A few years before, a circus elephant in south Russia had become uncontrollable and the local town council had decided that it must be destroyed. Accordingly they purchased a hundred cream cakes, of which the elephant, unlike Rasputin, was particularly fond. These were filled with potassium cyanide and given to the elephant, which duly consumed them. The poison took no effect whatsoever, and some days later the unfortunate beast had to be executed by firing squad.[8]

There is an alternative and possibly more plausible explanation. For potassium cyanide to take effect it has to react with the digestive juices. If the stomach contained a massive quantity of carbohydrate it might well be that the reaction would be delayed for a considerable time.

Whatever the reason, Rasputin's failure to die was rendering Yusupov desperate, very frightened, and embarrassed too. He could no longer continue the pretence of a conversation. Twice already he had excused himself and gone upstairs to tell his friends that the poison was not working and Rasputin must be enjoying supernatural protection. The tension up there was so great that Lazovert fainted and had to be revived in the snow. Rasputin, it was true, was not quite his usual self; he appeared tired, half asleep, and gratefully accepting the offer of a cup of tea observed that he was extraordinarily thirsty. Then, catching sight of a guitar, he asked Yusupov to sing for him. Reluctantly, for he was not in the mood, Yusupov sang a sad slow gypsy romance, while Rasputin rested his head wearily on the table. But the poison still showed no signs of killing him. Time was passing; they had been together for two long hours and nothing had happened. By rights Yusupov should have taken Rasputin up to Irina long ago, it was 2:30 A.M. and the evening was losing any point as both host and guest waited for something to happen.

Upstairs Dmitri Pavlovich, Purishkevich, and Sukhotin were getting increasingly restless, while Lazovert apologised nervously for his collapse. As they waited they grew noisier and Rasputin, hearing them, asked Yusupov what was going on. He replied that Irina's guests must be leaving, and that he would go upstairs to see. He went up for the third time and announced in jerky tones that the poison had still not worked and that Rasputin was getting restless. Something had to be done. They decided, as Purishkevich put it, to "stake their all" and mount a joint attack on Rasputin with blackjacks and Purishkevich's revolver. As they started to go downstairs together Yusupov observed that Rasputin would get suspicious if he saw them all at once, and that he would do better to shoot his guest himself. Accordingly he went back to his study, took a pocket Browning from his drawer, and went downstairs.

Rasputin had not moved from the table and was having trouble breathing. He said that he felt unwell and asked for more Madeira. This cheered him up and made him suggest a visit to the gypsies, to which Yusupov replied that it was too late. Rasputin had no inkling that he was about to die as Yusupov got out the gun, which he held behind his back. Yusupov walked over to a crystal and bronze Italian crucifix and stared at it for so long that Rasputin asked him what he was doing. Rasputin too went across and observed that, beautiful though it was, he preferred the inlaid chest that it stood on. "Grigorii Efimovich, you would do better to look at the crucifix and say a prayer," Yusupov observed.[9] As Rasputin looked at him, gently, almost submissively, at last understanding what was going on, Yusupov took the revolver from behind his back and shot him in the chest. Rasputin gave a cry and fell onto the bearskin.

The account of the shooting is a study in bizarre embarrassment, like something out of Dostoevsky. Rasputin was placid, feeling the ill effects of poison and slightly at a loss to know what he was doing *chez* Yusupov or when the fun would begin. Yusupov, who had hoped that he could kill at long distance, that in practical terms Rasputin would murder himself, found himself obliged to switch roles, from host to killer, a most embarrassing step for a dandy who had never known a shot fired in anger, let alone cold blood. Yet the soirée had reached a point when a new initiative was demanded of its host, who finally hit upon a suitable means of announcing his change of roles in the shape of the crucifix.

It must be said that Yusupov, in a subsequent conversation with Maklakov, put the crucifix in a different light:

> He conveyed to me the sense of horror which overcame him when Rasputin swallowed all the poison they had for him without any effects. Yusupov, who believed in supernatural powers, believed that one of them was protecting Rasputin. It might equally make a bullet harmless. He decided to exorcise it by a classic method—the sign of the cross. Leading Rasputin to the crucifix he reproached him for not crossing himself. And when Rasputin started to make the sign of the cross, thereby sending the dark protecting power away, Yusupov shot him.
>
> [The explanation] is in character; it struck me as the combination of potassium cyanide with the miraculous power of the sign of the cross; murder and God's blessing.[10]

As soon as they heard the shot—Yusupov had been gone some five minutes—the others came down and quickly lifted the body off the rug to prevent it from bleeding on it. It was 3:00 A.M. The plan was for Dmitri Pavlovich, Lazovert, and Sukhotin, dressed in Rasputin's hat and coat, to drive back to number 64 and give the impression that he had returned. They would then take his clothes to Purishkevich's train, where his wife would burn them while they returned for the body, which they would take and drop in the river. When they left, Yusupov and Purishkevich stayed behind and the latter lit a cigar. They were both feeling elated, confident that they had purged their country of a great evil.

Yusupov left Purishkevich for a while, saying he was going to his parents' quarters. In fact he had gone to look at the body, which exerted a powerful fascination over him. We only have his word for what happened next, and he cannot always be relied upon. Yusupov says that he bent over Rasputin and felt his pulse, which was lifeless, and then, taken with a fit of rage, he started to shake the corpse before letting it drop. Suddenly, to his horror, he saw Rasputin open first his left and then his right eye, and experienced that paralysis that comes from fear so total that, however hard one tries, one cannot make the muscles move. Suddenly Rasputin leapt to his feet and attacked him with a roar, trying to strangle him, foaming and bleeding at the mouth and repeating his name, "Felix, Felix," over and over again. Eventually Yusupov tore himself loose, leaving one of his shoulder straps behind him, and ran upstairs, calling to Purishkevich that Rasputin was still alive. The politician saw him, sickly pale, running off to his parents' quarters again. He then heard a second set of footsteps coming up the stairs and the sound of the door into the courtyard being opened. He grabbed his revolver and rushed down in time to see Rasputin moving fast across the courtyard calling, "Felix, Felix, I'll tell the tsarina." Purishkevich, who considered himself a good shot, fired twice and missed; the third shot caught Rasputin in the back and stopped him—he was some twenty paces away—and a fourth sent him to the ground. Purishkevich ran up and delivered a massive kick to the left temple, which left an ugly wound. This time it was finished.

Yusupov had recovered from his panic—he claimed to have gone round to cut Rasputin off should he reach the street—and joined Purishkevich standing over the body. The street seemed empty enough, but in fact the shots had been heard. A policeman, S. F. Vlassyuk, had been on duty on the other side of the Moika canal and he hurried towards the sound. A colleague told him that the shots appeared to have come from the palace. He went there, to find Yusupov together with his major-domo, G. A. Buzhinsky. Yusupov told him that he and his friends had had rather a riotous evening, at the end of which they had amused themselves by shooting Yusupov's dog. The officer returned to his post. Within fifteen minutes Buzhinsky approached him and invited him back to the house. There he found Yusupov, and:

> a gentleman who was a stranger to me wearing a cloak, military green in colour, and judging by his epaulettes he was a Councillor of State. He had close cropped reddish whiskers and a moustache of the same colour.[11]

Purishkevich, who was in no mood for discretion, asked Vlassyuk whether he was a good Christian who loved the tsar. When he replied in the affirmative, Purishkevich made himself known, proudly announced that he had just shot Rasputin and said that the policeman should hold his tongue for the sake of tsar and country. Vlassyuk agreed and twenty minutes later made a full report to his superintendent, Kalyadich. He did not believe that anything of the sort had taken place, assuming the whole affair to be the work of drunken grandees putting his loyalty to the test.[12]

Buzhinsky then announced to Felix that the corpse had been brought in and was lying on the landing—at which point Yusupov lost control. Repeating Rasputin's words, "Felix, Felix," he seized Maklakov's rubber blackjack, rushed to the body and began to beat it about the head in a frenzy till he fainted and was lifted away from it.

It may be that this was not all he did. It has been suggested that he mutilated the body, cutting off Rasputin's penis. Patte Barham, the co-author of Rasputin's daughter's last book, even claims to have seen it; preserved in a velvet container, it is said to be jealously guarded by some venerable White Russian ladies in Paris. There was also said to be a ring, with a magnificent diamond, which Yusupov cut off Rasputin's finger, and which is now the property of the poet Evtushenko. Certainly in the condition he was in Yusupov was capable of anything. Moreover, Rasputin seems to have had a horrid fascination for him, highly coloured by sexuality. However, the autopsy makes no mention of mutilation of any kind, stating that none of the wounds inflicted were in themselves mortal, whereas the removal of the penis would almost certainly have entailed Rasputin's bleeding to death. There was no mention of a finger being cut off to facilitate the removal of a ring, but then the ring might have come away of its own accord. However, we are essentially reliant upon the testimony of those present to discover what happened during the half hour or so that Yusupov could have been alone with the body. Certain cryptic hints in subsequent secondary accounts suggest that something strange may well have taken place. Maklakov writes, "I had another unusual conversation with Yusupov about the murder. I imagine that he remembers it well, but I will say nothing about it."[12] Most probably Yusupov abused the body sexually in some way, but if indeed there does exist a withered penis carefully preserved in some flat in Passy, it does not on the whole seem likely that it was once Rasputin's: the traffic in false relics has long been a feature of Orthodoxy.

At about 5:30 A.M. Sukhotin, Lazovert, and the grand duke returned for the body. They tied it in a canvas covering and placed it in the car. Yusupov was in no shape to do any more so the rest of the conspirators drove off together, north towards Petrovsky Island, the car making fresh tyre marks across the newly fallen snow. They still had Rasputin's coat and overshoes with them. These should have been burnt, but Purishkevich's wife had not wanted to go to the trouble of unstitching the furs, so they had contented themselves with burning a few minor items. They decided to throw the coat and shoes after the body and made a parcel of them. When they reached the Petrovsky bridge, they stopped the car and got the body out. Sukhotin, Purishkevich and Lazovert tried to heave it over the bridge parapet, which is a little over four feet high, but the first time they failed to clear it. It took a second attempt to get the height right, and the body splashed into the water. It was only then that they realised that they had forgotten to load their victim with the chains and weights. The conspirators had been worried that someone might see them throw Rasputin into the water. Fortunately, as they discovered when their headlights picked him up as they drove away, the sentry guarding the bridge was asleep. They had trouble on the way home, since the car kept on stopping, and when they reached Dmitri Pavlovich's residence they found bloodstains on the seat cover and one of Rasputin's overshoes, which had been left out of the parcel. Dmitri Pavlovich promptly gave orders to his staff for the overshoe and the seat cover to be burnt. Sukhotin, Lazovert, and Purishkevich then went back to the train to get what sleep they could, since the train was to be visited by members of the Duma at nine that morning.

CHAPTER 22

December 17, 1916

We are sitting here together—can you imagine our feelings—thoughts—our Friend has disappeared. Yesterday A. [i.e., Vyroubova] saw him and he said Felix asked him to come in the night, a motor would fetch him to see Irina. —A motor fetched him (military one) with two civilians and he went away.

This night big scandal in Yusupov's house, big meeting. Dmitri, Purishkevich etc. all drunk. Police heard shots, Purishkevich came out screaming to the Police that our Friend was killed. Police searching and Justice entered now in Yusupov's house . . .

Chief of Police has sent for Dmitri. Felix wished to leave tonight for Crimea. Begged [Protopopov] to stop him.

Our Friend was in good spirits but nervous these days . . . Felix pretends he never came to the house and never asked him . . . I can't and won't believe he has been killed. God have mercy.

Such utter anguish (am calm and can't believe it) . . .
Felix came often to him lately.

& Kisses,
Sunny[1]

This was the last letter Alexandra Fedorovna wrote to the tsar at headquarters. On receiving it he came straight to her and remained at her side till late in February. The letter gives a brief summary of the events of the seventeenth.

It was Constable Vlassyuk's report that had done the damage. It had gone straight up the chain of command to the chief of the Okhrana, Vassiliev, and from there to the minister of the interior himself. A visit by the police to Rasputin's house, both to check with the family and to remove any compromising documents that might be there (they found none), revealed that Rasputin had indeed left late the night before with Yusupov. His daughter Maria then got in touch with Vyroubova and Mounya Golovina, who in turn informed the tsarina. Mounya Golovina contacted Yusupov on the tsarina's behalf and asked him if he had seen Rasputin the night before. Felix still seems to have believed that he could get away with his deed. He told her that he had not seen Rasputin and then, together with Purishkevich and Dmitri, who had come to join him, he concocted a letter to the tsarina denying the whole affair. He said that he had had a dinner party that night, that Rasputin had telephoned at midnight suggesting a trip to the gypsies, but he had declined. Around 3:00 A.M. the guests had left and a shot had been heard: Dmitri Pavlovich had shot the porter's dog for fun.

In his attempts to get away with it Yusupov had spent all day directing the cleaning of his house and taking care of other details. He shot one of his own dogs through its open mouth, both to support his story and to provide some canine blood to cover Rasputin's bloodstains. But none of this helped much. When the police visited the palace they found traces of blood leading from the basement steps diagonally across the courtyard. There was too much for it to have come from the dead dog the staff obligingly produced, while the testimony of Yusupov's servants did not impress them as being truthful. It was therefore decided to pursue the investigation. The chief of police did not as yet accept that Rasputin was dead; he assumed that he had probably spent the night with friends, or with the gypsies on the islands, and set his agents scouring the restaurants, only to find that none of them had seen Rasputin the night before. In the meantime the search continued.

Late that evening the chief of police, V. V. Vassiliev, was informed that his agents had found traces of blood on the parapet of the Petrovsky bridge. The water below was not entirely frozen over, and on the edge of the ice they had also discovered an overshoe, which Rasputin's servants identified as belonging to him. It would appear, incredibly enough, that they had managed to trace the tyre tracks from Yusupov's palace on the Moika all the way to the bridge, a distance of over three miles, which gives an interesting glimpse of traffic conditions at the time. The chief of police was no longer in any uncertainty as to the murder, any doubts he might have had being dispelled by the news of a telegram the irrepressible Purishkevich had sent to Maklakov in Moscow saying that "It was all over."[2] Since the tsar was expected back from GHQ the next day he decided that, in the meantime, it would be prudent to forbid Yusupov or Dmitri Pavlovich to leave the capital.

They had some difficulty in finding the corpse, despite the use of divers, but it was eventually discovered a hundred *sazhens* (226 metres) downstream, having floated up under the ice. It was felt that the autopsy should be conducted as discreetly as possible, and that it would be unwise to transport the body through the city, for fear that it might inspire public unrest. It was taken in a covered ambulance to a naval hospital three miles out of town, and a guard was placed over it. Rasputin's daughters were permitted to view the corpse. It had to be thawed out before the autopsy could take place, and this took twenty-four hours. The body had been shot three times, and revealed numerous other wounds that looked like stabs. Traces of water in the lungs suggest that Rasputin was indeed still alive when he was thrown into the water, but accounts of the autopsy differ on this point. Some usually reliable sources suggest that he was dead on entering the water. The issue is one of some importance, since in Orthodoxy no one who dies by drowning can become a saint. However, there is no evidence to support the legend that he had twisted one hand free of his bonds and died making the sign of the cross.

News of Rasputin's murder spread rapidly, but it spread by word of mouth. The press was not permitted to cover the story explicitly, so it resorted to the traditional "Language of Aesop," whereby the reader had already to know what the paper was writing about in order to understand what it was saying. Press coverage of the murder gives us a remarkable insight into Petrograd as a city of rumour, half-truth, hints and suspicion. Thus the *Birzhevye Vedomosti* has no mention of the event until the twentieth, and even then its coverage relies upon its readers' knowledge of what took place:

> A heavy frost. The waters of the capital are held by ice, silent, dusted with snow are the gardens. But over the still capital hover strange nightmares. In the depths of the night shots ring out in a dead garden, secret cars hurry across the city carrying corpses and live men . . . Fantastic nightmares weave a poisonous fog and turn into horrid reality. For bloodshed is always horrible and smoking blood is always poisonous.

The same edition describes the finding of the corpse.

> The Krestovsky Island has come alive.
>
> Crowds gather there till nightfall.
>
> A watchman on a bridge is reported as saying that a diver went down into the bottle-green waters of the Neva for an hour but found nothing. The old riverman who knows how corpses drift tells them where to look. They first see a fur coat, hairs coming up through the ice. There was a lot of blood. His boot was a size sixteen, says the watchman. Your reporter then went to the Moika Palace, and looked up at the windows. It was dark upstairs, and the darkness of the wide window was just as secret and intriguing as the riddle of the secret events that have been occupying all our minds for the last three days.[3]

Another report was equally non-specific:

> A certain person visited another person with some other persons. After the first person vanished, one of the other persons

stated that the first person had not been at the house of the second person, although it was known that the second person had visited the first person late at night.[4]

In aristocratic circles, at least, news of the murder was cause for rejoicing; it was seen as a patriotic action that had removed a great evil from Russia. Some of the imperial family, it is true, felt that the killers had not gone far enough, and that as long as the tsarina and Protopopov were still at liberty their work was only half done. It argues a certain insensitivity to the taking of human life in cold blood, or indeed to a monstrous abuse of hospitality, that Yusupov and Dmitri Pavlovich were held by many to be heroic patriots. They were toasted in officers' messes, and one newspaper, *Day,* carried a story on its social page in which it mentioned that at a society gathering the songs of Sumarokov-Elston enjoyed a particular success.[5] According to one British officer in the capital at the time: "The very cabmen in the street are rejoicing over the removal of Rasputin and they and many others think that by this the German influence has received a check."[6]

There are numerous accounts of rejoicing at his death; in Pskov and in Kiev people embraced one another in the streets.[7] When I. V. Hessen, a distinguished editor of a liberal paper, learnt of the killing on the seventeenth, he immediately opened a bottle of Pinot Gris, a superb Crimean wine he had been saving for a special occasion, "not realising that the killing would simply accelerate the course of events."[8] For at the same time it began to be felt that there was something not altogether admirable about the circumstances of Rasputin's dispatch. It was a time of uncertainty and rumour, a time when anything appeared possible, with internal violence and violent change already in the air, a time of *bezvremenye,* "non-time," as Yusupov's father-in-law described it, and the first release of hysterical enthusiasm was another manifestation of that unhealthy climate. Besides, the rejoicing was far from universal. We have little record of the reaction of the common people to news of Rasputin's death, but the comments we have are anything but favourable. On hearing the news in hospital a wounded soldier observed: "He was the first peasant to come close to the tsar and tsarina, and look what happened, the high-ups killed him."[9] Although it is impossible to tell, one cannot help feeling that that soldier was not alone in his opinion. An entry in the diary of Maurice Paléologue, the French ambassador, is revealing. A certain Prince O . . . had just returned from the country and spoke of the impact of Rasputin's death upon the common people:

> It is a curious phenomenon and in keeping with Russian tradition. For the peasants Rasputin has become a martyr. He was from the people; he made the voice of the people known to the tsar; he defended the people against the court, and so courtiers killed him! That is what is being said in all the *izbas*.[10]

Nicholas hurried back to Tsarskoe Selo as soon as reports of the killing were confirmed. The tsarevich went with him, together with his French tutor, M. Gilliard, and when the latter reached the palace he was appalled at the sight of Alexandra:

> I will never forget the way I felt when I saw the empress. Despite herself her shattered face revealed how much she suffered. The pain was tremendous. Her trust had been betrayed, they had killed the only person who could save her child. Now he was gone any kind of disaster or catastrophe was possible. And now the waiting began, the waiting for a misfortune that could not be avoided.[11]

Gilliard's testimony comes as a timely reminder that the empress felt as dependent as ever on Rasputin, believing him to be the only person capable of keeping Aleksey alive. For all his wisdom, the God-sent quality of his advice, it was this more than any other attribute that mattered to her. We have little first-hand information about her feelings beyond this testimony—there were no more letters to Nicholas—but we do know that she was frightened, not for herself, but for Vyroubova, who, she feared, might be the next victim of an assassination.[12] We have little record of the children's reaction to news of Rasputin's death, except for one remark from Grand Duchess Olga Nicolaevna. "I know that he did much harm, but why did they treat him so cruelly?" she was heard to observe, with tears in her eyes.[13]

Nicholas was not appreciative of the "service" the killers had done tsar and country. As soon as he received his wife's letter he sent her a telegram: "Distressed and shaken, with you in prayers and thoughts."[14] He displayed no sympathy of any kind towards the killers, and this is scarcely surprising. Two of the best-connected young men in the country, a grand duke and the husband of an imperial princess, both of whom had been closer than anyone else of their age and sex to the inner circle of Tsarskoe Selo, had destroyed his wife's favourite, while it soon became clear that their intention, if not the details of their plot, were widely known in their immediate circle. To Nicholas their action must have appeared as the culmination of all the hostile criticism he had been receiving from his relations over the latter months, and as the beginning of a right-wing anti-dynastic coup. As the historian Melgunov has shown, there was indeed a plan to unseat the tsar, and it was only the events of February 1917 that prevented it from being put into action. If the Rasputin assassination was not part of it, it was at least a reflection of the attitudes that were to inspire such a conspiracy.

Its immediate consequence was to widen still further the rift between the grand dukes and the tsar, for there remained the awkward question of the fate of the young assassins. The day the body was discovered they were placed under house arrest and isolated, more or less, from the outside world. In fact they were able to see their immediate families. Dmitri Pavlovich's sister spent some time with him. Her first reaction on hearing news of his participation in the plot was pique–why had not her favourite brother kept her in the picture? When she met him afterwards she found him very tense. He told her that he had wanted to strike a blow for Russia at a time when no one was prepared to undertake anything, "to urge action, by example of action, all in one decisive stroke."[15] However, he was already somewhat subdued and beginning to have doubts as to the value of what he had done. He was rather disgusted by the popularity that his action had earned him. Yusupov, on the contrary, was as elated as ever:

> He was intoxicated by the importance of the part he had played, and saw in it a great political future . . . Yet in spite of his self-

> satisfaction and outward assurance there was in his words some anxiety both as to his own fate and Dmitri's.[16]

In fact both young men were very worried about what might become of them. They were not entirely beyond the law and in Dmitri's case there was also the growing feeling that he might have made a terrible mistake. The impression was confirmed by an interview he had with his father, the grand duke Paul. When they first met, Dmitri swore, perhaps a little disingenuously, that he had no actual blood on his hands, he was not a killer. He could not describe his exact role; all the participants were bound to one another by oath not to recount exactly what happened, taking collective responsibility, and the oaths held for the time being. Dmitri's father was relieved to learn that his son was not a murderer but felt his action to have been dreadfully unwise nonetheless:

> His attitude to what had happened was circumspect and entirely without enthusiasm. He acknowledged that Dmitri and Yusupov had been impelled by a patriotic motive, but contended that their action had been dangerous and thoughtless from many points of view. The deed, as he saw it, only deepened the abyss separating the imperial family from Russia, and the assassination which Yusupov had planned, and in which Dmitri had participated . . . was, in my father's opinion, both futile and hideous.[17]

This statesmanlike view of the whole sorry business is immediately qualified by an extraordinarily Machiavellian remark that suggests that the grand duke only objected to the way Rasputin was killed and not to the murder itself:

> He felt that Yusupov possessed sufficient means to permit him to choose another and more adequate way of getting rid of Rasputin, and blamed Yusupov for involving Dmitri in a deed which would bring such ugly notoriety.[18]

It is striking that no one ventured to express the view that Rasputin had as much right to stay alive as the next man. However, Dmitri

Pavlovich in years to come expressed the bitterest shame at having allowed himself to be involved in the killing.[19] Felix, on the other hand, remained unrepentant. Some years later he was asked whether his conscience ever pricked him. "No," Yusupov answered, smiling. "I shot a dog."[20]

Nicholas's immediate reaction was to banish Dmitri Pavlovich and Yusupov. The former was to serve with the Russian troops in Persia, the latter was sent to his estates in the Kursk area. In the meantime, investigation of the events of December 16 was continued, despite the tremendous pressure exerted upon the tsar by the grand dukes and their families. The tension increased steadily, until Grand Duke Andrey Vladimirovich could write in his diary:

> General discontent increases every day, the whole family is tremendously worked up, the young ones in particular, they will have to be held in check, to stop them getting out of control . . . Bad things are on the horizon.[21]

By "bad things" he meant a palace revolution. However, despite the tsar's properly sententious observation to the grand dukes who pressed for mercy that "No one is permitted to have a hand in murder, be it a grand duke or a peasant,"[22] the department of justice was in no hurry to conclude its investigation, since this could only lead to the most embarrassing of confrontations. Everyone concerned "worked to rule" and the investigation was still creeping slowly on when the revolution brought the whole affair to an end.

The fact remains that, at least in retrospect, the killing of Rasputin seemed to many to be the first step towards revolution, if only in that it signified that respect for the wishes of the tsar and tsarina had disappeared at the very highest of levels. This was already apparent to many people at the time. The young man who had hoped to take part in the killing but could not get leave passed a minister on the Duma stairs shortly after the event and the minister observed, "You will see this is the first shot of a revolution," while the reports of the secret police referred to the killers as the "swallows of the terror."[23] Curiously, as was the case with the French Revolution, it was a revolution of the right that was anticipated at this moment. Certainly many émigrés hold Yusupov responsible, in retrospect, for subsequent events. One old lady the author talked to, an ardent monarchist some ninety years old, observed that she could recall the imperial family so vividly that it might be yesterday, and that she grieved for their fate every night. She had never seen or spoken to Felix, who was a distant relative, since the deed, and felt that had it not been for him, "I would still be on my estates in the Tambov government and not sitting here in Chiswick." Another right-wing apologist, V. V. Shulgin, saw the killing as an attempt at a palace revolution. Since the number of revolutionaries was insufficient, they contented themselves with killing Rasputin. But the damage to the monarchy had been done already, and it was hopelessly poisoned; what was the point of killing the snake now?[24] As Dmitri Pavlovich's sister wrote:

> His death came too late to change the course of events. His dreadful name had become too thoroughly a symbol of disaster. The daring of those who killed him to save their country was miscalculated. All of the participants in the plot, with the exception of Prince Yusupov, later understood that in raising their hands to preserve the old regime they struck it, in reality, its fatal blow.[25]

Yet in view of the way in which numerous members of the tsar's family, including Dmitri Pavlovich's father, not to mention Alexandra's sister, had written and spoken to Nicholas and Alexandra in recent months, imploring them to get rid of Rasputin and institute reforms, only to be given the most hostile of receptions, there is a sense in which the assassination was truly a revolutionary act on the part of the "sons" avenging the rejection of the "fathers" by mounting a direct attack upon the dynasty. The last words belong to Rasputin himself, who wrote a letter to the empress in the last month of his life.

> The spirit of Grigorii Efimovich Rasputin of the village of Pokrovskoe. I write and leave behind me this letter at St. Petersburg. I feel that I shall leave my life before January 1. I wish to make known to the Russian people, to Papa, to the

> Russian mother and the children, to the land of Russia what they must understand. If I am killed by common assassins, and especially by my brothers the Russian peasants, you, tsar of Russia, will have nothing to fear for your children, they will reign in Russia for hundreds of years. But if I am murdered by nobles, and if they shed my blood, their hands will remain soiled with my blood and for twenty-five years they will leave Russia. Brothers will kill brothers, and they will kill each other and hate each other, and for twenty-five years there will be no nobles in this country. Tsar of the Russian land, if you have heard the sound of the bell which will tell you that Grigorii has been killed you must know this; if it was your relations who have brought about my death, then none of your family, that is to say none of your children or relatives, will remain alive for more than two years. They will all be killed by the Russian people. I go and feel in me the divine command to tell the Russian tsar how he must live if I have disappeared. You must reflect and act prudently. Think of your safety and tell your relatives that I have paid for them with my blood. I shall be killed, I am no longer among the living, pray, pray, be strong, think of your blessed family. Grigorii.[26]*

Rasputin was buried on December 22 in Tsarskoe Selo, in the centre aisle of a new church adjoining Anna Vyroubova's hospital for convalescents. The church was on her own property, and thus the imperial family could not be accused of taking Rasputin to themselves. The burial took place in the presence of the tsar, the tsarina, their children, Vyroubova, and one or two ladies-in-waiting. The empress was pale but began to cry when the plain oak coffin with a cross on the outside was taken out of the police van in which it arrived. Rasputin was buried with the icon the tsarina had brought to him from Novgorod, with signatures of herself and the children on the back, and Vyroubova's modestly scrawled "Anna" now added in

* Throughout 1917 Rasputin's prophecies to the effect that without him the imperial family would perish were taken as proof that he was a charlatan, since, for the time being, they were all still very much alive; but they would survive Rasputin by only a little over eighteen months.

the right-hand corner. The tsar made his own feelings clear in the terse little entry in his diary. "Just after eight the whole family went to the field where we were present at a sad spectacle; the coffin with the body of unforgettable Grigorii, killed on the night of the 16th by *savages* in the house of F. Yusupov, was let down into the grave."[27]

Although some of his earlier adherents lost faith in Rasputin when it became clear that he had failed to foresee that Yusupov would murder him, and even Anna Vyroubova was a little shaken by that failure, others stayed loyal. The empress remained unswerving in her devotion to her Friend, who she felt had undergone martyrdom on her behalf. A month after his death she had a dream in which she saw Rasputin in heaven looking down and giving his blessing to Russia. The same trust in him is reflected in a letter she wrote the day before the dynasty fell:

> The sun shines so brightly, and I feel such peace and calm when I visit his dear grave. He died to save us.[28]

Rasputin did not remain in his grave for long. Early in March 1917, at a time when the imperial family were prisoners in their own palace, orders were given to disinter the body. The work was carried out by members of Russia's anti-aircraft battery, which had been guarding Tsarskoe Selo. When the coffin was opened Rasputin's face had turned completely black. The empress's icon was discovered, and in due course was bought for a considerable sum by an American collector. The soldiers put the body into a packing case that had previously contained a piano and took it to Petrograd, where it was hidden in the old imperial stables. The next day it was loaded onto a lorry which drove out of town in the direction of Lesnoe. There it was burnt at the roadside a quarter of a mile from the forest of Pargolovo, in the presence of Captain Kolotseyev, a cavalry officer; Koupchinsky, a delegate of the provisional committee of the Duma; and six student militiamen. His ashes were then scattered. Rasputin, having died in water and been buried in earth, was now consigned to fire and the wind.

Rasputin may even be considered to have prophesied that consignment to fire. On one occasion late in 1916 he observed to a journalist:

> The fools don't understand who I am. A sorcerer, perhaps, a sorcerer may be. They burn sorcerers, and so let them burn me too. But there is one thing they do not realise. If they do burn me Russia is finished; they'll bury us together.[29]

CONCLUSION

AN ARTICLE IN *Birzhevye Vedomosti* in 1915 attacking Rasputin contains the phrase, "Yet what was there to exaggerate when the naked truth was worse than any lie?" When looking back on Rasputin's extraordinary career one may well feel that the truth, in so far as we have been able to bring it out, is, if not worse, then more fascinating than any of the legendary exaggerations with which Rasputin has been surrounded from the moment he first appeared upon the public stage right up to the present day. His legend presents him as a daemonic figure, possessed of supernatural powers, in the service of the forces of evil, the satyric lover of the Russian queen and a German spy to boot, a poison infecting the whole dynasty and a synonym for vice, magic, corruption and superhuman physical prepotency.

It would be preposterous to deny that he was in his way a very remarkable man, possessed of unusual powers. Perhaps the most noteworthy feat he performed was his "resurrection" of Vyroubova. Yet if we accept the possibility of healing by faith, we can see that Anna

Vyroubova would have been as susceptible as anyone to such treatment. Certainly noteworthy, it remained a relatively isolated incident, at least when compared to the accounts of persons who lay claims regularly to heal by faith. The story of Rasputin's life does not abound in such events; as faith healers go he was not all *that* remarkable. His ability to treat the tsarevich should be considered a special instance of folk medicine; indeed it is strange that the tsarina did not earlier seek the help of "whisperers" and peasant healers. However, he must be given credit for the consistency of his success, while the occasion on which he saved the boy's life, when Aleksey was lying in a Polish hunting lodge and Rasputin was in Siberia, poses a powerful challenge to rational belief.

Rasputin possessed clairvoyant powers of a sort. He saw death running after Stolypin in Kiev, but this was an isolated instance. On the whole his powers were more generalised. He had a strange apprehension of the future of the dynasty and the old regime that went beyond ordinary intuition. His confident assertion that the day would come when the imperial family would see his native village has an uncanny ring to it, as do his visions of the revolution to come. Yet here again his power was limited, generalised, and modest when compared to that of some other clairvoyants. There is, for example, in present-day Bulgaria an extraordinary clairvoyant woman of undisputed power named Vanga. She is blind, yet able to "see" her visitors, and to describe the appearance of their long-dead relatives in great detail. She has extraordinarily clear and comprehensive vision into the future. The Bulgarian government intended at one time to arrest her, but instead acknowledged the value of her powers and constructed an entire institute about her. Informed Bulgarian sources claim that she plays a considerable part in the planning of East bloc policy. Nor do Rasputin's healing powers compare with those of the old Georgian faith healer who, the Soviet government now freely admits, restored a practically dying Brezhnev to sprightly health just in time for the Moscow Olympics.

Such comparisons are not intended to disparage Rasputin's "powers," but merely to put them in perspective and show them to be circumscribed. To understand the man does not demand a belief in the paranormal world of supernature, lay-lines, reflexology and the Bermuda triangle. His real strength resided in a personality that, however unusual, remains within the scope of rational comprehension. He had the power to win the trust of certain persons, women for the most part, to inspire an unquestioning faith in him, and to ease their distress. In that respect he fulfilled the role of a priest or analyst.

It should also be recalled that he began his career as a man of God, a seeker after salvation and a pilgrim, and that he made a profound impression upon devout if gullible Christians for many years. He was capable of preaching a simple popular form of Christianity that had something of the joy, love, and celebration of God's creation that we find in the Dostoevsky of *The Brothers Karamazov*.

Yet when we consider all these qualities, the final impression we have is one of tragic waste. When we think how far this simple illiterate Siberian peasant got, there can be no escaping the fact that it all went sadly wrong. There is something distasteful about judging a man's life, putting one's finger on the reasons for his failure, and we do so reluctantly and because the reasons for that failure bring us close to the man himself. We have said that in many ways he possessed the kind of authority exerted by priests and analysts. Yet both the priesthood and analysis require years of training. Power is exercised within a carefully constructed framework, with a design that derives from a great accumulation of past experience. The authority is structured. The tragedy of Rasputin is that he operated alone. He lacked the conceptual intelligence and self-discipline to control his powers, and also lacked any sort of cultural framework that might have compensated for his personal deficiencies. Accordingly he became a classic example of the dangers of power without responsibility.

Looking back over his career, we can see how power corrupted him, turning him from a quest for the spiritual to a quest for pleasure, position, and consideration. He was spoilt by his contact with the high life, with consequences disastrous for all concerned.

It is easy enough to understand what happened to Rasputin when he reached the heights, harder to grasp how he got there. His rise must be seen against the background of a country that had "Official Christianity" as one of its fundamental tenets, and a culture that was still Christian, but only just. One of the most important features of European cultural history in the nineteenth and early twentieth centuries is the erosion of Christian values, both in public life and in individual consciousness. Imperial Russia had remained an overtly Christian culture for longer than most countries, but even there the hold of Orthodox Christianity was weakening. Rasputin's rise must be set against an age of religious decadence, in which the Orthodox required ever stronger and rarer experiences and began to flirt with heresy, sectarianism, and even paganism. Rasputin was in one sense the last of his kind, both a creation of Official Christianity and the sign of its termination. His authority was an index of the final collapse of Christendom, as the culture turned to strange gods and strange versions of God. His brand of religion was highly coloured by sectarian heresy—and yet there was more to it than that, it also possessed great warmth and simplicity. As a peasant he moved in a world of cosy belief, simple faith, the world of Bozhenka (the infinitely tender Russian diminutive form of God), which in the eyes of many people, and especially the tsarina, gave him great strength. His brand of faith, with its simplicity, its understanding both of spirituality and of weakness, appealed to many devout Christians of the age in their search for God.

Whatever the reasons for his rise to prominence, he lacked the temperament to cope with it. Very quickly he acquired the ambitions of a courtier who wished to be as close as possible to the monarch, no different in this respect from the French noblemen who sought to get as close as possible to the Sun King at Versailles. The ever-growing need for such closeness made him jealous of anyone threatening his position, and vindictive to boot. He found it impossible to see far beyond his own immediate self-interest, and his lack of political judgment made him encourage the imperial couple's own tendency to live in a closed world. In some respects he was the most powerful man in Russia—if only in the sense that he was able to make or break ministers. The extent of his influence is admirably summed up by Alexander Blok, who as secretary to the Muravyev Commission was better placed than any man to gain a bird's eye view of the last years of the regime:

People as diverse as Rodzyanko, General Ivanov . . . the Grand Dukes . . . spoke to the tsar about the damage Rasputin was doing. Although the view persons in power took of this illiterate *starets* differed widely they all agreed in one respect, they were all unflattering; yet at the same time it is clear that they all, in greater or lesser degree, were dependent upon him; whoever he might have been, the man's sphere of influence was colossal; his life was spent in an extraordinary atmosphere of hysterical adoration and limitless loathing: some prayed to him, others sought to destroy him; the utterly exceptional quality of the debauched peasant shot in the back at Yusupov's "gramophone party" is to be perceived most of all in the fact that the bullet that killed him hit the very heart of the ruling dynasty . . . The recluses of Tsarskoe Selo and Vyroubova's "little house" . . . were cut off from the world by a gulf which, according to Rasputin's will, narrowed sometimes, to give access to select influences, sometimes widened to become uncrossable even to relatives of the tsar.[1]

Rasputin made a substantial contribution to the fall of the dynasty, by alienating persons who could have advised the tsar and tsarina better, by encouraging the disastrous influence of Alexandra, by advocating the most injudicious ministerial appointments–Khvostov and Protopopov. He involved the imperial couple with persons they should have steered clear of, for instance Rubinstein. Certainly he allowed himself to be used by the most devious of political hustlers, such as Andronnikov. Yet most of his misdeeds were no more than errors of judgment, and much of his so-called influence was based upon bluff. Not all his advice was stupid nor was it all heeded by Nicholas. He had a certain clarity of vision, was always sensitive to the plight of peasant soldiers. He was fundamentally opposed to war, which meant for him no more, no less than needless bloodshed, and bitterly opposed to military action that sacrificed thousands of lives to secure a meaningless piece of territory. It is incidentally interesting to note that he spoke out against bloodshed–"enough blood has been spilt" he would remark–while his greatest skill was checking the flow of the blood of the tsarevich. He was a healer, not a wilful destroyer. On a more personal note the veneration acceded him by his disciples never gave him *folie de grandeur*. They remained his "fools," and while he was prepared to accept their adoration, since it was proffered, he never took it too seriously. "Take when they are giving, run when they are beating" (a Russian saying) remained his motto. He was selfish, limited, irresponsible, and wasted his powers. He reached the position he did thanks to the gullibility of others. The worst one can say of him is that he continued to exploit that gullibility out of naked self-interest.

If we have struck an apologetic note in this final consideration, it is to remind the reader that Rasputin was not wittingly destructive; he simply acted out of unenlightened self-interest–unenlightened in that he never learnt from his experiences, and always retained the horizons of a peasant. It was indeed because he was a peasant that his existence close to the throne was unacceptable to so many. Had he been a member of the nobility who achieved great prominence, acquired a hold over the tsarina, abused his position, was sexually dissolute and of poor political judgment, he would never have scandalised the nation. It was the fact of his being a peasant that created the scandal.

Although we have tried to lift Rasputin out of the web of legend that surrounds him, in the final analysis there *is* something legendary, mythic, about his historical role. Ever since the days of Peter the Great the gap between the Russian people and its rulers had widened steadily until, by the early twentieth century, it seemed unbridgeable. As Blok so clearly understood, it would not be the disaffected intelligentsia that would bring his country past the brink of chaos, but the *temniy narod,* her dark masses, who were so far removed from the thin veneer of civilization. In many respects the story of Rasputin is the strangest of modern Russian history, the sole instance of a genuine and prolonged meeting between the two Russias: civilization and the peasant world. For the first time the civilized world was penetrated by a very different kind of Russia, darkest Russia if you like, a penetration that both anticipated and assisted that civilization's downfall. Certainly it is in those terms that Marie Pavlovna, Dmitri Pavlovich's sister, summed him up:

> All that befell Russia through Rasputin's direct or indirect influence can, it seems to me, be regarded as the vengeful expression of a dark, terrible, all-sweeping hatred, kindling for centuries in the heart of the Russian peasant for the higher classes who never learned to understand him or win him over.[2]

That Rasputin, a dissolute peasant, should have enjoyed the confidence of the couple in ultimate command of the nation was enough to destroy their credibility in many eyes. Of course Rasputin was not the first peasant to try to reach the centre. Russia has known its share of failed peasant rebellions–Stenka Razin in the seventeenth century, and Pugachev in the eighteenth spring to mind. The failure of these peasant leaders to bring down the tsar has usually been characterised in military terms, by the failure of their armies to reach the capital. Rasputin was no rebel, yet the fact that he reached not just the capital, but the very heart of the empire, the seclusion and intimacy of Tsarskoe Selo, was enough to ensure that he succeeded where his predecessors had failed.

A [illegible] the Union [illegible] [illegible] [illegible] [illegible]
[illegible] it seems to me [illegible] of the [illegible] ex-
[illegible] [illegible] [illegible] all [illegible] [illegible]
[illegible] in the [illegible] of the Russian peasant [illegible]
[illegible] never [illegible] to [illegible] or win him over.

Thus [illegible] [illegible] [illegible] should [illegible]
[illegible] of the [illegible] [illegible] of the [illegible]
[illegible] that [illegible] in many ways. Of course [illegible]
was not the first [illegible] [illegible]
[illegible] of [illegible] [illegible] in the [illegible]
[illegible] and Pugachev in the [illegible] during so [illegible]. The failure
of these peasant [illegible] the [illegible] usually [illegible]
attributed [illegible] by the failure of their [illegible] to [illegible]
[illegible]. [illegible] was no rebel [illegible]
the [illegible], but [illegible] part of the empire, the [illegible] and
[illegible] of [illegible] enough to ensure that he succeeded
[illegible] peasant [illegible] had failed.

NOTES

CHAPTER 1

1. J. F. Fraser, *The Real Siberia* (London, 1904), p. 13.

2. Kennan, vol. i, pp. 89–90.

3. Talytsin, p. 11.

4. Novomeysky, p. 15.

5. Mintslov, *Debri,* pp. 6–7.

6. Kennan, vol. i, p. 68.

7. Fraser, p. 77.

8. Mintslov, *Debri,* p. 138.

9. Ibid., p. 131.

10. Zavarzine, p. 259.

11. Alexandra, p. 400.

12. See below, p. 46.

13. K. Marsden, *On Sledge and Horseback* (London, 1894), p. 79.

14. Preston, *Before the Curtain* (1956), pp. 48–49.

15. Dolgorukov, p. 273.

16. Dehn, pp. 110–11.

17. *Birzh. ved.,* 15 viii 15.

CHAPTER 2

1. Spiridovich, *Raspoutine,* pp. 10–11.

2. *Vop. ist.,* 1964, no. x, p. 119.

3. Spiridovich, *Raspoutine,* p. 12.

4. Rasputin, *My Father,* p. 30.

5. Kataev, p. 136.

6. *Vop. ist.,* 1964, no. x, p. 119.

7. Badmaev, p. 139.

8. Dillon, p. 24.

9. Bolotov, p. 218.

10. *Padenie,* vol. ii, p. 327.

11. Shakhovskoy, pp. 116–17.

12. Spiridovich, *Der. ann.,* vol. II, pp. 119–20.

13. *Vop. ist.,* 1964, no. x, p. 120.

14. Ibid.

15. Dehn, p. 112.

16. Rasputin, *The Real Rasputin,* p. 18.

CHAPTER 3

1. Dillon, pp. 154–55.
2. *Arkhiv russ. rev.*, 1925, no. xvi, p. 43.
3. Prugavin, *Raskol*, p. 12.
4. B. Fv., p. 247.
5. Prugavin, op. cit., pp. 40–42.
6. *Birzh. ved.*, 19 iv 15.
7. Spiridovich, *Raspoutine*, pp. 23–24.
8. Melnikov, *Sob. soch.*, vol. vi, p. 203.
9. Sévérac, pp. 14–15.
10. Melnikov, op. cit., p. 229.
11. Ibid., p. 224.
12. Ibid., p. 203.
13. Ibid., p. 270.
14. *Bogoslovskii vestnik*, July 1897, p. 584.
15. Sévérac, p. 66.
16. *Bogoslovskii vestnik*, April 1908, p. 731.
17. Ibid., p. 238.
18. Melnikov, op. cit., p. 240.
19. Bol'shakov, p. 86.
20. A. Mochulsky, *Andrey Bely* (New York, 1977), p. 133.
21. Melnikov, op. cit., p. 241.
22. Novoselov, p. 82.
23. Ibid., p. 95.
24. *Vop. ist.*, 1964, no. x, p. 121.
25. *Padenie*, vol. iv, pp. 499–500.

CHAPTER 4

1. Kamenskii, p. 12.
2. *Arkhiv russ. rev.*, 1925, no. xvi, p. 45.
3. Spiridovich, *Raspoutine*, p. 18.
4. Chaliapin, pp. 23–25.
5. Trufanov, pp. 154–56.
6. Ibid., pp. 156–57.
7. Spiridovich, *Der. ann.*, vol. I, p. 121.
8. Trufanov, p. 156.
9. Spiridovich, op. cit.
10. Yusupov, *La fin de Raspoutine*, p. 162.
11. Rasputin, *The Real Rasputin*, pp. 21–22.
12. Kennan, vol. i, pp. 20–21.
13. *Encyclopaedia Britannica*, 1886, vol. xiv, p. 22.
14. "Skitalets," p. 44.
15. Zhevakhov, pp. 265–66.
16. Spiridovich, *Raspoutine*, p. 397.
17. Ibid.
18. *Vop. ist.*, 1964, no. x, p. 121.
19. Marsden, pp. 12–13.
20. *Vop. ist.*, 1964, no. x, p. 121.
21. Dehn, pp. 100–1.
22. Spiridovich, *Raspoutine*, p. 214.
23. Witte, vol. i, p. 275.
24. Mintslov, *Peterburg*, p. 33.

CHAPTER 5

1. M. Buchanan, pp. 4–5.
2. Walpole, pp. 98–100.
3. Mintslov, *Peterburg*, p. 4.
4. Ibid., p. 50.
5. Ibid., p. 92.
6. Dobson, p. 111.
7. Mintslov, op. cit., p. 156.
8. Mossolov, p. 194.
9. Ibid., p. 191.
10. Ibid., p. 196.
11. Mintslov, op. cit., p. 85.
12. Ibid., p. 114.
13. Ibid., p. 226.
14. Ibid., p. 139.
15. Ibid., pp. 242–43.
16. Arsenev, pp. 70–71.
17. Zhevakhov, p. 235.
18. Mintslov, op. cit., pp. 36–37.
19. Ibid., pp. 86–87.
20. Trufanov, p. 165.

21. Mintslov, *Debri*, p. 238.
22. Mintslov, *Peterburg*, p. 80.
23. Essad Bey, p. 188.
24. Spiridovich, *Raspoutine*, p. 42.
25. Zhevakhov, p. 262.
26. Trufanov, pp. 87–88.
27. Ibid., pp. 90–91.
28. Zhevakhov, p. 263.
29. Ibid., p. 311.
30. Novomeysky, pp. 196–97.
31. Ibid.

CHAPTER 6

1. *Iskry*, 15 vi 14.
2. Vorres, p. 100.
3. Spiridovich, *Der. ann.*, vol. i, p. 98.
4. Aleksandr Mikhailovich, vol. i, pp. 167–68.
5. Vassili, pp. 214–15.
6. Iswolsky, p. 270.
7. Dillon, p. 355.
8. Aleksandr Mikhailovich, vol. i, p. 174.
9. Vassili, p. 215.
10. Mossolov, p. 9.
11. Kokovtsov, pp. 167–68.
12. Telyakovskii, p. 75.
13. Baryatinskaya, p. 32.
14. Marie Pavlovna, p. 21.
15. Ibid.
16. Gilliard, p. 67.
17. Essad Bey, p. 92.
18. Buxhoeveden, pp. 108–9.
19. Vorres, pp. 72–73.
20. Trewin, p. 38.
21. Marie Pavlovna, p. 34.
22. Mintslov, *Peterburg*, p. 70.
23. Kleinmichel, pp. 160–62.
24. Bogdanovich, p. 295.
25. Baryatinskaya, p. 138.
26. Bogdanovich, p. 397.
27. Spring Rice, vol. ii, p. 23.
28. Ibid., p. 14.
29. Mintslov, *Peterburg*, p. 137.
30. *Istoricheskii vestnik*, no. 147, 1917, pp. 151–59.
31. Murray, p. 27.
32. Dillon, pp. 155–56.
33. Ibid.
34. Mintslov, *Peterburg*, p. 18.
35. Bogdanovich, p. 49.
36. Pares, p. 131.
37. Ibid., p. 56–57.
38. Yusupov, *La fin de Raspoutine*, p. 11.
39. Buxhoeveden, p. 136.
40. Alexandra, p. 414.
41. Encausse, *Le maître Philippe*, p. 189.
42. Yusupov, *Lost Splendour*, p. 62.
43. Encausse, op. cit., pp. 221–22.
44. Pares, p. 134.
45. Spiridovich, *Der. ann.*, vol. i, p. 101.
46. Bogdanovich, p. 397.
47. Encausse, op. cit., p. 209.
48. Ibid., pp. 226–27.
49. *Istoricheskii vestnik*, 1917, no. 194, p. 53.

CHAPTER 7

1. Spiridovich, *Raspoutine*, pp. 48–49.
2. Ibid., p. 52.
3. Judas, p. 35.
4. Spiridovich, op. cit., p. 59.
5. Spiridovich, *Der. ann.*, vol. i, p. 290.
6. See above, p. 80.
7. Zhevakhov, p. 281.
8. Dehn, p. 99.
9. Spiridovich, *Raspoutine*, p. 88.
10. Dehn, p. 103.

11. *Russkoe proshloe,* 1923, no. iv, p. 109.
12. See below, p. 214.

CHAPTER 8

1. Alexander of Russia, pp. 184–85.
2. Sokolov, p. 64.
3. Spiridovich, *Raspoutine,* p. 71.
4. Ibid.
5. Shakhovskoy, p. 119.
6. Pasternak, *Doctor Zhivago* (London, 1958), pp. 329–300.
7. Katkov, pp. 281–82.
8. Spiridovich, *Raspoutine,* pp. 72–73.
9. Essad Bey, p. 191.
10. *Sov. zap.,* 1928, no. 347, p. 207.
11. Mel'nik, p. 8.
12. Dehn, p. 38.
13. Gilliard, pp. 67–68.
14. Bogdanovich, pp. 447–48, 452.
15. *Vop. ist.,* 1964, no. xi, pp. 91–92.
16. Bogdanovich, p. 453 (November 5, 1908).
17. Vorres, pp. 138–39.
18. *Vop. ist.,* 1964, no. x, p. 136.

CHAPTER 9

1. Zhevakhov, pp. 276–77.
2. Ibid.
3. Lemke, p. 263.
4. Sokolov, p. 77.
5. *Vop. ist.,* 1964, no. x, p. 130.
6. Spiridovich, *Der. ann.,* vol. ii, p. 296.
7. Rodzyanko, p. 11.
8. See below, p. 266.
9. Badmaev, p. 138.
10. Spiridovich, *Der. ann.,* vol. ii, p. 45.
11. Novoselov, in *Moskovskie vedomosti,* 30 iv 10.

CHAPTER 10

1. *Arkhiv russ. rev.,* 1925, no. xvi, pp. 24–25.
2. Ibid., p. 38.
3. Spiridovich, *Raspoutine,* p. 128.
4. Trufanov, p. 56.
5. Badmaev, p. 138.
6. *Peterburgskaya gazeta,* 11 iv 13.
7. Badmaev, p. 138.
8. Ibid.
9. Ibid.
10. Anon., *Nikolai II,* p. 88.
11. Zhevakhov, p. 270.
12. Trufanov, p. 137.
13. Kurlov, pp. 145–46.
14. Ibid.
15. M. Rasputin, *My Father,* pp. 75–77.
16. Ibid.
17. Bogdanovich, pp. 498–99.
18. Ibid.
19. *Vop. ist.,* 1964, no. x, p. 132.
20. Rasputin, *My Father,* p. 131.

CHAPTER 11

1. Badmaev, p. 143.
2. Ibid., p. 148.
3. Ibid., p. 159.
4. *Arkhiv russ. rev.,* 1925, vol. xvi, p. 30.
5. Ibid., p. 39.
6. Trufanov, p. 71.
7. Shulgin, pp. 96–97.

CHAPTER 12

1. *Vop. ist.,* 1965, no. i, p. 104.
2. *Byloe,* 1917, no. i (23), p. 60.
3. *Vop. ist.,* 1964, no. x, p. 131.
4. Milyukov, p. 100.

5. *Birzh. ved.*, 20 xii 16.
6. Bogdanovich, p. 496.
7. Mamontov, p. 233.
8. Milyukov, p. 102.
9. *Poslednie novosti,* 6 ix 36.
10. *Sovremennik,* no. iii, 1912.
11. *Padenie,* vol. iii, p. 435.
12. *Iskry,* 15 vi 14.
13. Bogdanovich, pp. 499–500.
14. Milyukov, p. 102.
15. Mintslov, *Debri,* p. 194.
16. Spiridovich, *Der. ann.*, vol. ii, p. 142.
17. Bogdanovich, p. 496.
18. *Padenie,* vol. iii, pp. 391–92.
19. Ibid., p. 389.
20. Ibid.
21. Mamontov, pp. 109–10.
22. Spiridovich, *Der. ann.*, vol. ii, p. 262.

CHAPTER 13

1. *Vechernee vremya,* 7 i 13.
2. Ibid., 3 i 13.
3. Vassili, p. 391.
4. Buxhoeveden, pp. 142–43.
5. Mamontov, p. 233.
6. Ibid., p. 114.
7. Sokolov, p. 71.
8. Zavarzine, pp. 143–44.
9. *Padenie,* vol. iv, p. 172.
10. *Arkhiv russ. rev.*, 1925, vol. xvi, p. 271.
11. *Padenie,* vol. iv, p. 334.
12. *Petrogradskaya gazeta,* 21 iii 17.
13. *Vop. ist.*, 1964, no. x, pp. 122–23.
14. Prugavin, *Leontii,* pp. 20–23.
15. *Petrogradskaya gazeta,* 21 iii 17.
16. *Russkoe proshloe,* 1923, no. iv, p. 100.
17. Teffi, p. 287.
18. *Russkoe proshloe,* 1923, no. iv, p. 100.
19. Dzhaunumova, p. 15.
20. M. Rasputin, *My Father,* p. 73.
21. Preston, p. 204.
22. Yusupov, *Lost Splendour,* p. 78.
23. Obolensky, pp. 43–44.
24. Bruce Lockhart, *Memoirs,* p. 60.

CHAPTER 14

1. Vassiliev, p. 136.
2. Ibid.
3. *Peterburgskaya gazeta,* 13 x 13.
4. Rodzyanko, p. 76.
5. Ibid.
6. *Vop. ist.*, 1964, no. x, p. 93.
7. Spiridovich, *Raspoutine,* p. 191.
8. Trufanov, p. 207.
9. Spiridovich, *Raspoutine,* p. 190.
10. *Vechernee vremya,* 13 ii 13.
11. Trufanov, p. 207.
12. Spiridovich, *Der. ann.*, vol. ii, p. 428.
13. *Padenie,* vol. vi, p. 266.
14. Melgunov, *Legenda,* p. 383.
15. Dehn, p. 106.
16. Simanovich, p. 196.
17. *Padenie,* vol. ii, p. 54.
18. Andrey Vladimirovich, p. 15.

CHAPTER 15

1. Makarov, p. 208.
2. Ibid., p. 284.
3. Ibid., p. 258.
4. Ibid., p. 245.
5. Mel'nik, p. 16.
6. Ibid.
7. Alexander of Russia, p. 293.

8. Bruce Lockhart, *Memoirs,* p. 97.
9. Ibid. Loc. cit.
10. Hoare, p. 49.
11. Solzhenitsyn, *August 1914.* (Paris, 1970), p. 554.
12. Alexandra, p. 421.
13. Ibid., pp. 17–18.
14. *Arkhiv russ. rev.,* 1923, no. xii, p. 16.
15. Ibid., p. 17.
16. Ibid., 1925, vol. xvi, p. 263.

CHAPTER 16

1. Makarov, p. 284.
2. *Birzh. ved.,* 10 iv 15.
3. Makarov, p. 289.
4. Melgunov, *Na putyakh,* p. 29.
5. Katkov, p. 58.
6. Alexandra, p. 321.
7. Ibid., p. 86–87.
8. Ibid.
9. Ibid., p. 434.
10. Ibid., p. 97.
11. Ibid.
12. Baryatinskaya, p. 251.
13. Alexandra, p. 94.
14. Ibid., p. 620.
15. Ibid., p. 379.
16. Ibid., p. 562.
17. Ibid., p. 221.
18. Ibid., p. 135.
19. Ibid., p. 385.
20. Ibid., p. 346.
21. Ibid., p. 399.
22. Ibid., p. 355.
23. Andrey Vladimirovich, p. 31.
24. Hessen, p. 320.
25. *Arkhiv russ. rev.,* 1925, no. xvi, pp. 264–65.
26. *Padenie,* vol. iv, p. 337.
27. Alexandra, p. 106.
28. *Birzh. ved.,* 15 viii 15.
29. *Arkhiv russ. rev.,* 1923, no. xvi, p. 52.

CHAPTER 17

1. *Padenie,* vol. iv, pp. 233–34.
2. Melgunov, *Legenda,* p. 19.
3. *Birzh. ved.,* 24 v 15.
4. Melgunov, op. cit., p. 34.
5. *Padenie,* vol. ii, p. 14.
6. Alexandra, p. 551.
7. Ibid., p. 175.
8. Ibid., p. 267.
9. *Padenie,* vol. iv, pp. 356–57.
10. Ibid., p. 349.
11. Ibid., vol. iii, p. 252.
12. Alexandra, p. 104.
13. Andrey Vladimirovich, p. 97.
14. *Padenie,* vol. iv, pp. 318–20.
15. Blok, p. 14.
16. *Padenie,* vol. iv, p. 362.
17. Ibid., vol. ii, p. 333.
18. Alexandra, p. 328.
19. Spiridovich, *Raspoutine,* p. 303.
20. *Padenie,* vol. i, p. 38.
21. Blok, p. 11.
22. *Padenie,* vol. i, p. 33.
23. Spiridovich, *Raspoutine,* p. 305.
24. Alexandra, p. 291.

CHAPTER 18

1. Utro rossii 8 viii 15, no 217.and.Ts.go ar. f. 601, op. 1. g. 263. 11 57-9. 7 f. 612. op. 1 g. 8 1 9.
2. *Padenie,* vol. i, p. 35.
3. Ibid., p. 55.
4. Ibid., vol. iv, p. 55.
5. *Arkhiv russ. rev.,* 1925, no. xvi, pp. 46–47.
6. Knox, p. 373.
7. Hanbury Williams, p. 53.
8. Marye, p. 228.

9. In V. Zlobin, *A Difficult Soul: Zinaida Gippius* (London, 1980), p. 2.
10. Gippius, *Sinyaya kniga*, p. 39.
11. *Birzh. ved.*, 19 ix 16.
12. Grave, p. 46.
13. Chaliapin, p. 260.
14. Grave, pp. 133–34.
15. Rodzyanko, p. 183.
16. Melgunov, *Legenda*, p. 385.
17. 6 delo pro. d co ch. 46.
18. Teffi, pp. 277–78.
19. Ibid., p. 274.
20. Purishkevich, pp. 248–49.
21. Rennikov, pp. 278–79.
22. Grünwald, p. 204.
23. Shakhovskoy, p. 56.
24. Grave, p. 142.
25. Kadmin, p. 47.
26. Rennikov, p. 279.
27. Grave, pp. 77–78.
28. Alexandra, p. 305.
29. Dzhaunumova, p. 35.
30. Paléologue, *Russie des tsars*, p. 251.
31. Blok, pp. 11–12.
32. Alexandra, pp. 328–29.
33. Ibid., p. 291.
34. Ibid., pp. 398–99.
35. Ibid., p. 397.
36. Ossendowsky, pp. 278–79.
37. *Padenie*, vol. ii, p. 67.
38. Melgunov, *Legenda*, p. 230.
39. Alexandra, p. 207.
40. Vuillamy, 9 ix 16.
41. *Padenie*, vol. ii, p. 300.
42. Blok, p. 11.
43. *Padenie*, vol. ii, p. 67.
44. Alexandra, p. 429.
45. Ibid., p. 437.
46. Ibid., p. 441.
47. Pares, p. 397.
48. Ibid., p. 25.

CHAPTER 19

1. Hoare, p. 81.
2. Gippius, *Sinyaya kniga*, p. 54.
3. Andrey Vladimirovich, p. 68.
4. Melgunov, *Na putyakh*, p. 168.
5. *Russkaya letopis'*, 1923, vol. iii, pp. 12–13.
6. Grünwald, p. 202.
7. Teffi, p. 290.
8. *Arkhiv russ. rev.*, 1925, no. xvi, p. 17.
9. Vassiliev, p. 151.
10. Melgunov, *Na putyakh*, p. 182.
11. Hanbury Williams, p. 59.

CHAPTER 20

1. Baryatinskaya, p. 47.
2. Yusupov, *Lost Splendour*, p. 96.
3. Mossolov, p. 8.
4. Yusupov, *Lost Splendour*, p. 95.
5. Marie Pavlovna, p. 154.
6. "Vassili," p. 239. Bogdanovich, pp. 51–52.
7. Alexandra, p. 237.
8. Englishman, pp. 190–92.
9. Yusupov, *La fin de Raspoutine*, pp. 110–11.
10. Melgunov, *Legenda*, pp. 386–87.
11. *Sov. zap.*, 1928, no. 34, p. 269.
12. Bogdanovich, p. 433.
13. Kokovtsov, p. 170.
14. *Golos Moskvy*, 1 iii 11.
15. Milyukov, p. 19.
16. *Gosudarstvennaia Duma chetverty sozyv*, Nov. 19, 1916, cols. 261, 265, 270, 286–88.
17. *Krasniy arkhiv.*, no. 14, pp. 123–24.

18. Zavarzine, p. 256.
19. Purishkevich, p. 33.
20. *Krasniy arkhiv.*, no. 14, p. 235.
21. Ibid., p. 239.
22. *Sov. zap.*, 1927–28, no. 34, pp. 269–75.
23. Ibid., p. 272.
24. Hoare, p. 68.
25. Spiridovich, *Raspoutine*, p. 373.
26. *Padenie*, vol. iv, pp. 503–4.
27. Alexandra, p. 465.
28. Simanovich, p. 268.
29. Spiridovich, *Raspoutine*, p. 273.

CHAPTER 21

1. Alexandra, p. 466.
2. Zhevakhov, p. 272.
3. *Padenie*, vol. iv, p. 503.
4. Melgunov, *Legenda*, p. 367.
5. Yusupov, *La fin de Raspoutine*, pp. 168–69.
6. Purishkevich, p. 70.
7. Vassiliev, p. 169.
8. Kataev, pp. 168–69.
9. Yusupov, *La fin de Raspoutine*, pp. 168–69.
10. *Sov. zap.*, 1927–28, no. 34, p. 281.
11. Vassiliev, p. 163.
12. Ibid., p. 164.

CHAPTER 22

1. Alexandra, pp. 469–70.
2. *Padenie*, vol. iv, p. 206.
3. *Birzh. ved.*, 20 xii 16.
4. Gippius, "La maisonette d'Ania."
5. Melgunov, *Legenda*, p. 373.
6. Hanbury Williams, pp. 145–46.
7. E.g., Marie Pavlovna, p. 250; Paley, pp. 131–32; Alexander of Russia, pp. 275–76.
8. *Arkhiv russ. rev.*, 1927, no. xxii, p. 352.
9. Melgunov, *Legenda*, p. 374.
10. Paléologue, *Russie des tsars*, p. 189.
11. Gilliard, p. 155.
12. Melgunov, *Legenda*, p. 377.
13. Spiridovich, *Der. ann.*, vol. ii, p. 452.
14. Melgunov, *Legenda*, p. 378.
15. Marie Pavlovna, p. 264.
16. Ibid., p. 265.
17. Ibid., p. 276.
18. Ibid.
19. Kseshinskaya, p. 159.
20. Mel'nik, p. 26.
21. Melgunov, *Legenda*, p. 376.
22. Aleksandr Mikhailovich, p. 310.
23. Blok, p. 27.
24. Shulgin, p. 109.
25. Marie Pavlovna, p. 253.
26. Pares, p. 397.
27. Melgunov, *Legenda*, p. 378.
28. Ibid.
29. Teffi, p. 299.

CONCLUSION

1. Blok, p. 10.
2. Marie Pavlovna, p. 252.

BIBLIOGRAPHY

Unless otherwise specified all English-language titles are published in London.

M. = Moscow, L. = Leningrad, St.P. = St. Petersburg, P. = Petrograd.

Aleksandr Mikhailovich. *Vospominaniya,* 3 vols. Paris, 1932.

Alexander of Russia. *Once a Grand Duke.* 1932.

Alexandra Fedorovna, "Correspondence."

Almazov. *Rasputin i rossiya.* Prague, 1922.

Anderson, V. *Staroobryadchestvo i sektantstvo.* St.P., 1909.

Andrey Vladimirovich. *Dnevnik.* L., 1925.

Anon. *Nikolai II.* P., 1917.

Anon. *Pokhozhdeniya Rasputina pri dvore.* s.l.n.d.

Arndt, A. *Das Sektenwesen in der Russischen Kirche.* Innsbruck, 1890.

Arsenev, N. *Russian Piety.* 1964.

Artsybashev, M. P. *Sanin.* Nice, 1909.

B. Fv. *Nicholas II und das Ende der Romanovs.* Leipzig, 1917.

Badmaev, P. A. *Za kulisami tsarisma.* s.l.n.d.

Balavanov, M. *Tsarskaya rossia 20-ovo veka.* Kharkov, 1927.

Bankoff, G. A. *Rasputin Speaks.* 1941.

Bargatinskaya, Princess A. M. *My Russian Life.* 1923.

Baring, M. *What I Saw in Russia.* 1927.

Bely, A. *Mezhdu dvukh revolyutsii.* L., 1937.

——. *Peterburg.* Berlin, 1923.

——. *Serebranniy golub.* Berlin, 1923.

Betskii, K. *Russkii Rokambol.* L., 1925.

Bienstock, J. W. *Rasputin la fin d'un régime.* Paris, 1918.

Blok, A. A. *Poslednie dni imperatorskoy vlasti.* M.-L., 1921.

Bogaevskaya, P. *Zametki o Sibirii.* Bryansk, 1895.

Bogdanovich, A. K. *Dnevnik.* M.-L., 1924.

Bolotov, A. V. *Svyatye i greshnye*. Paris, 1925.

Bol'shakov, G. *Russian Non-Conformity*. Philadelphia, 1940.

Bruce Lockhart, Sir Robert. *Diaries, 1915–38*. 1973.

——. *Memoirs of a Secret Agent*. 1975.

Brusilov, A. A. *A Soldier's Notebook: 1914–18*. 1930.

Buchanan, Sir George. *My Mission to Russia*, 2 vols. 1923.

Buchanan, M. "Recollections." s.l.n.d.

Buxhoeveden, Baroness Sophie. *The Life and Tragedy of Alexandra Fedorovna Empress of Russia*. 1928.

B. W. *Russian Court Memoirs*. 1917.

Chaliapin, F. *Man and Mask*. 1925.

Chetverinkov, I. A. *Ushedshaya Rossiya*. Berlin, n.d.

Danilovsky, A. *Vospominaniya*. Munich, 1954.

Dawe, R. E. *Memoir of an English Governess in Russia*. 1977.

Dehn, L. *The Real Tsaritsa*. 1923.

Dillon, E. J. *The Eclipse of Russia*. 1918.

Dobson, G. *St. Petersburg*. 1910.

Dolgorukov, V. A. *Putevoditel' po Sibirii*. St.P., 1903–4.

Dresler, A. *Rasputin*. Munich, 1929.

Dukes, Sir Paul. *The Unending Quest*. 1950.

Dyakin, B. C. *Russakaya burzhuasaya i tsarism vo gody pered mirovoy voiny*. L., 1967.

Dzhaunumova, E. F. *Moi vstrechi s. rasputinym*. Paris, 1923.

Encausse, P. *Le maître Philippe de Lyon*. Paris, 1955.

——. *Sciences occultes: Papus sa vie son oeuvre*. Paris, 1949.

Enden, Michel de. *Rasputine et le crépuscule de la monarchie en Russie*. Paris, 1976.

Englishman. *The Russian Diary of an Englishman*. P., 1915–17, 1919.

Essad Bey. *Nicholas II Prisoner of the Purple*. 1936.

Fleurot, A. D. *Through War to Revolution*. 1931.

Fulop Muller. *Rasputin der heilige Teufel*. Berlin, 1927.

Gilliard, P. *Le tragique destin de Nicolas II et sa famille* (Paris, 1921).

Gippius, Z. "La maisonette d'Ania." *Mercure de France*, August 1923.

——. *Sinyaya kniga*. Belgrade, 1929.

Gobron, R. *Raspoutine et l'orgie Russe*. Paris, 1930.

Grave, B. B. *Burzhuaziya na kanune fevral'skoi revolyutskii*. M.-L., 1927.

Grünwald, C. de. *Les nuits blanches de St. Petersbourg*. Paris, 1968.

Hanbury Williams, C. *The Emperor Nicholas II as I Knew Him*. 1922.

Heymann, R. *Rasputin*. Leipzig, 1917.
Hill, S S. *Travels in Siberia*. 1854.
Hoare, Sir Samuel. *The Fourth Seal*. 1930.
Iswolsky, A. *Memoirs*. 1920.
Jacoby, J. *Raspoutine*. Paris, 1934.
Judas, E. *Rasputin: Neither Devil nor Saint*. Los Angeles, 1942.
Kadmin, N. *Padenie dinastii*. M., 1917.
Kamenskii, S. *Vek minuvshii*. Paris, 1958.
Kataev, V. P. *A Mosaic of Life*. 1976.
Katkov, G. *Russia 1917*. 1967.
Kennan, G. *Siberia and the Exile System*, 2 vols. 1891.
Kinsky, Nora, Countess. *Russisches Tagebuch*. Stuttgart, 1976.
Kleinmichel, Countess M. *Memuary*. P., 1919.
Knox, Sir Alfred. *With the Russian Army*, 2 vols. 1921.
Kokovtsov, V. N. *Out of My Past*. 1935.
Krummer, R. *Rasputin ein Werkzeug der Juden*. Berlin, 1939.
Kurlov, A. *Gibel' imperatorskoi Rossii*. Paris, 1923.
Kutepov, K. V. *Sekty khlystov i skoptsov*. Stavropol, 1900.
Lemke, M. K. *250 dnei v tsarskoi stavke*. P., 1920.
Lipemann, H. *Rasputin, a New Judgement*. 1955.
Lurie, O. *La Russie 1914–17*. Lausanne, 1918.
Maire, G. F. *Raspoutine*. Paris, 1934.
Makarov, Yu. *Moya sluzhba v staroi gvardii*. Paris, 1951.
Mamantov, V. V. *Na gosudarevoy sluzhbe*. Tallin, 1926.
Marie Pavlovna. *Things I Remember*. 1931.
Marsden, G. V. *Rasputin and Russia, the Tragedy of a Throne*. 1920.
Marye, G. T. *Nearing the End of Imperial Russia*. 1928.
Massie, R. K. *Nicholas and Alexandra*. 1968.
Melgunov, P. *Na putyakh k dvortsomu perevorotu*. Paris, 1931.
——. *Legenda o separatnom mire*. Paris, 1957.
Mel'nik. *Vospominaniya o tsarskoi semi*. Belgrade, 1921.
Milyukov, P. *Vospominaniya*, 2 vols. 1955.
Minney, R. G. *Rasputin*. 1972.
Mintslov, S. R. *Debri zhizni*. Riga, 1929.
——. *Peterburg v 1903–10 godakh*. Riga, 1931.
Mossolov, A. A. *At the Court of the Last Tsar*. 1935.
Murat, Princess M. *Raspoutine et l'aube sanglante*. Paris, n.d.
Murray, G. *Matters of Life and Death*. 1953.
Nikolai II Materialy dlya kharakteristiki lichnosti i tsarstvovaniya. M., 1917.
Novomeysky, M. A. *My Siberian Life*. 1956.

Novoselov, P. I. *Grigorii Rasputin i misticheskoe rasputstvo.* Moscow, 1912.
Obolensky, S. *One Man in His Time.* 1960.
Oldenburg, S. S. *Tsarstvovanie imperatora Nikolaya II-ovo.* Munich, 1949.
Ossendowsky, F. *Beasts, Men and Gods.* 1923.
Padenie tsarskovo rezhima (Muravyev Commission). 6 vols. L., 1924–7.
Paléologue, M. *An Ambassador's Memoirs.* 1972.
——. *La Russie des tsars.* Paris, 1922.
Paley, Princess. *Memories of Russia 1916–19.* 1924.
Pares, Sir Bernard. *The Fall of the Russian Monarchy.* 1939.
Pethybridge, R. *Witnesses to the Russian Revolution.* 1964.
Pikul', V. *U poslednei cherty.* M.-L., 1979.
Prugavin, A. S. *Leontii Egorovich i evo poklonnitsy.* M., 1916.
——. *Raskol i sektantstvo.* M., 1905.
Purishkevich, V. M. *Dnevnik.* Riga, 1918.
——. *Comment j'ai tué Rasputine.* Paris, 1924.
Radziwill, Princess Catherine. *The Intimate Life of the Last Tsarina.* 1929.
Rasputin, M. *My Father.* 1934.
——. *The Real Rasputin.* 1929.
Rasputin, M., and Patte Barham. *Rasputin: The Man Behind the Myth.* 1977.
Rasputin. Original Akten zum Mord. Leipzig, n.d.
Rennikov, A. M. *Minuvhshie dni.* New York, n.d.
Rodzyanko, V. *The Reign of Rasputin.* 1934.
Romanovsky Krassinsky, Princess M. F. *Dancing in Petersburg.* 1960.
Rosen, Baron A. *40 Years of Diplomacy,* 2 vols. 1922.
Russian Supreme Monarchist Council. *Pravda o russkoi tsarskoi semi i tyemnykh silakh.* s.l.n.d.
Salisbury, H. *Black Night White Sun.* 1978.
Semennikov, V. *Monarkhiya pered krusheniyem.* M.-L., 1926.
Sévérac, G. *La secte russe des hommes de Dieu.* Paris, 1906.
Shakhovskoy, Prince V. N. *Sic transit gloria mundi.* Paris, 1952.
Shulgin, V. V. *Tage.* Berlin, 1928.
Simanovich. *Rasputin der allmächtige Bauer.* Berlin, 1928.
"Skitalets." *Publican and Serf.* 1906.
Sokolov, N. A. *Ubiistvo tsarskoy semi.* Berlin, 1925.
Spiridovich, A. I. *Les dernières années de la cour,* 2 vols. Paris, 1928.
——. *Raspoutine, 1863–1916.* Paris, 1935.

——. *Velikaya voina i fevral'skaya revolyutsiya,* 2 vols. New York, 1960–2.
Spring Rice, Sir C. *The Letters and Friendships of Sir Cecil Spring Rice,* ed. S. Gwynn, 2 vols. 1929.
Sukhomlinov, V. A. *Vospominaniya.* Berlin, 1924.
Suvorin, A. S. *Dnevnik.* M.-L., 1923.
Swann, H. *Home on the Neva.* 1956.
Talytsin, M. *Po tu storonu.* Paris, 1932.
Taube, Otto von. *Rasputin.* 1925.
Teffi, N. A. *Vospominaniya.* Paris, 1931.
Telyakovskii, V. A. *Vospominaniya.* Paris, 1924.
Thompson, G. *Der Zar Raspoutine und die Juden.* Hamburg, 1922.
Trewin, J. C. *Tutor to the Tsarevich.* 1975.
Trufanov, S. *The Mad Monk of Russia.* New York, 1918.
"Vassili," Count Paul. *Behind the Veil at the Russian Court.* 1913.
Vassiliev, V. *Vospominaniya.* Paris, 1930.
Volkonsky, S. *My Reminiscences.* 1945.
Volkov, A. A. *Souvenirs.* Paris, 1928.
Vonlyar-Larskaya, N. D. *The Russia that I Loved.* 1952.
Vorres, I. *The Last Grand Duchess.* 1964.
Vuillamy. *The Letters of the Tsar to the Tsarina, 1914–17.* 1929.
Vyroubova, A. A. *Memoirs of the Russian Court.* 1923.
——. *Stranitsy iz moyei zhizni.* Berlin, 1923.
Walpole, H. *The Dark Forest.* 1923.
Witte, S. Yu. *Vospominaniya,* 2 vols. Berlin, 1922.
Yusupov, F. *La fin de Raspoutine.* Paris, 1927.
——. *Lost Splendour.* 1953.
Zaitsov, K. I. *Pamyati poslednevo tsarya.* Shanghai, 1948.
Zancka, H. *Rasputin.* Berlin, 1917.
Zaslavskii, P. P. *Rytsar' chernoi sotni V. V. Shulgin.* M.-L., 1969.
Zavarzine, P. O. *Souvenirs d'un chef de l'okhrana.* Paris, 1930.
Zherebtsov, V. V. *Staraya Sibir' v vospominaniyakh sovremmenikov.* Irkutsk, 1933.
Zhevakhov, Prince N. D. *Vospominaniya,* 2 vols. Munich, 1923.

PERIODICALS CONSULTED

Arkhiv russkoy revolyutsii. (*Arkhiv russ. rev.*)
Birzhevye vedomosti. (*Birzh. ved.*)
Bogoslovskii vestnik.
Byloe.
Golos Moskvy.
Iskry.
Istoricheskii vestnik.

Krasniy arkhiv.
Moskovskie vedomosti.
Noviy Satirikon.
Novoe Vremya.
Peterburgskaya gazeta.
Peterburgskii zhurnal.
Petrogradskaya gazeta.
Poslednie novosti.
Revue de Paris.
Russkaya letopis'.
Russkoe proshloe.
Sovremennik.
Sovremennye zapiski. (*Sov. zap.*)
Vechernee vremya.
Voprosy istorii. (*Vop. ist.*)

INDEX

Note: No attempt has been made to index references to Rasputin, Nicholas II, or Alexandra. R. = Grigorii Efimovich Rasputin.